sweet mornings

sweet mornings

125 SWEET AND SAVORY BREAKFAST AND BRUNCH RECIPES

PATTY PINNER

MIDWAY
AN AGATE IMPRINT
CHICAGO

Printed in China

Photography by Peter McCullough.
Illustrations © CreativeMarket.com / OneVectorStock

Library of Congress Cataloging-in-Publication Data
Pinner, Patty, 1954- author.
Sweet mornings : 125 sweet and savory breakfast and brunch recipes / Patty Pinner.
pages cm
Includes index.
Summary: "A collection of sweet dessert recipes for breakfast and brunch, along with some savory dishes"-- Provided by publisher.
ISBN 978-1-57284-186-4 (hard cover) -- ISBN 1-57284-186-9 (hard cover)
1. Breakfasts. I. Title.
TX733.P64 2016
641.5'2--dc23
2015032001

10 9 8 7 6 5 4 3 2 1   16 17 18 19 20

Midway is an imprint of Agate Publishing. Agate books are available in bulk at discount prices.
agatepublishing.com

For my cousin, Ryan Sims; my son, Craig McAdams Sr.;
and my beloved grandchildren, Craig McAdams Jr.
and Amariona Murray-McAdams

Contents

Morning Savories

Introduction

For as long as I can remember, food has always been the dominant topic of conversation among the women in my family. Even now, when we get together, we share new recipes and encourage each other to try them. I've learned from these women that a delicious, home-cooked meal is a powerful way to bring peace to a household. My grandmother—we called her My My—used to tell us that breakfast was the most important meal in a love affair. She told me, "A nice breakfast for the one you love is the most intimate, tried-and-true way to season a relationship." My mother's cousin Evalene who only cooked one fine meal a day—breakfast—for her husband, Stanley, once told me, "I enjoy Stanley better in the morning. I start the day off madly in love with him, but as the day wanes, so does some of that love."

I am a firm believer that cooking for others is one of the best ways to express your love for them. I prefer to cook with the freshest and finest ingredients, and all good cooks know that love is the best spice. I even consider cooking for myself to be an act of love—I'm giving myself the gift of wonderful tastes and aromas and invoking the memories of people who meant so much to me during my childhood. The act of preparing a meal reminds me of who I am and where I'm from.

When I was growing up, my mother went out of her way to make our weekend mornings special. Her breakfasts usually included something sweet and delicious alongside her eggs, bacon, sausage, ham, and other breakfast items. Mama was one of those cooks who thought outside of the culinary box—she wouldn't think twice about serving a sweet for breakfast that was traditionally served as a dessert. She would say, "The only thing that differentiates breakfast from dinner is the time of day. You can't have a little sugar in the morning?"

Like Mama, I enjoy brightening my mornings with luscious enhancements to my breakfast main courses. There's nothing like filling the house with the tantalizing aroma of something sweet and spicy baking in the oven. My morning coffee is more rich and fulfilling when it's served with my homemade doughnuts, crumb cakes, and sweet rolls. When served on my most elegant dishes, my morning sweets come to life, adding an element of celebration.

I've been collecting sweet breakfast recipes for as long as I can remember. Most of them came from the women in my family, who guarded their recipes as if they were secret love potions. Many of my recipes go *way* back—they were passed down from my great-grannies, aunties, and cousins. Others came from neighborhood women famous in our community for their cooking. It gives me great pleasure to scour through my recipes and recall the stories of the women who gave them to me. My recipes are testimonials to all I've learned, listened to, and observed in the kitchens of other women. "Women sharpen women," my grandmother used to say.

Many of the recipes in this book reflect a time when folks lingered over their breakfast tables, rapt in conversation. They testify to my love of the sweet side of breakfast and are ideal for those weekend mornings when breakfast is served a little later than usual. Nothing soothes the soul or welcomes someone to the table like a good, hearty breakfast with a sweet treat on the side. I am pleased to share these recipes with you.

Miss Lillian's Cereal Toppers and Stir-Ins

WHEN I THINK OF MORNING FOOD, I often think of Miss Lillian, an older neighbor of my grandmother's. In the sixties, when I was growing up, Miss Lillian's way of tending to her husband's needs made other good wives say she was an old-fashioned wife—what her husband Logan said was the law. She'd even get out of bed in the middle of the night to make him a bowl of cereal. Though they were friends, the extent that Miss Lillian was willing to go to fulfill her wifely duties grated on my grandmother's nerves. While My My would indulge my grandfather with little niceties like a Sunday supper on a weeknight or a surprise platter of his favorite gingersnaps, she was not the kind of woman who would cater to his every whim. "You have to draw the line somewhere," she used to say. "Cause some men'll work the sap out of you if you don't."

A few months before I got married, I started putting together a little journal of recipes and ideas to help make my home a happier place for my husband to come home to. Miss Lillian came to mind immediately, so I gave her a call and asked if there was anything that she'd done to Mr. Logan's late-night bowls of cereal to make them special. She said, "No, sugah. It was never about the contents of the bowl that pleased him. He could've poured his own cereal. It was the fact that when he came home, there was somebody warm and welcoming waiting to greet him. I did for him the things that a loving wife would do."

UNSWEETENED DRY CEREAL TOPPERS

* Fresh fruits: sliced bananas, pears, peaches, strawberries
* Jam, jelly, marmalade
* Brown sugar
* Colored granulated sugars
* Granulated sugars flavored with extracts
* Syrup: chocolate, strawberry, maple
* Ground cinnamon
* Granola
* Blanched, sliced almonds
* Sweetened coconut

HOT CEREAL STIR-INS

* Stewed fruits
* Marshmallows
* Mixed dried fruits
* Chopped nuts: hazelnuts, walnuts, pecans
* Honey
* Fresh apple slices
* Applesauce
* Raisins or chopped and pitted dates
* Sweetened heavy cream
* Cottage cheese or yogurt

What Every Baker Needs

EVERY BAKER HAS HER OWN ESSENTIALS. Here are the ones I swear by:

UNSALTED BUTTER: I use butter to add flavor and texture. It brings out the richness in my baking. Unsalted butter allows me to add salt carefully—as much or as little as I need.

SALTED BUTTER: In some recipes, it doesn't matter if you use salted or unsalted butter. If a recipe just asks for butter, it won't make a whole lot of difference. If I'm using salted butter, I'll just take away some of the salt that the recipe calls for and get the same results.

LARGE EGGS: Eggs give color and flavor to baked goods. They also add structure and act as leavening agents. I use large eggs in all of my recipes.

ALL-PURPOSE FLOUR: For lighter, fluffier baked treats, I use cake flour. But for most morning treats, all-purpose flour is necessary. The best way to measure all-purpose flour is to spoon it into a measuring cup to overflowing and then use a knife to scrape any excess off the top.

SUGARS: I keep several types of sweeteners in my pantry for my baking—granulated sugar, baker's (or superfine) sugar, confectioners' sugar, light and dark brown sugar, and light and dark corn syrup. I also recommend keeping a good honey.

LEAVENERS: Yeast, baking soda, and baking powder are the ingredients that help my baked goods rise. I make sure they're all fresh. Once they are opened, most leaveners have a three-month shelf life. Most everything that I make calls for at least one of these ingredients.

SALT: Salt is a flavor enhancer that balances sweetness. I use salt in everything—sweet and savory recipes.

EXTRACTS: The pure extracts I use most often are vanilla and lemon. Of course, there are other important extracts, like orange, almond, chocolate, peppermint, and anise, but vanilla and lemon flavors always bring out the best in my baking.

MILK: Many baked goods call for whole or evaporated milk. I keep both stocked. I usually have either light or heavy cream and perhaps half-and-half available as well.

VEGETABLE OIL OR SHORTENING: Oils keep my sweet food moist and tender. Though I seldom deep-fry, when I do, I use vegetable oil.

Indispensable Baking Tools

While there are a lot of gadgets for the kitchen that you don't really need, there are a few absolutely necessary baking tools. Having the right tools is essential to delicious baking. As far as I am concerned, the following tools are indispensable:

MIXING BOWLS: I use them to mix everything from pancake and coffee cake batters to fruit cobblers and brownies.

SIEVES: I use mine for sifting dry ingredients like flour, baking powder, baking soda, and salt—anything that I want to be clump-free.

MEASURING SPOONS AND CUPS: Specific measuring spoons and cups ensure that I'm being accurate when I measure. Baking is exacting, and it requires most ingredients to be measured precisely.

SPATULAS AND TURNERS: I flip, turn, and extract things with spatulas and turners all day long. Rubber or silicone spatulas are generally used for mixing or stirring ingredients, while turners are used for turning food in pans and skillets.

BAKING PANS (GENERALLY METAL) AND DISHES (GENERALLY GLASS OR CERAMIC): Rimmed baking sheets, flat baking pans, round baking pans, muffin pans, cake pans, rectangular and square baking dishes—having a wide variety allows me to cook all kinds of morning treats. In particular, 9-inch × 13-inch baking dishes are perfect for baking, serving, and reheating sweets. I have Pyrex, stainless steel, and glazed ceramic versions. I bake coffee cakes, bars and squares, and brownies in mine, and they can go from the oven to the table with no difficulty.

WIRE RACK: They're necessary for success. Wire cooling racks allow sweets to cool quickly and evenly. If your treats cool on racks, they won't get soggy on the bottom or sides.

WHISKS: Whisks are important tools for incorporating both dry and wet ingredients. There isn't much that hard work and a big spoon can't stir, but I love whisks.

PASTRY BRUSHES: I use pastry brushes to apply egg washes, to butter crusts, and for greasing pans.

ROLLING PINS: Rolling pins allow me to roll or spread my dough to a uniform thickness. I use rolling pins to roll out crusts, cookies, and sweet roll doughs.

PARCHMENT PAPER: I use parchment paper to line my cake pans and baking tins. I buy the kind that is precut, lays flat, and is reusable. It's more expensive, but I don't have to mess with rolls of paper, and cleanup is easy.

RECIPES

Sweet Beginnings

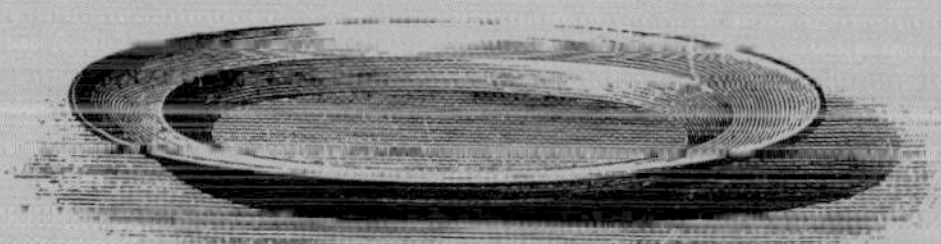

Mama's Brown Sugar and Pecan Coffee Cake

In the house where I grew up, our kitchen—*Mama's kitchen*—was the darkest room in the house, despite the fact that it had two windows. One of the windows overlooked the small porch, where Mama and I used to have our girl talks, and the other window was on the side of the house, in the shadow of our garage. What I remember most about Mama's kitchen was its air of mystery. The labels on her spice jars were turned around so that inquisitive eyes couldn't read their names, and her cookbooks and handwritten recipes were discreetly stored away.

Mama, who collected antiques—swaths of lace and linen, woven baskets, small kitchen gadgets, teacups and saucers, odd pieces of ceramic and china, and pots and pans—had a knack for bringing together a mishmosh of colors, patterns, and textures. Her kitchen had an old-world bazaar feel to it. Her counters featured ceramic jars and platters that held her homemade incense sticks, hand crafted soaps, and candles. It was a quiet kitchen, meditative and soulful. Each morning, it was always clean from the night before, and it always looked and felt like a cozy place to eat. Mama knew how to create a scene. Her kitchen was my favorite place to dream and imagine, especially in the mornings, when the day was young and sweet and full of possibilities.

When I was growing up, homemade coffee cake was a weekend morning staple. In fact, some of my most pleasurable morning experiences are linked to one of my mother's delicious coffee cakes and the sense of well-being that came from sitting in her warm, earthy kitchen. It was the perfect place for mornings with coffee cake and close friends.

Mama's Brown Sugar and Pecan Coffee Cake is delicious and easy to make. Its luscious aroma will scent your home while it's baking—an added treat. I'm sure this will become one of your favorite breakfast dessert recipes.

Makes 1 9-inch square coffee cake

BATTER

Nonstick cooking spray, for greasing

2 cups all-purpose flour, plus more for dusting

1 cup firmly packed light brown sugar

⅔ cup granulated sugar

1 teaspoon baking soda

½ teaspoon baking powder

¼ teaspoon salt

½ teaspoon freshly grated nutmeg

⅛ teaspoon ground cloves

1 cup buttermilk, room temperature

½ cup (1 stick) unsalted butter, melted and cooled

2 large eggs, room temperature

1 teaspoon pure vanilla extract

TOPPING

½ cup firmly packed light brown sugar

⅓ cup finely chopped pecans

1 teaspoon ground cinnamon

1. Preheat the oven to 350°F. Grease a 9-inch square baking dish with the cooking spray and dust with some flour. Set aside.

2. *To make the batter:* In a large mixing bowl, sift together the dry ingredients: the flour, brown and granulated sugars, baking soda, baking powder, and salt. Add the nutmeg and cloves and stir until well combined. Set aside.

3. In the bowl of a stand mixer fitted with the paddle attachment, add the wet ingredients: the buttermilk, butter, eggs, and vanilla extract. Beat together for 1 minute. Add the flour mixture to the bowl of the mixer ⅓ at a time, beating at low speed for 2 to 3 minutes, until just combined. Turn off the mixer. Transfer the batter to the prepared baking dish.

4. *To make the topping:* In a small mixing bowl, combine the brown sugar, pecans, and cinnamon. Mix well and sprinkle evenly over the batter in the dish.

5. Bake for 35 to 40 minutes, until the cake springs back when lightly touched in the center and a wooden toothpick inserted into the center of the cake comes out clean. Remove from the oven and set aside to cool on a wire rack for 10 minutes before serving.

6. Transfer to a serving platter, slice, and serve warm.

Cherry-Filled Coffee Cake

THIS RECIPE IS A SWEET ALTERNATIVE TO OTHER FLAVORS OF PIE filling that your coffee cakes may call for—apple, blueberry, and peach. You can substitute other flavors of pie filling in this recipe, but cherry adds a lovely summer note.

Makes 1 9-inch × 13-inch coffee cake

BATTER

Nonstick cooking spray, for greasing

2 cups all-purpose flour, plus more for dusting

1 cup (2 sticks) unsalted butter, room temperature

1 cup granulated sugar

3 large egg yolks, room temperature, lightly beaten

1 teaspoon baking powder

¼ teaspoon salt

1 cup sour cream, room temperature

1 teaspoon pure vanilla extract

3 large egg whites, stiffly beaten

1 (21-ounce) can cherry pie filling

TOPPING

½ cup firmly packed light brown sugar

½ cup all-purpose flour

2 tablespoons unsalted butter, room temperature

1 teaspoon ground cinnamon

Pinch salt

1. Preheat the oven to 350°F. Lightly grease a 9-inch × 13-inch baking dish with the cooking spray and dust with some flour. Set aside.

2. *To make the batter:* In the bowl of a stand mixer fitted with the paddle attachment, break up the butter by mixing on low speed for 1 minute. Add the granulated sugar and cream together the butter and sugar on medium speed for 2 to 3 minutes, until the mixture is light and fluffy. Scrape down the sides and bottom of the bowl to prevent lumps from forming. As the mixer is running, reduce the speed to low and slowly add the egg yolks, 1 at a time; after you add each egg, scrape down the sides of the bowl and resume beating on low speed for 30 seconds.

3. In a medium mixing bowl, sift together the dry ingredients: the flour, baking powder, and salt. Slowly add the flour mixture and the sour cream to the bowl of the running mixer 1/3 at a time, alternating back and forth, making sure to end with the flour mixture. As the mixer continues to run, add the vanilla extract and mix until thoroughly combined. Turn off the mixer. Using a rubber or silicone spatula, carefully and slowly fold the stiffly beaten egg whites into the batter.

4. Transfer 1/2 of the batter to the prepared baking dish. Spread the cherry pie filling over the batter, and then cover the cherry pie filling with the remaining batter.

5. *To make the topping:* In a medium mixing bowl, combine the brown sugar, flour, butter, cinnamon, and salt. Mix well and sprinkle evenly over the batter in the baking dish.

6. Bake for 45 to 55 minutes, until a wooden toothpick inserted into the center of the cake comes out clean. Remove from the oven and set aside to cool on a wire rack for 10 minutes before serving.

7. Transfer to a serving platter, slice, and serve warm.

Cousin Vercie's Snickerdoodle Scones

My mother's cousin Vercie maintained a kitchen that was always bright and sunny—so different from Mama's serene, dark, and secretive one. And when Cousin Vercie was in her kitchen, she generated a lot of noise. You could expect loud laughter and sometimes loud singing; you could hear the clanging of pots and pans. Vercie recited her recipes out loud and in the open—she didn't keep culinary secrets. She wouldn't hesitate to push aside whatever was on her kitchen table to make room for an impromptu card game with her girlfriends or to give her husband, Moe, a place to challenge one of his foundry buddies to a game of checkers.

Cousin Vercie was a wonderful, lively, and animated cook when she had an audience, and Cousin Moe was her most ardent spectator. When he watched his wife cook, wash dishes, or shell peas in that kitchen, he felt at peace, just as Vercie did as she cooked fine meals for Moe. When I was a young girl, I dreamed of having just that kind of kitchen, with all the aromas, flavors, and ambience that my family would enjoy.

Cousin Vercie's scones, topped with a mixture of granulated sugar and cinnamon, are simple to make and impressive to serve. They're a perfect little morning treat for someone you love.

Makes about 8 scones

BATTER

2 cups all-purpose flour, plus more for rolling

⅓ cup granulated sugar

1 teaspoon baking powder

½ teaspoon baking soda

¼ teaspoon ground cinnamon

¼ teaspoon salt

½ cup (1 stick) unsalted butter, cold, cut into ½-inch pieces

⅓ cup buttermilk, room temperature

1 large egg, room temperature

1 teaspoon pure vanilla extract

TOPPING

¼ cup granulated sugar

½ teaspoon ground cinnamon

1 tablespoon heavy cream, for brushing

1. *To make the batter:* In a large mixing bowl, sift together the dry ingredients: the flour, granulated sugar, baking powder, baking soda, cinnamon, and salt. Using your fingers, a pastry blender, or the tines of a fork, cut the butter into the flour mixture until it becomes coarse, like cornmeal.

2. In a small mixing bowl, whisk together the wet ingredients: the buttermilk, egg, and vanilla extract. Pour the buttermilk mixture into the flour mixture and stir gently with a fork until combined; a dough will form.

3. Turn out the dough onto a floured work surface. With floured hands, knead lightly by folding and gently pressing it 10 to 12 times, until it is nearly smooth. Form it into a ball.

4. Using a floured rolling pin, roll out the dough into a 1½-inch-thick, 11-inch-wide circle. Score the dough circle into 8 wedges, cover with plastic wrap, and transfer to the freezer to chill for 2 hours.

5. Preheat the oven to 350°F. Line an 11-inch × 17-inch baking pan with parchment paper. Set aside.

6. *To make the topping:* In a small mixing bowl, combine the granulated sugar and cinnamon and mix well. Set aside.

7. Remove the dough from the freezer. Using a sharp knife or a pizza cutter, cut the dough into 8 wedges, using the lines you scored as a guide. Place the wedges, about 2 inches apart, on the prepared pan. Brush the tops with the heavy cream. Sprinkle the sugar–cinnamon topping over each, gently pressing down to secure it to the scone.

8. Bake for 20 to 25 minutes, until the scones are a soft, golden color. Remove from the oven.

9. Transfer to a serving platter and serve warm.

Old-Fashioned Sour Cream Coffee Cake

ANOTHER OF COUSIN VERCIE'S CLAIMS TO FAME WAS HER WONDERFUL Old-Fashioned Sour Cream Coffee Cake. Cousin Moe would sit at the kitchen table watching her beating and whisking, laughing when she laughed, and talking serious when she talked serious. Cousin Vercie said she first sampled this tender coffee cake at a couples' church retreat that served a nice, down-home-styled breakfast. Said Cousin Moe loved it.

Makes 1 10-inch tube or Bundt cake

BATTER

Nonstick cooking spray, for greasing
All-purpose flour, for dusting
1 cup (2 sticks) unsalted butter
2 cups granulated sugar
2 large eggs, room temperature
1 cup sour cream, room temperature
1 teaspoon pure vanilla extract
2 cups cake flour
1 teaspoon baking powder
½ teaspoon salt

TOPPING

1 cup chopped pecans
2 tablespoons light brown sugar
1 teaspoon ground cinnamon
Sifted confectioners' sugar, for dusting

1. Preheat the oven to 350°F. Grease a 10-inch tube or Bundt pan with the cooking spray and dust with the all-purpose flour. Set aside.

2. *To make the batter:* In the bowl of a stand mixer fitted with the paddle attachment, break up the butter by mixing on low speed for 1 minute. Add the granulated sugar and cream together the butter and sugar on medium speed for 2 to 3 minutes, until the mixture is light and fluffy. Scrape down the sides and bottom of the bowl to prevent lumps from forming. As the mixer is running, reduce the speed to low and slowly add the eggs, 1 at a time; after you add each egg, scrape down the sides of the bowl and resume beating on low speed for 30 seconds. As the mixer continues to run, add the sour cream and vanilla extract and beat until just combined.

3. In a small mixing bowl, sift together the dry ingredients: the cake flour, baking powder, and salt. Add the flour mixture to the bowl of the mixer ⅓ at a time, beating each time at low speed for 2 to 3 seconds until just combined. Turn off the mixer.

4. *To make the topping:* In a small mixing bowl, combine the pecans, brown sugar, and cinnamon. Mix well.

5. Transfer ½ of the batter to the prepared pan. Evenly spread ½ of the topping over the batter and then cover the topping with the remaining batter. Evenly spread the remaining topping over the second layer of batter and press it lightly into the batter.

6. Bake for 45 to 50 minutes, until a wooden toothpick inserted into the center of the cake comes out clean. Remove from the oven and set aside to cool on a wire rack for 5 minutes before serving.

7. Invert onto a serving platter and dust with the confectioners' sugar. Slice and serve warm or at room temperature.

You could expect loud laughter and sometimes loud singing in Cousin Vercie's kitchen; you could hear the clanging of pots and pans.

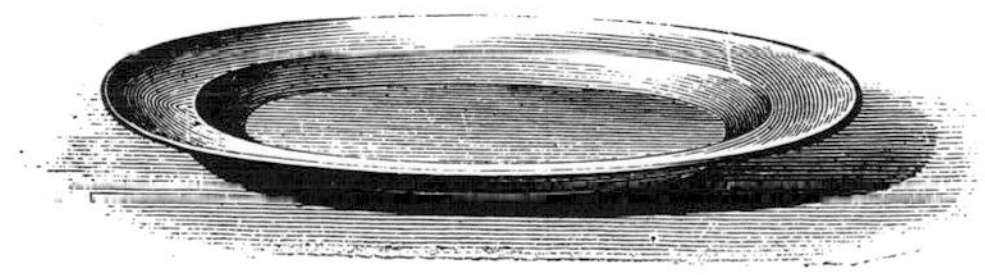

Chocolate Swirl Coffee Cake

My friend Edgina Foreman makes this delightful little chocolate coffee cake with a layer of cocoa powder and granulated sugar in the middle. It's so light and fluffy; a slice does a cup of hot coffee and conversation good. As far as I am concerned, there's nothing like good conversation and chocolate in the morning.

Makes 1 9-inch square coffee cake

- Nonstick cooking spray, for greasing
- 1½ cups all-purpose flour, plus more for dusting
- 1 cup granulated sugar (divided)
- ½ cup unsweetened cocoa powder
- ½ cup (1 stick) unsalted butter, room temperature
- 2 large eggs, room temperature
- 2 tablespoons baking powder
- ½ teaspoon salt
- ⅔ cup whole milk, room temperature
- 1 tablespoon pure vanilla extract

1. Preheat the oven to 350°F. Grease a 9-inch square baking dish with the cooking spray and dust with some flour. Set aside.

2. *To make the swirl:* In a small mixing bowl, whisk together 3 tablespoons of the granulated sugar and the cocoa powder. Set aside.

3. *To make the batter:* In the bowl of a stand mixer fitted with the paddle attachment, break up the butter by mixing on low speed for 1 minute. Add the remaining granulated sugar and cream together the butter and sugar on medium speed for 2 to 3 minutes, until the mixture is light and fluffy. Scrape down the sides and bottom of the bowl to prevent lumps from forming. As the mixer is running, reduce the speed to low and slowly add the eggs, 1 at a time; after you add each egg, scrape down the sides of the bowl and resume beating on low speed for 30 seconds.

4. In a medium mixing bowl, sift together the dry ingredients: the flour, baking powder, and salt.

5. In a small mixing bowl, combine the milk and vanilla extract. Add the flour mixture and the milk mixture to the bowl of the mixer ⅓ at a time, beating each time at low speed for 2 to 3 minutes, until just combined. Turn off the mixer.

6. Transfer ⅓ of the batter to the prepared baking dish. Evenly sprinkle ½ of the swirl over the batter and then cover the swirl with another ⅓ of the batter. Evenly sprinkle the remaining swirl over the second layer of batter and top it with the remaining ⅓ of the batter.

7. Bake for 25 to 30 minutes, until a wooden toothpick inserted into the center of the cake comes out clean. Remove from the oven and set aside to cool on a wire rack for 15 minutes before serving.

8. Transfer to a serving platter, slice, and serve warm.

As far as I am concerned, there's nothing like good conversation and chocolate in the morning.

Aunt Zaida's Almond Coffee Ring

EVERY YEAR DURING MY GIRLHOOD, MY PARENTS AND I WOULD TRAVEL to my father's birthplace, Paris, Tennessee. At least two or three times during each stay, my father's diminutive Aunt Zaida would invite us out to her sprawling farmhouse in the country. There, we would enjoy at least one of her memorable country meals. A typical breakfast might include cranberry-glazed ham, skillet-fried corn, homemade buttermilk biscuits, and one of her famously good almond coffee rings.

Aunt Zaida served all of her breakfasts—including on weekdays with her husband, Wallace, as her only guest—on fine china and porcelain. She was certainly a wonderful cook, but Aunt Zaida's fine place settings enhanced the flavor of her meals. I once heard her say, "Don't save all of your best—whether it be smiles or compliments—for company and strangers. Put some of that consideration to the side, and give it to your husband."

Uncle Wallace was powerfully built. As he approached the kitchen after being called in to breakfast, his shape as viewed through the screen door called Paul Bunyan to mind. Big, tall Uncle Wallace looked out of place sitting at the daintily set table. His muscular hands and arms always seemed a second away from knocking something over. But it never happened. Uncle Wallace accepted and passed the delicate dishes around the table with the grace of a ballerina. My mother used to tell me, "All men have a soft spot. Sometimes you have to help them find it." I guess serving Uncle Wallace's meals on fine china was Aunt Zaida's way of helping him find his.

I love making and serving pastry rings as a breakfast go-along. Not only are they delicious, they're also attractive and versatile. I've filled them with walnuts or pecans instead of almonds, and I've added coconut, orange zest, dried cherries, and raisins to the fillings at various times.

When I serve Aunt Zaida's Almond Coffee Ring, someone always asks for a pencil, some paper, and the recipe.

recipe continues

Makes 1 ring (6–8 servings)

FILLING

½ cup firmly packed light brown sugar

½ cup slivered almonds, toasted

4 tablespoons unsalted butter, melted and cooled

1 large egg yolk, room temperature, lightly beaten

⅛ teaspoon pure almond extract

DOUGH

3½–4 cups all-purpose flour (divided), plus more for kneading

2¼ teaspoons (1 ¼-ounce package) active dry yeast

1 cup half-and-half

½ cup (1 stick) unsalted butter

⅓ cup granulated sugar

½ teaspoon salt

1 large egg, room temperature, beaten

½ teaspoon pure vanilla extract

Nonstick cooking spray, for greasing

GLAZE AND GARNISH

1 cup sifted confectioners' sugar

1½ teaspoons unsalted butter, melted

⅛ teaspoon pure vanilla extract

2–3 tablespoons half-and-half, room temperature, as needed

½ cup sliced almonds, toasted

1. *To make the filling:* In a small mixing bowl, whisk together the brown sugar, almonds, butter, egg yolk, and almond extract. Set aside.

2. *To make the dough:* In a large mixing bowl, combine 2 cups of the flour and the yeast and set aside.

3. In a large saucepan over low heat, combine the half-and-half, butter, granulated sugar, and salt and cook, stirring constantly, for 2 minutes, until the mixture reaches 120°F to 130°F and the butter has nearly melted. Remove from the heat.

4. To the bowl of a stand mixer fitted with the paddle attachment, add the flour–yeast mixture. As the mixer is running at medium speed, gradually add the half-and-half mixture to its bowl. Beat for 2 to 3 minutes, scraping down the sides and bottom of the bowl occasionally. Add the egg and vanilla extract and continue beating until the mixture is well blended.

5. As the mixer continues to run at medium speed, add 1 cup of the remaining flour and continue beating for 2 minutes, until the dough is thick and smooth. Gradually add the remaining flour as needed until the dough becomes soft.

6. Turn out the dough onto a floured work surface. With floured hands, knead lightly for 4 to 5 minutes, until the dough is smooth, satiny, and elastic. Form it into a smooth ball. Place the ball of dough in a well-greased bowl and turn it so all sides of the dough are greased. Cover with a slightly damp kitchen towel and set aside to rest and rise in a warm, draft-free place for 45 minutes to 1 hour, until the dough has doubled in size.

7. Remove the dough from the bowl, return it to the floured work surface, and gently punch it down. Knead lightly for 5 minutes. Return it to the greased bowl, cover with the slightly damp kitchen towel, and set aside to rest for 15 minutes.

8. Preheat the oven to 350°F. Line a baking sheet with parchment paper and spray the parchment with the cooking spray. Set aside.

9. Turn out the dough onto the floured work surface. Using a floured rolling pin, roll and gently stretch the dough into an 18-inch × 12-inch rectangle that is 1/4 inch thick. Evenly spread the prepared filling over the dough, leaving a 1/2-inch margin around its edges. Starting with the long side of the dough, roll it up tightly, jelly-roll style, and pinch the edges together to seal.

10. Place the rolled dough, seam side down, on the prepared baking sheet. Shape the dough into a ring and pinch the ends together to seal. Using a pair of kitchen scissors, make neat, diagonal cuts on the outside edge of the dough ring at 1-inch intervals 3/4 of the way toward the dough's center. These slices prevent the filling from seeping out at the bottom. (Take care not to slice all the way through.) Slightly separate the cuts, gently bending and overlapping each cut so the filling shows.

11. Bake for 25 to 30 minutes, until the coffee ring is light golden brown. Remove from the oven and set aside to cool on the baking sheet for 5 minutes.

12. *To make the glaze:* In a small mixing bowl, whisk together the confectioners' sugar, butter, and vanilla extract. Continue whisking and add the half-and-half as needed until the mixture reaches a smooth consistency.

13. Carefully remove the coffee ring from the baking sheet and place it on a wire rack. Drizzle the glaze over the coffee ring while still warm. Sprinkle the almonds over the top of the glaze.

14. Transfer to a serving platter, slice, and serve warm.

Glazed Cinnamon–Raisin Biscuits

THIS RECIPE FOR GLAZED CINNAMON–RAISIN BISCUITS CAME TO ME from my aunt Mildred Thompson; they were her family's favorite. The name alone makes me think of Aunt Mildred, her cooking sisters, and her delicious glazed cinnamon biscuits. The confectioners' sugar glaze really makes the biscuits unforgettable. But Aunt Mildred says, "This recipe was already old when they gave it to me."

Makes about 8–10 biscuits

DOUGH

Nonstick cooking spray, for greasing

2 cups all-purpose flour, plus more for kneading

2 tablespoons granulated sugar

1 tablespoon ground cinnamon

1 teaspoon baking powder

½ teaspoon salt

⅓ cup vegetable shortening, room temperature

½ cup raisins

⅔ cup whole milk, room temperature

GLAZE

1⅓ cups sifted confectioners' sugar

3 tablespoons whole milk, room temperature

½ teaspoon pure vanilla extract

1. Preheat the oven to 450°F. Grease a baking sheet with the cooking spray and set aside.

2. *To make the dough:* In a large mixing bowl, sift together the dry ingredients: the flour, granulated sugar, cinnamon, baking powder, and salt. Using your fingers, a pastry blender, or the tines of a fork, cut the shortening into the flour mixture until its texture resembles peas.

3. Fold the raisins into the mixture. Slowly add the milk, stirring constantly, until the dough pulls away from the sides of the bowl.

4. Turn out the dough onto a floured work surface. With floured hands, knead lightly for about 2 minutes, until the dough's surface is no longer damp. Form the dough into a ½-inch-thick square.

5. Using a 2-inch round biscuit cutter, cut the dough into 8 to 10 circles. Place the dough circles on the prepared baking sheet about 1 inch apart.

6. Bake for 12 to 15 minutes, until the biscuits are golden brown. Remove from the oven and set aside to cool on the baking sheet for 5 minutes.

7. *To make the glaze:* In a small mixing bowl, whisk together the confectioners' sugar, milk, and vanilla extract. Drizzle the glaze over the biscuits while they are still warm.

8. Transfer to a serving platter and serve warm.

Chocolate Cinnamon Rolls

MAMA ALWAYS USED TO SAY THAT SHE WASN'T A "TRENDY" COOK, BUT she often surprised us with these chocolate cinnamon rolls at breakfast. Mama also used to say, "A woman has to show herself in many different ways."

Makes 12 rolls

DOUGH

½ cup warm water (110°F–115°F)

1 tablespoon active dry yeast

½ cup granulated sugar

4 tablespoons unsalted butter, melted and cooled

1 teaspoon salt

½ cup warm whole milk (110°F–115°F)

2 large eggs, room temperature, beaten

3½–4½ cups all-purpose flour, plus more for kneading

½–⅔ cup unsweetened cocoa powder

Nonstick cooking spray, for greasing

FILLING

1 cup firmly packed light brown sugar

¾ cup (1½ sticks) unsalted butter, melted and cooled

¾ cup chopped pecans

½ cup light corn syrup

1 tablespoon ground cinnamon

6 ounces bittersweet chocolate pieces, chopped

GLAZE

¾ cup sifted confectioners' sugar

1–2 tablespoons whole milk, room temperature

½ teaspoon pure vanilla extract

1. *To make the dough:* In a large mixing bowl, allow the yeast to dissolve in the warm water until it becomes frothy. Add the granulated sugar, butter, and salt. Slowly add the milk, stirring constantly, until the sugar has dissolved. Add the eggs, 1 at a time, stirring constantly, until the ingredients are fully combined.

2. Place a hand mixer in the bowl and set it at medium speed. Add the flour and cocoa powder and beat for 3 minutes, until a soft dough forms.

3. Turn out the dough onto a floured work surface. With floured hands, knead lightly for 6 to 8 minutes, until the dough is smooth, satiny, and elastic. Form it into a smooth ball. Place the ball of dough in a well-greased bowl and turn it so all sides of the dough are greased. Cover with a slightly damp kitchen towel and set aside to rest and rise in a warm, draft-free place for 45 minutes to 1 hour, until the dough has doubled in size.

4. *To make the filling:* In a small mixing bowl, whisk together the brown sugar, butter, pecans, corn syrup, and cinnamon. Set aside.

5. Remove the dough from the bowl, return it to the floured work surface, and gently punch it down. Knead lightly for 2 to 3 minutes. Return it to the greased bowl, cover with the slightly damp kitchen towel, and set aside to rest for 10 minutes.

6. Turn out the dough onto a floured work surface. Using a floured rolling pin, roll and gently stretch the dough into a 15-inch × 9-inch rectangle that is 1/4 inch thick. Evenly spread the prepared filling over the dough, leaving a 1/2-inch margin around its edges. Sprinkle the chocolate pieces evenly over the dough, gently pressing them into place. Starting with the long side of the dough, roll it up tightly, jelly-roll style, and pinch the edges together to seal.

7. Line a baking sheet with parchment paper and spray the parchment with the cooking spray. Place the rolled dough, seam side down, on the prepared baking sheet. Cover with the slightly damp kitchen towel and set aside in a warm, draft-free place for 45 minutes to 1 hour, until the dough has doubled in size.

8. Preheat the oven to 350°F.

9. Using a serrated knife, cut the dough into 12 equally sized pieces. Place the rolls, cut side down, on the prepared baking sheet and bake for 20 minutes, until they are cooked through and golden brown. Remove from the oven and set aside.

10. *To make the glaze:* In a small mixing bowl, whisk together the confectioners' sugar, milk, and vanilla extract.

11. Transfer the rolls to a wire rack. Drizzle the glaze over the rolls while they are still warm. Set aside to cool for 5 minutes.

12. Using a wide spatula, remove the rolls from the rack. Transfer to a serving platter and serve warm.

Old-Fashioned Rice Pudding Squares

In our home, rice pudding was a well-loved weekday comfort dessert. Mama would serve it after a baked chicken or glazed pork chop supper or one of her hearty one-pot meals. Her rice pudding was especially wonderful on winter mornings—it warmed our bodies and our souls. When I think of that rice pudding, I think of Cousin Paul.

When I was seven, Paul came to Michigan to find a job at the General Motors foundry in our town. For a year or so, Cousin Paul resided in a set of spare rooms upstairs that Mama had converted into an apartment. Truth be told, he was a delightful addition to our home. Besides being attractive—tall, built, and brown as a chocolate bar—Cousin Paul was thoughtful and *industrious*, a word that Mama used to describe a person who worked hard inside his home and out.

It should come as no surprise that word spread quickly through the neighborhood that a fine, hardworking, and *single* man was living in the spare rooms above our home. Every matchmaking mother, grandmother, and auntie on our block descended on our house with the quickness. To hear them tell it, each one had a beautiful daughter, a virtuous granddaughter, or a domestic-goddess niece. I once heard Daddy tell Cousin Paul, "Take your time choosing a woman. The wrong woman can sneak more out your back door than you can bring through the front."

Cousin Paul did take his time sorting through the women—Maxine, Ruby, Eartha, and Josette, to name a few—who would come to our door bearing fresh, homemade goodies and would leave with armloads of Paul's dirty laundry. They wooed him in their tightest dresses and their highest heels. They washed his dishes and swept his floors and bought him pretty things, like a monogrammed cigarette lighter, a pair of gold cuff links, and bottles of cologne packaged in elegant wrapping. Every woman who visited his apartment would hint that it needed a woman's touch, and that *she* was the perfect woman to administer that touch. Mama would say, "They're goin' about it the wrong way. When you're running after a man, you have to be discreet with it. You can't let him see you coming."

As we watched Cousin Paul's ladyfriends come and go, we often speculated about which one he'd settle down with. We knew for sure that she would have to be a good cook; in particular, her breakfast rice pudding would have to taste as good as Mama's. We knew that because he said so.

Makes about 6 servings

Nonstick cooking spray, for greasing

1½ cups water

1 cup short-grain white rice (I prefer Arborio), rinsed and drained

2 large eggs, room temperature

2 cups evaporated milk

⅔ cup granulated sugar

½ teaspoon ground cinnamon

¼ teaspoon freshly grated nutmeg

¼ teaspoon salt

½ vanilla bean, split, seeds scraped and set aside

2 tablespoons unsalted butter, melted and cooled

Boiling water, as needed

Whipped cream or topping (optional)

1. Preheat the oven to 325°F. Lightly grease a 9-inch square baking dish with the cooking spray and set aside.

2. In a medium saucepan over medium-high heat, bring the water and rice to a boil. Cover the saucepan. Reduce the heat to medium-low and simmer for 15 to 20 minutes, until the rice is tender and the water has fully absorbed. Remove from the heat and set aside to cool slightly.

3. In a large mixing bowl, beat the eggs until they are light and fluffy. Add the evaporated milk, granulated sugar, cinnamon, nutmeg, salt, and vanilla bean seeds to the bowl and stir well. Add the cooked rice and the butter to the bowl and stir until fully combined.

4. Transfer the contents of the mixing bowl to the prepared baking dish. Place the baking dish inside a larger pan. Add boiling water to the larger pan until the water level reaches halfway up the sides of the baking dish.

5. Bake for 35 minutes. Remove from the oven and stir gently in order to redistribute the rice. Return to the oven and bake for 1½ hours, until the rice is lightly browned and has set. Remove from the oven. Remove the baking dish from the larger pan and place on a wire rack to cool for at least 20 minutes.

6. Slice the rice pudding into squares and, if desired, top each square with a dollop of whipped cream or topping. Serve warm.

Red Velvet Pancakes

THESE PILLOWY PANCAKES WITH A CREAM CHEESE GLAZE ARE PERFECT for a special breakfast. My Aunt Helen used to refer to signature dishes like these as "honey traps"—little niceties that wives and girlfriends make to endear themselves to the men they love.

Makes 12 pancakes (3 pancakes per serving)

BATTER

1½ cups all-purpose flour

3 tablespoons light brown sugar

2 tablespoons unsweetened cocoa powder

1½ teaspoons baking powder

½ teaspoon baking soda

½ teaspoon salt

¼ teaspoon ground cinnamon

2 large egg yolks, room temperature, lightly beaten

1 cup buttermilk, room temperature

3 tablespoons unsalted butter, melted and slightly cooled

1 tablespoon red food coloring

1 teaspoon pure vanilla extract

2 large egg whites

Nonstick cooking spray, for greasing

GLAZE

1 (8-ounce) package cream cheese, room temperature

4 tablespoons unsalted butter, melted and cooled

1–2 tablespoons heavy cream, room temperature

1 cup sifted confectioners' sugar

1 teaspoon pure vanilla extract

GARNISH

Confectioners' sugar, for dusting

1. *To make the batter:* In a large mixing bowl, sift together the dry ingredients: the flour, brown sugar, cocoa powder, baking powder, baking soda, salt, and cinnamon. Set aside.

2. In a separate large mixing bowl, beat together the egg yolks with the wet ingredients: the buttermilk, butter, food coloring, and vanilla extract. Continue beating until the mixture is smooth.

3. Whisking constantly, gradually add the buttermilk mixture to the flour mixture. Continue whisking until the batter is just combined.

4. Slowly fold the egg whites into the batter, which should end up with a few lumps in it. Set aside and let rest for 10 to 15 minutes.

5. *To make the glaze:* In the bowl of a stand mixer fitted with the paddle attachment, combine the cream cheese, butter, and heavy cream. Beat on medium-low speed for 2 to 3 minutes, until the mixture is smooth. Reduce the mixer speed to low and gradually add the confectioners' sugar and then the vanilla extract to the mixture. Beat for 1 to 2 minutes, until the mixture is well combined. Feel free to add more heavy cream to achieve a smooth consistency.

6. Place a lightly greased large griddle or skillet over medium heat. Once the surface is hot, ladle on a ½ cup of the batter for each pancake, cooking 4 at a time. Cook for 2 to 3 minutes, until bubbles form on the surface of the batter, the sides of the pancakes are slightly browned, and the bottoms are set. Flip the pancakes over and continue to cook for 1 to 2 minutes, until they are soft and pillowy to the touch. Remove from the griddle or skillet and place 1 pancake each on 4 separate serving plates. Spread a layer of the glaze over each pancake. Using a paper towel, clean the griddle or skillet.

7. Repeat step 6, stacking the fresh pancakes on top of the 4 on the serving plates and spreading another layer of glaze over them.

8. Repeat steps 6 and 7 until all the batter has been used.

9. Dust each stack of pancakes with the confectioners' sugar and serve hot.

Miss Ruthie's Butter Pecan Loaf

My mother's best friend was an older woman named Ruth Gowens who lived across the street from us. Miss Ruthie, who enjoyed cooking and having people stop in for morning coffee, was quite a socialite in our town and had inherited an entire block of fashionable two-story houses that she renovated into multifamily dwellings.

A stout woman, Miss Ruthie wore mink coats and long chandelier earrings as she made her way down the block, collecting her rents. She served all of her food—even her weekday meals—on fancy china. Her ornate forks and spoons, gravy bowls and soup tureens, and butter dishes and sugar bowls would have made the Queen of England green with envy.

When we lived in the old neighborhood, Miss Ruthie would occasionally invite our family to wonderful weekend breakfasts. She was a gracious and accommodating hostess who went out of her way to feed us a quality meal replete with freshly squeezed orange juice and bacon that came from Canada.

On our way home, everybody had something to say. The women in my family praised the meal and the men complained about bumping their elbows against all that fine china.

Now that I'm grown, I look back on those elegant mornings at Miss Ruthie's with great fondness. I remember the dress clothes we wore, the privilege of sitting at a table while grown folks talked about the things that grown folks talked about, the wonderful baked goods that accompanied her morning meals, and how her sugar treats served on fine china made us feel so relaxed . . . well, at least, most of us felt relaxed.

Makes 1 9-inch × 5-inch × 3-inch loaf

- ½ cup (1 stick) unsalted butter
- ½ cup chopped pecans
- 2 cups all-purpose flour, plus more for dusting
- 1½ teaspoons baking powder
- ½ teaspoon ground cinnamon
- ¼ teaspoon freshly grated nutmeg
- ¼ teaspoon salt
- Nonstick cooking spray, for greasing
- 2 large eggs, room temperature, beaten
- 1 cup granulated sugar
- ¼ cup firmly packed light brown sugar
- 1 teaspoon pure vanilla extract
- 1 cup buttermilk, room temperature

1. In a medium saucepan over medium–low heat, melt the butter. Add the pecans and cook, stirring frequently, for 3 to 4 minutes, until the butter has browned and the pecans are lightly toasted. Remove from the heat.

2. Place a sieve over a small bowl. Pour the contents of the saucepan into the sieve, allowing the pecans to drain and reserving the butter. Set the butter aside to cool to room temperature.

3. In a large mixing bowl, sift together the dry ingredients: the flour, baking powder, cinnamon, nutmeg, and salt. Set aside.

4. Preheat the oven to 350°F. Grease a 9-inch × 5-inch × 3-inch loaf pan with the cooking spray and line the bottom of the pan with parchment paper. Grease the parchment and dust the sides and bottom of the pan with some flour. Shake out the excess flour. Set the pan aside.

5. In the bowl of a stand mixer fitted with the whisk attachment, beat the eggs, 1 at a time, on medium speed for 30 seconds each. While the mixer continues to run, add the granulated and brown sugars and vanilla extract and beat for 4 to 5 minutes, until the mixture is light and fluffy. Add the buttermilk and continue to beat until just blended.

6. Reduce the mixer speed to low and gradually add the flour mixture. Scrape down the sides and bottom of the bowl to prevent lumps from forming. Beat for 2 to 3 minutes, until the batter is just blended. Turn off the mixer. Fold in the chopped pecans and then the reserved butter.

7. Transfer the batter to the prepared pan and bake for 45 to 50 minutes, until the cake is golden and springs back when touched. Remove from the oven and set aside to cool in the pan on a wire rack for about 10 minutes.

8. Remove from the pan and set aside on the wire rack to cool for least 3 hours before slicing.

9. Transfer to a serving platter, slice, and serve at room temperature.

My My's Old-Fashioned Crumb Cake

My grandmother, My My, was an old-fashioned woman with modern, practical sensibilities. She could weave lattice pie tops that looked like works of art and could create high, fluffy cakes unrivaled by the best cooks in our community. She had a wise and sure stewardship over her kitchen, planning her Saturday morning grocery shopping excursions around a week's worth of menus put together the night before. Her pots and pans, and dishes and utensils, were cleared and promptly washed as soon as they'd served their purpose; every trinket had its own resting place in her spotless kitchen. Unlike so many women of her generation, my grandmother wasn't the self-depriving, submissive type. My My had clothes, lots of suits, dresses, hats, and purses. Behind my grandfather's back, she once said, "A man expects a woman to want nice and pretty things; why disappoint him?"

As a young child, it seemed to me that My My was made of flour, sugar, butter, and eggs—all the ingredients that went into the wonderful sweet things she created. When she wasn't shopping or primping in the mirror of her chiffonier, she was in the kitchen sifting and stirring, mixing and creaming. I was amazed with the luscious things she could create. My My's crumb cake recipe is an old family favorite that's been passed down through the generations. This decadent, warming treat is best served on a cold, frosty morning with mugs of steaming-hot coffee.

Makes 1 9-inch × 13-inch cake (16–20 squares) or 1 10-inch tube or Bundt cake

recipe continues

My My's Old-Fashioned Crumb Cake *CONTINUED*

TOPPING

2½ cups all-purpose flour

1 cup granulated sugar

1 cup firmly packed light brown sugar

½ teaspoon ground cinnamon

½ teaspoon salt

1 cup (2 sticks) unsalted butter

1 teaspoon pure vanilla extract

BATTER

Nonstick cooking spray, for greasing

2 cups all-purpose flour, plus more for dusting

3 teaspoons baking powder

½ teaspoon salt

½ cup (1 stick) unsalted butter, room temperature

1 cup granulated sugar

½ cup firmly packed dark brown sugar

2 large eggs, room temperature

½ cup whole milk, room temperature

1 teaspoon pure vanilla extract

1 teaspoon ground cinnamon

GARNISH (OPTIONAL)

Confectioners' sugar, for dusting

1. *To make the topping:* In a medium mixing bowl, sift together the dry ingredients: the flour, granulated and brown sugars, cinnamon, and salt. Set aside.

2. In a small saucepan over low heat, melt the butter. Remove from the heat and stir in the vanilla extract. Set aside to allow the butter to cool slightly.

3. Slowly drizzle the butter mixture into the flour mixture and toss gently with a fork. Continue to toss until all of the butter is absorbed and the mixture has formed into moist clumps about ¼ inch to ½ inch in size. Set aside.

4. Preheat the oven to 350°F. Grease a 9-inch × 13-inch baking dish or a 10-inch tube or Bundt pan with the cooking spray and dust the sides and bottom of the dish or pan with some flour. Shake out the excess flour. Set the dish or pan aside.

5. *To make the batter:* In a medium mixing bowl, sift together the dry ingredients: the flour, baking powder, and salt. Set aside.

As a young child, it seemed to me that My My was made of flour, sugar, butter, and eggs—all the ingredients that went into the wonderful sweet things she created.

6. In the bowl of a stand mixer fitted with the paddle attachment, break up the butter by mixing on low speed for 1 minute. Add the granulated and brown sugars and cream together the butter and sugars on medium speed for 2 to 3 minutes, until the mixture is light and fluffy. Scrape down the sides and bottom of the bowl to prevent lumps from forming. As the mixer is running, reduce the speed to low and slowly add the eggs, 1 at a time; after you add each egg, scrape down the sides of the bowl and resume beating on low speed for 30 seconds. Add the milk, vanilla extract, and cinnamon and beat at low speed for 2 to 3 seconds, until just incorporated. Add the flour mixture to the bowl of the mixer ⅓ at a time, beating each time at low speed for 2 seconds until just combined. Turn off the mixer.

7. Transfer the batter to the prepared baking dish or pan. Using a rubber or silicone spatula or a butter knife, evenly spread the batter in the pan. Using your fingers, scatter the crumb topping over the batter, covering it evenly and completely. Bake for 45 to 55 minutes (rotating the pan at 15-minute intervals), until a wooden toothpick inserted into the center of the cake comes out clean. Remove from the oven and set aside to cool in the pan on a wire rack for at least 30 minutes.

8. Carefully transfer to a serving platter, crumb side up. Dust with the confectioners' sugar, if desired, and slice and serve warm.

Zucchini Bread

THIS RECIPE PUTS ZUCCHINI FROM THE GARDEN TO DELICIOUS USE. The orange juice and zest that it calls for set it apart from other recipes. My grandmother made this bread often when zucchini from the garden was plentiful. My grandfather would always ask her what she was going to do with all that zucchini, but of course, he knew she'd turn it into cobblers and breads. In those days, folks didn't throw away anything.

Makes 1 9-inch × 5-inch × 3-inch loaf

Nonstick cooking spray, for greasing
2 small, young zucchini
2 cups all-purpose flour
1 teaspoon baking powder
1 teaspoon baking soda
1 teaspoon ground cinnamon
½ teaspoon ground allspice
½ teaspoon salt
1 cup granulated sugar
½ cup firmly packed light brown sugar
½ cup (1 stick) unsalted butter, melted and cooled
2 large eggs, room temperature
¼ cup sour cream, room temperature
1 tablespoon freshly squeezed orange juice
1 teaspoon pure vanilla extract
1 teaspoon freshly grated orange zest
½ cup walnuts, toasted and coarsely chopped

1. Preheat the oven to 350°F. Lightly grease a 9-inch × 5-inch × 3-inch loaf pan with the cooking spray and set aside.

2. Using a box grater's large-holed side, grate the zucchini. Place the zucchini between several layers of paper towels to absorb any excess liquid and set aside.

3. In a large mixing bowl, sift together the dry ingredients: the flour, baking powder, baking soda, cinnamon, allspice, and salt. Set aside.

4. In a medium mixing bowl, whisk together the granulated and brown sugars, butter, eggs, sour cream, orange juice, vanilla extract, and orange zest. Add the zucchini and stir well until it is evenly distributed.

5. Using a rubber or silicone spatula, gently fold the zucchini mixture into the flour mixture until the batter is well combined. Fold in the chopped walnuts. (Do not overmix.)

6. Transfer the batter to the prepared pan. Use the spatula to smooth the top of the batter and spread it evenly in the pan. Bake for 55 to 60 minutes, until a wooden toothpick inserted into the center of the loaf comes out clean. Remove from the oven and set aside to cool in the pan on a wire rack for 10 minutes.

7. Turn out the loaf onto the wire rack and allow to cool completely.

8. Transfer to a serving platter, slice, and serve at room temperature.

Chocolate–Macadamia Waffles

My paternal grandfather's sister Frances had a Martha Stewart–type personality. She cooked, crafted, and gardened like a goddess, and her front porch was always crowded with potted plants that looked as though they could have won ribbons. Whenever we traveled to Paris, Tennessee, to visit Daddy's family, Mama and I always tried to spend a night or two (without Daddy) at her house. There was so much girly stuff to see and do, and she was always working on something new—a quilt, crocheted doilies for her tabletops, tatting for the hem of an apron, her side yard flower bed, a stenciling project. A measly hour or two didn't give us the time we needed to take it all in. The women on Daddy's side of the family were much better at crafts than the women on Mama's side, who were much better cooks. Aunt Frances's feminine artisanship appealed to my emerging inner domestic goddess.

At the end of each visit, Aunt Frances would section off pieces of the projects that she was working on to help get us started on our own projects. We would leave with a large brown grocery bag crammed with blocks of quilt starters, scraps of fabric from old dresses, hand-sketched quilt patterns, small pieces of crochet, and at least seven or eight plant clippings wrapped in wet newspaper.

Aunt Frances was also a great Southern cook. During our visits, she'd serve decadent, old-fashioned country breakfasts replete with dishes like country-fried chicken and onion gravy, homemade yeast rolls, sautéed potatoes, smoked ham slices, egg pie, blackberry dumplings, and sometimes her delicious Chocolate–Macadamia Waffles. To me, these brownie-like waffles were king. She always used to say that she reserved these waffles for special occasions, so when she included them in her breakfast offerings to us, she made us feel royal.

recipe continues

Chocolate–Macadamia Waffles *CONTINUED*

Makes about 12 4-inch waffles

Nonstick cooking spray, for greasing
2 large egg whites, room temperature
2 cups all-purpose flour
½ cup granulated sugar
3 teaspoons baking powder
½ teaspoon salt
2 large egg yolks, room temperature
1 cup whole milk, room temperature
½ cup vegetable oil
2 squares semisweet chocolate, melted
¼ cup heavy cream, room temperature
1 teaspoon pure vanilla extract
½ cup finely chopped macadamia nuts
Confectioners' sugar, for dusting (optional)

1. Preheat a lightly greased waffle iron according to the manufacturer's directions.

2. Using a hand mixer set at medium speed, beat the egg whites in a small mixing bowl until stiff peaks form. Set aside.

3. In a medium mixing bowl, sift together the dry ingredients: the flour, granulated sugar, baking powder, and salt. Make a well in the center of the mixture and set aside.

4. In a separate medium mixing bowl, lightly beat the egg yolks. Add the milk, vegetable oil, melted chocolate, heavy cream, and vanilla extract and stir until combined.

5. Add the chocolate mixture to the flour mixture and stir until just moistened. (Do not overmix; the batter should be lumpy.) Add the nuts and stir until evenly blended.

6. Fold the beaten egg whites into the batter and set aside to rest for at least 5 minutes.

7. Pour a ladleful of the batter on the prepared waffle iron and cook according to the manufacturer's directions. Once the waffle is properly cooked, use the tines of a fork to lift it off the iron and place on a serving platter.

8. Repeat step 7 until all the batter has been used.

9. Serve warm, with a dusting of the confectioners' sugar, if desired.

Mama's French Toast Casserole

EVERYONE HAS A FAVORITE HOLIDAY TRADITION. WHEN I THINK OF MINE, comfort food, like Mama's French Toast Casserole, is at the top of my list. When I was a child, the aroma of sugar and spices baking in the oven on a holiday morning was always intoxicating. This dish always makes me think of Mama, who worked tirelessly to create holidays that were flavorful and fragrant.

Makes about 12 servings

½ cup (1 stick) unsalted butter, melted
2 cups half-and-half, room temperature
8 large eggs, room temperature, lightly beaten
1 cup whole milk, room temperature
1 cup firmly packed light brown sugar
⅓ cup chopped pecans
1 teaspoon pure vanilla extract
1 teaspoon ground cinnamon
½ teaspoon salt
¼ teaspoon freshly grated nutmeg
1 (1-pound) loaf French bread, cut into 1-inch cubes
Maple syrup, for serving (optional)

1. Evenly pour the butter into a 9-inch × 13-inch baking dish. Set aside.

2. In a large mixing bowl, combine the half-and-half, eggs, milk, brown sugar, pecans, vanilla extract, cinnamon, salt, and nutmeg and whisk until well combined. (Do not overmix.)

3. Layer ½ of the bread cubes on the bottom of the baking dish. Pour ½ of the egg mixture over the bread cubes. Layer the remaining bread cubes on top and pour the remaining egg mixture over them, making sure all bread cubes are evenly covered. Cover with plastic wrap and refrigerate for 1 hour or overnight.

4. Remove the dish from the refrigerator 30 minutes before baking. Preheat the oven to 350°F.

5. Remove the plastic wrap from the baking dish and discard. Cover the baking dish with aluminum foil and bake for 30 minutes. Uncover and bake for an additional 15 minutes, until a wooden toothpick inserted near the center of the casserole comes out clean. Remove from the oven and let stand for 5 minutes.

6. Transfer to a serving platter, slice, and serve warm, with the maple syrup, if desired.

COOKS' NOTE: *For an added touch, drizzle a small amount of maple syrup on top of the casserole and return it to the oven for 5 to 6 minutes, until the syrup has caramelized.*

Brown Sugar and Cinnamon Swirl Pancakes

I'VE SERVED A LOT OF PANCAKES THROUGH THE YEARS, BUT THESE ARE the pancakes my family and friends ask for most often. Nearly everyone says the delicious ribbon of cinnamon and brown sugar reminds them of eating a slice of old-fashioned coffee cake.

Makes about 8 4-inch pancakes

FILLING

⅓ cup firmly packed light brown sugar

4 tablespoons unsalted butter, melted and slightly cooled

1½ teaspoons ground cinnamon

GLAZE

4 tablespoons unsalted butter

4 ounces cream cheese, room temperature

1 cup sifted confectioners' sugar

½ teaspoon pure vanilla extract

2–3 tablespoons (or as needed) heavy cream, room temperature, for thinning

BATTER

1¼ cups all-purpose flour

2 teaspoons baking powder

¼ teaspoon salt

1 cup whole milk, room temperature

1 large egg, room temperature, lightly beaten

1 tablespoon vegetable oil

Nonstick cooking spray, for greasing

1. *To make the filling:* In a medium mixing bowl, stir together the brown sugar, butter, and cinnamon. Transfer the filling to a quart-sized resealable plastic bag and set aside.

2. *To make the glaze:* In a small saucepan over low heat, warm the butter until it melts. Remove from the heat and add the cream cheese. Stir until the mixture is almost smooth. Add the confectioners' sugar to the saucepan and stir until well combined. Add the vanilla extract and stir until well combined. Thin the mixture with the heavy cream as needed to achieve a smooth consistency. Set aside.

recipe continues

Brown Sugar and Cinnamon Swirl Pancakes *CONTINUED*

3. *To make the batter:* In a large mixing bowl, sift together the dry ingredients: the flour, baking powder, and salt. Whisk the milk, egg, and vegetable oil into the mixture until the batter is just moistened—a few small lumps are OK.

4. Place a lightly greased large griddle or skillet over medium heat. Once the surface is hot, ladle on ⅓ cup of the batter for each pancake, cooking 4 at a time.

5. Snip off one of the lower corners of the resealable bag and pinch it shut until ready to use. After 1 minute of cooking time for the pancakes, gently squeeze the bag to pipe a small amount of the cinnamon filling on top of each pancake in a swirl pattern. Cook for 2 to 3 minutes, until bubbles form on the surface of the batter, the sides of the pancakes are slightly browned, and the bottoms are set. Flip the pancakes over and continue to cook for 1 to 2 minutes, until they are soft and pillowy to the touch. Remove from the griddle or skillet and place 1 pancake each on 4 separate serving plates. Using a paper towel, clean the griddle or skillet.

6. Repeat step 4, stacking the fresh pancakes on top of the 4 on the serving plates and placing a layer of glaze over them.

7. Repeat steps 4 and 5 until all the batter has been used.

8. Serve warm.

Tuesday Morning Blueberry Loaf

On the first Monday of every month, my grandmother deep-cleaned her house. She raised the windows to air the rooms, even in the thick of winter. She soaked, rinsed, and starched the curtains and hung them in the sun. She waxed the wood furniture and floors.

At the end of the day, she'd bake something sweet and wrap and store it for the next day, as the Tuesday after deep-cleaning day was her morning of rest. She'd sleep later than usual and wouldn't throw herself into domesticity the way she did every other morning. Instead, she'd go into her sanctuary, her kitchen, and unwrap the sweet she'd made and display it on one of her many dessert pedestals. She'd spend most of the morning in the family room with a cup of tea or coffee and a slice of her sweet, reading women's magazines and cookbooks. We didn't drop in or call to discuss our husband or boyfriend woes or any other *urgent* matter that could wait until later, because everybody knew that the first Tuesday morning of every month, my grandmother rested.

When blueberries were in season, she'd usually make one of her lovely blueberry loaves. The granulated sugar sprinkled on top of the batter before baking gives this loaf a nice little crust.

Makes 1 9-inch × 5-inch × 3-inch loaf (about 12 servings)

Nonstick cooking spray, for greasing

2 cups all-purpose flour (divided), plus more for dusting

2 cups fresh or frozen blueberries, thawed and drained

2 teaspoons baking powder

¼ teaspoon freshly grated nutmeg

¼ teaspoon salt

½ cup (1 stick) unsalted butter, room temperature

1 cup granulated sugar

½ cup firmly packed light brown sugar

2 large eggs

2 teaspoons freshly grated lemon zest (about 2 medium lemons)

1 teaspoon pure vanilla extract

½ cup whole milk, room temperature

¾ cup chopped walnuts

Additional granulated sugar, for sprinkling

recipe continues

Tuesday Morning Blueberry Loaf *CONTINUED*

1. Preheat the oven to 350°F. Grease a 9-inch × 5-inch × 3-inch loaf pan with the cooking spray and line the bottom of the pan with parchment paper. Grease the parchment and dust the sides and bottom of the pan with some flour. Shake out the excess flour. Set the pan aside.

2. In a medium mixing bowl, toss the blueberries with 1 tablespoon of the flour. Set aside.

3. In a large mixing bowl, sift together the dry ingredients: the remaining flour, baking powder, nutmeg, and salt. Set aside.

4. In the bowl of a stand mixer fitted with the paddle attachment, break up the butter by mixing on low speed for 1 minute. Add the granulated and brown sugars and cream together the butter and sugars on medium speed for 2 to 3 minutes, until the mixture is light and fluffy. Scrape down the sides and bottom of the bowl to prevent lumps from forming. As the mixer is running, reduce the speed to low and slowly add the eggs, 1 at a time; after you add each egg, scrape down the sides of the bowl and resume beating on low speed for 30 seconds. Add the lemon zest and vanilla extract and beat until combined.

5. Reduce the mixer speed to low and add the flour mixture and the milk to the bowl of the mixer in alternating thirds, starting and ending with the flour. Continue beating until smooth. (Do not overbeat.)

6. Remove the bowl from the mixer and, using a rubber or silicone spatula, fold the blueberries and walnuts into the batter.

7. Transfer the batter to the prepared pan. Using the spatula or a butter knife, smooth the top of the batter and sprinkle it with the additional granulated sugar. Bake for 60 to 70 minutes, until a wooden toothpick inserted into the center of the loaf comes out clean. (If necessary, cover the loaf with an aluminum foil tent at the 55-minute point to prevent overbrowning.) Remove from the oven and set aside to cool in the pan on a wire rack for 30 minutes.

8. Turn out the loaf onto the wire rack and allow to cool completely.

9. Transfer to a serving platter, slice, and serve at room temperature.

Aunt Bulah's Brown Sugar–Hazelnut Biscuits

AUNT BULAH, MY GRANDMOTHER'S ENTERPRISING YOUNGER SISTER, owned and operated a popular community grocery store in New Orleans. She always made me feel as though I was the most special person in the world. Once, when Mama and I went to visit her, Aunt Bulah took me to the home of a local dressmaker, Miss Beatrice, as she had commissioned her to design and sew four Sunday dresses for me. I was seven years old, and the thought of wearing pretty dresses designed especially for me made me feel like a movie star. In my mind, Miss Beatrice was the famous Hollywood dressmaker Edith Head and I was the beautiful actress Dorothy Dandridge. Aunt Bulah told me, "Girls need lots of lovely dresses."

Today, when I go into a dress shop, I often get carried away and walk out feeling guilty because I've exceeded my budget. But Aunt Bulah's words always come rushing back to me—"Girls need lots of lovely dresses"—and then I don't feel so bad.

Makes 10 biscuits

Nonstick cooking spray, for greasing
1 cup firmly packed light brown sugar
¾ cup (1½ sticks) unsalted butter
½ cup dark corn syrup
1½ cups coarsely chopped hazelnuts
1 (10-count) tube refrigerated biscuit dough, separated

1. Preheat the oven to 350°F. Grease a 9-inch square baking dish with the cooking spray and set aside.

2. In a medium saucepan over low heat, combine the brown sugar, butter, and corn syrup and cook until the butter has melted. Raise the heat to high and bring the mixture to a soft boil. Cook, uncovered, for 3 to 4 minutes, until the mixture thickens. Remove from the heat and stir in the hazelnuts.

3. Pour the hazelnut mixture into the prepared baking dish and spread it evenly in the dish. Arrange each round of biscuit dough on top of the hazelnut mixture.

4. Bake for 10 to 12 minutes, until the biscuits are golden brown and puffy and the hazelnut syrup is bubbling. Remove from the oven.

5. Transfer to a serving platter and serve warm.

Aunt Evelyn's Banana–Macadamia Bread

AUNT EVELYN—MY MY'S BABY SISTER—WAS AN EXCEPTIONAL COOK AND baker. Her stews and gumbos were the talk of our family, and we simply couldn't visit New Orleans without asking her to make some. She used to tell us that she put a "little bit of *this*, and a little bit of *that*" in her food to make it taste so good. We didn't ask for most of her prized recipes, but I did ask for this Banana–Macadamia Bread recipe. I couldn't help myself—not *just* because it belonged to my great-aunt but also because this bread is so popular with family and friends.

Makes 1 9-inch × 5-inch × 3-inch loaf (about 12 servings)

Nonstick cooking spray, for greasing

½ cup (1 stick) unsalted butter, room temperature

½ cup granulated sugar

½ cup firmly packed light brown sugar

2 large eggs

1 cup mashed ripe bananas (about 2–3 bananas)

1 teaspoon pure vanilla extract

2 cups all-purpose flour

1 teaspoon baking powder

1 teaspoon baking soda

¼ teaspoon salt

½ cup buttermilk, room temperature

1 cup finely chopped macadamia nuts

Fresh fruit or yogurt, for serving

1. Preheat the oven to 350°F. Grease a 9-inch × 5-inch × 3-inch loaf pan with the cooking spray. Set aside.

2. In the bowl of a stand mixer fitted with the paddle attachment, break up the butter by mixing on low speed for 1 minute. Add the granulated and brown sugars and cream together the butter and sugars on medium speed for 2 to 3 minutes, until the mixture is light and fluffy. Scrape down the sides and bottom of the bowl to prevent lumps from forming. As the mixer is running, reduce the speed to low and slowly add the eggs, 1 at a time; after you add each egg, scrape down the sides of the bowl and resume beating on low speed for 30 seconds. Add the bananas and vanilla extract and beat until combined. Turn off the mixer.

3. In a medium mixing bowl, sift together the dry ingredients: the flour, baking powder, baking soda, and salt.

4. Set the mixer speed to low and add the flour mixture and the buttermilk to the bowl of the mixer in alternating thirds, starting and ending with the flour mixture. Continue beating until the mixture is just moistened. (Do not overbeat.) Fold in the macadamia nuts.

5. Transfer the batter to the prepared pan. Using a rubber or silicone spatula or a butter knife, smooth the top of the batter. Bake for 55 to 60 minutes, until a wooden toothpick inserted into the center of the bread comes out clean. Remove from the oven and set aside to cool in the pan on a wire rack for 15 minutes.

6. Turn out the bread onto the wire rack and allow to cool completely.

7. Transfer to a serving platter, slice, and serve at room temperature with the fresh fruit or yogurt.

Mama's Strawberry Coffee Cake

MAMA'S STRAWBERRY COFFEE CAKES WERE ALWAYS DELICIOUSLY FRAgrant, their scent wafting through our house on summer mornings. Daddy and I would *ooh* and *ahh* our way through every crumb. Mama would say, "Go on, now! You're making me feel like I'm 10 feet tall." But we knew Mama really didn't mind us carrying on over her strawberry cake or any of the special delicacies that she cooked for us. Truth be told, we knew she anticipated our joyful noises, and that she cooked with her freshest butter and her sweetest sugar so we would *ooh* and *ahh* and ask for seconds. Cooks love to be appreciated; they want you to praise their dishes.

This coffee cake, bursting with fresh strawberries, is topped with a delicious streusel. Streusel always makes things taste better.

Makes 1 9-inch square coffee cake

BATTER

Nonstick cooking spray, for greasing

1½ cups all-purpose flour

1 teaspoon baking powder

1 teaspoon baking soda

½ teaspoon salt

2 tablespoons unsalted butter, melted

½ cup granulated sugar

1 large egg, room temperature

½ teaspoon pure vanilla extract

½ cup half-and-half, room temperature

2 cups fresh strawberries, hulled and chopped

TOPPING

½ cup all-purpose flour

½ cup granulated sugar

½ cup chopped walnuts

½ cup (1 stick) unsalted butter

½ teaspoon ground cinnamon

1. Preheat the oven to 350°F. Grease a 9-inch square baking dish with the cooking spray and set aside.

2. *To make the batter:* In a large mixing bowl, sift together the dry ingredients: the flour, baking powder, baking soda, and salt. Set aside.

recipe continues

3. In the bowl of a stand mixer fitted with the paddle attachment, break up the butter by mixing on low speed for 1 minute. Add the granulated sugar and cream together the butter and sugar on medium speed for 2 to 3 minutes, until the mixture is light and fluffy. Scrape down the sides and bottom of the bowl to prevent lumps from forming. As the mixer is running, reduce the speed to low and add the egg, making sure that it is thoroughly incorporated into the mixture. Add the vanilla extract and beat until combined. (Do not overbeat.) Turn off the mixer.

4. Set the mixer speed to low and add the flour mixture and the half-and-half to the bowl of the mixer in alternating thirds, starting and ending with the flour mixture. Continue beating until the mixture is just moistened. (Do not overbeat.)

5. *To make the topping:* In a small mixing bowl, combine the flour, granulated sugar, walnuts, butter, and cinnamon and, using your hands, stir until well blended.

6. Transfer the batter to the prepared baking dish and arrange the strawberries evenly on top of the batter. Evenly sprinkle the topping on top of the strawberries. Bake for 40 to 50 minutes, until a wooden toothpick inserted into the center of the cake comes out clean. Remove from the oven and set aside to cool in the baking dish on a wire rack for 10 minutes.

7. Turn out the cake onto the wire rack and allow to cool completely.

8. Transfer to a serving platter. Slice and serve at room temperature.

Applesauce Spice Loaf

My father's father, Jack Pinner, was an entertaining, talkative man. He was the kind of man who had so many life stories that he could transition from one story to another without pausing. Grandpa Jack also used the freedom of speech that's afforded to old people as justification for speaking his mind.

Grandpa Jack, who was divorced from Daddy's mother, Mary Lee, came to live with my parents for the last stretch of his life. By that time, he'd spent most of his savings on the things old men spend their money on—thick slabs of delicatessen cheese and bologna, fishing tackle and hunting gear, and younger women. Once, we were sitting down to a late breakfast, and Mama had baked one of her tasty applesauce loaves. Grandpa Jack turned to Daddy and said, in front of everybody, "Son, your wife might be a little on the uppity side, but she sure can make a tasty loaf." Everybody got a chuckle out of it—even Mama, who chose to focus on the compliment rather than the snide remark.

The way I remember it, Grandpa loved Mama's Applesauce Spice Loaf better than any of her other sweet loaves. It has a comforting, old-fashioned, down-home flavor that no doubt reminded him of the treats that he'd grown up with.

This loaf calls for simple pantry ingredients that you probably already have on hand. I love it when simple things come together to produce something delicious.

Makes 1 9-inch × 5-inch × 3-inch loaf (about 12 servings)

TOPPING

2 teaspoons granulated sugar

¼ teaspoon ground cinnamon

BATTER

Nonstick cooking spray, for greasing

2 cups all-purpose flour, plus more for dusting

1 teaspoon ground cinnamon

1 teaspoon baking powder

½ teaspoon baking soda

¼ teaspoon freshly grated nutmeg

¼ teaspoon salt

⅛ teaspoon ground allspice

1 cup unsweetened applesauce

½ cup (1 stick) unsalted butter, melted and slightly cooled

½ cup granulated sugar

⅓ cup firmly packed light brown sugar

1 whole large egg, room temperature

1 large egg yolk, room temperature

2 tablespoons apple cider (not sparkling)

1 teaspoon pure vanilla extract

½ cup chopped pecans or walnuts

recipe continues

Applesauce Spice Loaf *CONTINUED*

1. *To make the topping:* In a small mixing bowl, combine the granulated sugar and cinnamon and stir well. Set aside.

2. Preheat the oven to 350°F. Grease a 9-inch × 5-inch × 3-inch loaf pan with the cooking spray and line the bottom of the pan with parchment paper. Grease the parchment and dust the sides and bottom of the pan with some flour. Shake out the excess flour. Set the pan aside.

3. *To make the batter:* In a large mixing bowl, sift together the dry ingredients: the flour, cinnamon, baking powder, baking soda, nutmeg, salt, and allspice. Set aside.

4. In a separate large mixing bowl, whisk together the applesauce, butter, granulated and brown sugars, egg, egg yolk, apple cider, and vanilla extract until the mixture is smooth. Gently stir the flour mixture into the applesauce mixture ⅓ at a time until just combined. Fold the nuts into the batter until well distributed.

5. Transfer the batter to the prepared pan. Evenly sprinkle the batter with the topping and bake for 45 to 50 minutes, until a wooden toothpick inserted into the center of the loaf comes out clean. Remove from the oven and set aside to cool in the pan on a wire rack for 15 minutes.

6. Turn out the loaf onto the wire rack and allow to cool completely.

7. Transfer to a serving platter, slice, and serve at room temperature.

Old-Fashioned Raisin Buns with Vanilla Glaze

My maternal great-grandmother, Ella, had a reputation for being the kind of cook who could make a tasty breakfast out of next to nothing. Her Raisin Buns with Vanilla Glaze were a classic in our family. There are a lot of different bun flavors, but Great-Grandma Ella's raisin buns are timeless and delicious with a cup of tea or coffee or a glass of milk. When I make them for people who stop in, it tastes as though Great-Grandma Ella is still in the kitchen. They can be eaten hot or at room temperature.

Makes about 15 buns

DOUGH

Nonstick cooking spray, for greasing

1 cup hot water

¾ cup raisins

3 cups all-purpose flour, plus more for kneading

½ cup granulated sugar

2 teaspoons baking powder

1 teaspoon baking soda

½ teaspoon salt

¼ teaspoon freshly grated nutmeg

¾ cup (1½ sticks) unsalted butter, cold, cut into small pieces

½ cup whole milk, room temperature

2 large eggs, room temperature, well beaten

1 teaspoon pure vanilla extract

GLAZE

2 cups sifted confectioners' sugar

1 tablespoon unsalted butter, melted and cooled

1–2 tablespoons whole milk

1 teaspoon pure vanilla extract

Great-Grandma Ella's raisin buns are timeless and delicious with a cup of tea or coffee or a glass of milk.

1. Preheat the oven to 375°F. Lightly grease a large baking sheet with the cooking spray and set aside.

2. In a small mixing bowl, soak the raisins in the hot water for 10 minutes. Drain the raisins and set aside.

3. *To make the dough:* In a large mixing bowl, whisk together the dry ingredients: the flour, granulated sugar, baking powder, baking soda, salt, and nutmeg. Using your fingers, a pastry blender, or the tines of a fork, cut the butter into the flour mixture until it resembles coarse crumbs. Add the milk, eggs, and vanilla extract, stirring just until the mixture is blended. (Do not overmix.) Gently fold the raisins into the dough.

4. Turn out the dough onto a floured work surface. With floured hands, knead for 2 minutes, until it is smooth. Form it into a ball.

5. Using a floured rolling pin, roll out the dough into a 1½-inch-thick, 9-inch × 14-inch rectangle. Using a 3-inch round biscuit cutter or the rim of a drinking glass, cut out the buns.

6. Place the buns on the prepared baking sheet and bake for 10 to 12 minutes, until the buns are light golden brown.

7. *To make the glaze:* In a small mixing bowl, combine the confectioners' sugar, the butter, 1 tablespoon of the milk, and the vanilla extract and stir until the glaze is smooth. Add up to 1 tablespoon more of the milk if needed to reach a smooth consistency.

8. Remove the baking sheet from the oven. Use a spatula to transfer the buns to a wire rack. Drizzle the buns with the glaze while they are still hot.

9. Transfer to a serving platter and serve hot or at room temperature.

Chocolate–Hazelnut Granola

My mother's eldest sister, Marjell, once told me that it was a disgrace to mistreat a house guest—especially a man who had come to call. She said it was in the Bible. Aunt Marjell, who was our family's chocolate expert, always kept something sweet on hand for her morning guests to nibble. For example, she always had a container full of her homemade Chocolate–Hazelnut Granola nearby . . . especially for her men friends.

Makes about 6 cups

3 cups old-fashioned rolled oats
1 cup blanched, slivered almonds
½ cup unsweetened cocoa powder
¼ cup wheat germ
½ teaspoon fine sea salt
¾ cup virgin coconut oil
¾ cup pure maple syrup
½ teaspoon pure vanilla extract
1 cup raw hazelnuts, roughly chopped

1. Preheat the oven to 300°F. Line a large rimmed baking sheet with parchment paper. Set aside.

2. In a large mixing bowl, stir together the rolled oats, almonds, cocoa powder, wheat germ, and salt. Set aside.

3. In a small saucepan over medium–low heat, combine the coconut oil, maple syrup, and vanilla extract and stir until the mixture is melted and well blended. Add the oil mixture to the oat mixture and stir well.

4. Spread the mixture onto the prepared baking sheet. Bake for 15 minutes and stir well. Return to the oven for 15 minutes and stir again. Bake for 5 to 10 minutes more, until the mixture is dry and toasted. Remove from the oven, fold in the hazelnuts, and set aside to cool completely. (The granola will crisp as it cools.)

5. Serve or store the granola at room temperature in an airtight container.

Wilma Vickory's Chocolate Streusel Coffee Cake

MISS WILMA, AN OLDER LADY WHO LIVED IN A TIDY BROWN AND WHITE house in our neighborhood, was a friend and confidante to the younger wives who lived on the block. Miss Wilma relished consoling and advising her young and inexperienced charges. She would invite the young wives to morning coffee and cake, and tell them things like, "Don't worship your husband. You can put him on a pedestal, you can warm his slippers and keep them by the bed, but don't worship at his feet." Or, "A lot of good men are ruined because their women give 'em too much coddling."

The young wives would rush home and begin putting their newfound wisdom to good use. And before long, the young wives would return to Wilma Vickory's kitchen for her tried-and-true recipes. Breakfast is a special event when you bring Wilma Vickory's moist and delicious Chocolate Streusel Coffee Cake to the table. As with most things, the streusel topping really sets it off.

Makes 1 9-inch coffee cake

FILLING AND TOPPING

- Nonstick cooking spray, for greasing
- 1 cup finely chopped pecans
- ½ cup firmly packed light brown sugar
- 1 tablespoon instant coffee granules
- 1 teaspoon ground cinnamon
- 1 cup semisweet chocolate chips
- ¼ cup all-purpose flour
- ¼ cup unsweetened cocoa powder
- ½ cup (1 stick) unsalted butter, cold, cut into small pieces

BATTER

- 1 cup (2 sticks) unsalted butter, room temperature
- 1⅓ cups granulated sugar
- 3 large eggs, room temperature
- 1½ teaspoons pure vanilla extract
- 2½ cups all-purpose flour, plus more for dusting
- 1½ teaspoons baking powder
- 1½ teaspoons baking soda
- ¼ teaspoon salt
- 1 cup sour cream, room temperature

recipe continues

1. Preheat the oven to 350°F. Grease the bottom and sides of a 9-inch springform pan with the cooking spray and dust the sides and bottom of the pan with some flour. Shake out the excess flour. Set the pan aside.

2. *To make the filling and topping:* In a medium mixing bowl, combine the pecans, brown sugar, coffee granules, and cinnamon and mix well.

3. Transfer ¾ cup of the pecan mixture to a small mixing bowl and stir in the chocolate chips. This will be the filling. Set aside.

4. Add the flour and cocoa powder to the pecan mixture in the medium mixing bowl and stir until combined. Using your fingers, a pastry blender, or the tines of a fork, cut the butter into the flour–pecan mixture until it forms small, moist clumps. This will be the topping. Set aside.

5. *To make the batter:* In the bowl of a stand mixer fitted with the paddle attachment, break up the butter by mixing on low speed for 1 minute. Add the granulated sugar and cream together the butter and sugar on medium speed for 2 to 3 minutes, until the mixture is light and fluffy. Scrape down the sides and bottom of the bowl to prevent lumps from forming. As the mixer is running, reduce the speed to low and slowly add the eggs, 1 at a time; after you add each egg, scrape down the sides of the bowl and resume beating on low speed for 30 seconds. Add the vanilla extract and resume beating on low speed for 30 seconds. Turn off the mixer.

6. In a medium mixing bowl, sift together the dry ingredients: the flour, baking powder, baking soda, and salt.

7. Turn the mixer speed to low and slowly add the flour mixture and the sour cream to the bowl of the running mixer ⅓ at a time, alternating back and forth, making sure to end with the flour mixture. Once the mixture is smooth, turn off the mixer.

8. Transfer ½ of the batter into the prepared pan and smooth the top with a rubber or silicone spatula or a butter knife. Sprinkle the filling evenly over the batter. Spread the remaining batter over the filling from step 3 and smooth the top. Sprinkle with the topping from step 4.

9. Set the springform pan on a baking sheet and place the baking sheet in the center of the oven, directly on the middle shelf. Bake for 30 minutes. Remove from the oven. Place a sheet of aluminum foil loosely over the top of the pan to keep the cake from browning too quickly. Return to the oven for 35 to 40 minutes, until a wooden toothpick inserted into the center of the cake comes out clean. Remove from the oven and remove the foil. Transfer the pan to a wire rack and set aside to cool to room temperature, about 1 hour.

10. Loosen the cake from the springform pan by sliding an offset spatula around the inside ring. Remove the springform pan from the cake.

11. Transfer to a serving platter and serve hot or warm.

Breakfast is a special event when you bring Wilma Vickory's moist and delicious Chocolate Streusel Coffee Cake to the table.

Orange-Filled Crescents

I ALWAYS FEEL UPLIFTED WHEN I SMELL THE AROMA OF ORANGES, especially in the morning. Orange is such a bright, crisp, and pleasing flavor. These sweet crescent-shaped rolls are a delightful morning treat. They have an orange-flavored filling, chopped pecans, bits of grated orange zest, and a drizzle of orange glaze on top. These rolls really brighten up a plate of bacon and eggs.

Makes 24 rolls

DOUGH

½ cup granulated sugar (divided)

¼ cup warm water (110°F–115°F)

2¼ teaspoons (1¼-ounce package) active dry yeast

½ cup buttermilk, room temperature

2 large eggs, room temperature

½ cup (1 stick) melted unsalted butter (divided)

2 tablespoons freshly grated orange zest

½ teaspoon salt

⅛ teaspoon baking soda

3¾–4 cups all-purpose flour, plus more kneading

Nonstick cooking spray, for greasing

FILLING

¾ cup granulated sugar

½ cup finely chopped pecans

4 tablespoons unsalted butter, melted and cooled

1 tablespoon freshly grated orange zest

GLAZE

¾ cup granulated sugar

½ cup (1 stick) unsalted butter, melted and cooled

½ cup sour cream, room temperature

2 tablespoons freshly squeezed orange juice

½ teaspoon pure vanilla extract

1. *To make the dough:* In a small mixing bowl, combine ¼ cup of the granulated sugar, the warm water, and the yeast. Stir until the yeast and sugar dissolve. Set aside at room temperature for 10 minutes, until the mixture becomes foamy.

recipe continues

2. In the bowl of a stand mixer fitted with the paddle attachment, combine the buttermilk, the eggs, 6 tablespoons of the butter, the remaining granulated sugar, the orange zest, the salt, and the baking soda and blend on low speed for 1 minute. Using a wooden spoon, stir the yeast mixture and 1½ cups of the flour into the mixture. Beat the mixture for 30 seconds on low speed; raise the speed to high and beat for 3 minutes. While the mixer continues to run, add more of the flour, ½ cup at a time, to the bowl. Continue beating until a soft ball of dough forms. (Use only as much flour as you need to reach this consistency.) Turn off the mixer.

3. Turn out the dough onto a floured work surface. With floured hands, knead the dough lightly for 7 to 8 minutes, until it is smooth and elastic. (If necessary, dust with additional flour, 1 tablespoon at a time, to prevent the dough from sticking.) Form it into a smooth ball. Place the ball of dough in a well-greased bowl and turn it so all sides of the dough are greased. Cover with a slightly damp kitchen towel and set aside to rest and rise in a warm, draft-free place for 1½ hours, until the dough has doubled in size.

4. Grease 2 baking sheets with the cooking spray or line with parchment paper. Set aside.

5. *To make the filling:* In a small mixing bowl, combine the granulated sugar, pecans, butter, and orange zest and mix well. Set aside.

6. Remove the dough from the bowl, return it to the floured work surface, and gently punch it down. Divide the dough in half. Roll each half into a ¼-inch-thick 12-inch disk. Brush the tops of the disks with the remaining butter. Evenly sprinkle ½ of the filling on top of each disk of dough.

7. Cut each disk into 12 pie-shaped wedges. Starting with the wide end, roll up each wedge to its pointy tip. Curve the ends down, forming a crescent-roll shape. Place the filled rolls, 2 inches apart, on the prepared baking sheets, with the tips pointing down. Cover the rolls with a slightly damp kitchen towel and let them rise for 1½ hours, until they have doubled in size.

8. Preheat the oven to 350°F.

9. *To make the glaze:* In a small, heavy saucepan over medium–high heat, combine the granulated sugar, butter, sour cream, and orange juice. Bring the mixture to a gentle boil, stirring constantly, and cook for 3 minutes. Remove from the heat, stir in the vanilla extract, and set aside to cool slightly.

10. Place the rolls in the oven and bake for 15 to 20 minutes, until the rolls are golden brown. Remove from the oven and immediately transfer the rolls from the baking sheets to a wire rack. Drizzle the still-warm glaze over them and set aside to cool for 2 minutes.

11. Transfer to a serving platter and serve warm.

Big Mama's Zucchini–Walnut Bread

When I was a little girl, my grandmother's cousins, Houston and Clifton Porter, and their wives, Myrlie and Leora, were very important people in our family. Cousin Houston pastored a large and prosperous church in New York City, and his brother, Clifton, owned and operated a successful dry-cleaning business in Chicago. My grandmother used to say, "Aunt Etta's boys have done well for themselves. They both have pull and money."

Way before I had met them in person, I knew all about our cousins' accomplishments through secondhand accounts from my mother, aunts, and grandmother. I knew that Myrlie taught high school English, as had her mother and her mother's mother, and that she was active in her church and community. I knew that she had been romantically involved with a prominent blues guitarist before she married Cousin Cliff, and that she was a well-coiffed woman, with never a nail chipped or a hair out of place. I knew that Leora was the perfect pastor's wife. I knew that she wore stunning, lush church hats, and long movie-star gloves to match, and that she was tall—taller than most women—which gave her an unmistakable air of nobility. I knew that she was soft spoken and smiled often, and that she referred to everyone as "my beloved." I knew that they were pillars of their communities, the elite. Our family thought they were the cream of the crop and loved to cite and praise their endeavors whenever we gathered.

One day, my grandmother announced that the Porter brothers and their elegant wives were coming to Michigan. Though their visit with us would be short—a few hours—I was thrilled. Finally, I would meet the fabulous Porters, and the women in my family would cook their best company food. Who wouldn't be thrilled?

The conversations about who would host the Porters centered on location, house space, and family rank. My great-aunt—we called her Big Mama—won hands down. Her house was the largest and most ornate. Big Mama mopped her kitchen floors and dusted her picture frames every morning and used Brillo pads to shine the bottoms of her pots and pans every night. Safe and reliable, she served on the Usher Board, the Breath of Life Committee, and the Cup of Water Program. She was active in her church's Tuesday Night Prayer Meeting, the Sisters' Bible Study Club, and the Neighborhood Women's Action League. Big Mama also had a flair for organizing church and community charity events, so if anyone could hold court with the highfalutin Porters, it was Big Mama. She could talk *their* talk.

Finally, the highly anticipated Saturday morning arrived. Big Mama draped a crisp, white linen tablecloth across her dining room table and set out her sparkling company glassware. They arrived in two black Cadillacs. From the living room window, we watched them emerge from their vehicles—the men first, and then their wives. I remember hearing things like, "Look at *that* hat!" and "That fur is way too long and bulky for little Myrlie! Looks like she been swallowed by a bear." The Porters were ushered inside and immediately swallowed up in hugs, kisses, and handshakes. After exchanging a quick round of obligatory greetings, they were helped out of their coats and led into Big Mama's dining room. Myrlie may have had her educational pedigree and social clubs and Leora her exquisite hats, majestic height, and reign as first lady of her husband's megachurch, but the women in my family were at the height of their powers when they were feeding people. It was time for them to show off. It was time to eat.

I remember a Southern breakfast of homemade sausage patties, thick-cut smoked bacon strips, sautéed potatoes and onions, Cheesy Scrambled Eggs (see recipe on p. 226), Fried Green Tomatoes (see recipe on p. 234), buttermilk biscuits, and home-canned apple preserves. As a treat, Big Mama made a loaf of her famous zucchini bread. She placed it in the center of the table on a glass cake stand, impossible to ignore. Cousin Leora couldn't stop marveling at how delicious the zucchini loaf looked. "My beloveds, you've outdone yourselves," she said.

The rest of that morning went by in a flurry of serving plates being passed around the table and the chatter of family memories. It doesn't matter who you are, or who you *think* you are, sitting over an old-fashioned breakfast conjures up memories and puts you in a talking mood. I listened intently, turning my head from one speaker to the next; even as a child, the part of a visit that I enjoyed most was listening to family stories.

recipe continues

Big Mama's Zucchini–Walnut Bread *CONTINUED*

Before long, it was time for the cousins to leave. They stood in Big Mama's foyer and said their farewells, vowing to be better at keeping in touch. Cousin Houston said, "It's a shame that we rarely get a chance to sit down and enjoy communion with our families." Cousin Clifton said, "At the end of the day, family is all we've got." Cousin Leora said, "My beloveds, you made us feel at home."

As I look back, that day was one of the most important days of my childhood. It embodied what family gatherings are supposed to be: getting together with the people you love, eating fabulous food, and sharing family memories. Our elite cousins had come to Saginaw and had given us *and* our food their stamp of approval. Cousin Myrlie had said, "The food was so rich and delicious." Compliments didn't come any sweeter than that.

Yet Big Mama let it be known that she wasn't in awe that the high-class Porters had come to our humble neck of the woods to eat a meal. She said, "There's an old saying: *No matter how high a bird flies, it still has to come down to earth to eat.*"

As a parting gift, Big Mama wrapped the entire zucchini loaf in foil and sent it off with the Porters. To this day, I don't know if she'd set it on a pedestal and placed it in the middle of the table as a tease or if she'd decided to do it when Cousin Leora said, "That zucchini loaf is the best-looking loaf I've ever seen."

Makes 1 8½-inch × 4½-inch loaf

- Nonstick cooking spray, for greasing
- 1½ cups all-purpose flour
- 1 teaspoon ground cinnamon
- ¾ teaspoon baking powder
- ½ teaspoon baking soda
- ½ teaspoon salt
- ¼ teaspoon freshly grated nutmeg
- ½ cup vegetable oil
- ½ cup granulated sugar
- ½ cup firmly packed light brown sugar
- 1 large egg, room temperature, lightly beaten
- 1½ teaspoons pure vanilla extract
- 1 cup finely grated, unpeeled zucchini
- ½ cup finely chopped walnuts

1. Preheat the oven to 350°F. Grease the bottom and sides of an 8½-inch × 4½-inch loaf pan with the cooking spray. Set aside.

2. In a large mixing bowl, sift together the dry ingredients: the flour, cinnamon, baking powder, baking soda, salt, and nutmeg. Set aside.

3. In a medium mixing bowl, whisk together the wet ingredients: the vegetable oil, granulated and brown sugars, egg, and vanilla extract. Add the grated zucchini and walnuts. Slowly add the oil mixture to the flour mixture, stirring until just combined.

4. Spread the batter into the prepared pan and bake for 45 to 50 minutes, until a wooden toothpick inserted into the center of the loaf comes out clean. Remove from the oven and set aside to cool in the pan for 10 minutes.

5. Turn out onto a wire rack to cool completely.

6. Transfer to a serving platter, slice, and serve at room temperature.

"No matter how high a bird flies, it still has to come down to earth to eat." —Big Mama

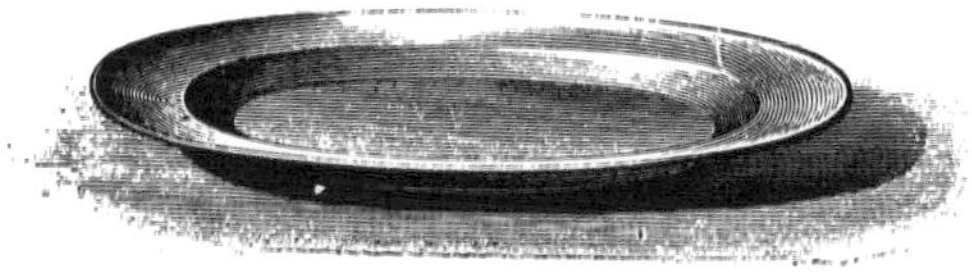

Fruitcake Loaf

When it comes to fruitcakes, you either like them or you don't. I love them, and most of the people I hang around with love them too. During the winters of my girlhood, my mother frequently made fruitcakes in the form of morning loaf cakes. Whenever I saw bags of mixed fruit on the kitchen counter, I knew they were going into one of her luscious loaves, and I looked forward to their spiciness and tenderness. Mama had a gentle and delicious way with her Fruitcake Loaf.

Makes 1 9-inch × 5-inch loaf

Nonstick cooking spray, for greasing

1½ cups all-purpose flour

2 teaspoons baking powder

½ teaspoon salt

1 teaspoon ground cinnamon

¼ teaspoon freshly grated nutmeg

⅛ teaspoon ground cloves

½ cup (1 stick) unsalted butter, room temperature

1 cup granulated sugar

2 large eggs

1 cup whole milk, room temperature

1 teaspoon pure vanilla extract

1 cup chopped mixed dried fruits (apricots, ginger, pineapple chunks, raisins, figs, pears, apples)

½ cup chopped walnuts

½ cup chopped pecans

½ cup maraschino cherries, drained and cut in half

1½ tablespoons coarse sugar, for sprinkling

1. Preheat the oven to 350°F. Lightly grease a 9-inch × 5-inch loaf pan with the cooking spray and set aside.

2. In a large mixing bowl, sift together the dry ingredients: the flour, baking powder, and salt. Add the cinnamon, nutmeg, and cloves and stir until well combined.

Whenever I saw bags of mixed fruit on the kitchen counter, I knew they were going into one of Mama's luscious loaves.

3. In the bowl of a stand mixer fitted with the paddle attachment, break up the butter by mixing on low speed for 1 minute. Add the granulated sugar and cream together the butter and sugar on medium speed for 2 to 3 minutes, until the mixture is light and fluffy. Scrape down the sides and bottom of the bowl to prevent lumps from forming. As the mixer is running, reduce the speed to low and add the eggs, 1 at a time; after you add each egg, scrape down the sides of the bowl and resume beating on low speed for 30 seconds. Add the milk and vanilla extract and beat at low speed for 2 to 3 seconds, until just incorporated. Add the dry ingredient mixture to the bowl of the mixer ⅓ at a time and beat at low speed for 2 to 3 seconds, until just combined. Turn off the mixer.

4. Carefully add the dried fruits, walnuts, and pecans to the batter and stir until just distributed. Fold in the maraschino cherries, stirring only until moistened.

5. Transfer the batter to the prepared pan and evenly sprinkle the top of the batter with the coarse sugar. Bake for 60 minutes, until a wooden toothpick inserted into the center of the cake comes out clean. Remove from the oven and set aside to cool in the pan on a wire rack for 10 minutes. Remove from the pan and transfer to the wire rack to cool completely.

6. Transfer to a serving platter, slice, and serve at room temperature.

Apricot Coffee Bread

THIS WONDERFUL BREAD IS EASY TO MAKE—THERE'S NO KNEADING. Apricot Coffee Bread is made in a round tube pan and looks beautiful on a nice platter. I serve it for company at the kitchen table with cups of hot coffee.

Makes 1 10-inch tube or Bundt bread

TOPPING

½ cup all-purpose flour

½ cup firmly packed light brown sugar

1 teaspoon ground cinnamon

4 tablespoons unsalted butter, cold, cut into small pieces

BATTER

Nonstick cooking spray, for greasing

3 cups all-purpose flour, plus more for dusting

1½ teaspoons baking powder

½ teaspoon baking soda

½ teaspoon salt

¾ cup (1½ sticks) unsalted butter, room temperature

1½ cups granulated sugar

3 large eggs

1 cup sour cream, room temperature

1 teaspoon pure vanilla extract

1 cup dried apricots, chopped into small pieces

½ cup chopped pecans

GARNISH

Confectioners' sugar, for dusting

1. *To make the topping:* In a small mixing bowl, combine the flour, brown sugar, and cinnamon and stir until well combined. Using your fingers, a pastry blender, or the tines of a fork, cut the butter into the flour mixture until it resembles small crumbs. Set aside.

2. Preheat the oven to 350°F. Grease a 10-inch tube or Bundt pan with the cooking spray and dust with some flour. Set aside.

3. *To make the batter:* In a large mixing bowl, sift together the dry ingredients: the flour, baking powder, baking soda, and salt. Set aside.

4. In the bowl of a stand mixer fitted with the paddle attachment, break up the butter by mixing on low speed for 1 minute. Add the granulated sugar and cream together the butter and sugar on medium speed for 2 to 3 minutes, until the mixture is light and fluffy. Scrape down the sides and bottom of the bowl to prevent lumps from forming. As the mixer is running, reduce the speed to low and slowly add the eggs, 1 at a time; after you add each egg, scrape down the sides of the bowl and resume beating on low speed for 30 seconds. Add the sour cream and vanilla extract and beat at low speed for 2 to 3 seconds, until just incorporated. Turn off the mixer.

5. Carefully add the apricots and pecans to the batter and stir until just distributed.

6. Transfer the batter to the prepared pan and evenly sprinkle the top of the batter with the topping. Bake for 55 to 60 minutes, until a wooden toothpick inserted into the center of the bread comes out clean. Remove from the oven and set aside to cool in the pan on a wire rack for 10 minutes.

7. Using a serrated knife, separate the bread from the tube pan and invert onto the wire rack to cool completely.

8. Transfer to a serving platter and dust with the confectioners' sugar. Slice and serve at room temperature.

Pan-Fried Biscuit Doughnuts

A GOOD BREAKFAST DOESN'T HAVE TO BE COMPLICATED OR EXPENSIVE to make. Here's an incredibly delicious, easy-to-make, and inexpensive breakfast treat that starts with store-bought biscuit dough. As an added bonus, these doughnuts are coated with a pleasing combination of granulated sugar and cinnamon. I can't remember a good, weekday company breakfast that didn't include some sort of pan-fried doughnuts; my grandmother made these doughnuts for guests all the time.

Makes 10 doughnuts and 10 doughnut holes

TOPPING

½ cup granulated sugar

1 teaspoon ground cinnamon, or more to taste

DOUGHNUTS

Vegetable oil, for frying

1 (10-count) tube refrigerated buttermilk biscuit dough (Pillsbury home-style biscuits are a good choice), separated

All-purpose flour, for rolling

GLAZE

1½ cups sifted confectioners' sugar

2 tablespoons half-and-half

½ teaspoon pure vanilla extract

I can't remember a good, weekday company breakfast that didn't include some sort of pan-fried doughnuts.

1. *To make the topping:* In a paper bag, combine the granulated sugar and cinnamon. Shake to thoroughly combine. Set aside.

2. *To make the doughnuts:* In a large, deep skillet or Dutch oven, pour a 2-inch-deep quantity of the vegetable oil. Heat the oil to 350°F. Line a plate with several layers of paper towels and set aside.

3. Place the rounds of biscuit dough on a floured cutting board. (If any are irregular in height or shape, gently pat them until they are uniform.) Using a 1-inch round cookie cutter or the plastic cap of a 2-liter soda bottle, cut a hole in the center of each dough round, reserving the extra dough to make doughnut holes.

4. *To make the glaze:* In a small mixing bowl, whisk together the confectioners' sugar, half-and-half, and vanilla extract until the mixture is smooth.

5. When the oil reaches 350°F, working in batches of 3 or 4 at a time, carefully drop the doughnuts and doughnut holes into the hot oil. Fry for 1½ minutes per side, until they are light golden brown on both sides. Using a slotted spoon or long tongs, remove the doughnuts and holes from the oil and immediately transfer to the prepared plate, draining as much of the oil as possible.

6. Repeat step 5 until all the doughnuts and holes are fried.

7. Drop one of the warm doughnuts in the paper bag containing the topping and shake vigorously. Using tongs, remove the coated doughnut from the bag and place it on a cutting board.

8. Repeat step 7 with the remaining doughnuts and holes.

9. Drizzle the glaze over the doughnuts and holes.

10. Transfer to a serving platter and serve immediately.

Triple-Berry Parfait

Layers of fresh fruit, whipped cream, and granola come together deliciously in this bright, refreshing summer morning delight. This is one of those versatile dishes that's pretty enough for company and humble enough for every day. When berries are in season, I make berry parfaits every chance I get, especially on the weekends. You might even say it's a family tradition.

When I was growing up, my grandmother felt strongly about maintaining family traditions. She used to say, "Our family traditions bind us together like glue. If we didn't come together and honor them, I suspect I wouldn't know the whereabouts of half of y'all, with your busy schedules and all."

Makes 4 servings

2 cups fresh blueberries
1 cup fresh raspberries
1 cup sliced fresh strawberries
1 tablespoon freshly squeezed lime juice
1 tablespoon freshly squeezed lemon juice
¼ vanilla bean, split, seeds scraped and set aside
2 tablespoons plus 2 teaspoons granulated sugar (divided)
1½ cups heavy cream, cold
¾ cup granola without raisins, for garnish

1. Place the bowl of a stand mixer in the freezer to chill for at least 30 minutes.

2. In a medium mixing bowl, combine the blueberries, raspberries, strawberries, lime and lemon juices, vanilla bean seeds, and 2 tablespoons of the granulated sugar. Allow the mixture to macerate for at least 30 minutes, until thick juices develop.

3. In the prepared mixer bowl, beat the heavy cream with the whisk attachment until it is thick and stiff peaks form. As the mixer continues to run, carefully add the remaining granulated sugar. Continue beating until the mixture is well combined. Set the whipped cream aside.

4. Among 4 dessert glasses, spoon ⅓ cup of the berry mixture. Evenly spread the whipped cream in each glass and top each with the remaining berry mixture. Sprinkle evenly with the granola.

5. Serve immediately.

Lemon–Coconut Bread

I LOVE QUICK BREADS FOR THOSE DAYS WHEN I'M SHORT ON TIME BUT still want to sit down to something pretty and delicious. Truth be told, I love them for when I want to be perceived as a goddess in the kitchen, and this Lemon–Coconut Bread makes that happen. It's moist and sweet and has a bit of lemon flavor in every bite. When I serve it to my morning guests, they think I'm something special.

This recipe was one of my mother's favorites for when her neighborhood girlfriends stopped over for morning coffee after their husbands had gone to work. When Mama was feeling swanky, she would sometimes top her bread with walnuts. I like the nut topping variation best; the combination of lemon, shredded coconut, and chopped walnuts is so delicious. I suggest that you experiment to discover exactly how you like yours.

Makes 1 9-inch × 5-inch × 3-inch loaf (about 12 servings)

GLAZE

2 cups sifted confectioners' sugar

2 tablespoons evaporated milk, plus more as needed

2 tablespoons freshly squeezed lemon juice

1 teaspoon unsalted butter, melted and cooled

BATTER

Nonstick cooking spray, for greasing

2½ cups all-purpose flour

2 teaspoons baking powder

½ teaspoon salt

1 cup granulated sugar

1 cup shredded, sweetened coconut

¾ cup evaporated milk

½ cup freshly squeezed lemon juice

2 large eggs, room temperature, lightly beaten

¼ cup buttermilk, room temperature

1 tablespoon freshly grated lemon zest

1 teaspoon pure vanilla extract

½ cup (1 stick) unsalted butter, melted

TOPPING (OPTIONAL)

½ cup finely chopped walnuts

¼ cup firmly packed light brown sugar

1. Preheat the oven to 350°F. Lightly grease a 9-inch × 5-inch × 3-inch loaf pan with the cooking spray and set aside.

2. *To make the glaze:* In a medium mixing bowl, place the confectioners' sugar. Stir in the evaporated milk, lemon juice, and butter until the mixture is smooth. Add more evaporated milk, 1 teaspoon at a time, if needed to reach a smooth consistency. Set aside.

3. *To make the batter:* In a large mixing bowl, sift together the dry ingredients: the flour, baking powder, and salt. Add the granulated sugar and coconut and stir until well combined. Set aside.

4. In a medium mixing bowl, whisk together the wet ingredients: the evaporated milk, lemon juice, eggs, buttermilk, lemon zest, and vanilla extract. Slowly add the milk mixture to the flour mixture, stirring until just combined. Add the butter and stir until the batter is smooth. Transfer the batter to the prepared pan.

IF NOT USING THE TOPPING:

5. Bake for 50 minutes, until a wooden toothpick inserted into the center of the bread comes out clean. Remove from the oven. Set aside to cool in the pan on a wire rack for 10 minutes.

6. Remove from the pan and transfer to the wire rack to cool completely.

7. Drizzle the glaze over the top of the bread.

8. Transfer to a serving platter, slice, and serve at room temperature.

IF USING THE TOPPING:

5. *To make the topping:* In a small mixing bowl, combine the walnuts and brown sugar and stir until well combined.

6. Bake for 15 minutes. Remove from the oven and quickly and evenly sprinkle the topping over the batter. Return the pan to the oven and bake for 10 to 15 minutes, until a wooden toothpick inserted into the center of the bread comes out clean. Remove from the oven. Set aside in the pan to cool on a wire rack for 10 minutes.

7. Remove from the pan and transfer to the wire rack to cool completely.

8. Drizzle the glaze over the top of the bread.

9. Transfer to a serving platter, slice, and serve at room temperature.

Ava Joy's Lemon Streusel Coffee Cake

AVA JOY MALONE WAS A QUINTESSENTIAL NEIGHBORHOOD BEAUTY. SHE had beautiful bone structure, perfect satiny skin, and a full and shapely mouth. Her iridescent, cat-like brown eyes were so captivating that it was hard to meet them with your own when she focused on you. She had a certain charm, that *je ne sais quoi*—an enchanting and elusive quality that is pleasing to the senses but hard to fully explain. Every woman wanted to look, walk, and talk like her, and every man just wanted to look at her.

Many neighborhood women would say mean things about Miss Ava Joy in front of their husbands and boyfriends, hoping to redirect their attention away from her beauty and toward her imperfections. But Mama liked Miss Ava Joy and would say so in front of anybody, including Daddy. Mama used to tell me, "The more you try to draw a man's attention away from a pretty woman by constantly publicizing her flaws and limitations, the more attention the man is going to pay her. The more you talk—good or bad—about a rival, the more you're puttin' her on his mind."

But Miss Ava Joy was much more than just a beauty. She had an engaging personality too. She wasn't stuck on her beauty, nor did she apologize for it. She walked with a slink, had excellent taste, and wore pretty clothes that accentuated her features and her gestures. She made beautiful crafts. When I was a little girl, I thought Miss Ava was an exotic creature to be studied.

When I was 10, my mother asked Miss Ava Joy to teach me to make beaded jewelry. On summer mornings, I would walk the two blocks to Miss Ava Joy's house, where she would have jars of beads and cards of embroidery string already laid out on the kitchen table. I was charmed by the entire visit each time, but perhaps the best part came at the end. At the end of our classes, Miss Ava Joy always pulled something sweet and delicious from her oven that was my reward, she would say, for being a good student.

On Miss Ava Joy's kitchen wall, just above the table where we sat, hung a flea-market find: a painting of Samia Gamal, the famous Egyptian belly dancer who was famous for her veil work, graceful arm movements, and poise. There was a clear similarity between the two women—not a physical resemblance,

recipe continues

but more in their feminine deportment. Samia Gamal wore high heels while she danced. Ava Joy Malone wore high heels while she cooked. Samia Gamal used her hips to tap out a story. Ava Joy Malone used her hips to close her refrigerator door.

Of all the loaves, buns, and sweet rolls that Miss Ava Joy served after our morning sessions, her Lemon Streusel Coffee Cake was my favorite. Like the woman herself, this is a warm and lovely treat.

Makes 1 9-inch × 13-inch coffee cake

TOPPING

½ cup all-purpose flour

½ cup finely chopped pecans

⅓ cup firmly packed light brown sugar

1 teaspoon ground cinnamon

4 tablespoons unsalted butter, cold

BATTER

Nonstick cooking spray, for greasing

¾ cup (1½ sticks) unsalted butter, room temperature

1 cup granulated sugar

3 large eggs, room temperature, lightly beaten

1 cup sour cream, room temperature

1 tablespoon freshly grated lemon zest

1 tablespoon freshly squeezed lemon juice

1 teaspoon pure vanilla extract

2¼ cups all-purpose flour, plus more for dusting

1½ teaspoons baking powder

½ teaspoon baking soda

½ teaspoon salt

1 cup lemon pie filling, prepared from a box mix

GARNISH (OPTIONAL)

Confectioners' sugar, for dusting

1. Preheat the oven to 350°F. Lightly grease a 9-inch × 13-inch baking dish with the cooking spray and dust with some flour. Set aside.

2. *To make the topping:* In a small mixing bowl, combine the flour, pecans, brown sugar, and cinnamon. Using your fingers, a pastry blender, or the tines of a fork, cut the butter into the mixture until it resembles coarse crumbs. Cover the bowl with plastic wrap and place it in the refrigerator until ready to use.

3. *To make the batter:* In the bowl of a stand mixer fitted with the paddle attachment, break up the butter by mixing on low speed for 1 minute. Add the granulated sugar and cream together the butter and sugar on medium speed for 2 to 3 minutes, until the mixture is light and fluffy. Scrape down the sides and bottom of the bowl to prevent lumps from forming. As the mixer is running, reduce the speed to low and slowly add the eggs, 1 at a time; after you add each egg, scrape down the sides and bottom of the bowl and resume beating on low speed for 30 seconds. Add the sour cream, lemon zest and juice, and vanilla extract and beat until fully incorporated.

4. In a large mixing bowl, sift together the dry ingredients: the flour, baking powder, baking soda, and salt. Reduce the mixer speed to low and gradually add the dry ingredient mixture to the bowl of the mixer ⅓ at a time. Beat at low speed for 2 to 3 seconds, until just combined. Turn off the mixer.

5. Transfer ½ of the batter into the prepared baking dish and smooth the top with a rubber or silicone spatula or a butter knife. Evenly spread the lemon pie filling over the batter. Spread the remaining batter over the filling and smooth the top. Sprinkle with the topping. Bake for 45 to 50 minutes, until the topping is golden brown. Remove from the oven and set aside to cool to room temperature in the pan on a wire rack.

6. Carefully transfer to a serving platter. Sprinkle with the confectioners' sugar, if desired, and slice and serve at room temperature.

Peach Cobbler

In our family, coffee hour is a time for talking. We usually honor it with something sweet and simple, like this Peach Cobbler. While one family member tells a family story, another can make a pot of coffee, and yet another can make this quick treat. Everybody else can either laugh or listen along or both.

Makes 1 9-inch × 13-inch casserole (about 10–12 servings)

½ cup (1 stick) unsalted butter

2 cups peeled, sliced peaches with their natural juices (fresh or canned)

1 cup self-rising flour

1 cup granulated sugar

¼ teaspoon freshly grated nutmeg

¼ teaspoon salt

1 cup whole milk, room temperature

1. Preheat the oven to 350°F. Place the butter in a 9-inch × 13-inch casserole dish and place the dish in the oven to allow the butter to melt. Remove from the oven. Transfer the peaches and their juices to the dish, pouring them over the butter. Spread the peaches out but do not stir.

2. In a large mixing bowl, sift together the flour, granulated sugar, nutmeg, and salt. Add the milk and whisk until the batter is smooth.

3. Pour the batter evenly over the peaches and return the dish to the oven. Bake for 30 to 40 minutes, until the cobbler is puffy and golden brown on top. Remove from the oven.

4. Serve warm.

Dezarae Triplett's Pumpkin–Praline French Toast

A YOUNG NEIGHBOR OF OURS, DEZARAE TRIPLETT, WAS A NATURAL beauty and a gifted homemaker. A brilliant self-taught artist, she created pretty needlepoint pieces and exquisite ceramic adornments for her garden. She also turned out baked goods so delicious they rivaled those of even the most experienced cooks in our neighborhood.

Miss Dezarae had a way about her that charmed everybody, including her gorgeous young husband, Sterling, who was a permanent mama's boy, and all our other neighbors, who measured a woman's worth by her housekeeping and culinary prowess. Everybody spoke lovingly about Dezarae—everybody, that is, except Alma Triplett, Dezarae's overbearing live-in mother-in-law.

According to the neighbors, Miss Alma actually purchased and supervised the lovely clothes and trinkets—minks, real pearls, and diamonds—that Dezarae wore so well. Miss Alma treated poor Dezarae as though she were competing against her daughter-in-law for her son's affections, doing everything she could to cause tension between Dezarae and Sterling. Among her comments: "It's not natural for a wife to be taller than her husband." "Is it *really* necessary to kiss and hug Sterling every time he comes through the door?" "It'll surprise me if the two of you last. Sterl's so easygoing, and you're like a cat on a hot tin roof. You can't keep still—you're always fiddlin' around the house and in the garden." More than once, I heard Miss Alma tell pretty Miss Dezarae, "You sure are lucky to have a fine-looking man like my Sterling. Before he married you, women used to throw themselves at him." Sterling was Miss Alma's golden boy, and Miss Dezarae was the woman who stole him from her. Mama used to say, "Before you marry a man, study his family—*especially* his mother. Some women can't let their sons go. There's nothing worse than being tangled up with a man whose mother is the kind of woman who meddles in her son's marriage."

It didn't help that Miss Dezarae was a *way* better cook than Miss Alma. In fact, Miss Alma was a dreadful cook—her macaroni and cheese was soupy, her meatloaf bland and brittle. It offended Miss Alma that time and again, Dezarae's

recipe continues

tasty cooking was the focus of Sterling's attention. To conceal her jealousy and resentment, Miss Alma insulted everything that Miss Dezarae put on the table. "You put too much meat in the collards." "The bread salad doesn't go with the rest of the meal." "The coffee is too bitter." Of course, none of it was true.

Years ago, long after Miss Alma had passed away, Mama and Miss Dezarae got together to reminisce about old times. Mama said, "That Alma Triplett was something special. Was there *anything* that she didn't criticize?" Miss Dezarae laughed. "I'll have to think about it," she said. A few days later, Miss Dezarae sent Mama her recipe for Pumpkin–Praline French Toast. At the bottom of the recipe, she had inscribed, *Mother Triplett loved this. She actually asked for the recipe*. This melt-in-your-mouth sweet breakfast indulgence serves up to 10 and is perfect for lazy Saturday mornings in autumn when the weather is turning chilly.

Makes about 10 servings

- 1 cup plus 2 tablespoons firmly packed light brown sugar (divided)
- ½ cup light corn syrup
- 4 tablespoons unsalted butter
- 1 cup coarsely chopped pecan pieces
- 1 (1-pound) loaf French or sourdough bread, cut into 1-inch slices
- 2 cups whole milk, room temperature
- 1 cup pumpkin purée
- 3 large eggs, room temperature
- ½ cup heavy cream, room temperature
- 1 tablespoon all-purpose flour
- 1 teaspoon pure vanilla extract
- 1 teaspoon pumpkin pie spice
- Pinch coarse salt
- Butter and maple syrup, for serving

1. In a medium saucepan over medium heat, combine 1 cup of the brown sugar, the corn syrup, and the butter. Cook, stirring constantly, for 5 minutes, until the mixture is bubbly. Stir in the pecan pieces and remove from the heat.

2. Spread the pecan mixture over the bottom of a 9-inch × 13-inch casserole dish. Arrange the bread slices over the pecan mixture in a single layer.

3. In a large mixing bowl, combine the milk, the pumpkin purée, the eggs (1 at a time, beating after each addition), the heavy cream, the remaining brown sugar, the flour, the vanilla extract, the pumpkin pie spice, and the salt and stir until well combined.

4. Slowly pour the mixture over the bread, parting the slices to allow the liquid to fall between them. Using the back of a large spoon, press down on each slice of bread to make sure each piece is completely saturated. Cover the dish with plastic wrap and refrigerate for at least 8 hours or overnight.

5. Preheat the oven to 350°F. Remove the plastic wrap from the baking dish.

6. Bake for 45 to 50 minutes, until the casserole is golden brown and set in the middle. Remove from the oven.

7. Transfer to a serving platter by first running a knife around the edges of the baking dish and placing the platter on top of the dish. Carefully invert onto the platter. Slice and serve warm with the butter and maple syrup.

Morning Apple Crisp

My maternal grandmother always took special care when she made breakfast on Saturdays for the family. Saturday breakfast at her house was an occasion for the whole family, and our best friends and favorite neighbors were always welcome too. Sometimes breakfast was late; sometimes it was early—Saturdays at My My's house were usually full of *go*, with grocery shopping, piano lessons with Miss Rosa, and Scout meetings with Mr. Branch and Miss Margaret. Everybody always had somewhere else to be.

My My would serve either bacon, eggs, and grits or homemade sausage patties and Hash-Brown Potatoes (see recipe on p. 230). Alongside, we'd have either buttermilk biscuits from scratch or creamed corn fritters and always a special homemade sweet treat. Sometimes, that special treat was her delicious Morning Apple Crisp topped with a golden-brown cinnamon and brown sugar oat crumble.

We would always tell My My that she shouldn't have gone to so much trouble, and she would say, "Nothing gives me more enjoyment than when we sit together for a meal."

Makes 6–8 servings

TOPPING

1 cup old-fashioned rolled oats

¾ cup all-purpose flour

¾ cup firmly packed light brown sugar

¼ teaspoon ground cinnamon

¼ teaspoon salt

6 tablespoons unsalted butter, cold, cut into 1-inch cubes

FILLING

7 to 8 medium baking apples, peeled, cored, and cut into ¼-inch slices (I prefer Fuji, Golden Delicious, or Granny Smith)

½ cup firmly packed light brown sugar

3 tablespoons unsalted butter, melted

2 tablespoons apple cider (not sparkling)

1 tablespoon freshly squeezed lemon juice

½ teaspoon ground cinnamon

½ teaspoon pure vanilla extract

Freshly grated nutmeg, to taste

1. Preheat the oven to 350°F.

2. *To make the topping:* In a medium mixing bowl, combine the oats, flour, brown sugar, cinnamon, and salt. Using your fingers, a pastry blender, or the tines of a fork, cut the butter into the mixture until it resembles coarse crumbs. Cover the bowl with plastic wrap and place it in the refrigerator until ready to use.

3. *To make the filling:* Place the apple slices in an ungreased 9-inch square glass baking dish. Add the brown sugar, butter, apple cider, lemon juice, cinnamon, vanilla extract, and nutmeg. Toss until the apples are thoroughly coated with the mixture.

4. Evenly sprinkle the topping over the filling. Every ½ inch or so, push the topping down into the filling. Bake for 35 to 45 minutes, until the apples are tender and bubbly and the topping is golden brown. Remove from the oven and set aside to cool in the dish on a wire rack for 15 minutes before serving.

5. Slice and serve warm.

"Nothing gives me more enjoyment than when we sit together for a meal." — My My

Cousin Lillie Bea's Orange Coffee Cake

My grandmother's cousin Lillie Bea seemed out of place in our family. Whenever the other women gathered to talk about their recipes, Cousin Lillie would be off to the side, wrapped up in her fashion magazines or filing and polishing her nails. Domesticity wasn't in Cousin Lillie's nature. She was a glamour-girl type, always smoothing the wrinkles on her neck or rubbing scented oils on her arms and legs. Big Mama, whose daily makeup routine went no further than a dash of red lipstick and a smidgen of rouge, used to say of Cousin Lillie, "Don't make no sense for a middle-aged woman to carry on so . . . you can't hold age back—you can't smooth it away or rub it away; sooner or later it'll catch up with you."

Though Cousin Lillie wasn't an everyday cook, she was a reliable special-occasion cook who brought lovely dishes to family gatherings and holiday suppers. She would, on occasion, persuade us to stop over for coffee and homemade sweet rolls or breakfast cake.

This coffee cake recipe calls for refrigerated biscuits, which makes it easy to prepare, and the orange flavor makes it a rich and flavorful morning treat.

Makes 1 10-inch tube or Bundt cake

BATTER

- Nonstick cooking spray, for greasing
- 1 cup granulated sugar
- ⅓ cup minced pecans
- ¼ cup firmly packed light brown sugar
- 1 tablespoon freshly grated orange zest
- 4 tablespoons unsalted butter, melted and cooled
- 1 tablespoon freshly squeezed orange juice
- 2 (12-ounce) tubes refrigerated buttermilk biscuit dough, separated

GLAZE

- 1½ cups sifted confectioners' sugar
- 3–4 tablespoons freshly squeezed orange juice
- 1½ teaspoons freshly grated orange zest

1. Preheat the oven to 350°F. Grease a 10-inch fluted tube or Bundt pan with the cooking spray and set aside.

2. *To make the batter:* In a small mixing bowl, whisk together the granulated sugar, pecans, brown sugar, and orange zest. Set aside.

3. In a separate small mixing bowl, whisk together the butter and orange juice. Set aside.

4. Dip 1 round of biscuit dough in the orange juice mixture. Transfer the round to the sugar mixture and roll it around until it is well coated. Set the dough round upright in the prepared pan. Repeat with the remaining dough rounds until the tube pan is filled and then sprinkle the remaining sugar mixture over the dough rounds.

5. Bake for 20 to 25 minutes, until the cake's top is golden brown and a wooden toothpick inserted into the center of the cake comes out clean.

6. *To make the glaze:* In a small mixing bowl, whisk together the confectioners' sugar and orange juice and zest until the mixture is smooth.

7. Remove from the oven and set aside to cool in the pan on a wire rack for 5 minutes before serving.

8. Using a serrated knife, separate the cake from the tube pan and invert onto a serving platter. Drizzle with the glaze. Slice and serve warm.

Mama's Rustic Pear Tart

I GREW UP IN A HOUSE WITH A LARGE GARDEN AND THREE FRUIT TREES—apple, peach, and pear. Daddy had a natural joy for gardening; he could make any type of plant grow and thrive. He pruned and fertilized his plants and trees with precision and love. When he was working in the garden or with the fruit trees in our backyard, we saw the radiant look of a man who had separated from himself and become one with the nature growing on his figurative 40 acres.

I would often watch my mother observe my father in his garden from the kitchen window. She once said, "He works hard for us . . . to keep a roof over our heads and food on our table. The least that I can do is show him my appreciation by making some of his favorite dishes out of the food that he brings in from the field."

Fresh pear slices tossed in a mixture of granulated sugar, butter, and spices work together deliciously to make Mama's Rustic Pear Tart. Daddy always came to breakfast with sparks in his eyes when he knew that one of her tarts was on the menu.

Makes about 6–8 servings

DOUGH

1⅓ cups all-purpose flour, plus more for rolling

1 tablespoon granulated sugar

¼ teaspoon salt

⅛ teaspoon baking powder

½ cup (1 stick) unsalted butter, cold, cut into small pieces

2–3 tablespoons cold water

FILLING

4 medium-firm but ripe Bartlett pears, peeled, cored, and sliced ¼ inch thick

3 tablespoons granulated sugar

1 tablespoon freshly squeezed lemon juice

2 teaspoons cornstarch

¼ teaspoon ground cinnamon

⅛ teaspoon freshly grated nutmeg

1 tablespoon unsalted butter, cut into small dice

TOPPING

1 large egg white, room temperature

1 teaspoon water

1 tablespoon coarse sugar

1. *To make the dough:* In a medium mixing bowl, sift together the dry ingredients: the flour, granulated sugar, salt, and baking powder. Using your fingers, a pastry blender, or the tines of a fork, cut the butter into the flour mixture until it resembles coarse crumbs. Gradually add the cold water, 1 tablespoon at a time, until the mixture is just moistened. Gather the dough into a ball and pat it into a 4-inch-wide disk. Wrap the disk in plastic wrap and refrigerate for at least 30 minutes.

2. Turn out the dough onto a floured work surface. Using a floured rolling pin, roll out the dough into a 14-inch-wide circle. Line a 14-inch baking pan with parchment paper and transfer the dough to the prepared pan. Loosely cover the pan with plastic wrap and place in the refrigerator until ready to use.

3. Preheat the oven to 375°F.

4. *To make the filling:* In a large mixing bowl, toss together the pears, granulated sugar, lemon juice, cornstarch, cinnamon, and nutmeg until the pears are well coated with the mixture. Set aside.

5. *To make the topping:* In a small mixing bowl, beat together the egg white and water until the mixture is well combined. Set aside.

6. Remove the pan from the refrigerator and spoon the filling over the dough, leaving a 2-inch border. Dot the top of the filling with the butter. Fold the edges of the crust over the filling, making pleats in the dough every 2 inches or so and leaving the center of the tart uncovered. Using a pastry brush, brush the topping over the exposed dough and sprinkle with the coarse sugar. Bake for 30 to 35 minutes, until the crust is golden brown and the pears are fork tender and lightly caramelized. Remove from the oven and set aside to cool on a wire rack for 15 minutes before serving.

7. Slice and serve warm.

Miss Earline's Rhubarb Coffee Cake

NOBODY COULD MAKE SOFT AND TENDER RHUBARB COFFEE CAKE THE way Miss Earline, my aunt's neighbor, could. My entire family said so.

Makes 1 9-inch × 13-inch coffee cake

BATTER

Nonstick cooking spray, for greasing
2 cups all-purpose flour, plus more for dusting
1 teaspoon baking powder
1 teaspoon baking soda
¼ teaspoon salt
½ cup (1 stick) unsalted butter
½ cup firmly packed light brown sugar
1 cup sour cream, room temperature
1 large egg, room temperature
1 teaspoon pure vanilla extract
2½ cups finely chopped rhubarb

TOPPING

¾ cup granulated sugar
½ cup all-purpose flour
½ cup (1 stick) unsalted butter, melted and cooled
½ teaspoon ground cinnamon

1. Preheat the oven to 350°F. Lightly grease a 9-inch × 13-inch baking dish with the cooking spray and dust with some flour. Set aside.

2. *To make the batter:* In a large mixing bowl, sift together the dry ingredients: the flour, baking powder, baking soda, and salt. Set aside.

3. In a separate large mixing bowl, using a hand mixer set at low speed, break up the butter for 1 minute. Increase the speed to medium, add the brown sugar, and cream together the butter and sugar for 2 to 3 minutes. Add the sour cream, egg, and vanilla extract and beat until well blended. Turn off the mixer.

4. Slowly add the sour cream mixture into the flour mixture, stirring by hand until the mixture is just combined.

5. *To make the topping:* In a small mixing bowl, stir together the granulated sugar, flour, butter, and cinnamon until the mixture is crumbly.

6. Transfer the batter to the prepared baking dish and spread the rhubarb over the batter. Sprinkle the topping over the rhubarb. Bake for 45 minutes, until the coffee cake is a soft golden color and a wooden toothpick inserted into the center of the cake comes out clean. Remove from the oven and set aside to cool in the pan on a wire rack for 30 minutes.

7. Carefully transfer to a serving platter. Slice and serve warm or at room temperature.

Southern Tea Cakes

In my family, Southern-style tea cakes, with their warm undertones of vanilla and nutmeg, have always been regarded as a special treat. The women in my family made these cakes—a cross between a cookie and a sweet biscuit—in batches large enough to please our family and friends during the holiday season and for family picnics and reunions. Sometimes they made them just because someone yearned for a down-home, comforting snack. When My My made tea cakes, news spread quickly. Our entire family would flock to her house hoping to get there before they were gone.

My My told us once that when she was young, her sister Bulah sold tea cakes at the counter in her community grocery market in New Orleans on Saturday mornings. By noon, she'd always sell out. Mama told me that when she was a little girl, she would help her older cousin, Eunice, select patterns and fabric for the summer church dresses that Cousin Eunice hand-stitched for a wealthy woman who lived in town, and that Cousin Eunice always paid her for her labor in tea cakes. Our Cousin Flossie, who was always so clean and meticulous, once used a white cloth to wipe away the excess flour collected on the bottoms of the 12 dozen tea cakes she'd baked for a church social—dusted each one until she'd raised it to her standards.

To this day, when I make tea cakes, these old family stories come to mind. Today, I bake them mostly during the winter holiday season, when I want the kitchen to have a nice and enticing aroma, or on those weekday mornings when I have a taste for an unassuming snack that imparts a delicate hint of nutmeg in each bite. These tea cakes are perfect with coffee or tea or a glass of cold milk. You can experiment with flavors by substituting almond or lemon extract for the vanilla.

Makes 36 tea cakes

Vegetable shortening, for greasing

1 cup (2 sticks) unsalted butter, room temperature

1½ cups granulated sugar

3 large eggs, room temperature

3½–5 cups all-purpose flour, plus more for rolling

2 teaspoons baking powder

1 teaspoon baking soda

½ teaspoon freshly grated nutmeg

½ cup buttermilk, room temperature

⅓ cup light molasses

1 teaspoon pure vanilla extract

recipe continues

Southern Tea Cakes *CONTINUED*

1. Preheat the oven to 350°F. Lightly grease 2 baking sheets with the shortening. Set aside.

2. In the bowl of a stand mixer fitted with the paddle attachment, break up the butter by mixing on low speed for 1 minute. Add the granulated sugar and cream together the butter and sugar on medium speed for 2 to 3 minutes, until the mixture is light and fluffy. Scrape down the sides and bottom of the bowl to prevent lumps from forming. As the mixer is running, reduce the speed to low and slowly add the eggs, 1 at a time; after you add each egg, scrape down the sides of the bowl and resume beating on low speed for 30 seconds.

3. In a large mixing bowl, sift together the dry ingredients: 3½ cups of the flour, the baking powder, the baking soda, and the nutmeg. Set aside.

4. In a medium mixing bowl, combine the buttermilk, molasses, and vanilla extract and stir until well combined.

5. Change the mixer attachment to the dough hook and slowly add the dry ingredients and the buttermilk mixture to the bowl of the running mixer ⅓ at a time, alternating back and forth, making sure to end with the flour mixture. Mix until thoroughly combined. If needed, add more flour, ½ cup at a time, until a smooth dough forms. Turn off the mixer.

6. Turn out the dough onto a floured work surface. Roll it out into a large circle and then form it into a ball. Repeat 3 or 4 more times and then roll the dough out 1 last time into a large circle that is ½ inch thick. Using a drinking glass, round cookie cutter, or jar lid, cut 36 disks out of the dough and place them on the prepared baking sheets.

7. Bake for 8 to 10 minutes, until the cakes' bottoms are slightly browned. Remove from the oven and set aside to cool on the baking sheets for 5 minutes. Transfer the cakes to a wire rack and allow to cool completely.

8. Transfer to a serving platter and serve at room temperature.

Morning Cake

Our family preferred morning sweets that were light, tender, fine textured, and laden with sugar. We wanted our sweets to go along with hot coffee or tea and slices of bacon or links of pork sausage—versatile cakes that went with bright summer mornings and cold winter ones alike. We wanted cake recipes that didn't require time for the yeast to rise and that were as delicious on an average morning as they were on a special one.

Thank you, Susan Howell, for this old-fashioned Morning Cake recipe that accomplishes all of those things.

Makes 1 9-inch square cake

BATTER

Nonstick cooking spray, for greasing

½ cup (1 stick) unsalted butter, room temperature

1 cup granulated sugar

2 large eggs, room temperature

2 cups all-purpose flour, plus more for dusting

2 teaspoons ground cinnamon

1 teaspoon baking soda

½ teaspoon salt

¾ cup whole milk, room temperature

TOPPING

½ cup firmly packed light brown sugar

2 tablespoons unsalted butter, melted

1. Preheat the oven to 350°F. Grease a 9-inch square baking dish with the cooking spray and dust with some flour. Set aside.

2. *To make the batter:* In the bowl of a stand mixer fitted with the paddle attachment, break up the butter by mixing on low speed for 1 minute. Add the granulated sugar and cream together the butter and sugar on medium speed for 2 to 3 minutes, until the mixture is light and fluffy. Scrape down the sides and bottom of the bowl to prevent lumps from forming. As the mixer is running, reduce the speed to low and slowly add the eggs, 1 at a time; after you add each egg, scrape down the sides of the bowl and resume beating on low speed for 30 seconds.

Our family preferred morning sweets that were light, tender, fine textured, and laden with sugar. This old-fashioned recipe accomplishes all of those things.

3. In a medium mixing bowl, sift together the dry ingredients: the flour, cinnamon, baking soda, and salt. Slowly add the flour mixture and the milk to the bowl of the running mixer ⅓ at a time, alternating back and forth, making sure to end with the flour mixture. Mix until thoroughly combined. Turn off the mixer.

4. *To make the topping:* In a small mixing bowl, whisk together the brown sugar and butter.

5. Transfer the batter to the prepared baking dish and evenly sprinkle the top of the batter with the topping. Bake for 30 minutes, until the cake is golden brown. Remove from the oven and set aside to cool in the baking dish on a wire rack for 10 minutes.

6. Transfer to a serving platter, slice, and serve warm.

Strawberry Bread

Miss Hatfield, a meticulous older woman who lived up the street from us in a tall white house, often seemed rather remote. But when her sickly mother, known to us as Old Lady Hatfield, passed away, Miss Hatfield delivered incredibly delectable homemade treats—jelly pies, spiced cakes, berry breads—to her neighbors' homes, including ours. I suppose that baking for the neighbors she'd ignored during her mother's ailments was her way of showing us that she was an ordinary person.

On summer mornings, when strawberries were in season, Mama used to make Miss Hatfield's Strawberry Bread recipe. She'd slice us up nice portions and serve them on pretty plates. Daddy loved Miss Hatfield's bread with his hot coffee, and I loved it with tall glasses of cold milk.

Makes 1 9-inch × 13-inch loaf

DOUGH

Nonstick cooking spray, for greasing

3⅛ cups all-purpose flour, plus more for dusting

2 cups granulated sugar

2 teaspoons ground cinnamon

1 teaspoon baking soda

½ teaspoon freshly grated nutmeg

½ teaspoon salt

2½ cups hulled, chopped fresh strawberries

1 cup vegetable oil

4 large eggs, room temperature, beaten

2 teaspoons pure vanilla extract

1 tablespoon freshly grated lemon zest

1¼ cups chopped walnuts

GLAZE

1 cup sifted confectioners' sugar

2 tablespoons freshly squeezed lemon juice

1. Preheat the oven to 350°F. Grease a 9-inch × 13-inch baking dish with the cooking spray and lightly dust with some flour. Set aside.

2. *To make the dough:* In a large mixing bowl, sift together the dry ingredients: the flour, granulated sugar, cinnamon, baking soda, nutmeg, and salt. Set aside.

3. In a separate large mixing bowl, combine the strawberries, vegetable oil, eggs, vanilla extract, and lemon zest and stir until well combined. Gradually add the strawberry mixture to the flour mixture, stirring until the dough is just moistened. Fold in the walnuts.

4. Transfer the dough to the prepared baking dish. Bake for 30 minutes, until a wooden toothpick inserted into the center of the bread comes out clean. Remove from the oven and set aside in the pan to cool on a wire rack for 5 minutes.

5. *To make the glaze:* In a small mixing bowl, whisk together the confectioners' sugar and lemon juice until well combined. Drizzle the glaze over the warm bread while it remains in the pan. Set aside to cool in the pan on the wire rack for 10 minutes before serving.

6. Transfer to a serving platter, slice, and serve warm.

Daddy loved Miss Hatfield's bread with his hot coffee, and I loved it with tall glasses of cold milk.

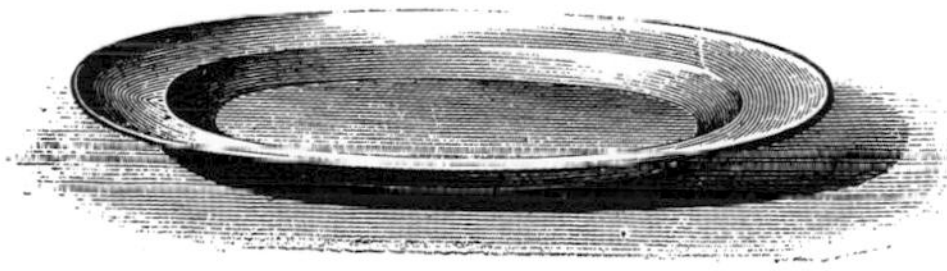

Mama's Coffee Cake Muffins

I BELIEVE THAT COOKING FOR MY FATHER WAS MY MOTHER'S MOST enjoyable expression of love. Her spice cabinet bulged with seasonings that pleased his palate. Her recipe collection was full to bursting with recipes he loved, written on the backs of envelopes and grocery store receipts, checked off and noted in her cookbooks. Shopping for the ingredients for Daddy's supper was her favorite hobby.

Mama, who was an avid reader, had read somewhere that cinnamon was a natural aphrodisiac, so naturally it was one of her staples. Most of her prized dessert recipes called for a pinch of it, at least. There's just enough cinnamon in these muffins to give them an appetizing flavor and a welcoming fragrance. Mama used to tell me, "A dish should smell as good as it tastes."

Makes 12 muffins

TOPPING AND BATTER

- Nonstick cooking spray, for greasing
- 2½ cups all-purpose flour (divided)
- ⅓ cup firmly packed light brown sugar
- 1½ teaspoons ground cinnamon (divided)
- ½ cup (1 stick) unsalted butter, melted and cooled (divided)
- 2 teaspoons baking powder
- ½ teaspoon salt
- ¾ cup granulated sugar
- 1 teaspoon pure vanilla extract
- ¾ cup sour cream, room temperature
- 2 large eggs, room temperature, beaten
- 1 teaspoon baking soda

GLAZE

- 1 cup sifted confectioners' sugar
- 2–3 tablespoons whole milk, room temperature
- 1 teaspoon pure vanilla extract

1. Preheat the oven to 350°F. Grease a 12-count muffin pan with the cooking spray. Set aside.

2. *To make the topping:* In a medium mixing bowl, combine ½ cup of the flour, the brown sugar, and ½ teaspoon of the cinnamon. Using your fingers, a pastry blender, or the tines of a fork, cut 4 tablespoons of the butter into the flour mixture until it becomes crumbly. Set aside.

recipe continues

3. *To make the batter:* In the bowl of a stand mixer fitted with the paddle attachment, sift together the remaining 2 cups of flour, the remaining 1 teaspoon of cinnamon, the baking powder, and the salt. Add the granulated sugar, the remaining butter, and the vanilla extract and mix for 2 to 3 minutes on low speed. Set aside.

4. In a small mixing bowl, combine the sour cream, eggs, and baking soda. Stir until well combined. With the mixer running at low speed, slowly add the sour cream mixture to the flour mixture ⅓ at a time and beat for 2 to 3 minutes, until well combined. Turn off the mixer.

5. Divide the batter evenly among the cups of the prepared pan, filling each about ⅔ full. Sprinkle each evenly with the topping. Bake for 20 to 25 minutes, until a wooden toothpick inserted into the center of a muffin comes out clean. Remove from the oven and set aside to cool in the pan on a wire rack for 10 minutes.

6. *To make the glaze:* In a small mixing bowl, whisk together the confectioners' sugar, milk, and vanilla extract until fully combined. Drizzle the glaze over the muffins.

7. Using a serrated knife, separate the muffins from the pan and then tap the pan gently on the counter to release them.

8. Transfer to a serving platter and serve warm.

Puffed Cherry Pancake Casserole

In my girlhood, I often used to travel to Flint, Michigan, to visit my Aunt Helen. Aunt Helen's neighbor and friend, Gladys Bass, had three pretty daughters named Vivica, Marianne, and Hope, and the Bass sisters were the darlings of Aunt Helen's neighborhood. They had everything that little girls coveted: fair complexions; long, wavy hair; pink canopy beds; Easy-Bake Ovens; toy kitchen sets; a real Coca-Cola dispenser; pink and white tricycles; Chatty Cathy dolls; baton sets; foldaway doll houses with complete rooms of furniture; transistor radios with earphones; and Barbie dolls with striking wardrobes (Miss Gladys was a master seamstress). Because the Bass girls and I were close in age, and because Miss Gladys said she admired my visiting manners, I would spend large portions of the days of my visits playing with the sisters. Many times, I spent the night; truth be told, I felt honored that Gladys Bass would have me.

Though I was young, I was aware that the Bass household was a household of women and that Gladys Bass was its fierce protector, preparing her beautiful daughters for survival in a world run by men. In the presence of her girls—and me—Miss Bass, newly divorced, talked about men bluntly as though they were objects to be conquered before they conquered you. She would remind her daughters that they had nice things because she was an independent and hard-working woman, and that a woman didn't have to subject herself to abuse from a man in order to put a sack of potatoes or a loaf of bread in her cupboard. When I'd see or hear her talking to men—the butcher, the mailman, the insurance man, her ex-husband—she'd wear a stony expression and sometimes would speak with contempt in her voice.

Contrary to Miss Bass's cold and unapproachable demeanor toward men, Aunt Helen expressed a warm and gracious spirit around them—especially her husband, Joe. Though their philosophies differed, Miss Bass wasn't the kind of woman who resented Aunt Helen's happy marriage or kept her best recipes from her friend. This is one of them.

recipe continues

Puffed Cherry Pancake Casserole *CONTINUED*

Makes 8–10 servings

½ cup (1 stick) unsalted butter
1 cup all-purpose flour
3 tablespoons granulated sugar
½ teaspoon ground cinnamon
¼ teaspoon salt
6 large eggs, room temperature
1¼ cups whole milk, room temperature
1 teaspoon pure vanilla extract
1 cup pitted fresh sour cherries
Confectioners' sugar, for dusting

1. Preheat the oven to 425°F. Place the butter in a 9-inch × 13-inch casserole dish and place the dish in the oven to allow the butter to melt. Remove from the oven. Using a pastry brush, spread the butter over the bottom and up the sides of the dish.

2. In a large mixing bowl, sift together the dry ingredients: the flour, granulated sugar, cinnamon, and salt. While whisking constantly, add the eggs, 1 at a time, to the bowl; continue whisking until the mixture is smooth. Resume whisking and add the milk and vanilla extract; continue whisking until the mixture is well combined. Stir in the cherries.

3. Transfer the batter to the baking dish, spread evenly, and return the dish to the oven. Bake for 20 minutes, until the casserole is puffy and golden brown on top. Remove from the oven.

4. Dust with the confectioners' sugar, slice, and serve hot.

Claudette Cotton's Banana–Yogurt Coffee Cake with Cream Cheese Glaze

CLAUDETTE COTTON, OUR NEIGHBOR FROM THE OLD NEIGHBORHOOD, was not the kind of wife who stayed at home to cook meals and decorate the house. Miss Claudette was the kind who drove her husband, Russell, to work in the mornings and, from there, kept on going for the rest of the day. She had hair and nail appointments, exercise class appointments, and sometimes, Miss Claudette, who resembled a young Etta James—complete with dyed-blond hair and a small mole above her upper lip—cruised around town just for the fun of it.

My mother was the opposite. Miss Claudette was forward; Mama was reserved. Miss Claudette was adventurous and spontaneous; Mama was cautious and consistent. Miss Claudette wore her dresses short and tight; Mama wore hers proper and ladylike. Although they were as different as cotton is from sandpaper, Mama liked Miss Claudette, and Miss Claudette liked Mama.

With Daddy, though, it was a different story. "She's loud and fast and runs the street while her husband's at work," Daddy said. "I don't think you oughta be around a woman like that. She sets a bad example." My mother had a lot of old-fashioned qualities, but allowing a man to supervise her friendships wasn't one of them. Mama continued to be friendly with Miss Claudette.

Years later, when Claudette Cotton's name came up during a conversation, Mama told me, "An assertive, experienced woman is a big challenge for a lot of men. Most men don't want their wives being friendly with an experienced woman—they're afraid that a woman like that will enlighten their wives about things . . . insightful things about men and relationships, things that they don't want their wives to know a great deal about." As far as I was concerned, Miss Claudette was a perfect balance of bold and charming.

She often called us over to sample something that she'd made from scratch; our favorite was this, her light and decadent Banana–Yogurt Coffee Cake.

Makes 1 10-inch tube or Bundt cake

BATTER

Nonstick cooking spray, for greasing

All-purpose flour, for dusting

¾ cup (1½ sticks) unsalted butter, room temperature

1 cup firmly packed light brown sugar

½ cup granulated sugar

2 large eggs, room temperature

1¼ cups plain Greek yogurt, room temperature

1 cup mashed ripe bananas (about 3 medium bananas)

½ teaspoon pure vanilla extract

¼ teaspoon pure banana extract

2 cups cake flour

1 teaspoon baking powder

1 teaspoon baking soda

½ teaspoon salt

½ cup chopped pecans

TOPPING

1 cup all-purpose flour

½ cup firmly packed light brown sugar

1 teaspoon ground cinnamon

½ cup (1 stick) butter, cold, cut into cubes

GLAZE

1 cup sifted confectioners' sugar

3 ounces cream cheese, room temperature

3 tablespoons whole milk, room temperature, plus more as needed

2 tablespoons unsalted butter, room temperature

1 teaspoon pure vanilla extract

1. Preheat the oven to 350°F. Grease a 10-inch tube or Bundt pan with the cooking spray and dust with the all-purpose flour. Set aside.

2. *To make the batter:* In the bowl of a stand mixer fitted with the paddle attachment, break up the butter by mixing on low speed for 1 minute. Add the brown and granulated sugars and cream together the butter and sugars on medium speed for 2 to 3 minutes, until the mixture is light and fluffy. Scrape down the sides and bottom of the bowl to prevent lumps from forming. As the mixer is running, reduce the speed to low and slowly add the eggs, 1 at a time; after you add each egg, scrape down the sides of the bowl and resume beating on low speed for 30 seconds. As the mixer continues to run, add the Greek yogurt, bananas, and vanilla and banana extracts and beat until thoroughly combined.

recipe continues

Claudette Cotton's Banana–Yogurt Coffee Cake with Cream Cheese Glaze *CONTINUED*

3. In a medium mixing bowl, sift together the dry ingredients: the cake flour, baking powder, baking soda, and salt. Add the flour mixture to the bowl of the mixer ⅓ at a time, beating each time at low speed for 2 to 3 seconds until just combined. Turn off the mixer. Carefully fold the pecans into the batter.

4. *To make the topping:* In a medium mixing bowl, combine the flour, brown sugar, and cinnamon. Using your fingers, a pastry blender, or the tines of a fork, cut the butter into the flour mixture until it forms small, moist clumps.

5. Transfer the batter to the prepared pan, spread evenly, and sprinkle the topping over the batter. Bake for 45 to 50 minutes, until a wooden toothpick inserted into the center of the cake comes out clean. Remove from the oven and set aside to cool completely in the pan on a wire rack.

6. *To make the glaze:* In a small mixing bowl, mix together the confectioners' sugar, cream cheese, milk, butter, and vanilla extract. Add more milk, as needed, to reach a smooth consistency.

7. Using a serrated knife, separate the cake from the tube pan and invert onto a serving platter. Drizzle with the glaze. Slice and serve at room temperature.

Old-Fashioned Gingerbread Waffles

FLAVORED WITH BROWN SUGAR, MOLASSES, AND WARM SPICES, Old-Fashioned Gingerbread Waffles are a perfect winter-morning treat. I like to serve mine with warmed maple syrup, sliced pears, and a hearty helping of scrambled eggs and bacon—a delicious breakfast for any occasion.

Makes 8–10 waffles

Nonstick cooking spray, for greasing
3 large eggs, room temperature
1 cup buttermilk, room temperature
½ cup molasses
¼ cup firmly packed brown sugar
2 cups all-purpose flour
1 teaspoon ground ginger
1 teaspoon baking powder
1 teaspoon baking soda
½ teaspoon ground cinnamon
½ teaspoon salt
¼ teaspoon freshly grated nutmeg
¼ teaspoon ground cloves
6 tablespoons unsalted butter, melted and cooled

1. Preheat a lightly greased waffle iron according to the manufacturer's directions.

2. In a medium mixing bowl, whisk the eggs until they are light and frothy. Add the buttermilk, molasses, and brown sugar and continue whisking until well combined. Set aside.

3. In a large mixing bowl, sift together the dry ingredients: the flour, ginger, baking powder, baking soda, cinnamon, salt, nutmeg, and cloves. Gradually stir the buttermilk mixture into the flour mixture until the batter is smooth. Add the butter and stir until well combined.

4. Pour a ladleful (⅓ cup) of the batter on the prepared waffle iron and cook according to the manufacturer's recommendations. Once the waffle is properly cooked, use the tines of a fork to lift it off the grid and transfer to a serving platter.

5. Repeat step 4 until all the batter is used.

6. Serve warm.

Banana Streusel Coffee Cake

I DO HAVE A FIXATION WITH BANANAS: SLICED ON TOP OF CEREAL, baked into bread, or served any other way is just fine with me. Anything made with bananas is great to start the day.

My My made the best banana dishes—she had a nose for it. Her Banana Streusel Coffee Cake was particularly moist and rich. I remember serving this cake as one of my first attempts at baking for someone outside my family. It is as moist and rich today as it was in my childhood.

Makes 1 10-inch tube or Bundt cake

BATTER

Nonstick cooking spray, for greasing

All-purpose flour, for dusting

1 cup (2 sticks) unsalted butter, room temperature

1 cup granulated sugar

¾ cup firmly packed light brown sugar

2 large eggs, room temperature

1⅓ cups mashed ripe bananas (about 3 large bananas)

1 teaspoon pure vanilla extract

2½ cups cake flour

1 teaspoon baking powder

1 teaspoon baking soda

½ teaspoon salt

1½ teaspoon freshly grated orange zest

1 cup sour cream, room temperature

FILLING

½ cup chopped pecans, toasted

½ cup confectioners' sugar

1 teaspoon ground cinnamon

1. Preheat the oven to 350°F. Grease a 10-inch tube or Bundt pan with the cooking spray and dust with the all-purpose flour. Set aside.

2. *To make the batter:* In the bowl of a stand mixer fitted with the paddle attachment, break up the butter by mixing on low speed for 1 minute. Add the granulated and brown sugars and cream together the butter and sugars on medium speed for 2 to 3 minutes, until the mixture is light and fluffy. Scrape down the sides and bottom of the bowl to prevent lumps from forming. As the mixer is running, reduce the speed to low and slowly add the eggs, 1 at a time; after you add each egg, scrape down the sides of the bowl and resume beating on low speed for 30 seconds. As the mixer continues to run, add the bananas and vanilla extract and beat until thoroughly combined.

3. In a medium mixing bowl, sift together the dry ingredients: the cake flour, baking powder, baking soda, and salt. Stir in the orange zest. Slowly add the dry ingredients and the sour cream to the bowl of the running mixer ⅓ at a time, alternating back and forth, making sure to end with the flour mixture. Mix until thoroughly combined. Turn off the mixer.

4. *To make the filling:* In a small mixing bowl, combine the pecans, confectioners' sugar, and cinnamon. Mix well.

5. Transfer ½ of the batter to the prepared pan. Sprinkle the filling over the batter and then cover the filling with the remaining batter.

6. Bake for 50 to 60 minutes, until a wooden toothpick inserted into the center of the cake comes out clean. Remove from the oven and set aside to cool in the pan on a wire rack for 25 minutes.

7. Using a serrated knife, separate the cake from the pan and invert onto a serving platter. Slice and serve warm.

Anything made with bananas is great to start the day.

Lemon–Cornmeal Muffins

YELLOW CORNMEAL AND ALL-PURPOSE FLOUR COME TOGETHER perfectly in these lovely muffins. I loved cornmeal muffins as a child, and they're still a special treat. Truth be told, I've never met anyone, child or adult, who doesn't like these muffins. They're easy to put together on a rushed morning, but people think you've spent the entire morning standing in front of a hot oven. To me, that's what good cooking is all about.

Makes 12 muffins

BATTER

Nonstick cooking spray, for greasing

1 cup fine yellow cornmeal

1 cup all-purpose flour

1 cup granulated sugar

2 tablespoons cornstarch

½ teaspoon salt

Freshly grated zest and freshly squeezed juice of 1 small lemon, divided

¾ cup buttermilk, room temperature

½ cup (1 stick) unsalted butter, melted and cooled

2 large eggs, room temperature

1 teaspoon pure vanilla extract

¾ cup fresh or frozen blueberries, thawed and drained

GLAZE

1½ cups sifted confectioners' sugar

Freshly squeezed juice of 1 lemon

1. Preheat the oven to 350°F. Grease a 12-count muffin pan with the cooking spray and set aside.

2. *To make the batter:* In a large mixing bowl, sift together the dry ingredients: the cornmeal, flour, granulated sugar, cornstarch, salt, and lemon zest. Set aside.

3. In a medium mixing bowl, whisk together the wet ingredients: the buttermilk, butter, eggs, lemon juice, and vanilla extract. Gradually add the buttermilk mixture to the cornmeal mixture, stirring until the batter is just combined. Carefully fold the blueberries into the batter.

4. Divide the batter evenly among the cups of the prepared pan, filling each about ⅔ full. Bake for 15 to 20 minutes, until a wooden toothpick inserted into the center of a muffin comes out clean. Remove from the oven and set aside to cool in the pan on a wire rack for 5 minutes.

5. *To make the glaze:* In a small mixing bowl, whisk together the confectioners' sugar and lemon juice until fully combined.

6. Using a serrated knife, separate the muffins from the pan and then tap the pan gently on the counter to release them. Transfer the muffins to the wire rack. Prick each with a wooden toothpick or the tines of a fork and drizzle the glaze over each muffin. Leave on the wire rack for 1 hour, until cooled completely.

7. Transfer to a serving platter and serve at room temperature.

Sherry Hannah's Pistachio Coffee Cake

My friend Sherry Hannah lives on three beautifully manicured acres in Bridgeport Township, Michigan. Sherry's knack for gardening is well known; once a year, Sherry invites a few of her best girlfriends to a morning walk through her gorgeous wooded garden. The garden bends, dips, and turns, and its cozy, rustic seating arrangements encourage reflection and conversation. We talk about flowers and plants, and how to love and care for them, and we talk about husbands and lovers, and how to love and care for them.

As much as I enjoy the harmonious morning treks through Sherry's lovely garden, I can't wait until they're over. At the end of each stroll, Sherry leads us to her kitchen, where there's always a delicious homemade treat waiting for us. As far as I'm concerned, that's when the garden party really starts to bloom.

Despite the fact that this coffee cake recipe calls for store-bought cake mix and instant pudding mix, it is moist and delicious, with a homemade taste and appearance. The pistachio pudding mix gives it a pretty tint of green, perfect for a summer morning garden party, and three or four drops of green food coloring added to the batter will make it an even prettier shade of garden green.

Makes 1 10-inch tube or Bundt cake

TOPPING

¾ cup shelled, skinned, and minced pistachios

½ cup granulated sugar

¼ cup firmly packed light brown sugar

1½ teaspoons ground cinnamon

1 tablespoon unsalted butter, melted

½ teaspoon pure vanilla extract

PISTACHIO DUST

1 cup shelled and skinned pistachios

¾ cup granulated sugar

2 tablespoons ground cinnamon

BATTER

Nonstick cooking spray, for greasing

1 (18-ounce) box yellow cake mix, without the pudding

1 cup sour cream, room temperature

4 large eggs, room temperature

¾ cup vegetable oil

1 (3½-ounce) package instant pistachio pudding mix

½ teaspoon pure vanilla extract

½ teaspoon pure almond extract

3–4 small drops of green food coloring (optional)

1. *To make the topping:* In a medium mixing bowl, combine the pistachios, granulated and brown sugars, and cinnamon and mix well. Stir in the butter and vanilla extract. Set aside.

2. Preheat the oven to 350°F. Grease a 10-inch fluted tube or Bundt pan with the cooking spray and set aside.

3. *To make the pistachio dust:* In the bowl of a food processor, combine the pistachios, granulated sugar, and cinnamon and process until the mixture is finely ground. Coat the bottom and sides of the prepared pan with 1/4 cup of the pistachio dust and reserve the rest.

4. *To make the batter:* In a large mixing bowl, using a hand mixer set at medium speed, beat together the cake mix, sour cream, eggs (1 at a time), vegetable oil, pudding mix, vanilla and almond extracts, and food coloring for 3 minutes, until thoroughly combined. Transfer 1/3 of the batter into the prepared pan and coat with half of the remaining pistachio dust. Transfer another 1/3 of the batter into the pan and coat with the remaining pistachio dust. Transfer the remaining 1/3 of the batter into the pan and sprinkle with the topping.

5. Bake for 45 to 50 minutes, until a wooden toothpick inserted into the center of the cake comes out clean. Remove from the oven and set aside to cool in the pan on a wire rack for 15 minutes.

6. Using a serrated knife, separate the cake from the pan and invert onto the wire rack to cool completely.

7. Transfer to a serving platter, slice, and serve at room temperature.

Aunt Betty Jean's Orange–Pecan Bread

My Aunt Betty Jean's Orange–Pecan Bread matches perfectly with her traditional breakfast: bacon, eggs, and sautéed potatoes. This rich, pretty bread is a staple on her morning table. I ask her to make it for me all the time.

Makes 1 9-inch × 5-inch × 3-inch loaf

Nonstick cooking spray, for greasing

2¼ cups all-purpose flour, plus more for dusting

¾ cup granulated sugar

2 tablespoons baking powder

½ teaspoon salt

2 large eggs, room temperature

1 cup whole milk, room temperature

1½ cups (1 12-ounce jar) thick orange marmalade

½ cup vegetable oil

1 tablespoon freshly grated orange zest

½ cup chopped pecans

1. Preheat the oven to 325°F. Grease a 9-inch × 5-inch × 3-inch loaf pan with the cooking spray and line the bottom of the pan with parchment paper. Grease the parchment and dust the sides and bottom of the pan with flour. Shake out the excess flour. Set the pan aside.

2. In a large mixing bowl, sift together the dry ingredients: the flour, granulated sugar, baking powder, and salt. Set aside.

3. In the bowl of a stand mixer fitted with the whisk attachment, beat the eggs, 1 at a time, on medium speed for 30 seconds each. Change the mixer attachment to the paddle and add the milk, almost all of the marmalade (reserving a small amount for brushing the bread after it bakes), the vegetable oil, and the orange zest and beat for 2 to 3 minutes, until the mixture is light and fluffy. Turn off the mixer. Gradually stir the flour mixture into the milk mixture until the batter is just moistened. Gently fold the pecans into the batter.

4. Transfer the batter to the prepared pan and bake for 1 hour, until a wooden toothpick inserted into the center of the bread comes out clean. Remove from the oven and set aside to cool in the pan on a wire rack for 10 minutes.

5. Remove from the pan and brush the top of the bread with the remaining marmalade. Set aside to cool completely on the wire rack.

6. Transfer to a serving platter, slice, and serve at room temperature.

Miss Katie's Cinnamon Rolls

My mother's friend and neighbor, Katie Falls, had a reputation for being an amazing baker. For years, Mama and Miss Katie got together at Christmastime to make cinnamon rolls for their respective families and friends. I've always loved cinnamon rolls made from scratch; I relished being in the kitchen while my mother and Miss Katie were kneading, rolling, and spreading the dough with cinnamon and sugar. Afterward, the sight of every table and available counter covered with pans of baked rolls draped in cotton bread cloths would send me into a tailspin of anticipation.

The cinnamon roll recipe they used was Miss Katie's. Miss Katie was a lot older than my mother, so naturally she had a trove of tried-and-true recipes my mother coveted. According to Mama, who had been collecting and testing cinnamon roll recipes for years, Miss Katie's delicious, soft, and chewy rolls were among the best.

They weren't just for Christmas: Mama would often make these cinnamon rolls when she was planning breakfast for overnight guests. Through the years, many folks have left our house saying that Mama's morning food was the best part of their stay.

Makes 12 large rolls

DOUGH

Vegetable shortening, for greasing
2¼ teaspoons (1 ¼-ounce package) active dry yeast
⅓ cup granulated sugar (divided)
¼ cup warm water (105°F–115°F)
1 cup evaporated milk
4 tablespoons unsalted butter
2 large eggs, room temperature, beaten
½ teaspoon salt
4 cups all-purpose flour, plus more for kneading

FILLING

¾ cup firmly packed light brown sugar
¼ cup granulated sugar
1½ tablespoons ground cinnamon
⅛ teaspoon ground cloves
Pinch salt
2 tablespoons unsalted butter, melted, for spreading
¾ cup chopped pecans

ICING

1½ cups sifted confectioners' sugar
4 ounces cream cheese, room temperature
1 tablespoon unsalted butter, melted
1 teaspoon pure vanilla extract
Pinch salt
2–3 tablespoons evaporated milk, plus more as needed

recipe continues

Miss Katie's Cinnamon Rolls *CONTINUED*

1. Lightly grease a 9-inch × 13-inch baking dish with the shortening. Set aside.

2. *To make the dough:* In a large mixing bowl, dissolve the yeast and 1 teaspoon of the granulated sugar in the warm water, stirring constantly with a wooden spoon to hasten the process. Set aside to bloom for 10 minutes, until the mixture turns frothy.

3. In a saucepan over medium–low heat, warm the milk and butter to 100°F to 110°F. (The butter need not melt completely.) Transfer the contents of the saucepan to the bowl with the yeast mixture.

4. While stirring constantly, add the remaining granulated sugar, eggs, and salt to the bowl with the yeast mixture. Slowly stir in the flour, 1 cup at a time, stopping when the dough has pulled together and becomes soft and somewhat sticky.

5. Turn out the dough onto a floured work surface. With floured hands, knead lightly for 8 to 10 minutes, until it is smooth, satiny, and no longer sticky. (Do not overknead—the dough is ready as soon as it holds an indentation when you touch it.) Form it into a smooth ball. Place the ball of dough in a well-greased bowl and turn it so all sides of the dough are greased. Cover with plastic wrap and set aside to rest and rise in a warm, draft-free place for 45 minutes to 1 hour, until the dough has doubled in size.

6. Remove the dough from the bowl, return it to the floured work surface, and gently punch it down. Return the dough to the greased bowl and recover with plastic wrap to allow it rise again for 45 minutes.

7. *To make the filling:* In a small mixing bowl, stir together the brown and granulated sugars, cinnamon, cloves, and salt. Set aside.

8. Turn out the dough onto a lightly floured work surface. With floured hands, knead the dough 4 or 5 times. Using a floured rolling pin, roll and gently stretch the dough into a 17-inch × 14-inch rectangle. Using a pastry brush, spread the butter over the top of the dough, leaving an uncoated ½-inch rim around the edges. Evenly spread the prepared filling over the dough, leaving the ½-inch margin around its edges clear of filling. Sprinkle the pecans over the filling, keeping the ½-inch margin. Lightly press the filling and pecans into the dough. Starting with the long side of the dough, roll it up tightly, jelly-roll style, and pinch the edges together to seal.

9. Using a serrated knife, slice the dough into 12 equal slices. Place the slices, spiral side up, about ½ inch apart in the prepared baking dish. Cover the dish lightly with plastic wrap and allow to rise in a warm, draft-free place for 30 minutes, until the rolls are slightly puffy.

10. Preheat the oven to 375°F.

11. Remove the plastic wrap from the dish and bake for 25 to 30 minutes, until the rolls are cooked through and are a light golden brown. Remove from the oven and set aside to cool in the dish on a wire rack for 5 minutes.

12. *To make the icing:* In a small mixing bowl, vigorously beat together the confectioners' sugar, cream cheese, butter, vanilla extract, and salt. As you continue beating the mixture, slowly add the evaporated milk, 1 tablespoon at a time, until the icing is smooth and reaches a smooth consistency.

13. Using a butter knife, gently remove the rolls from the baking dish and transfer to a wire rack on top of a sheet of parchment paper. Spread the icing on the warm rolls, gently pushing it into the rolls' swirls.

14. Transfer to a platter and serve warm or at room temperature.

Apple Fritters

No collection of breakfast desserts would be complete without my favorite autumn-morning comfort food, apple fritters. My father loved them, so Mama made them often.

Makes about 12–16 fritters

- 1¼ cups sifted cake flour
- 1 tablespoon light brown sugar
- 1 teaspoon baking powder
- ½ teaspoon ground cinnamon
- ½ teaspoon sea salt
- ⅛ teaspoon freshly grated nutmeg
- ½ cup buttermilk, room temperature
- 1 large egg, room temperature, beaten
- 2 tablespoons unsalted butter, melted and cooled
- 1 teaspoon pure vanilla extract
- 2 fresh, firm, medium Golden Delicious or honeycrisp apples, peeled, cored, and cut into ½-inch-thick chunks
- ⅓ cup vegetable shortening, for frying
- Cinnamon sugar, for rolling (optional)
- Confectioners' sugar, for dusting (optional)

1. In a large mixing bowl, whisk together the dry ingredients: the flour, brown sugar, baking powder, cinnamon, salt, and nutmeg. Set aside.

2. In a separate large mixing bowl, whisk together the wet ingredients: the buttermilk, egg, butter, and vanilla extract. Stir the buttermilk mixture into the flour mixture until a smooth batter forms and everything is well combined. Set aside to rest for 10 minutes.

3. Using paper towels, blot the apple chunks dry. Gently fold them into the batter.

4. Line a few plates with several layers of paper towels and set aside.

5. In a large skillet over medium–high heat, heat the shortening until it is hot but not smoking. Drop spoonfuls of the batter into the hot shortening, a few at a time, and fry for 1 to 2 minutes, until the fritters become golden brown on one side. Using a slotted spoon, turn each over and continue frying for another 1 to 2 minutes, until both sides are golden brown. Remove the fritters from the hot oil and allow them to drain on the prepared plates.

6. Repeat step 5 until all the batter has been used. Remove from the heat.

7. If using, roll each warm fritter in the cinnamon sugar or dust each with the confectioners' sugar. Transfer to a serving platter and serve warm.

Date–Nut Coffee Cake

WHENEVER MAMA PUT ONE OF HER DATE–NUT COFFEE CAKES ON THE breakfast table, it always had the final word. It's delicious plain but also tastes amazing served with a smidgen of cream cheese.

Makes 1 9-inch square coffee cake

BATTER

Nonstick cooking spray, for greasing
All-purpose flour, for dusting
2 cups cake flour
1 cup granulated sugar
1 teaspoon baking powder
1 teaspoon baking soda
½ teaspoon salt
2 large eggs, room temperature
1 cup buttermilk, room temperature
½ cup (1 stick) unsalted butter, melted and cooled
1 cup pitted and finely chopped dates
1 teaspoon pure vanilla extract

TOPPING

½ cup granulated sugar
½ cup chopped walnuts
1 teaspoon ground cinnamon
4 tablespoons unsalted butter, melted and cooled

1. Preheat the oven to 350°F. Lightly grease a 9-inch square baking dish with the cooking spray and dust with the all-purpose flour. Set aside.

2. *To make the batter:* In a large mixing bowl, sift together the dry ingredients: the cake flour, granulated sugar, baking powder, baking soda, and salt. Set aside.

3. In a medium mixing bowl, slightly beat the eggs. Add the buttermilk and butter and whisk until fully combined. Gradually add the egg mixture to the flour mixture, stirring until the batter is well combined. Add the dates and vanilla extract and stir until well combined.

4. *To make the topping:* In a small mixing bowl, combine the granulated sugar, walnuts, and cinnamon and stir until combined.

5. Transfer the batter to the prepared baking dish. Sprinkle the topping over the batter and then drizzle the melted butter over the topping. Bake for 35 to 40 minutes, until a wooden toothpick inserted into the center of the cake comes out clean. Remove from the oven and set aside to cool in the dish on a wire rack for 10 minutes.

6. Slice into squares and serve warm.

Plum Crostata

For the women in my family, 1963 was a very good year. That year, Mama's baby sister, Betty Jean, married her kind-hearted beau, Clyde, and my grandmother's young cousin Imogene divorced her spiteful husband, John. Aunt Marjell bought her first house, and Mama, who believed that a woman should be highly skilled and capable of supporting herself, enrolled in a shorthand class at the Adult Education Center.

That same year, the Plum Crostata was all the rage in our family. My maternal grandfather, Pop, grew plums in his yard. It was my grandmother's job to use them in cakes, breads, and pies. We'd watch Pop bring in the fruit and then watch My My transform them into succulent creations. But we never told Pop how effortless the crostata really was to make. My My liked to make him think she'd spent the entire morning in the kitchen making something nice with his plums.

Makes 1 crostata (6 servings)

CRUST

1½ cups all-purpose flour, plus more for rolling

½ cup granulated sugar

½ teaspoon salt

6 tablespoons unsalted butter, cold, cut into small pieces

2 large egg yolks

1 tablespoon ice water, plus more if needed

FILLING

3 cups fresh, firm, ripe, sliced, and pitted sugar plums (or other variety, about 1½ pounds before pitting), juices reserved

1-2 tablespoons granulated sugar (depending on the sweetness of the plums)

1½ tablespoons cornstarch

1 tablespoon pure vanilla extract

Freshly grated zest of 1 small lemon

Pinch salt

GLAZE

1 large egg yolk, beaten

1 tablespoon cold water

TOPPING

2 tablespoons coarse sugar, for sprinkling

1. *To make the crust:* In a large mixing bowl, sift together the dry ingredients: the flour, granulated sugar, and salt. Using your fingers, a pastry blender, or the tines of a fork, cut the butter into the flour mixture until it becomes coarse, like cornmeal.

Add the egg yolks, one at a time, stirring until the mixture is well blended. (Do not overmix.) Gently sprinkle the ice water into the dough and massage it in. The dough should hold together; if not, add more ice water, 1 teaspoon at a time. Gather the dough into a ball and pat it into a disk. Wrap the disk in plastic wrap and refrigerate for at least 1 hour. (The disk will keep for 3 days in the refrigerator and up to 3 months in the freezer.)

2. Turn out the dough onto a floured work surface. Using a floured rolling pin, roll out the dough into a 14-inch-wide circle. Line a baking sheet with parchment paper and transfer the circle to the prepared baking sheet. Place the baking sheet with the dough in the refrigerator while you make the filling. (The disk will keep for 3 days in the refrigerator and up to 3 months in the freezer.)

3. Preheat the oven to 450°F.

4. *To make the filling:* In a large mixing bowl, gently toss the plum slices with the granulated sugar, cornstarch, vanilla extract, lemon zest, and salt until well blended. Set aside for 1 to 2 minutes.

5. Remove the dough from the refrigerator. Spoon the filling into the center of the dough, leaving a 1½-inch border. Fold the border over once, pleating it to help hold in the filling.

6. *To make the glaze:* In a small mixing bowl, combine the egg yolk and water and mix well.

7. Using a pastry brush, brush the plum slices with the reserved plum juice and then brush the rim of the dough around the outside of the crostata with the glaze. Sprinkle the entire top of the crostata with the coarse sugar.

8. Bake for 20 to 25 minutes, until the crust is golden brown and the plums are fork tender. Remove from the oven and set aside to cool on the baking sheet on a wire rack for about 5 minutes. Using 2 large spatulas, remove from the baking sheet and place on the wire rack.

9. Transfer to a serving platter, slice, and serve warm or at room temperature.

Great-Aunt Martha's Blackberry–Oatmeal Squares

When we were children, my cousins and I loved to spend weekends in Chicago with our Great-Aunt Martha. She was a quintessential morning person; mornings at her house were bold and bright and full of promise. She would rise early, throw open the drapes—just like in the movies—and thrill us with suggestions for the day: perhaps a picnic in Wicker Park, a trip to Navy Pier, or a day at the Lincoln Park Zoo. As soon as our feet hit the floor, Great-Aunt Martha would have us turn a series of pirouettes, usually in time with a Maria Callas album playing in the background. Afterward, we'd dance the Twist or the Jerk or groove to Sly and the Family Stone's "Hot Fun in the Summertime." Great-Aunt Martha was a genuine eccentric—truth be told, she was a lovable hot mess.

Great-Aunt Martha never did give us a picnic in Wicker Park, take us on a trip to Navy Pier, or treat us to a day at the Lincoln Park Zoo, but that didn't diminish our love for her. Just being with her was all we needed. Great-Aunt Martha's handmade book of breakfast recipes contained a lot of tasty treats, and this one, for Blackberry–Oatmeal Squares, was one of our favorites.

Makes 16–18 squares

CRUST AND TOPPING

Nonstick cooking spray, for greasing

½ cup (1 stick) unsalted butter, room temperature

¾ cup firmly packed light brown sugar

1 large egg, room temperature

1 teaspoon pure vanilla extract

2 cups old-fashioned rolled oats

¾ cup all-purpose flour

¼ teaspoon baking soda

¼ teaspoon ground cinnamon

¼ teaspoon salt

FILLING

2½ cups fresh blackberries

¼ cup firmly packed light brown sugar

2 tablespoons water

1 tablespoon freshly squeezed lemon juice

1 tablespoon cornstarch

½ teaspoon ground cinnamon

recipe continues

Aunt Martha's Blackberry–Oatmeal Squares *CONTINUED*

1. Preheat the oven to 350°F. Lightly grease a 9-inch square baking dish with the cooking spray and set aside.

2. *To make the crust and topping:* In the bowl of a stand mixer fitted with the paddle attachment, break up the butter by mixing on low speed for 1 minute. Add the brown sugar and cream together the butter and sugar on medium speed for 2 to 3 minutes, until the mixture is light and fluffy. Scrape down the sides and bottom of the bowl to prevent lumps from forming. As the mixer is running, reduce the speed to low and add the egg and vanilla extract and beat for 30 seconds. Turn off the mixer.

3. Add the oats, flour, baking soda, cinnamon, and salt; using your fingers, blend the dry ingredients into the mixture until it forms pea-sized crumbs. Remove 1 cup of the mixture from the bowl and reserve it in the refrigerator for use as the topping.

4. Press the remaining oat mixture into the bottom of the prepared baking dish. Bake for 15 to 20 minutes, until the crust is slightly golden. Remove from the oven and set aside to cool. Leave the oven on.

5. *To make the filling:* In a medium saucepan over medium–high heat, bring the blackberries, brown sugar, water, lemon juice, cornstarch, and cinnamon to a boil. Reduce the heat to medium and simmer, uncovered and stirring frequently, for 10 minutes, until the mixture thickens slightly. Remove from the heat and set aside.

6. Carefully spread the filling on top of the baked crust. Remove the reserved topping from the refrigerator. Sprinkle the topping evenly over the filling and lightly press the topping into the filling. Bake for 25 to 30 minutes, until the topping is golden brown. Remove from the oven and set aside to cool in the baking dish on a wire rack for 5 minutes.

7. Slice into squares and serve warm.

Banana Bread French Toast with Buttermilk Syrup

MY BANANA BREAD FRENCH TOAST ALWAYS LIGHTS UP A BREAKFAST table. As far as I'm concerned, there's no reason to wait for the weekend to enjoy French toast when I can put a loaf of banana bread to good use and whip up this irresistible breakfast for myself or for guests in no time.

Makes 4–6 servings

SYRUP

1½ cups granulated sugar

¾ cup buttermilk

⅓ cup unsalted butter

2 tablespoons light corn syrup

1 teaspoon baking soda

1 teaspoon pure vanilla extract

FRENCH TOAST

3 large eggs, room temperature

¼ cup half-and-half, room temperature

1 teaspoon pure vanilla extract

1 loaf banana bread, cut into ½-inch-thick slices

2 tablespoons unsalted butter (optional)

1. *To make the syrup:* In a medium saucepan over medium heat, bring the sugar, buttermilk, butter, corn syrup, and baking soda to a simmer and cook for 5 or 7 minutes, until the sugar has dissolved. Remove from the heat and vigorously whisk in the vanilla extract. Set aside.

2. *To make the French toast:* In a shallow mixing bowl, whisk together the eggs and half-and-half until well blended. Add the vanilla extract and continue whisking until well blended.

3. Warm a nonstick skillet over medium–high heat. Dip 1 slice of the banana bread in the egg mixture and make sure each side is thoroughly coated. Remove from the mixture, place in the skillet, and cook for 2 to 3 minutes, until lightly golden brown on one side. Flip over and cook on the other side for 2 to 3 minutes, until golden brown. Transfer to a serving platter. Repeat until all slices of the banana bread have been used. Remove from the heat.

4. Pour the still-warm syrup over the platter of prepared French toast slices and serve warm. Top with the butter, if using.

Apricot Galette

NOTHING ABOUT A FREE-FORM GALETTE HAS TO BE PERFECT. THAT'S why I like making them so much—they are soulful and rustic. Galettes are festive and pretty enough to make for guests, yet simple enough to whip up on a weekday morning.

Makes 1 galette (6–8 servings)

CRUST

1¾ cups all-purpose flour, plus more for rolling

3 tablespoons granulated sugar

1 large egg yolk

¼ teaspoon salt

¾ cup (1½ sticks) unsalted butter, cold, cut into ½-inch cubes

3½ tablespoons ice water, plus more if needed

FILLING

3 cups fresh apricots, halved, pitted, and thinly sliced (about 1½–2 pounds before pitting)

2–4 tablespoons granulated sugar (depending on the sweetness of the apricots)

1½ tablespoons cornstarch

½ cup apricot jam or preserves, melted

½ teaspoon pure vanilla extract

TOPPING

2 tablespoons heavy cream

¼ cup minced almonds

1. *To make the crust:* In a large mixing bowl, combine the flour, granulated sugar, egg yolk, and salt. Using your fingers, a pastry blender, or the tines of a fork, cut the butter into the flour mixture until it becomes coarse, like cornmeal. Gently sprinkle the ice water into the dough and massage it in. The dough should hold together; if not, add more ice water, 1 teaspoon at a time. Gather the dough into a ball and pat it into a disk. Wrap the disk in plastic wrap and refrigerate for at least 1 hour. (The disk will keep for 3 days in the refrigerator and up to 3 months in the freezer.)

2. Turn out the dough onto a floured work surface. Using a floured rolling pin, roll out the dough into a 14-inch-wide circle. Line a baking sheet with parchment paper and transfer the circle to the prepared baking sheet. Place the baking sheet with the dough in the refrigerator while you make the filling.

3. Preheat the oven to 350°F.

4. *To make the filling:* In a large mixing bowl, gently toss the apricot slices with the granulated sugar and cornstarch. Set aside for 10 minutes, stirring occasionally.

5. Add the apricot jam and vanilla extract to the apricot mixture and stir until well blended. Spoon the filling into the center of the dough, leaving a 2-inch border. Fold the border over once, pleating it to help hold in the fruit.

6. *To make the topping:* Using a pastry brush, brush the rim of dough around the outside of the galette with the heavy cream. Sprinkle the entire top of the galette with the minced almonds.

7. Bake for 40 to 55 minutes, until the crust is golden brown and the apricots are fork tender. Remove from the oven and set aside to cool on the baking sheet on a wire rack for about 5 minutes.

8. Using 2 large spatulas, remove from the baking sheet and place on the wire rack to cool for 5 minutes.

9. Transfer to a serving platter, slice, and serve warm or at room temperature.

Baked Grape-Nuts Pudding

If you love the heady flavor of Grape-Nuts, you'll really love this pudding with your cup of morning coffee. This recipe is from my maternal Great-Aunt Laura, who worked as a beautician. Try it either warm or cold with a dollop of whipped cream.

Makes 8 servings

4 cups whole milk, scalded

2 cups Grape-Nuts cereal

Nonstick cooking spray, for greasing

2 large eggs, room temperature, yolks and whites separated

Pinch ground cinnamon

Pinch freshly grated nutmeg

⅓ cup packed light brown sugar

1 teaspoon pure vanilla extract

⅛ teaspoon salt

1 cup chopped walnuts

½ cup golden raisins

½ cup pitted and chopped dates

1. In a large mixing bowl, pour the scalded milk over the cereal and set aside to cool to room temperature.

2. Preheat the oven to 350°F. Grease a 2-quart ovenproof casserole dish with the cooking spray and set aside.

3. In a small mixing bowl, beat the egg whites until stiff and set aside.

4. In a medium mixing bowl, beat together the egg yolks with the cinnamon and nutmeg. Add the sugar, vanilla extract, and salt and stir together until well combined. Add the egg yolk mixture to the cereal mixture and stir until combined.

5. Add the walnuts, raisins, and chopped dates and gently fold them into the mixture. Then, gently fold in the egg whites.

6. Transfer the mixture to the prepared casserole dish. Bake for 50 minutes to 1 hour, until a knife inserted into the center of the pudding comes out clean. Remove from the oven.

7. Slice into squares and serve warm.

Miss Dottie's Nutmeg Coffee Cake

OF ALL MY MOTHER'S FRIENDS, MISS DOTTIE WAS THE MOST FASCINATING. She traveled everywhere, from Europe to the West Indies, and had pen pals around the world.

I once heard Miss Dottie tell Mama that nutmeg was her favorite spice. Long ago, rich people carried nutmeg as a show of wealth and would use intricate, tiny personal graters to grate their own at fancy eateries. She had a collection of these graters, and she used them to make her Nutmeg Coffee Cake extra delicious.

Makes 1 9-inch square coffee cake

Nonstick cooking spray, for greasing
2 cups all-purpose flour
1½ cups firmly packed light brown sugar
1 tablespoon baking powder
½ teaspoon salt
¾ cup (1½ sticks) unsalted butter, cold, cut into small pieces
1 cup whole milk, room temperature
1 large egg, room temperature, lightly beaten
1 teaspoon freshly grated nutmeg
¾ cup finely chopped walnuts
Maple syrup, for serving

1. Preheat the oven to 350°F. Grease a 9-inch square baking dish with the cooking spray and set aside.

2. In a large mixing bowl, sift together the dry ingredients: the flour, brown sugar, baking powder, and salt. Using your fingers, a pastry blender, or the tines of a fork, cut the butter into the flour mixture until it becomes crumbly and resembles peas. Press ½ of the mixture into the bottom of the prepared baking dish.

3. In a small mixing bowl, whisk together the milk, egg, and nutmeg until the mixture is well blended. Gently fold the walnuts into the mixture. Gently stir the milk mixture into the remaining flour mixture until just combined.

4. Transfer the batter to the prepared baking dish. Bake for 40 to 45 minutes, until a wooden toothpick inserted into the center of the cake comes out clean. Remove from the oven and set aside to cool in the baking dish on a wire rack for 5 minutes. Remove from the baking dish, transfer to the wire rack, and allow to cool completely.

5. Transfer to a serving platter, slice into squares, and serve at room temperature with the maple syrup.

Cowboy Coffee Cake

OUR COUSIN JOHN AND HIS WIFE FLORENCE LIVED IN A SPACIOUS BRICK house on the west side of Detroit. Florence was a city girl through and through, and John adored her. His face would light up like the moon whenever she sashayed into the room.

Behind her back, the women in my family claimed that Cousin Florence had a reputation—that she'd worn glitter and gone to nightclub soirees and house parties. Cousin John, an older bachelor, had met her at one of them.

Mama loved Cousin Florence, who made wonderful breakfasts. Her table linens were always starched, and her finest china was always used when we came over. We especially liked her Cowboy Coffee Cake (she used to call Cousin John her cowboy).

Makes 1 10-inch tube or Bundt cake

GLAZE

1 cup sifted confectioners' sugar

2–3 tablespoons whole milk, room temperature

2 tablespoons unsalted butter, melted

½ teaspoon pure almond extract

COFFEE CAKE

Nonstick cooking spray, for greasing

1 (12-ounce) tube refrigerated biscuit dough (not the flaky type), separated

1 cup firmly packed light brown sugar

½ cup finely chopped pecans

⅓ cup unsalted butter

¼ cup whole milk

1 teaspoon ground cinnamon

1. *To make the glaze:* In a small mixing bowl, stir together the confectioners' sugar, 2 tablespoons of the milk, the butter, and the almond extract. Add more milk, up to 1 tablespoon, as needed to reach a smooth consistency. Set aside.

2. Preheat the oven to 350°F. Grease a 10-inch fluted tube or Bundt pan with the cooking spray and set aside.

3. *To make the coffee cake:* Place the rounds of biscuit dough in the bottom of the prepared pan. Set aside.

4. In a medium saucepan over medium-low heat, combine the brown sugar, pecans, butter, milk, and cinnamon and cook for 2 to 3 minutes, until the butter has melted. Remove from the heat.

5. Pour the brown sugar mixture over the rounds of biscuit dough in the pan. Bake for 25 to 30 minutes, until the coffee cake is golden brown. Remove from the oven. Set aside to cool in the pan on a wire rack for 5 minutes.

6. Using a serrated knife, separate the cake from the pan and invert onto a serving platter. Drizzle with the topping.

7. Slice and serve warm.

Aunt Helen's Pumpkin Bread

A NICE SLICE OF PUMPKIN BREAD AND A CUP OF HOT COFFEE IS SO satisfying on a dark, chilly fall morning. My Aunt Helen, whose cooking was rich and sultry, made pumpkin bread for family and for girlfriends during the holidays as gifts.

Aunt Helen's Pumpkin Bread recipe calls for 1 cup of pumpkin purée. Feel free to use the stuff in the can from the supermarket or some fresh from the middle of your Halloween pumpkin—as long as the pumpkin is little and sweet.

Makes 1 9-inch × 5-inch × 3-inch loaf

Nonstick cooking spray, for greasing
All-purpose flour, for dusting
1½ cups cake flour
1 cup granulated sugar
1 teaspoon baking soda
½ teaspoon baking powder
½ teaspoon ground cinnamon
½ teaspoon freshly grated nutmeg
½ teaspoon salt
¼ teaspoon ground allspice
2 large eggs, room temperature
1 cup pumpkin purée
½ cup vegetable oil
¼ cup whole milk, room temperature
½ cup chopped walnuts
½ cup currants

1. Preheat the oven to 350°F. Grease a 9-inch × 5-inch × 3-inch loaf pan with the cooking spray and line the bottom of the pan with parchment paper. Grease the parchment and dust the sides and bottom of the pan with the all-purpose flour. Shake out the excess flour. Set the pan aside.

2. In a large mixing bowl, sift together the dry ingredients: the cake flour, granulated sugar, baking soda, baking powder, cinnamon, nutmeg, salt, and allspice. Set aside.

3. In the bowl of a stand mixer fitted with the whisk attachment, beat the eggs, 1 at a time, on low speed for 30 seconds each. While the mixer continues to run, add the pumpkin purée, vegetable oil, and milk and beat for 2 to 3 minutes, until the mixture is light and fluffy. Turn off the mixer.

A nice slice of pumpkin bread and a cup of hot coffee is so satisfying on a dark, chilly fall morning.

4. Gradually stir the blended dry ingredients into the egg mixture. Fold the walnuts and currants into the batter.

5. Transfer the batter to the prepared pan and bake for 65 to 70 minutes, until a wooden toothpick inserted into the center of the bread comes out clean. Remove from the oven and set aside to cool in the pan on a wire rack for about 10 minutes.

6. Remove from the pan and set aside to rest and cool on the wire rack for least 3 hours before slicing.

7. Transfer to a serving platter, slice, and serve at room temperature.

COOKS' NOTE: *If you do use a Halloween pumpkin, don't forget to roast its seeds in a cast-iron skillet. They're a delicious snack!*

Biscuits and Strawberries

THIS IS A WONDERFUL SOUTHERN RECIPE. BIG MAMA MADE BISCUITS and Strawberries all the time—they were cheap and tasty to fix in the morning. We used to have Biscuits and Strawberries mostly in the summer, when the strawberries were in season. As she made them, Mama would tell me stories about Big Mama; I never got tired of hearing them.

Makes 8 servings

1 cup very ripe strawberries, hulled and diced
2 tablespoons plus ¼ cup granulated sugar (divided)
2 cups all-purpose flour, plus more for rolling
2 teaspoons baking powder
½ teaspoon baking soda
½ teaspoon salt
½ cup (1 stick) unsalted butter, cold
1 cup heavy cream

1. In a small mixing bowl, combine the strawberries and 2 tablespoons of the sugar. Transfer the bowl to the refrigerator and allow the mixture to macerate for at least 1 hour.

2. Preheat the oven to 425°F. Line a baking sheet with parchment paper and set aside.

3. In a large mixing bowl, sift together the dry ingredients: the flour, the remaining ¼ cup granulated sugar, the baking powder, the baking soda, and the salt. Using your fingers, a pastry blender, or the tines of a fork, cut the butter into the flour mixture until it becomes coarse, like cornmeal. Remove the strawberries from the refrigerator and fold them into the flour mixture. Carefully stir in the heavy cream. With floured hands, knead the mixture once or twice, but do not overmix.

4. Turn out the dough onto a generously floured work surface. Using a floured rolling pin, roll and gently stretch it into a 9-inch × 5-inch rectangle that is ¾ inch thick. Using a floured 2-inch round biscuit cutter, cut 8 disks out of the dough.

5. Place the disks on the prepared baking sheet. Bake for 10 to 20 minutes, until the biscuits are golden brown at the edges and the strawberries' juices are just bubbling. Remove from the oven and set aside to cool on the baking sheet on a wire rack for 1 minute.

6. Transfer to a serving platter and serve warm or at room temperature.

Real Hot Chocolate

I CRAVE A MUG OF STEAMING HOT CHOCOLATE ON COLD, WINTRY MORNINGS. I'll choose real homemade hot chocolate over the store-bought variety any day. It is truly one of my favorite indulgences.

Makes 4 servings

- 2 cups water
- 6 cups whole milk
- 6 ounces good-quality unsweetened baking chocolate, shaved
- ½ cup heavy cream
- 6 tablespoons granulated sugar
- ½ teaspoon pure vanilla extract
- Pinch salt
- Sweetened whipped cream, for serving

1. Place the water in a saucepan over medium-high heat and bring to a boil. Place a medium heatproof stainless-steel bowl on top of the boiling water. In the bowl, combine the milk, chocolate, heavy cream, granulated sugar, vanilla extract, and salt. Vigorously whisk the mixture until it becomes frothy. Remove from the heat.

2. Ladle the hot chocolate into 4 mugs and top each mug with a spoonful of the sweetened whipped cream. Serve immediately.

Stuffed Pecan Pie French Toast

THIS DELICIOUS STUFFED PECAN PIE FRENCH TOAST IS A MELT-IN-your-mouth morning pleasure that I make often. I got this recipe from Mama, who usually made the treat on Sunday mornings before church.

Makes 8 servings

BREAD

½ cup (1 stick) unsalted butter, plus more for greasing

1 cup firmly packed light brown sugar

1 (15-ounce) loaf cinnamon-swirl bread, sliced (16 slices)

BATTER

2 cups whole milk, room temperature

1 cup granulated sugar

3 large eggs, room temperature

1½ teaspoons pure vanilla extract

½ teaspoon salt

FILLING

2 cups chopped pecans, toasted

1 cup packed light brown sugar

½ cup (1 stick) unsalted butter, melted and cooled

½ cup light corn syrup

2 large eggs, room temperature

1 teaspoon pure vanilla extract

½ teaspoon ground cinnamon

GARNISH

Confectioners' sugar, for dusting

1. Preheat the oven to 350°F. Grease a rimmed baking sheet with butter and set aside.

2. *To make the bread:* In a small saucepan over medium–high heat, bring the brown sugar and butter to a boil. Remove from the heat and set aside.

3. Place the slices of bread on the prepared baking sheet. Bake for 5 minutes, until the slices are lightly toasted. Remove from the oven and set aside.

4. *To make the batter:* In a large mixing bowl, combine the milk, granulated sugar, eggs, vanilla extract, and salt and whisk until well blended.

5. Dip 1 slice of the bread in the batter and make sure each side is thoroughly coated. Remove from the batter and return the slice to the baking sheet. Repeat until all slices of the bread have been dipped in the batter. Set aside.

6. *To make the filling:* In a separate large mixing bowl, combine the pecans, brown sugar, butter, corn syrup, eggs, vanilla extract, and cinnamon and stir until well combined.

7. Spread 1 to 2 tablespoons of the filling on each of 8 slices of the dipped bread, reserving 1/4 cup of the filling. Place an unfilled, dipped slice of bread on top of each filled slice. Bake for 15 to 20 minutes, until the French toast is hot and cooked through. Remove from the oven.

8. Transfer to a serving platter. Top each serving with an equal portion of the reserved filling, dust with the confectioners' sugar, and serve hot.

COOKS' NOTE: *If you do add the reserved filling to the top of each serving, be aware that it contains raw eggs. There are some risks to consuming raw eggs, but who among us hasn't eaten a little batter from time to time? Consider this, particularly if you are cooking for young children, the elderly, or folks with compromised immune systems.*

Glazed Coffee Bars

THESE GLAZED BARS ARE PERFECT FOR ANYONE WHO LOVES THE TASTE of coffee.

Makes 12 bars

BATTER

Nonstick cooking spray, for greasing

½ cup (1 stick) unsalted butter, room temperature

1 cup firmly packed light brown sugar

2 large eggs, room temperature

⅓ cup hot, strong coffee

1¾ cups all-purpose flour

1 teaspoon ground cinnamon

1 teaspoon baking powder

½ teaspoon baking soda

¼ teaspoon salt

1 cup semisweet chocolate chips

½ cup chopped walnuts

GLAZE

¾ cup sifted confectioners' sugar

1 teaspoon unsalted butter, melted and cooled

¼ teaspoon pure vanilla extract

3–4 teaspoons cold coffee

1. Preheat the oven to 350°F. Grease an 8-inch square baking dish with the cooking spray and set aside.

2. *To make the batter:* In the bowl of a stand mixer fitted with the paddle attachment, break up the butter by mixing on low speed for 1 minute. Add the brown sugar and cream together the butter and sugar on medium speed for 2 to 3 minutes, until the mixture is light and fluffy. Scrape down the sides and bottom of the bowl to prevent lumps from forming. As the mixer is running, reduce the speed to low and slowly add the eggs, 1 at a time; after you add each egg, scrape down the sides of the bowl and resume beating on low speed for 30 seconds. Add the hot coffee and resume beating on low speed for 30 seconds. Turn off the mixer.

3. In a medium mixing bowl, sift together the dry ingredients: the flour, cinnamon, baking powder, baking soda, and salt. Gradually stir the flour mixture into the bowl of the mixer. Using a rubber or silicone spatula, gradually fold the chocolate chips and the walnuts into the batter.

4. Transfer the batter to the prepared baking dish. Bake for 30 to 35 minutes, until a wooden toothpick inserted into the center of the dish comes out clean. Remove from the oven and set aside to cool on a wire rack for 5 minutes before serving.

5. *To make the glaze:* In a small mixing bowl, combine the confectioners' sugar, butter, and vanilla extract and mix well. Gradually stir in the cold coffee, starting with 3 teaspoons, adding another 1 teaspoon as needed, until you reach a smooth consistency.

6. Pour the glaze evenly over the bars. Set aside to cool completely.

7. Slice and serve at room temperature.

Apple Blintzes

THIS RECIPE FOR APPLE BLINTZES CAME TO ME AROUND 30 YEARS AGO from a neighbor, Carrie Brown. When we lived next door to her, Miss Carrie, as we called her, was well into her 80s and refused to let her husband of 60 years call her by any name other than Carrie. "I won't let him take me for granted. I'm more dignified than that," Miss Carrie used to tell me. "Very few girls these days set those standards for themselves."

The crêpes in Miss Carrie's recipe can also be filled with meats or vegetables, but I've always used fresh fruits—especially chopped apples. Served with hot coffee or tea, these Apple Blintzes make a wonderful breakfast treat.

Makes 6–8 servings

FILLING

3 large, tart apples, peeled, cored, and coarsely chopped

½ cup granulated sugar

¼ cup water

1 teaspoon cornstarch

½ teaspoon ground cinnamon

⅛ teaspoon freshly grated nutmeg

CRÊPES

¾ cup whole milk, room temperature, plus more as needed

½ cup cold water

3 large egg yolks, room temperature

2 tablespoons unsalted butter, melted

½ teaspoon pure vanilla extract

1 cup all-purpose flour

¼ teaspoon kosher salt

Vegetable oil, for cooking

Confectioners' sugar, for dusting

1. *To make the filling:* In a medium saucepan over low heat, combine the apples, sugar, water, cornstarch, cinnamon, and nutmeg and simmer over low heat for 15 minutes, until the apples are fork tender. Remove from the heat and set aside.

2. *To make the crêpes:* In a medium mixing bowl, whisk together the milk, water, egg yolks, butter, and vanilla extract. Gradually whisk in the flour and salt. The mixture should be thin; if it is not, add more milk, 1 tablespoon at a time, until it reaches the desired consistency. Cover with plastic wrap and refrigerate for 2 hours.

3. Lightly grease a 12-inch nonstick skillet with the vegetable oil and place it over medium–high heat. Once the surface is hot, pour ¼ cup of the batter into the skillet and immediately tilt it so that the skillet's bottom and a small portion of its sides are covered. Cook for 1 minute, until the top is no longer moist. Flip the crêpe over and cook on the other side for 20 seconds, until the crêpe is golden brown. Remove from the skillet and place on a plate.

4. Repeat step 3 until all of the batter has been used.

5. Place 1 heaping tablespoon of the filling in the center of 1 crêpe. Fold the sides of the crêpe over the filling and roll the crêpe up, forming a blintz. Place the blintz on a warmed serving platter. Continue with the remaining crêpes and filling until all the crêpes and filling have been used.

6. Dust the blintzes with the confectioners' sugar and serve warm.

The crêpes in Miss Carrie's recipe can also be filled with meats or vegetables.

Brownie Muffins

MAMA'S FRIEND MISS LENA HAD LOTS OF BEAUTIFUL THINGS: FINE alligator pumps, delicate French handbags, and precious jewelry. Most of these things were given to her by her boyfriend, Harvey, who did so in appreciation for her fine cooking. Miss Lena made Harvey tender pot roasts, sweet collard greens, delicious sweet potato pies, luscious banana puddings, and homemade soups and stews that rivaled his mother's. Like Mr. Harvey, we loved Miss Lena's cooking, and we told her so.

Makes 12 muffins

Nonstick cooking spray, for greasing
½ cup (1 stick) unsalted butter
½ cup semisweet cocoa powder
1 cup granulated sugar
1 cup all-purpose flour
3 large eggs, room temperature, lightly beaten
1 teaspoon pure vanilla extract
½ teaspoon baking powder
¼ teaspoon salt
¼ cup chopped pecans
¼ cup semisweet chocolate chips

1. Preheat the oven to 350°F. Grease a 12-count muffin pan with the cooking spray. Set aside.

2. In a small saucepan over medium–low heat, melt the butter and cocoa powder. Remove from the heat and set aside to cool.

3. In a large mixing bowl, combine the granulated sugar, flour, eggs, vanilla extract, baking powder, and salt and stir until well combined. Pour the cooled butter mixture into the bowl and stir until well combined. Fold in the pecans.

4. Divide the batter evenly among the cups of the prepared pan, filling each about ⅔ full. Sprinkle each evenly with the chocolate chips. Bake for 15 to 20 minutes, until a wooden toothpick inserted into the center of a muffin comes out clean. Remove from the oven and set aside to cool in the pan on a wire rack for 7 minutes.

5. Using a serrated knife, separate the muffins from the pan and then tap the pan gently on the counter to release them. Transfer the muffins to the wire rack and allow them to cool completely.

6. Transfer to a serving platter and serve at room temperature.

Jam Muffins

I'M SO GLAD MY FRIEND JOCELYN NEWSOME GAVE ME THIS RECIPE YEARS ago. Children and grown folks alike love the swirl of jam that's baked inside of each of these muffins; they make a perfect morning snack.

Makes 24 mini muffins

BATTER

Nonstick cooking spray, for greasing

1½ cups all-purpose flour

⅓ cup granulated sugar

2 teaspoons baking powder

½ teaspoon salt

½ cup whole milk, room temperature

4 tablespoons unsalted butter, melted and cooled

1 large egg, room temperature, beaten

1 teaspoon pure vanilla extract

¼ cup chopped walnuts

½ cup fruit jam, room temperature

TOPPING

2 tablespoons unsalted butter, melted

¼ cup granulated sugar

1. Preheat the oven to 350°F. Grease 2 12-count mini-muffin pans with the cooking spray. Set aside.

2. *To make the batter:* In a large mixing bowl, sift together the dry ingredients: the flour, granulated sugar, baking powder, and salt. Set aside.

3. In a separate large mixing bowl, combine the wet ingredients: the milk, butter, egg, and vanilla extract and stir until well combined. Fold in the walnuts. Gradually add the milk mixture to the flour mixture, stirring until just combined.

4. Divide the batter evenly among the cups of the prepared pans, filling each cup about ⅔ full. Top each cup with 1 teaspoon of the jam. Using a wooden toothpick, gently swirl the jam into the batter. Bake for 15 to 20 minutes, until a wooden toothpick inserted into the center of a muffin comes out clean. Remove from the oven and set aside to cool in the pans on a wire rack for 7 minutes.

5. *To make the topping:* Brush the top of each muffin with the butter. Sprinkle with the granulated sugar.

6. Using a serrated knife, separate the muffins from the pans and then tap the pans gently on the counter to release the muffins.

7. Transfer to a serving platter and serve warm.

Cherry Granola

CHERRY GRANOLA HAS A MARVELOUS AROMA—IT MAKES MY WHOLE HOUSE smell good. Old-fashioned oats, slivered almonds, chopped pecans, and coconut flakes are sweetened with dark brown sugar and maple syrup and then roasted to perfection. The granola is brightened with dried tart cherries, cinnamon, and a smidgen of nutmeg—what a wonderful combination of sweet, tart, and spice! Homemade granola tastes a lot better than the kind you buy in stores.

Makes 8 cups

4 cups old-fashioned rolled oats
1 cup slivered almonds
1 cup pecans, roughly chopped
½ cup unsweetened coconut flakes
½ cup firmly packed dark brown sugar
6 tablespoons unsalted butter, melted and cooled
¼ cup maple syrup
1 teaspoon pure vanilla extract
½ teaspoon ground cinnamon
⅛ teaspoon freshly grated nutmeg
2 cups dried tart cherries
Milk, cream, or yogurt, for serving (optional)

1. Preheat the oven to 350°F. Line a baking sheet with parchment paper or aluminum foil and set aside.

2. In a large mixing bowl, combine the oats, almonds, pecans, and coconut.

3. In a separate large mixing bowl, stir together the brown sugar, butter, maple syrup, vanilla extract, cinnamon, and nutmeg. Pour the sugar mixture over the oat mixture and toss until the mixture is well blended.

4. Evenly spread the mixture onto the prepared baking sheet. Bake, tossing the granola and rotating the baking sheet occasionally, for 15 to 20 minutes, until the mixture becomes lightly toasted and fragrant. Remove from the oven and stir in the cherries until they are evenly distributed. Set aside to cool completely.

5. Transfer to a tightly sealed container. Serve with the milk, cream, or yogurt, or eat by the handful.

Blueberry–Cornmeal Coffee Cake with Streusel Topping

THIS BLUEBERRY–CORNMEAL COFFEE CAKE WITH STREUSEL TOPPING is one of those delicious, moist, and rich breakfast or brunch treats that looks best on a pretty cake pedestal. It's full of blueberry sweetness, and the streusel topping is simple and delicious. My friend Maya Bradshaw gave me this outstanding recipe years ago. It was given to Maya by her mother, Margaret Flowers, who got it from her mother, Mae.

Makes 1 9-inch square coffee cake

BATTER

Nonstick cooking spray, for greasing

1 cup all-purpose flour, plus more for dusting

½ cup (1 stick) unsalted butter, room temperature

1 cup granulated sugar

2 large eggs, room temperature

⅓ cup heavy cream, room temperature

Freshly grated zest of 1 lemon

½ teaspoon pure vanilla extract

½ cup finely ground yellow cornmeal

2 teaspoons baking powder

½ teaspoon baking soda

½ teaspoon salt

2 cups fresh, ripe blueberries, patted dry

TOPPING

½ cup granulated sugar

¼ cup all-purpose flour

2 tablespoons finely ground yellow cornmeal

1 teaspoon ground cinnamon

⅛ teaspoon salt

3 tablespoons unsalted butter, cold, cut into small pieces

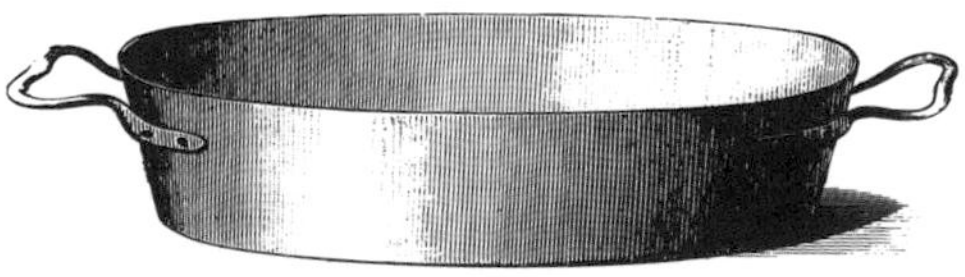

1. Preheat the oven to 350°F. Grease a 9-inch square baking dish with the cooking spray and dust with some flour. Set aside.

2. *To make the batter:* In the bowl of a stand mixer fitted with the paddle attachment, break up the butter by mixing on low speed for 1 minute. Add the granulated sugar and cream together the butter and sugar on medium speed for 2 to 3 minutes, until the mixture is light and fluffy. Scrape down the sides and bottom of the bowl to prevent lumps from forming. As the mixer is running, reduce the speed to low and slowly add the eggs, 1 at a time; after you add each egg, scrape down the sides of the bowl and resume beating on low speed for 30 seconds. Add the heavy cream, lemon zest, and vanilla extract and resume beating on low speed for 30 seconds. Turn off the mixer.

3. In a small mixing bowl, whisk together the dry ingredients: the flour, cornmeal, baking powder, baking soda, and salt. Gradually stir the flour mixture into the bowl of the mixer.

4. *To make the topping:* In a small mixing bowl, whisk together the granulated sugar, flour, cornmeal, cinnamon, and salt. Using your fingers, a pastry blender, or the tines of a fork, cut the butter into the mixture until it becomes coarse, like cornmeal.

5. Transfer ½ of the batter to the prepared baking dish and sprinkle the blueberries over the batter. Sprinkle ½ of the topping over the blueberries. Carefully spread the remaining batter over the topping and then sprinkle the remaining topping over the batter. Bake for 35 to 40 minutes, until a wooden toothpick inserted into the center of the cake comes out clean. Remove from the oven and set aside to cool on a wire rack for 5 minutes.

6. Run a serrated knife or spatula around the edges of the dish to loosen the cake. Slice into squares. Return to the wire rack and allow to cool completely.

7. Serve at room temperature.

Orange Sweet Rolls

My father's cousin Rosemarie was a wonderful cook, and she *knew it.* We coveted her glazed Orange Sweet Rolls and always begged her to bring a batch each time she came to one of our family breakfasts.

Mama once asked Cousin Rosemarie why her food tasted so good. She replied, "I always carefully check how ingredients look and feel at the grocery store. If the purples, reds, and oranges don't feel good to the touch, I know they won't taste good either. I don't bring 'em home." From that day forward, Mama did as Cousin Rosemarie had suggested.

Makes 12 rolls

DOUGH

2¼ teaspoons (1¼-ounce package) active dry yeast

½ cup warm water (about 110°F–115°F)

3–4 cups all-purpose flour, as needed, plus more for kneading

½ cup sour cream

½ cup granulated sugar

4 tablespoons unsalted butter, melted and cooled

1 large egg, room temperature, lightly beaten

½ teaspoon salt

1 cup warm whole milk (about 110°F–115°F)

Nonstick cooking spray, for greasing

FILLING

¾ cup granulated sugar

½ cup (1 stick) unsalted butter, melted and cooled

2 tablespoons freshly grated orange zest

1 teaspoon pure orange extract

GLAZE

1 cup sifted confectioners' sugar

2 teaspoons unsalted butter, melted and cooled

2–3 tablespoons freshly squeezed orange juice

½ teaspoon pure orange extract

1. Line a baking sheet with parchment paper or aluminum foil and set aside.

2. *To make the dough:* In a large mixing bowl, allow the yeast to dissolve in the warm water until it becomes frothy. Add 3 cups of the flour, the sour cream, the granulated sugar, the butter, the egg, and the salt. Slowly add the milk, stirring constantly until the sugar has dissolved.

3. Place a hand mixer in the bowl and set it at medium speed. Beat for 3 minutes, until a soft, smooth dough forms. Add up to 1 cup more of the flour as needed to reach the desired consistency.

4. Turn out the dough onto a floured work surface. With floured hands, knead lightly for 6 to 8 minutes, until it is smooth, satiny, and elastic. (If needed, you may add more flour, 1 tablespoon at a time, to prevent the dough from sticking to your hands.) Form the dough into a smooth ball. Place the ball of dough in a well-greased bowl and turn it so all sides of the dough are greased. Cover with a slightly damp kitchen towel and set aside to rest and rise in a warm, draft-free place for 1 hour, until the dough has doubled in size.

5. *To make the filling:* In a small mixing bowl, stir together the granulated sugar, butter, and orange zest and extract. Set aside.

6. Remove the dough from the bowl, return it to the floured work surface, and gently punch it down. With floured hands, knead lightly for 5 to 6 minutes. Return it to the greased bowl, cover with the slightly damp kitchen towel, and set aside to rest for 10 minutes.

7. Turn out the dough onto a floured work surface. Using a floured rolling pin, roll and gently stretch the dough into a 12-inch × 9-inch rectangle that is ½ inch thick. Evenly spread the prepared filling over the dough, leaving a ½-inch margin around its edges. Starting with the long side of the dough, roll it up tightly, jelly-roll style, and pinch the edges together to seal.

8. Using a serrated knife, cut the dough into 12 equally sized pieces. Arrange the rolls, cut side up, on the prepared baking sheet. Cover and set aside in a warm, draft-free place to rest for 30 minutes.

9. Preheat the oven to 350°F.

10. *To make the glaze:* In a small mixing bowl, whisk together the confectioners' sugar, the butter, 2 tablespoons of the orange juice, and the orange extract. Add more orange juice as needed to reach a smooth consistency. Set aside.

11. Bake for 25 to 30 minutes, until the rolls are golden brown. Remove from the oven and set aside to cool on the baking sheet on a wire rack for 5 minutes.

12. Drizzle the glaze over the rolls while they are still warm. Remove from the baking sheet and transfer to the wire rack. Allow to cool for 5 minutes.

13. Using a wide spatula, remove from the wire rack. Transfer to a serving platter and serve warm.

Miss Hatfield's Old-Fashioned Sunday Morning Coffee Cake

MISS HATFIELD'S COFFEE CAKE WAS A CLASSIC, SIMPLE, NO-FUSS, old-fashioned coffee cake, with a nice cinnamon and sugar crumb topping that sliced nicely for company.

Miss Hatfield started passing out food and inviting us to breakfast regularly after her mother, cantankerous Old Lady Hatfield, passed away. She would serve us coffee cake early in the morning with a cup of coffee or tea or, if we didn't go to Sunday school, later in the morning with a glass of cold milk.

Makes 1 9-inch × 13-inch coffee cake

Nonstick cooking spray, for greasing
3 cups all-purpose flour, plus more for dusting
1 teaspoon baking powder
1 cup (2 sticks) unsalted butter, room temperature
1 cup granulated sugar
1 cup firmly packed brown sugar
¾ cup chopped pecans
1 teaspoon ground cinnamon
1 cup buttermilk, room temperature
2 large eggs, room temperature
1 teaspoon pure vanilla extract
1 teaspoon baking soda
½ teaspoon salt

1. Preheat the oven to 350°F. Lightly grease a 9-inch × 13-inch baking dish with the cooking spray and dust with some flour. Set aside.

2. In a medium mixing bowl, sift together the dry ingredients: the flour and baking powder. Set aside.

3. In the bowl of a stand mixer fitted with the paddle attachment, break up the butter by mixing on low speed for 1 minute. Add the granulated and brown sugars and cream together the butter and sugars on medium speed for 2 to 3 minutes, until the mixture is light and fluffy. Turn off the mixer.

4. Add the pecans and cinnamon to the flour mixture and stir until well combined. Add the flour mixture to the bowl of the mixer ⅓ at a time, stirring after each addition, until well combined. Remove and reserve 1 cup of this mixture for later use as a topping.

5. Add the buttermilk, eggs, vanilla extract, baking soda, and salt to the bowl of the mixer and stir until the mixture is lumpy but well combined.

6. Transfer the batter to the prepared baking dish. Using your fingers, scatter the reserved topping over the batter, covering it evenly and completely. Bake for 30 minutes, until a wooden toothpick inserted into the center of the cake comes out clean. Remove from the oven and set aside to cool in the pan on a wire rack for at least 30 minutes.

7. Carefully transfer to a serving platter, crumb side up. Slice and serve warm.

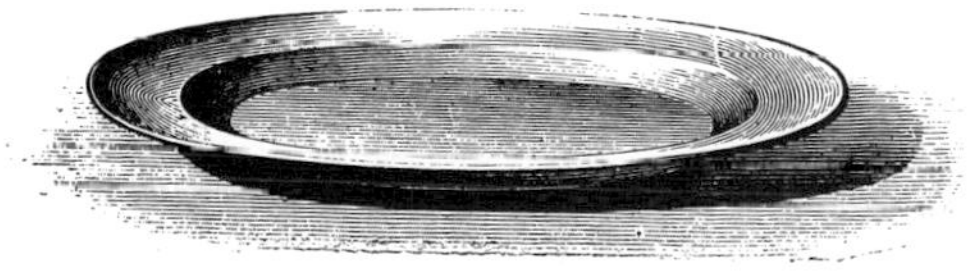

Broiled Pineapple

FRESH PINEAPPLE IS NO-FUSS DELICIOUS, OF COURSE. BUT DRESS IT with butter, brown sugar, and a dollop of vanilla yogurt and you'll give breakfast a striking new look.

Makes 8 servings

1 large pineapple, cored, peeled, and sliced lengthwise into 8 thick spears

2 tablespoons unsalted butter

½ cup firmly packed light brown sugar

Vanilla yogurt, for serving

1. Set the oven rack 4 inches from the heat source. Set the oven to broil.

2. Brush the pineapple spears with the butter and place them on a baking sheet in a single layer. Broil the spears for 3 to 5 minutes, until the spears are golden brown. Remove from the oven and immediately sprinkle the pineapple spears with the brown sugar.

3. Transfer to serving plates and serve warm with the vanilla yogurt.

Blueberry Buttermilk Pancakes with Blueberry Syrup

IN THE SUMMER, WHEN BLUEBERRIES ARE IN SEASON, THE MEN IN MY family—fathers, brothers, uncles, cousins, and grandsons—love waking up to a fresh batch of blueberry pancakes. They don't know that it takes only about 15 minutes to whip them up. My grandmother used to tell us, "A man doesn't need to know everything. Keep some of your business to yourself."

Like the men in my family, a stack of fresh Blueberry Buttermilk Pancakes makes me feel like nothing else can. The hint of buttermilk that this recipe calls for adds flavor and tender flake to them. They're delicious topped with butter and maple syrup, but my Blueberry Syrup really makes them special.

Makes 4 servings

SYRUP

2 cups fresh, ripe blueberries (divided)

½–¾ cup granulated sugar, depending on the sweetness of the blueberries

½ cup water

2 teaspoons freshly squeezed lime or lemon juice

⅛ teaspoon ground cinnamon

⅛ teaspoon ground cloves

⅛ teaspoon salt

BATTER

1½ cups all-purpose flour

⅓ cup granulated sugar

2 teaspoons baking powder

1 teaspoon baking soda

¼ teaspoon salt

1½ cups buttermilk, room temperature

2 large eggs, room temperature, well beaten

4 tablespoons unsalted butter, melted and cooled

½ teaspoon pure vanilla extract

1½ cup fresh, ripe blueberries, patted dry

Confectioners' sugar, for dusting

Softened butter, for serving

1. *To make the syrup:* In a medium saucepan over medium–low heat, combine 1 cup of the blueberries, the granulated sugar, the water, the lime or lemon juice, the cinnamon, the cloves, and the salt. Cook, stirring constantly, for 10 minutes, until the mixture thickens.

2. Stir in the remaining blueberries and cook, stirring occasionally, for 2 to 3 minutes, until the blueberries become tender. Remove from the heat and set aside.

3. *To make the batter:* In a large mixing bowl, sift together the dry ingredients: the flour, granulated sugar, baking powder, baking soda, and salt. Set aside.

4. In a medium mixing bowl, stir together the buttermilk, eggs, and butter. Add the buttermilk mixture to the flour mixture, stirring until the ingredients are just combined. Stir in the vanilla extract. Carefully fold in the blueberries. (Do not overmix.)

5. Place a large, heavy, and lightly greased skillet over medium heat. Once the surface is hot, transfer ½ cup of the batter to the skillet. Cook for 2 to 3 minutes, until the surface of the pancake begins to bubble. Flip over and cook for 2 minutes on the other side, until both sides are golden brown. Transfer the pancake to a warmed, covered platter.

6. Repeat step 5 until all the batter has been used. Remove from the heat.

7. Transfer the pancakes to 4 serving plates. Dust with the confectioners' sugar and serve warm with the butter and syrup.

COOKS' NOTE: *You can cover and refrigerate the remaining syrup for up to 1 week.*

Eggnog Crumb Coffee Cake

IN OUR SMALL TOWN, STORE-BOUGHT EGGNOG IS AVAILABLE ONLY around Christmastime. After New Year's Day, I can't find it anywhere. It's a holiday drink and has been for as long as I can remember. I love the taste of eggnog in pies, cookies, and morning crumb cakes. It's rich and creamy and makes my baked goods taste like the holidays.

Makes 1 9-inch × 13-inch coffee cake

TOPPING

⅓ cup firmly packed light brown sugar

1 tablespoon all-purpose flour

1 tablespoon unsalted butter, melted and cooled

½ teaspoon freshly grated nutmeg

BATTER

Nonstick cooking spray, for greasing

2 cups all-purpose flour

1 tablespoon baking powder

1 teaspoon salt

½ teaspoon freshly grated nutmeg

1 cup thick eggnog, room temperature

1 cup granulated sugar

½ cup (1 stick) unsalted butter, melted and cooled

¼ cup firmly packed light brown sugar

2 large eggs, room temperature

1 teaspoon pure vanilla extract

GLAZE

½ cup sifted confectioners' sugar

1–2 tablespoons thick eggnog

1. *To make the topping:* In a small mixing bowl, combine the brown sugar, flour, butter, and nutmeg and stir until well combined. Set aside.

2. Preheat the oven to 350°F. Grease a 9-inch × 13-inch baking dish with the cooking spray and set aside.

3. *To make the batter:* In a medium mixing bowl, sift together the dry ingredients: the flour, baking powder, salt, and nutmeg. Set aside.

4. In a large mixing bowl, stir together the eggnog, granulated sugar, butter, and brown sugar until the mixture is well combined. Whisking constantly, add the eggs, 1 at a time and then the vanilla. Slowly add the flour mixture to the eggnog mixture ⅓ at a time, stirring constantly. Continue stirring until the batter is well combined.

recipe continues

5. *To make the glaze:* In a separate small mixing bowl, stir together the confectioners' sugar and eggnog until the mixture is smooth and has reached a smooth consistency. Refrigerate until ready to use.

6. Transfer ½ of the batter to the prepared baking dish. Sprinkle ½ of the topping over the batter. Carefully spread the remaining batter over the topping and then sprinkle the remaining topping over the batter. Bake for 35 to 45 minutes, until a wooden toothpick inserted into the center of the cake comes out clean. Remove from the oven and set aside to cool in the baking dish on a wire rack for 5 minutes.

7. Using a wooden toothpick, prick holes all over the surface of the cake and pour the glaze over the cake. Run a serrated knife or spatula around the edges of the dish to loosen the cake and slice into squares. Return to the wire rack and allow to cool completely.

8. Transfer to a serving platter and serve at room temperature.

Nut Bread

WHEN I WAS GROWING UP, NUT BREAD WAS SOMETHING THAT MAMA made during the winter months. She'd use whatever nuts she had on hand—pecans, walnuts, almonds, peanuts, or hazelnuts—and sometimes, she added fruit, like apples, bananas, dates, or pumpkin purée. There was no better aroma than Mama's homemade bread floating through the house early in the morning.

Mama always served this traditional Southern bread with cream cheese.

Makes 1 9-inch × 5-inch × 3-inch loaf

- Nonstick cooking spray, for greasing
- 2 cups all-purpose flour
- 1¼ cups granulated sugar
- 1 teaspoon baking powder
- ½ teaspoon salt
- 1 cup buttermilk, room temperature
- ½ cup (1 stick) unsalted butter, melted and cooled
- 1 large egg, room temperature, well beaten
- 1 teaspoon pure vanilla extract
- ½ teaspoon baking soda
- ¾ cup chopped toasted almonds, pecans, or walnuts

1. Preheat the oven to 350°F. Grease the bottom and ½ inch up the sides of a 9-inch × 5-inch × 3-inch loaf pan with the cooking spray. Set aside.

2. In a large mixing bowl, sift together the dry ingredients: the flour, granulated sugar, baking powder, and salt. Make a well in the center of the mixture and set aside.

3. In a medium mixing bowl, combine the buttermilk, butter, egg, vanilla extract, and baking soda and stir until well combined.

4. Add the buttermilk mixture to the flour mixture and stir until just moistened. (Do not overmix; the batter should be lumpy.) Carefully fold in the nuts.

5. Transfer the batter to the prepared pan. Bake for 50 to 55 minutes, until a wooden toothpick inserted into the center of the bread comes out clean. Remove from the oven and set aside to cool in the pan on a wire rack for 10 minutes.

6. Remove from the pan and cool completely on the wire rack.

7. Transfer to a serving platter, slice, and serve at room temperature.

Hot Cooked Apples

NOTHING TASTES BETTER THAN SAUTÉED FRUIT SPOONED OVER WAFFLES, pancakes, or hot buttered biscuits just out of the oven. Hot Cooked Apples are easy and inexpensive to make. When I was young, Mama used to spoon them on top of my oatmeal and slices of French toast. Talk about tasty—it was way better than store-bought syrup.

Makes 4–6 servings

4 tablespoons unsalted butter

2 tablespoons granulated sugar, plus more as needed

1 tablespoon firmly packed light brown sugar, plus more as needed

½ teaspoon ground cinnamon

⅛ teaspoon freshly grated nutmeg

⅛ teaspoon ground cloves

Pinch salt

4 large, firm, and ripe Golden Delicious apples, peeled, cored, and cut into ¼-inch slices

1. In a large, heavy skillet over medium–low heat, melt the butter. Add the granulated and brown sugars, cinnamon, nutmeg, cloves, and salt and stir until well combined.

2. Gently toss the apple slices in the butter mixture until they are well coated. Raise the heat to medium and cook, turning the apples over once or twice, or as needed, for 8 to 10 minutes, until the apples are fork tender and well glazed. Do not overcook. Remove from the heat.

3. Transfer to a serving bowl and serve warm.

COOKS' NOTE: *I like to serve this dish on the side with a plate of bacon, grits, and buttered toast.*

Pan-Fried Peaches

EASY, TASTY PAN-FRIED PEACHES ARE A HEAVENLY WAY TO ENJOY fresh peaches. Cooked with butter, granulated and brown sugars, cinnamon, and nutmeg, they taste fantastic over pancakes and waffles or by themselves with a serving of pork sausage and scrambled eggs.

Makes 6 servings

¼ cup firmly packed light brown sugar

1 tablespoon granulated sugar

Dash ground cinnamon, or to taste

Dash freshly grated nutmeg, or to taste

2 tablespoons unsalted butter

6 ripe, but firm, fresh peaches, peeled, pitted, and split in half

1. In a small mixing bowl, stir together the brown and granulated sugars, cinnamon, and nutmeg. Set aside.

2. In a large, heavy skillet over medium–low heat, melt the butter. Place the peach halves, cut side down, in the skillet in a single layer. Sprinkle ½ of the sugar mixture over the peaches. Cover and cook for 5 minutes, until the edges of the peaches have browned.

3. Turn over the peaches and sprinkle with the remaining sugar mixture, making sure the peaches and their cavities are well coated. Reduce the heat to low, cover, and cook, stirring often to prevent sticking and burning, for 2 to 3 minutes, until the peaches are fork tender. Remove from the heat.

4. Transfer to a serving bowl and serve warm.

Almond Crescent Rolls

THESE QUICK AND EASY CRESCENT ROLLS ARE SEASONED WITH SLICED almonds. I love to serve them to guests, as they're always surprised that I've made them such a delicious and special treat. That they take so little time to prepare is my secret.

Makes 8 rolls

DOUGH

1 (8-count) tube refrigerated crescent roll dough, separated and unrolled

FILLING

½ cup ground almonds

⅓ cup unsalted butter, melted and cooled

⅓ cup granulated sugar

2 teaspoons ground cinnamon

½ teaspoon pure almond extract

GLAZE

⅓ cup sifted confectioners' sugar

2 tablespoons unsalted butter, melted

2 tablespoons whole milk, cold, plus more as needed

½ teaspoon pure almond extract

TOPPING

¼ cup blanched, slivered almonds

1. Preheat the oven to 350°F. Place the unrolled pieces of dough on an ungreased, rimmed baking sheet.

2. *To make the filling:* In a small mixing bowl, stir together the ground almonds, butter, granulated sugar, cinnamon, and almond extract.

3. Evenly spread the butter mixture over the unrolled pieces of dough and tightly roll up each piece of dough, starting with the wide end. Shape the rolls into crescents.

4. Bake for 12 to 15 minutes, until the rolls are golden brown. Remove from the oven. Using a spatula, transfer the rolls to cool on a wire rack while you make the glaze.

5. *To make the glaze:* In a small mixing bowl, stir together the confectioners' sugar, the butter, 2 tablespoons of the milk, and the almond extract until smooth (add more milk if needed to achieve a smooth consistency).

6. Drizzle the glaze over the warm rolls and sprinkle with the slivered almonds. Allow to cool completely.

7. Transfer to a serving platter and serve at room temperature.

Apple Pie Crescent Rolls

CANS OF STORE-BOUGHT DOUGH AND APPLE PIE FILLING HELP YOU FIX up this simple morning delight in no time. The spices give the dish a taste of old-fashioned apple pie.

Makes 16 rolls

Nonstick cooking spray, for greasing

1 (21-ounce) can apple pie filling

1 tablespoon firmly packed light brown sugar

½ teaspoon pure vanilla extract

½ teaspoon ground cinnamon

¼ teaspoon freshly grated nutmeg

⅛ teaspoon ground cloves

1 (8-count) tube refrigerated crescent roll dough, separated, unrolled, and sliced in half

1 large egg white, room temperature, beaten

Granulated sugar, for sprinkling

1. Preheat the oven to 350°F. Grease a 9-inch round baking pan with the cooking spray and set aside.

2. In a medium mixing bowl, combine the apple pie filling, brown sugar, vanilla extract, cinnamon, nutmeg, and cloves and stir until well combined.

3. Place about 1 teaspoon of the filling mixture near the large end of each dough triangle. Starting with the large end, roll up the triangle and, using a pastry brush, seal the edges with the egg white. Repeat with the remaining pieces of dough until you have made 16 rolls. Reserve the unused filling mixture for topping the rolls.

4. Place the rolls in the prepared pan in a crescent shape with the points facing toward the center. Evenly top each roll with the remaining filling mixture. Sprinkle the tops of each roll with the granulated sugar.

5. Bake for 12 to 15 minutes, until golden brown. Remove from the oven and set aside to cool in the pan on a wire rack for 5 minutes.

6. Transfer to a serving platter and serve warm.

Fruit Salad

FRESH FRUIT SALAD IS DELICIOUS AND EFFORTLESS TO PREPARE. It's perfect for summer mornings on the patio.

Makes 8 servings

⅓ cup freshly squeezed orange juice

¼ cup superfine sugar

2 tablespoons cornstarch

1 tablespoon freshly squeezed lime juice

1 (20-ounce) can pineapple chunks, juice drained and reserved

1 (15-ounce) can unpeeled apricot halves, juice drained and reserved

2 cups fresh blueberries, patted dry

2 kiwifruit, patted dry, peeled, and sliced

1 cup ripe strawberries, patted dry, hulled, and halved

1 cup green grapes, patted dry and halved

1 cup red grapes, patted dry and halved

1 medium Red Delicious apple, patted dry and thinly sliced

1 medium Granny Smith apple, patted dry and thinly sliced

2 large, firm bananas, peeled and thinly sliced

1. In a small saucepan over medium–high heat, whisk together the orange juice, superfine sugar, cornstarch, lime juice, pineapple juice, and apricot juice until well combined. Bring the mixture to a boil and then reduce the heat to medium. Cook, stirring constantly, for 2 minutes, until the mixture is smooth. Remove from the heat, cover, and refrigerate for at least 1 hour.

2. In a large serving bowl, combine the pineapple, apricot halves, blueberries, kiwifruit, strawberries, grapes, and apples and toss until well blended.

3. Remove the juice mixture from the refrigerator and pour it over the fruit. Gently stir in the sliced bananas.

4. Serve immediately.

Cinnamon-Toast Rolls

MY MOTHER MADE CINNAMON-TOAST ROLLS FOR DADDY AND ME ALL the time. They're a lot more dolled up than regular cinnamon toast, and they make a wonderful breakfast.

Makes 12 mini rolls

Nonstick cooking spray, for greasing
12 slices day-old white bread
½ cup (1 stick) unsalted butter, melted
½ cup granulated sugar
2 tablespoons ground cinnamon

1. Preheat the oven to 375°F. Grease a 12-count mini-muffin pan with the cooking spray. Set aside.

2. Trim the crust from the slices of bread. Using a rolling pin, flatten out the bread slices until they are very thin. Coat both sides of the bread with the butter.

3. In a small mixing bowl, mix together the granulated sugar and cinnamon. Generously sprinkle one side of the bread with the sugar mixture, making sure to cover the bread very well. Fold 1 slice of bread in half, hold the folded slice from the top, and gently roll it up, cylinder-style. Repeat with the remaining slices of bread and place the rolls in the prepared pan.

4. Bake for 15 to 20 minutes, until the rolls are golden brown. Remove from the oven. Remove the pan and place on a wire rack to cool slightly before serving.

5. Transfer to a serving platter and serve warm.

Honey and Spice Loaf

Our cousin Pearl, who suffered from high blood pressure, was known for her bland dinners—she didn't use salt, pepper, or any other seasonings in her food. So we'd bring our own seasonings to her house and, when she wasn't looking, spice up our suppers to our liking.

It wasn't easy to get a good night's sleep at Pearl's house. She slept with all the lights on and with the TV blaring. But interestingly enough, when it came to breakfast food, she'd set aside her health concerns and sweeten and spice things to our liking. Her Honey and Spice Loaf was lovely, kissed with honey, cinnamon, ginger, cloves, and nutmeg.

Makes 1 9-inch × 5-inch × 3-inch loaf

BATTER

Nonstick cooking spray, for greasing
2 cups all-purpose flour
1½ teaspoons ground cinnamon
1 teaspoon baking soda
½ teaspoon salt
½ teaspoon ground ginger
¼ teaspoon ground cloves
¼ teaspoon freshly grated nutmeg
¾ cup finely chopped walnuts
⅔ cup honey
½ cup whole milk, room temperature
½ cup granulated sugar
½ cup vegetable oil
2 large eggs, well beaten
1 tablespoon freshly grated orange zest

TOPPING

¾ cup confectioners' sugar
1 tablespoon freshly squeezed orange juice

1. Preheat the oven to 350°F. Grease the bottom and ½ inch up the sides of a 9-inch × 5-inch × 3-inch loaf pan with the cooking spray. Set aside.

2. *To make the batter:* In a medium mixing bowl, sift together the dry ingredients: the flour, cinnamon, baking soda, salt, ginger, cloves, and nutmeg.

3. In a large mixing bowl, combine the walnuts, honey, milk, granulated sugar, vegetable oil, eggs, and orange zest and stir until well combined. Gently stir the flour mixture into the walnut mixture, ½ cup at a time, until well combined.

4. Transfer the batter to the prepared pan and, using a rubber or silicone spatula, smooth the top of the batter. Bake for 40 to 50 minutes, until a wooden toothpick inserted near the center of the loaf comes out clean. Remove from the oven and set aside to cool in the pan on a wire rack for 10 minutes.

5. *To make the topping:* In a medium mixing bowl, whisk together the confectioners' sugar and orange juice.

6. Remove from the pan and place on a wire rack. Drizzle the topping over the loaf and allow to cool completely.

7. Transfer to a serving platter, slice, and serve at room temperature.

Blackberry Buckle

My mother's friend Eudora Hawkins was an excellent seamstress. She had a beautiful collection of homemade aprons she'd made from leftover bric-a-brac and fabric. Whenever we'd stop by, Miss Eudora would whisk Mama into her cramped sewing room to look at swatches of material and patterns she was working on. While they'd be deep in conversation, I'd look over Miss Eudora's apron collection.

When they were through with their business, Miss Eudora always had a morning treat for us. She could bake as well as she could sew. "I've got a treat for you, Dearie," Miss Eudora would tell me. (She called everybody "Dearie.")

This is her delicious Blackberry Buckle, a wonderful morning treat with just the right amount of cinnamon. You might not think of a buckle as a morning treat that goes well with a cup of hot coffee—but it is and it does.

Makes 6–8 servings

TOPPING

½ cup granulated sugar

⅓ cup all-purpose flour

4 tablespoons unsalted butter, melted and cooled

½ teaspoon ground cinnamon

BATTER

Nonstick cooking spray, for greasing

1 cup all-purpose flour, plus more for dusting

4 tablespoons unsalted butter, room temperature

½ cup granulated sugar

1 large egg, room temperature

1½ teaspoons baking powder

⅛ teaspoon salt

½ cup buttermilk, room temperature

½ teaspoon pure vanilla extract

2 cups sweetened blackberries

You might not think of a buckle as a morning treat that

1. *To make the topping:* In a small mixing bowl, combine the granulated sugar, flour, butter, and cinnamon. Stir together until the mixture is crumbly and set aside.

2. Preheat the oven to 350°F. Grease a 9-inch glass baking dish with the cooking spray and dust with some flour. Set aside.

3. *To make the batter:* In the bowl of a stand mixer fitted with the paddle attachment, break up the butter by mixing on low speed for 1 minute. Add the granulated sugar and cream together the butter and sugar on medium speed for 2 to 3 minutes, until the mixture is light and fluffy. Scrape down the sides and bottom of the bowl to prevent lumps from forming. As the mixer is running, reduce the speed to low, add the egg, and beat on low speed for 30 seconds.

4. In a separate small mixing bowl, sift together the dry ingredients: the flour, baking powder, and salt. Slowly add the buttermilk and the flour mixture to the bowl of the running mixer ⅓ at a time, alternating back and forth, making sure to end with the flour mixture. Stir in the vanilla extract.

5. Transfer the batter to the prepared baking dish and scatter the blackberries over the batter. Sprinkle the topping over the blackberries. Bake for 30 to 35 minutes, until the topping is golden brown and the blackberries are bubbling at the edges. Remove from the oven and set aside to cool in the dish on a wire rack for 10 minutes.

6. Slice and serve warm or at room temperature.

goes well with a cup of hot coffee—but it is and it does.

Aunt Sarah's Sweet Potato Muffins

My My's sister Sarah rarely gave out her recipes, but she did share this Sweet Potato Muffin recipe with my grandmother years ago. Of course, My My wanted her girls to stand out in the kitchen, so she quickly passed the recipe to her daughters. And when I was newly married, Mama passed it to me, saying, "Put this in your breakfast file. These muffins are easy to whip up on those mornings when you want to serve a sweet little something with your bacon and eggs."

Makes 12 muffins

BATTER

Nonstick cooking spray, for greasing

2 cups all-purpose flour

1½ teaspoons baking powder

1 teaspoon ground cinnamon

½ teaspoon pumpkin pie spice

½ teaspoon salt

½ cup (1 stick) unsalted butter, room temperature

¾ cup firmly packed dark brown sugar

½ cup granulated sugar

2 large eggs, room temperature

1½ cups mashed baked sweet potato (about 1 large sweet potato)

⅔ cup whole milk, room temperature

1 teaspoon pure vanilla extract

¾ cup finely chopped walnuts

TOPPING

2 tablespoons granulated sugar

¼ teaspoon ground cinnamon

These muffins are easy to whip up on those mornings when you want to serve a sweet little something with your bacon and eggs.

1. Preheat the oven to 350°F. Grease a 12-count muffin pan with the cooking spray. Set aside.

2. *To make the batter:* In a medium mixing bowl, sift together the dry ingredients: the flour, baking powder, cinnamon, pumpkin pie spice, and salt. Set aside.

3. In the bowl of a stand mixer fitted with the paddle attachment, break up the butter by mixing on low speed for 1 minute. Add the brown and granulated sugars and cream together the butter and sugars on medium speed for 2 to 3 minutes, until the mixture is light and fluffy. Scrape down the sides and bottom of the bowl to prevent lumps from forming. As the mixer is running, reduce the speed to low and slowly add the eggs, 1 at a time; after you add each egg, scrape down the sides of the bowl and resume beating on low speed for 30 seconds. Add the sweet potato, milk, and vanilla extract and beat at low speed for 2 to 3 minutes, until just incorporated. Turn off the mixer.

4. Add the flour mixture to the bowl of the mixer ⅓ at a time, gently stirring as you do so. Stop when the last of the flour mixture is just combined. (Do not overmix.) Gently fold in the walnuts.

5. *To make the topping:* In a small mixing bowl, whisk together the granulated sugar and cinnamon until fully combined.

6. Divide the batter evenly among the cups of the prepared pan, filling each about ⅔ full. Sprinkle each evenly with the topping. Bake for 20 to 25 minutes, until the centers of the muffins spring back when touched. Remove from the oven and set aside to cool in the pan on a wire rack for 5 minutes.

7. Using a serrated knife, separate the muffins from the pan and then tap the pan gently on the counter to release them. Transfer the muffins to a wire rack and allow them to cool completely.

8. Transfer to a serving platter and serve at room temperature.

Pineapple Upside-Down Biscuits

THIS OLD-FASHIONED FAVORITE HAS MADE A COMEBACK. TRADITIONALLY, pineapple upside-down cake is usually made in a cast-iron skillet, but these Pineapple Upside-Down Biscuits make preparation a breeze, using premade buttermilk biscuit dough and a quick bake in a muffin pan.

Makes 10 biscuits

Nonstick cooking spray, for greasing

½ cup firmly packed light brown sugar

4 tablespoons unsalted butter, melted and cooled

½ teaspoon ground cinnamon

¾ cup crushed pineapple, drained, juice reserved

10 pecan halves

1 (10-count) tube refrigerated buttermilk biscuit dough, separated

1. Preheat the oven to 400°F. Grease 10 cups of a 12-count muffin pan with the cooking spray. Set aside.

2. In a small mixing bowl, combine the brown sugar, butter, and cinnamon and stir until well combined. Using a fork to thoroughly combine the mixture, add the crushed pineapple (but not the juice).

3. Divide the pineapple mixture evenly among the cups of the prepared pan. Place 1 pecan half in the middle of each filled cup. Place 1 round of biscuit dough in each of the cups and brush the biscuits with the reserved pineapple juice.

4. Bake for 10 to 12 minutes, until the biscuits are golden brown. Remove from the oven and set aside to cool in the muffin pan for 1 to 2 minutes. Using a fork, remove the biscuits from the pan.

5. Transfer to a serving platter, fruit side up, and serve warm.

Baked Oatmeal Squares with Brown Sugar and Cinnamon

BAKED OATMEAL SQUARES ARE ONE OF MY ALL-TIME FAVORITES because they are both flavorful and filling. You'll love them, too!

Makes about 4–6 servings

Nonstick cooking spray, for greasing
2 cups quick-cooking oats
1 teaspoon baking powder
½ teaspoon salt
½ teaspoon ground cinnamon
½ teaspoon ground allspice
¼ cup chopped pecans
¼ cup raisins
2 cups whole milk, room temperature
½ cup firmly packed light brown sugar
3 tablespoons unsalted butter, melted and cooled
1 large egg, room temperature, lightly beaten
Confectioners' sugar, for dusting

1. Preheat the oven to 350°F. Lightly grease an 8-inch square baking dish with the cooking spray and set aside.

2. In a medium mixing bowl, stir together the dry ingredients: the oats, baking powder, salt, cinnamon, and allspice. Add the pecans and raisins and stir until well combined. Set aside.

3. In a large mixing bowl, whisk together the wet ingredients: the milk, brown sugar, butter, and egg. Add the oat mixture to the milk mixture ⅓ at a time, stirring until well combined.

4. Transfer the batter to the prepared baking dish. Bake for 25 minutes, until the mixture is a light golden brown along the edges. Remove from the oven and set aside to cool in the baking dish on a wire rack for 10 minutes.

5. Dust the baking dish with the confectioners' sugar. Slice into squares and serve warm.

Old-Fashioned Gingerbread

GINGERBREAD WAS MY MATERNAL GRANDFATHER'S FAVORITE TREAT. My grandmother made it for him all the time. He loved to have his with a glass of cold buttermilk.

Makes 8 servings

- Nonstick cooking spray, for greasing
- 2 cups all-purpose flour, plus more for dusting
- 1½ teaspoons ground ginger
- 1 teaspoon ground cinnamon
- 1 teaspoon baking soda
- ½ teaspoon salt
- ¼ teaspoon ground cloves
- ¼ teaspoon freshly grated nutmeg
- ½ cup (1 stick) unsalted butter, melted
- ½ cup granulated sugar
- 1 cup light molasses
- 1 large egg, room temperature
- ½ teaspoon pure vanilla extract
- 1 cup buttermilk, room temperature
- ¼ cup cold water

1. Preheat the oven to 350°F. Grease a 9-inch square pan with the cooking spray and dust with some flour. Set aside.

2. In a medium mixing bowl, sift together the dry ingredients: the flour, ginger, cinnamon, baking soda, salt, cloves, and nutmeg. Set aside.

3. In the bowl of a stand mixer fitted with the paddle attachment, break up the butter by mixing on low speed for 1 minute. Add the granulated sugar and cream together the butter and sugar on medium speed for 2 to 3 minutes, until the mixture is light and fluffy. Scrape down the sides and bottom of the bowl to prevent lumps from forming. As the mixer is running, reduce the speed to low; add the molasses, egg, and vanilla extract and beat at low speed for 2 to 3 minutes, until just incorporated. Add the buttermilk and beat at low speed for 1 to 2 minutes, until just incorporated. Turn off the mixer.

4. Add the flour mixture to the bowl of the mixer ⅓ at a time, gently stirring as you do so. Stop when the last of the flour mixture is just combined. (Do not overmix.) Add the cold water and stir until the mixture is evenly moistened.

5. Transfer the batter to the prepared pan. Bake for 30 to 35 minutes, until the gingerbread begins to pull away from the edges of the pan. Remove from the oven and set aside to cool in the pan on a wire rack for 15 minutes.

6. Transfer to a serving platter. Slice and serve warm or at room temperature.

Carrot Cake Muffins

THESE TENDER CARROT CAKE MUFFINS ARE DELICIOUS. I FILL MINE with spices, crushed pineapple, and chopped walnuts and top them with a glaze. I'm glad my friend Dorothy Culpepper gave me this recipe years ago, as these muffins routinely add a touch of delight to ordinary breakfasts and brunches in my house.

Makes 12 muffins

BATTER

- Nonstick cooking spray, for greasing
- 2¼ cups all-purpose flour
- 1 teaspoon baking powder
- 1 teaspoon baking soda
- 1 teaspoon ground cinnamon
- ½ teaspoon salt
- ¼ teaspoon freshly grated nutmeg
- ¼ teaspoon ground allspice
- 1 cup granulated sugar
- ⅔ cup firmly packed light brown sugar
- 2 cups finely grated carrots
- ½ cup vegetable oil
- ½ cup buttermilk, room temperature
- ½ cup crushed pineapple, with the juice
- 2 large eggs, room temperature, lightly beaten
- 1½ teaspoons pure vanilla extract
- ½ cup chopped walnuts

GLAZE

- ½ cup sifted confectioners' sugar
- 2–3 tablespoons buttermilk, plus more as needed
- 1 teaspoon ground cinnamon
- ¼ teaspoon pure vanilla extract

1. Preheat the oven to 375°F. Grease a 12-count muffin pan with the cooking spray. Set aside.

2. *To make the batter:* In a large mixing bowl, sift together the dry ingredients: the flour, baking powder, baking soda, cinnamon, salt, nutmeg, and allspice. Stir in the granulated and brown sugars, make a well in the center of the mixture, and set aside.

3. In a separate large mixing bowl, combine the wet ingredients: the carrots, vegetable oil, buttermilk, pineapple, eggs, and vanilla extract. Stir until very well combined. Slowly add the carrot mixture to the flour mixture, stirring until the batter is well combined and moistened. Gently fold in the walnuts.

4. *To make the glaze:* In a small mixing bowl, whisk together the confectioners' sugar, 2 tablespoons of the buttermilk, the cinnamon, and the vanilla extract. Add more buttermilk if needed to achieve a smooth consistency. Refrigerate for 30 minutes or more to allow the glaze to thicken.

5. Divide the batter evenly among the cups of the prepared pan, filling each about 3⁄4 full. Bake for 15 to 20 minutes, until a wooden toothpick inserted into the center of a muffin comes out clean. Remove from the oven and set aside to cool in the pan on a wire rack for 5 minutes.

6. Remove the glaze from the refrigerator. Using a serrated knife, separate the muffins from the pan and then tap the pan gently on the counter to release them. Transfer the muffins to the wire rack, drizzle them with the glaze, and allow them to cool completely.

7. Transfer to a serving platter and serve at room temperature.

Buttermilk Coffee Cake

NO TWO COFFEE CAKES ARE ALIKE. THE BUTTERMILK IN THIS RECIPE makes the cake moist and extra delicious, and the cake's filling and topping give it a satisfying crunch.

Makes 1 9-inch × 13-inch coffee cake

FILLING AND TOPPING

¼ cup firmly packed light brown sugar

¼ cup granulated sugar

2 tablespoons all-purpose flour

¾ teaspoon ground cinnamon

½ teaspoon freshly grated nutmeg

1 cup chopped pecans

⅓ cup butter, cold, cut into small pieces

BATTER

Nonstick cooking spray, for greasing

3 cups all-purpose flour, plus more for dusting

2 teaspoons baking powder

1 teaspoon baking soda

½ teaspoon salt

½ cup (1 stick) unsalted butter, room temperature

1 cup firmly packed light brown sugar

¾ cup granulated sugar

2 large eggs, room temperature

1½ cups buttermilk, room temperature

1. *To make the filling and topping:* In a medium mixing bowl, whisk together the brown and granulated sugars, flour, cinnamon, and nutmeg until well blended. Fold in the chopped pecans. Using your fingers, a pastry blender, or the tines of a fork, cut the butter into the flour mixture until it resembles peas. Set aside.

2. Preheat the oven to 350°F. Lightly grease a 9-inch × 13-inch baking dish with the cooking spray and dust with some flour. Set aside.

3. *To make the batter:* In a medium mixing bowl, sift together the dry ingredients: the flour, baking powder, baking soda, and salt. Set aside.

4. In the bowl of a stand mixer fitted with the paddle attachment, break up the butter by mixing on low speed for 1 minute. Add the brown and granulated sugars and cream together the butter and sugars on medium speed for 2 to 3 minutes, until the

mixture is light and fluffy. Scrape down the sides and bottom of the bowl to prevent lumps from forming. As the mixer is running, reduce the speed to low and slowly add the eggs, 1 at a time; after you add each egg, scrape down the sides of the bowl and resume beating on low speed for 30 seconds. Add the flour mixture and buttermilk to the bowl of the mixer in alternating thirds, starting and ending with the flour mixture. Turn off the mixer.

5. Transfer ½ of the batter to the prepared baking dish. Using a rubber or silicone spatula or a butter knife, evenly spread the batter in the pan. Using your fingers, scatter ½ of the filling and topping over the batter, covering it evenly and completely. Carefully spread the remaining batter on top of the crumb mixture, and then spread the remaining filling and topping over the batter. Bake for 25 minutes, until a wooden toothpick inserted into the center of the cake comes out clean. Remove from the oven and set aside to cool in the pan on a wire rack for 10 minutes.

6. Carefully transfer to a serving platter, slice, and serve warm.

COOKS' NOTE: *Sometime I make a glaze to drizzle over the warm topping. In a small mixing bowl, whisk together 1 cup sifted confectioners' sugar and 2½ tablespoons buttermilk. Drizzle over the warm cake.*

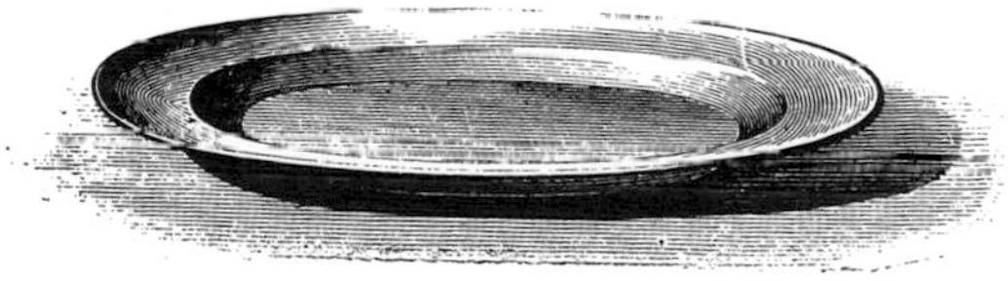

Puffed Berry Pancake

ANY COMBINATION OF FRESH BERRIES WILL DO, BUT I PREFER BLUEBERRIES and raspberries in my Puffed Berry Pancake. You know it's done perfectly when it puffs up in the oven and then quickly deflates once it comes out. Serve it on a pretty platter or right in the pie dish you made it in.

Makes 6 servings

2 tablespoons unsalted butter

4 large egg yolks, room temperature, whites reserved for another use

1 cup whole milk, room temperature

½ teaspoon pure vanilla extract

1 cup all-purpose flour

3 tablespoons granulated sugar

½ teaspoon freshly grated lemon zest

⅛ teaspoon sea salt

1 cup fresh blueberries

1 cup fresh halved raspberries

3 large egg whites

2 tablespoons confectioners' sugar, for dusting

1. Preheat the oven to 300°F. Place the butter in a 12-inch ovenproof deep pie dish and warm it in the oven until the butter melts. Remove the dish from the oven and raise the temperature to 400°F.

2. In a small mixing bowl, whisk together the wet ingredients: the egg yolks, milk, and vanilla extract.

3. In a large mixing bowl, combine the dry ingredients: the flour, granulated sugar, lemon zest, and salt. While whisking constantly, slowly add the egg yolk mixture to the flour mixture. Continue whisking until the batter is smooth. Carefully fold in first the blueberries, then the raspberries. Set aside.

4. In a separate large mixing bowl, beat the egg whites until stiff. Gently fold the beaten egg whites into the batter.

5. Transfer the batter to the prepared pie dish. Bake for 15 to 20 minutes, until the pancake's sides are crisp and golden brown. Remove from the oven.

6. Dust the pancake generously with the confectioners' sugar and serve immediately, either in the pie dish or on a serving platter.

COOKS' NOTE: *A large ovenproof skillet works just fine if you don't have an ovenproof deep pie dish.*

Banana–Pecan Loaf

AUNT MARJELL IS THE BANANA BREAD BAKER IN OUR FAMILY. SHE keeps the legacy going with her delicious loaves. Mama and I often visited Aunt Marjell for coffee and stimulating conversation; she always had interesting stories to tell about the small Mississippi town where she'd grown up and our relatives who lived there.

I don't know if we went for Aunt Marjell's stories or for her Banana–Pecan Loaf. Both were worthwhile reasons to visit.

Makes 1 9-inch × 5-inch × 3-inch loaf

Nonstick cooking spray, for greasing
1½ cups all-purpose flour
1 teaspoon baking powder
½ teaspoon baking soda
½ teaspoon salt
3 ripe bananas
1 cup granulated sugar
1 cup (2 sticks) unsalted butter, melted and cooled
2 large eggs, room temperature
1 teaspoon pure vanilla extract
½ cup finely chopped pecans

1. Preheat the oven to 350°F. Lightly grease a 9-inch × 5-inch × 3-inch loaf pan with the cooking spray and set aside.

2. In a medium mixing bowl, sift together the dry ingredients: the flour, baking powder, baking soda, and salt. Set aside.

3. In the bowl of a stand mixer fitted with the paddle attachment, combine the bananas, granulated sugar, and butter and mix on medium speed for 1 to 2 minutes, until the mixture is smooth and just combined. As the mixer is running, reduce the speed to low and slowly add the eggs, 1 at a time; after you add each egg, scrape down the sides and bottom of the bowl and resume beating on low speed for 30 seconds. As the mixer continues to run, add the vanilla extract and beat until just combined. Add the flour mixture to the bowl of the mixer ⅓ at a time, beating at low speed for 2 to 3 minutes until just combined. Turn off the mixer and gently fold in the pecans. (Do not overmix.)

4. Transfer the batter to the prepared pan. Bake for 25 minutes, until a wooden toothpick inserted into the center of the loaf comes out clean. Remove from the oven and set aside to cool in the pan on a wire rack for 10 minutes.

5. Carefully transfer to a serving platter, slice, and serve warm.

Sweet Potato Scones

WHEN I WAS A LITTLE GIRL, MY MOTHER TAUGHT ME HOW TO DO ALL sorts of delicious things with leftover sweet potatoes. These Sweet Potato Scones make a delicious morning treat or a great side dish for a fall brunch. They make the house smell terrific . . . and as an added benefit, the aroma will drift into the bedrooms and wake everyone up.

Makes 8 scones

BATTER

Nonstick cooking spray, for greasing

2 cups all-purpose flour, plus more for rolling

½ cup firmly packed light brown sugar

2 teaspoons baking powder

½ teaspoon ground cinnamon

½ teaspoon freshly grated nutmeg

½ teaspoon salt

½ cup (1 stick) unsalted butter, cold

⅓ cup buttermilk, room temperature

1 large egg, room temperature

1 teaspoon pure vanilla extract

1 cup mashed baked sweet potato (about 1 medium)

GLAZE

½ cup sifted confectioners' sugar

2 tablespoons light brown sugar

¼ teaspoon pure vanilla extract

2–3 tablespoons whole milk, cold, plus more as needed

1. Preheat the oven to 400°F. Lightly grease a baking sheet with the cooking spray and set aside.

2. *To make the batter:* In a large mixing bowl, sift together the dry ingredients: the flour, brown sugar, baking powder, cinnamon, nutmeg, and salt. Using your fingers, a pastry blender, or the tines of a fork, cut the butter into the flour mixture until it resembles coarse crumbs. Set aside.

3. In a small mixing bowl, whisk together the wet ingredients: the buttermilk, egg, and vanilla extract. Stir the buttermilk mixture into the flour mixture until it is just moistened. Add the sweet potato to the batter and stir until just combined.

4. Turn out the dough onto a lightly floured work surface. With floured hands, knead the dough 7 or 8 times. Pat the dough into an 8-inch circle and slice it into 8 equal wedges. Place the wedges 1 inch apart on the prepared baking sheet.

5. *To make the glaze:* In a small mixing bowl, whisk together the confectioners' and brown sugars, the vanilla extract, and 2 tablespoons of the milk. Add more milk if needed to reach a smooth consistency.

6. Bake for 15 to 20 minutes, until the scones are golden brown. Remove from the oven and set aside to cool on the baking sheet on a wire rack for 5 minutes.

7. Drizzle the glaze over the scones while they are still warm. Transfer to the wire rack and allow them to cool for 5 minutes.

8. Transfer to a serving platter and serve warm.

Cinnamon–Pecan Sticky Bun Ring

WHENEVER I MAKE THESE STICKY BUNS, MY GUESTS ASK FOR THE RECIPE. They taste like homemade goodness, but the convenience of refrigerated biscuit dough and breakfast syrup means you can whip them up in no time.

Makes 10 servings

Nonstick cooking spray, for greasing

All-purpose flour, for dusting

¾ cup chopped pecans

3 tablespoons breakfast syrup

½ cup firmly packed light brown sugar

3 tablespoons unsalted butter, melted and cooled

1 teaspoon ground cinnamon

2 (10-count) tubes refrigerated buttermilk biscuit dough, separated

1. Preheat the oven to 375°F. Grease a 10-inch tube or Bundt pan with the cooking spray and dust with some flour. Sprinkle the pecans and breakfast syrup into the pan.

2. In a small mixing bowl, stir together the brown sugar, butter, and cinnamon. Sprinkle ⅓ of the sugar mixture into the prepared pan.

3. Split each round of biscuit dough in half and arrange the halves horizontally in the prepared pan. Sprinkle the remaining sugar mixture on top of the rounds of dough.

4. Bake for 12 to 15 minutes, until the ring is golden brown. Remove from the oven and set aside to cool in the pan on a wire rack for 1 to 2 minutes.

5. Invert onto a serving platter and serve warm.

Ricotta Hot Cakes with Berries

MY COUSIN OPHELIA HAD LOVELY HAIR AND LONG, SOFT HANDS. BEHIND her back, My My called her "Po' Cud'n 'Phelia" because she'd never been married.

I envied Cousin Ophelia. She owned a successful tailoring shop, drove a Chrysler New Yorker, and lived in a big brick house on the west side of town. She bought herself fancy hand soaps and lotions and came and went as she pleased.

Ricotta Hot Cakes with Berries was one of her best recipes.

Makes 6–8 servings

1½ cups ricotta cheese, room temperature

5 large eggs, yolks and whites separated

½ cup (1 stick) unsalted butter, melted and cooled

¼ cup granulated sugar

2 tablespoons freshly grated lemon zest (about 3–4 medium lemons)

½ teaspoon pure vanilla extract

½ cup all-purpose flour

½ teaspoon salt

Vegetable oil, for frying

2 cups fresh strawberries, raspberries, blueberries, blackberries, or other berries of your choice

Confectioners' sugar, for dusting

1. In a large mixing bowl, whisk together the ricotta cheese, egg yolks, butter, granulated sugar, lemon zest, and vanilla extract until the mixture is well blended. While whisking constantly, slowly add the flour, about 1 tablespoon at a time. Continue whisking until the mixture is well blended.

2. In a small mixing bowl, beat the egg whites with the salt until stiff peaks form. Gently fold ¼ of the egg white mixture into the ricotta mixture. Add the remaining egg white mixture to the ricotta mixture and gently fold together. (Do not overmix.)

3. In a large, heavy, and deep skillet over medium–high heat, warm about 3 inches of the oil. Once the oil is hot, carefully drop heaping tablespoons of the batter into the skillet; they will spread out into small cakes. Cook the cakes for 1 to 2 minutes on each side, until they are golden brown. Transfer the cooked cakes to a large, warmed platter lined with paper towels and tented with aluminum foil.

4. Repeat step 3 until all the batter has been used.

5. Transfer to a serving platter and top with the berries. Dust with the confectioners' sugar and serve warm.

Cranberry–Orange Walnut Loaf

THE ORANGE ZEST THIS RECIPE CALLS FOR GIVES IT ITS MILD ORANGE scent. It'll sweet-talk anyone out of a warm bed.

Makes 1 9-inch × 5-inch × 3-inch loaf

Nonstick cooking spray, for greasing
2 cups all-purpose flour
1½ cups fresh cranberries, chopped
½ cup granulated sugar
½ cup firmly packed light brown sugar
1½ teaspoons baking powder
1 teaspoon baking soda
1 teaspoon freshly grated orange zest
½ teaspoon salt
½ cup whole milk, room temperature
½ cup freshly squeezed orange juice
4 tablespoons unsalted butter, melted
1 large egg, room temperature, beaten
¾ cup coarsely chopped walnuts

1. Preheat the oven to 350°F. Lightly grease a 9-inch × 5-inch × 3-inch loaf pan with the cooking spray and set aside.

2. In a large mixing bowl, stir together the flour, cranberries, granulated and brown sugars, baking powder, baking soda, orange zest, and salt until well combined. Set aside.

3. In a separate large mixing bowl, whisk together the milk, orange juice, butter, and egg. Stir the milk mixture into the flour mixture until the batter is well combined. Carefully fold in the walnuts.

4. Transfer the batter to the prepared pan. Bake for 1 hour, until a wooden toothpick inserted into the center of the loaf comes out clean. Remove from the oven and set aside to cool in the pan on a wire rack for 10 minutes.

5. Carefully transfer to a serving platter, slice, and serve warm.

Mama's Honey-Bun Coffee Cake

MAMA MADE THIS COFFEE CAKE ALL THE TIME. IT CALLS FOR A CAKE MIX—something Mama didn't often use—but the mix made it so easy to make. Once it's doctored up, you can't taste the cake mix; it tastes just as good as a cake made from scratch.

Makes 1 9-inch × 13-inch coffee cake

FILLING

¾ cup firmly packed light brown sugar

6 tablespoons unsalted butter, melted and cooled

1 tablespoon ground cinnamon

BATTER

Nonstick cooking spray, for greasing

All-purpose flour, for dusting

1 (18-ounce) box yellow cake mix, without the pudding

1 cup sour cream, room temperature

4 large eggs, room temperature

¾ cup vegetable oil

TOPPING

½ cup honey

½ cup firmly packed light brown sugar

¼ cup unsalted butter, melted and cooled

1½ cups coarsely chopped pecans

1. *To make the filling:* In a small mixing bowl, combine the brown sugar, butter, and cinnamon. Stir well. Set aside.

2. Preheat the oven to 350°F. Lightly grease a 9-inch × 13-inch baking dish with the cooking spray and dust with some flour. Set aside.

3. *To make the batter:* In a large mixing bowl, combine the cake mix, sour cream, and eggs and stir until well combined. Add the vegetable oil and stir until well combined.

4. Transfer ½ of the batter into the prepared baking dish and sprinkle the filling over the batter. Spread the remaining batter over the filling. Using a butter knife, create swirls of the filling in the batter. Bake for 30 minutes, until a wooden toothpick inserted into the center of the cake comes out clean. Remove from the oven and set aside to cool in the baking dish on a wire rack for 10 minutes.

5. *To make the topping:* In a small mixing bowl, whisk together the honey, brown sugar, and butter. Gently fold in the pecans.

6. Using a pastry brush, brush the topping over the top of the warm cake. Allow to cool for 20 minutes.

7. Slice into squares, transfer to a serving platter, and serve at room temperature.

Apple–Cinnamon Bear Claws

Bear claws are delicious. I love how people forget all about the refrigerated biscuits that the recipe calls for and, instead, focus on the marvelous taste that each claw exhibits.

Makes 10 bear claws

BEAR CLAWS

Nonstick cooking spray, for greasing

1 cup apple pie filling

1½ teaspoons ground cinnamon (divided)

All-purpose flour, for rolling

1 (10-count) tube refrigerated buttermilk biscuit dough, separated

1 tablespoon granulated sugar

GLAZE

¼ cup sifted confectioners' sugar

2 tablespoons whole milk, room temperature

TOPPING

¼ cup sliced almonds

1. Preheat the oven to 375°F. Lightly grease a large baking sheet with the cooking spray and set aside.

2. *To make the bear claws:* In a medium mixing bowl, combine the apple pie filling and 1 teaspoon of the cinnamon. Stir together and set aside.

3. On a lightly floured surface, roll out each round of biscuit dough into a 6-inch-diameter circle. Spoon 2 tablespoons of the filling into the center of each circle. Fold the dough over the filling, pinching the edges to seal. At even intervals, cut 3 1-inch-long slits on the sides of the pressed dough to add claw-like decoration to each bear claw. (Do not cut all the way through.)

4. In a small mixing bowl, combine the granulated sugar and remaining cinnamon and stir well. Sprinkle over the bear claws.

5. Place the bear claws about 2 inches apart on the prepared baking sheet. Bake for 10 to 12 minutes, until the bear claws are golden brown. Remove from the oven and set aside to cool on the baking sheet on a wire rack for 10 minutes.

6. *To make the glaze:* In a small mixing bowl, whisk together the confectioners' sugar and milk.

7. Transfer to a serving platter. Drizzle the glaze over the warm bear claws and sprinkle with the sliced almonds. Serve warm.

Hazelnut Rolls

HAZELNUTS REMIND ME OF DADDY, AS HE LOVED THEM. HE'D SIT IN THE living room with a big bowl of them, cracking them open one after another. He'd eat them by themselves, but Mama would put them in cookies, pies, and cakes. Sometimes, she'd put them in rolls.

Mama's Hazelnut Rolls were simple and quick, but all the same, when he knew she was making them, he'd keep coming to the kitchen door asking if they were done yet. I guess he wanted to enjoy them while they were still hot and sticky.

Makes 10 rolls

FILLING

¾ cup hazelnuts, toasted and coarsely chopped

¾ cup firmly packed dark brown sugar

¼ cup granulated sugar

½ teaspoon ground cloves

⅛ teaspoon salt

2 tablespoons unsalted butter, melted and cooled

DOUGH

Nonstick cooking spray, for greasing

2½ cups all-purpose flour, plus more for rolling

½ cup ground hazelnuts

3 tablespoons granulated sugar

2 tablespoons baking powder

½ teaspoon salt

⅛ teaspoon ground cloves

1 cup buttermilk, room temperature

6 tablespoons unsalted butter, melted and cooled (divided)

1 large egg, room temperature

1 teaspoon pure vanilla extract

GLAZE

¾ cup sifted confectioners' sugar

3½ ounces cream cheese, room temperature, softened

3–4 tablespoons whole milk, room temperature

1 teaspoon pure vanilla extract

1. *To make the filling:* In a small mixing bowl, combine the hazelnuts, brown and granulated sugars, cloves, and salt. Add the butter and whisk until the mixture comes together. Set aside.

2. Preheat the oven to 350°F. Line a baking sheet with parchment paper and spray the parchment with the cooking spray. Set aside.

3. *To make the dough:* In a large mixing bowl, whisk together the dry ingredients: the flour, hazelnuts, granulated sugar, baking powder, salt, and cloves. Make a well in the center of the bowl and set aside.

4. In a medium mixing bowl, combine the wet ingredients: the buttermilk, 5 tablespoons of the butter, the egg, and the vanilla extract. Stir until just combined. Slowly add the buttermilk mixture to the flour mixture, stirring until just combined.

5. Turn out the dough onto a floured work surface and, with floured hands, knead it until a smooth dough forms. If the dough is too sticky or wet, place it in a lightly floured bowl, cover with plastic wrap, and refrigerate for 30 minutes.

6. Using a floured rolling pin, roll and gently stretch the dough into a 12-inch × 9-inch rectangle that is ¼ inch thick. Brush the dough with the remaining butter and evenly spread the filling over the dough, leaving a ½-inch margin around its edges. Starting with the long side of the dough, roll it up tightly, jelly-roll style. Gently press the dough as you go along, making a very tight log, and pinch the edges together to seal. Slice the dough into 10 equal 1½-inch-wide rolls. Arrange the rolls, evenly spaced apart and placed cut side down, on the prepared baking sheet.

7. *To make the glaze:* In a medium mixing bowl, whisk together the confectioners' sugar, the cream cheese, 3 tablespoons of the milk, and the vanilla extract. Continue whisking and add as much as 1 tablespoon more of the milk as needed until the mixture reaches a smooth consistency.

8. Bake for 20 to 25 minutes, until the tops of the rolls are golden brown. Remove from the oven and set aside in the pan to cool on a wire rack for 5 minutes.

9. Carefully remove from the baking sheet and place on the wire rack positioned over a sheet of parchment paper. Drizzle the glaze over the rolls while they are still warm.

10. Transfer to a serving platter and serve warm.

Crumb-Topped Blackberry Muffins

In 1965, jazz was everywhere. It floated out of project buildings and penthouse windows alike. Daddy listened to Thelonious Monk, John Coltrane, Louis Armstrong, and Count Basie on homemade 8-track cartridges he bought from Mr. Manning, who made them in his garage. I guess you could say that making tapes was Mr. Manning's hustle.

Sarah Vaughan was Mama's favorite singer. She loved Miss Vaughan's lush voice and played Miss Vaughan's "My Favorite Things" over and over on a small stereo in the kitchen. Mama baked while Miss Vaughan's velvety voice sang on. And the music came out in her cooking—the morning sweets she made were as plush and smooth as cool jazz. These Crumb-Topped Blackberry Muffins are a case in point.

Makes 16 muffins

TOPPING

3 tablespoons all-purpose flour

¼ cup granulated sugar

½ teaspoon ground cinnamon

¼ teaspoon salt

2 tablespoons unsalted butter, cold, cut into small pieces

MUFFINS

Nonstick cooking spray, for greasing

2 cups all-purpose flour

¾ cup granulated sugar

2 teaspoons baking powder

½ teaspoon baking soda

½ teaspoon ground cinnamon

½ teaspoon freshly grated lemon zest

¼ teaspoon salt

1 cup plain yogurt

½ cup (1 stick) unsalted butter, melted and cooled

2 large eggs, room temperature, lightly beaten

1 teaspoon pure vanilla extract

1½ cups fresh blackberries

1. *To make the topping:* In a small mixing bowl, combine the flour, granulated sugar, cinnamon, and salt. Using your fingers, a pastry blender, or the tines of a fork, cut the butter into the flour mixture until it becomes crumbly. Set aside.

2. Preheat the oven to 400°F. Grease 2 8-count muffin pans with the cooking spray. Set aside.

3. *To make the batter:* In a large mixing bowl, sift together the dry ingredients: the flour, granulated sugar, baking powder, baking soda, cinnamon, lemon zest, and salt. Make a well in the center of the mixture and set aside.

4. In a small mixing bowl, combine the wet ingredients: the yogurt, butter, eggs, and vanilla extract. Add the yogurt mixture to the flour mixture and stir until the batter is moistened. (Do not overmix; the batter should be lumpy.) Carefully fold in the blackberries, ensuring they are evenly distributed and that the fruit does not become broken up.

5. Divide the batter evenly among the cups of the prepared pans, filling each about ½ full. Sprinkle each evenly with the topping. Bake for 25 to 30 minutes, until a wooden toothpick inserted into the center of a muffin comes out clean. Remove from the oven and set aside to cool in the pans on a wire rack for 10 minutes.

6. Using a serrated knife, separate the muffins from the pans and then tap the pans gently on the counter to release the muffins.

7. Transfer to a serving platter and serve warm.

The morning sweets Mama made were as plush and smooth as cool jazz.

Key Lime Squares

I LOVE THE TASTE OF KEY LIMES. MY FRIEND BETTY RASCO MAKES THESE cool, creamy, and tart squares whenever I come over for a morning chat.

Makes 20 squares

CRUST

Nonstick cooking spray, for greasing

2 cups all-purpose flour, plus more for dusting

½ cup confectioners' sugar

¼ teaspoon salt

1 cup (2 sticks) unsalted butter, cold, cut into small pieces

FILLING

4 large eggs, room temperature

2 cups granulated sugar

⅓ cup freshly squeezed Key lime juice

½ teaspoon freshly grated Key lime zest

⅛ teaspoon salt

1 tablespoons cornstarch

½ teaspoon baking powder

GARNISH

Confectioners' sugar, for dusting

1. Preheat the oven to 350°F. Lightly grease a 9-inch × 13-inch baking dish with the cooking spray and dust with some flour. Set aside.

2. *To make the crust:* In a medium mixing bowl, sift together the flour, confectioners' sugar, and salt. Using your fingers, a pastry blender, or the tines of a fork, cut the butter into the flour mixture until it becomes coarse, like cornmeal.

3. Press the crust into the bottom and the sides of the baking dish. Bake for 15 to 20 minutes, until the edges of the crust is lightly golden brown. Remove from the oven and set aside. Keep the oven on.

4. *To make the filling:* In a large mixing bowl, beat the eggs by hand until they are light in color. Add the granulated sugar, Key lime juice and zest, and salt and beat by hand for 2 to 3 minutes, until the mixture is frothy. Add the cornstarch and baking powder and whisk until thoroughly combined.

5. Evenly pour the filling over the hot crust. Return to the oven and bake for 20 minutes, until the filling is set. Remove from the oven and set aside in the baking dish on a wire rack to cool to room temperature.

6. Refrigerate for 4 hours or overnight.

7. Remove from the refrigerator. Dust with the confectioners' sugar, slice into squares, and serve.

Cream Cheese French Toast Bake

THIS RECIPE REMINDS ME WHY BREAKFAST IS MY FAVORITE MEAL OF the day. It calls for cubed French bread, blueberries, half-and-half, and cinnamon and spends the night marinating in the fridge. Cream Cheese French Toast Bake really is an overnight sensation.

Makes 8 servings

- Nonstick cooking spray, for greasing
- All-purpose flour, for dusting
- 1 (12-ounce) loaf French bread, cubed into 1-inch pieces
- 1 (8-ounce) package cream cheese, cubed into 1-inch pieces, room temperature
- 2 cups fresh blueberries
- 2 cups half-and-half
- 5 large eggs, room temperature, lightly beaten
- ½ cup granulated sugar
- 1 teaspoon pure vanilla extract
- ½ teaspoon ground cinnamon

1. Lightly grease a 9-inch × 13-inch baking dish with the cooking spray and dust with some flour. Place ½ of the bread cubes in the dish and place ½ of the cream cheese cubes on top of the bread cubes. Sprinkle 1 cup of the blueberries over the top and add the remaining bread cubes on top. Sprinkle the remaining blueberries over the bread cubes. Add the remaining cream cheese cubes on top of the blueberries.

2. In a medium mixing bowl, combine the half-and-half, eggs, granulated sugar, vanilla extract, and cinnamon and beat until well blended. Pour over the mixture in the baking dish, cover with plastic wrap, and refrigerate overnight.

3. Preheat the oven to 350°F. Remove the baking dish from the refrigerator, uncover, and set aside on the counter for 30 minutes.

4. Bake for 25 to 35 minutes, until the center of the Cream Cheese French Toast Bake is firm and the top is a light golden brown. Remove from the oven and set aside to cool in the baking dish on a wire rack for 10 minutes.

5. Slice and serve warm.

Almond–Nutmeg Sticky Rolls

ON THOSE CRAZY MORNINGS WHEN I DON'T HAVE THE TIME TO MAKE A yeast dough from scratch, these easy sticky rolls are a great option. Because this recipe uses refrigerated crescent roll dough, I'm off to a fast start. The sweet filling in the middle and the delicious glaze on top get my family going on any morning, even if snow is falling. These rolls are especially good with hot coffee or tea.

Makes 16 rolls

TOPPING

Nonstick cooking spray, for greasing

All-purpose flour, for dusting

⅔ cup sliced almonds

½ cup light corn syrup

FILLING

⅓ cup granulated sugar

4 tablespoons unsalted butter

1 tablespoon freshly squeezed lemon juice

1 teaspoon freshly grated lemon zest

½ teaspoon freshly grated nutmeg

ROLLS

2 (8-count) tubes refrigerated crescent roll dough, unrolled but not separated

4 tablespoons unsalted butter, melted, for brushing

GLAZE

⅓ cup sifted confectioners' sugar

2–3 tablespoons whole milk, room temperature

1 tablespoon unsalted butter, melted and cooled

¼ teaspoon pure almond extract`

1. Preheat the oven to 350°F. Lightly grease a 9-inch × 13-inch baking dish with the cooking spray and dust with some flour.

2. *To make the topping:* Sprinkle the almonds and corn syrup in the bottom of the prepared baking dish. Set aside.

3. *To make the filling:* In a small saucepan over medium–high heat, combine the granulated sugar, butter, lemon juice and zest, and nutmeg and bring to a boil. Reduce the heat to medium and simmer, stirring occasionally, for 3 minutes, until the sugar has completely dissolved. Remove from the heat and pour the mixture over the almonds and corn syrup in the prepared baking dish.

4. *To make the rolls:* On a lightly floured surface, form the unrolled crescent roll dough into 2 14-inch-long rectangles. Firmly press out any perforations. Using a pastry brush, brush the dough with the butter and evenly spread the filling over the dough, leaving a ½ inch margin around its edges. Starting with the long side of the dough, roll it up tightly, jelly-roll style. Gently press the dough as you go along, making a very tight log, and pinch the edges together to seal. Slice the dough equally into 16 1-inch-wide rolls and arrange the rolls, evenly spaced apart and placed cut side down, in the prepared baking dish.

5. Bake for 17 to 20 minutes, until the rolls are golden brown. Remove from the oven and set aside to cool in the baking dish on a wire rack for 1 minute.

6. *To make the glaze:* In a small mixing bowl, stir together the confectioners' sugar, 2 tablespoons of the milk, the butter, and the almond extract. Add more milk, up to 1 tablespoon, as needed to reach a smooth consistency.

7. Using a serrated knife, loosen the rolls from the baking dish. Invert the dish over a serving platter and transfer the rolls to the platter.

8. Drizzle the glaze over the rolls. Slice and serve warm.

Glazed Apple Cider Doughnuts

Our grandmother's neighbor and friend, Vera Genwright, made these wonderful Glazed Apple Cider Doughnuts for her husband, Forrest. Miss Vera once told My My, "He doesn't ask for much. The least I can do is make doughnuts for his Saturday morning supper." My My nodded knowingly. Making delicious doughnuts that a man asked for by name was right up her alley.

I like Miss Vera's doughnuts because the cake flour and buttermilk make them so soft and tender. People don't expect fried doughnuts made from scratch in the morning. Surprise them with these.

Makes 18 doughnuts

DOUGH

1 cup apple cider (not sparkling)

2¾ cups cake flour

2 teaspoons baking powder

1 teaspoon baking soda

½ teaspoon ground cinnamon

½ teaspoon salt

⅛ teaspoon freshly grated nutmeg

4 tablespoons unsalted butter, room temperature

1 cup granulated sugar

2 large eggs, room temperature

½ cup buttermilk, room temperature

All-purpose flour, for rolling

Vegetable oil or shortening, for frying

GLAZE

1 cup sifted confectioners' sugar

2 tablespoons apple cider (not sparkling), room temperature

1. Line a baking sheet with parchment paper and set aside.

2. *To make the dough:* In a small saucepan over medium-high heat, bring the apple cider to a simmer and cook for 7 to 10 minutes, until the cider's volume reduces by ⅔. Remove from the heat and set aside.

3. In a large mixing bowl, sift together the dry ingredients: the cake flour, baking powder, baking soda, cinnamon, salt, and nutmeg. Set aside.

4. In the bowl of a stand mixer fitted with the paddle attachment, break up the butter by mixing on low speed for 1 minute. Add the granulated sugar and cream together the butter and sugar on medium speed for 2 to 3 minutes, until the mixture is light and fluffy. Scrape down the sides and bottom of the bowl to prevent lumps from forming. As the mixer is running, reduce the speed to low and slowly add the eggs, 1 at a time; after you add each egg, scrape down the sides of the bowl and resume beating on low speed for 30 seconds. Add the reduced cider and buttermilk and beat at low speed for 30 seconds, until just incorporated. Add the flour mixture to the bowl of the mixer ⅓ at a time, beating each time at low speed for 1 minute until the dough comes together. Turn off the mixer.

5. Turn out the dough onto a floured work surface. Using a floured rolling pin, roll and gently stretch the dough into a 13-inch × 9-inch rectangle that is ½ inch thick. Using a doughnut cutter, cut out 18 doughnuts; in order to make that many, you may have to pick up any excess dough, roll it into a ball, and roll it out again.

6. Place the doughnuts on the prepared baking sheet. Refrigerate for 15 minutes.

7. *To make the glaze:* In a small mixing bowl, whisk together the confectioners' sugar and apple cider until the mixture is smooth.

8. Line a few plates with several layers of paper towels and set aside.

9. In a large skillet over medium-high heat, heat the vegetable oil until it is hot but not smoking. Drop 2 or 3 of the doughnuts at a time into the hot oil and fry for 1 to 2 minutes, until the doughnuts become golden brown on 1 side. Using a slotted spoon, turn each over and continue frying for another 1 to 2 minutes, until both sides are golden brown. Remove the doughnuts from the hot oil and allow them to drain on the prepared plates.

10. Repeat step 9 until all the doughnuts have been fried. Remove from the heat.

11. Transfer to a serving platter. Drizzle with the glaze and serve warm.

Banana–Nut Waffles

BANANA–NUT WAFFLES ARE THE EPITOME OF A GOOD BREAKFAST—MY father, who loved them, sure thought so. He wanted Mama to make them as often as she could. She would serve her banana waffles hot with lots of store-bought syrup, pats of sweet butter, and slices of soft bananas.

Makes 6 servings

Nonstick cooking spray, for greasing
3 large egg yolks and whites, room temperature, separated
1¾ cups all-purpose flour
½ cup firmly packed light brown sugar
2 tablespoons granulated sugar
1 teaspoon baking powder
½ teaspoon salt
½ teaspoon ground cinnamon
¼ teaspoon freshly grated nutmeg
1½ cups buttermilk, room temperature
2 ripe bananas, mashed
½ cup (1 stick) unsalted butter, melted and cooled
1 teaspoon baking soda
1 teaspoon pure vanilla extract
⅔ cup coarsely chopped walnuts
Breakfast syrup, pats of butter, and sliced bananas, for serving

1. Preheat a lightly greased waffle iron according to the manufacturer's directions.

2. In a small mixing bowl, beat the egg whites until stiff peaks form. Set aside.

3. In a large mixing bowl, sift together the dry ingredients: the flour, brown and granulated sugars, baking powder, salt, cinnamon, and nutmeg. Make a well in the center of the mixture and set aside.

4. In a medium mixing bowl, combine the buttermilk, bananas, butter, egg yolks, baking soda, and vanilla extract and stir until well blended.

5. Add the buttermilk mixture to the flour mixture and stir until just moistened. (Do not overmix; the batter should be lumpy.) Add the walnuts and stir until evenly blended.

6. Fold the stiff egg whites into the batter and set aside to rest for at least 5 minutes.

7. Pour ⅓ cup of the batter on the prepared waffle iron and cook according to the manufacturer's recommendations. Once the waffle is properly cooked, use the tines of a fork to lift it off the grid and place on a serving platter.

8. Repeat step 7 until all the batter has been used.

9. Serve hot with the breakfast syrup, pats of butter, and banana slices.

French Toast Sandwiches

MAMA SAID ONCE THAT MEN DIDN'T MAKE FRENCH TOAST SANDWICHES. When I want my family to indulge in a decadent, home-cooked breakfast, I make French Toast Sandwiches.

Makes 4 servings

Nonstick cooking spray, for greasing

1 cup whole milk, room temperature

3 large eggs, room temperature

½ teaspoon pure vanilla extract

¼ teaspoon ground cinnamon

⅛ teaspoon salt

2 tablespoons freshly squeezed orange juice

Freshly grated zest of 1 orange

1 loaf brioche or other egg bread, cut into 8 thick slices

4 ounces cream cheese, room temperature, beaten

6 tablespoons orange marmalade

Confectioners' sugar, for dusting

Butter and maple syrup, for serving (optional)

1. Preheat the oven to 350°F. Grease a rimmed baking sheet with the cooking spray and set aside.

2. In a large mixing bowl, beat together the milk, eggs, vanilla extract, cinnamon, and salt until well blended. Add the orange juice and zest and whisk until well blended.

3. Slice each piece of the bread on the diagonal. Carefully dip both sides of the 16 pieces of bread in the milk mixture and place ½ of the slices of the dipped bread on a large plate. Spread the cream cheese first and then the marmalade evenly over these slices and then top each cream cheese–marmalade slice with the remaining 8 pieces of dipped bread, sandwich style. You will now have 4 sandwiches total, each cut in ½ on the diagonal.

4. Place the sandwiches on the prepared baking sheet and bake for 3 to 4 minutes, until they are golden brown on one side. Flip them over and bake for another 3 to 4 minutes, until golden brown on the other side. Remove from the oven.

5. Transfer to a serving platter. Dust with the confectioners' sugar and serve hot with the butter and maple syrup, if using.

Baked Doughnuts

When I was a little girl, my family owned a rental property in Flint, Michigan. Daddy would go to Flint often to check on the property, and each time he did, he'd stop by Dawn Donuts and pick up a bag of their Chop Suey Fritters, just for the two of us.

Mama never tried to make those fritters—I think she kept them as special treats for my father and me. But on quiet mornings, she would make us these wonderful Baked Doughnuts, brushed with butter and swirled in a sugar mixture. I loved them just as much.

Makes 12 doughnuts

BATTER

Nonstick cooking spray, for greasing

2 cups all-purpose flour

1¼ cups granulated sugar

2 teaspoons baking powder

½ teaspoon freshly grated nutmeg

½ teaspoon salt

1 cup whole milk, room temperature

2 large eggs, room temperature, lightly beaten

⅓ cup unsalted butter, melted

2 teaspoons pure vanilla extract

TOPPING

½ cup (1 stick) unsalted butter, melted

¼ cup granulated sugar

¼ cup firmly packed light brown sugar

1 tablespoon ground cinnamon

1. Preheat the oven to 350°F. Lightly grease a baking sheet with the cooking spray and set aside.

2. *To make the batter:* In a large mixing bowl, sift together the dry ingredients: the flour, granulated sugar, baking powder, nutmeg, and salt. Make a well in the center of the bowl and set aside.

On quiet mornings, Mama would make us these wonderful Baked Doughnuts, brushed with butter and swirled in a sugar mixture.

3. In a small mixing bowl, whisk together the wet ingredients: the milk, eggs, butter, and vanilla extract. Slowly and gently fold the milk mixture into the flour mixture until just combined.

4. Transfer the batter to a pastry bag or a plastic resealable bag with ½ inch snipped off 1 corner. Using the bag, pipe the batter onto the baking sheet in the shape of 12 doughnuts set 1 inch apart.

5. *To make the topping*: In a small mixing bowl, place the butter. In a separate small mixing bowl, combine the granulated and brown sugars and the cinnamon and stir well. Set aside.

6. Bake for 15 minutes, until the doughnuts are light golden brown. Remove from the oven. Turn out the doughnuts onto a wire rack to cool for 5 minutes.

7. Using a pastry brush, brush the still-warm doughnuts with the butter and then dip each doughnut in the sugar mixture until well coated.

8. Serve immediately; the doughnuts are best eaten the same day that they are made.

Lemon Drizzle Coffee Cake

THIS COFFEE CAKE IS ONE OF MY FAVORITES. I LOVE SURPRISING MORNING guests with a nice slice of it and a cup of hot coffee, and telling them, "This was one of those mornings when I had a taste for something sweet and tangy."

The recipe for this moist, delicious cake comes from Alice Worthy, one of my mother's quilting friends. Miss Alice would often visit on Thursday mornings; Mama provided the coffee and Miss Alice brought the cake.

Makes 1 10-inch tube or Bundt cake

STREUSEL

½ cup sifted all-purpose flour

3 tablespoons light brown sugar

1 teaspoon pure lemon extract

Pinch salt

2 tablespoons unsalted butter, cold, cut into small pieces

BATTER

Nonstick cooking spray, for greasing

All-purpose flour, for dusting

½ cup (1 stick) unsalted butter, room temperature

½ cup granulated sugar

3 large eggs, room temperature

Freshly grated zest and freshly squeezed juice of 1 large lemon

1¼ cups self-rising flour

1 teaspoon baking powder

1 teaspoon pure vanilla extract

GLAZE

1 cup sifted confectioners' sugar

½ cup freshly squeezed lemon juice

1. *To make the streusel:* In a small mixing bowl, combine the flour, brown sugar, lemon extract, and salt and stir until well combined. Using your fingers, a pastry blender, or the tines of a fork, cut the butter into the flour mixture until it becomes crumbly. Set aside.

2. Preheat the oven to 350°F. Grease a 10-inch tube or Bundt pan with the cooking spray and dust with the flour. Set aside.

3. *To make the batter:* In the bowl of a stand mixer fitted with the paddle attachment, break up the butter by mixing on low speed for 1 minute. Add the granulated sugar and cream together the butter and sugar on medium speed for 2 to 3 minutes, until the mixture is light and fluffy. Scrape down the sides and bottom of the bowl to prevent lumps from forming. As the mixer is running, reduce the speed to low and slowly add the eggs, 1 at a time; after you add each egg, scrape down the sides of the bowl and resume beating on low speed for 30 seconds. Add the lemon zest and juice and beat at low speed for 1 minute, until just incorporated. Add the flour to the bowl of the mixer ⅓ at a time, beating each time at low speed for 2 to 3 minutes until just combined. Add the baking powder and vanilla extract and continue beating for 1 minute, until fully combined. Turn off the mixer.

4. Transfer ½ of the batter to the prepared pan. Using a rubber or silicone spatula or a butter knife, evenly spread the batter in the pan. Sprinkle the streusel over the batter, covering it evenly and completely. Evenly spread the remaining batter over the streusel. Bake for 30 to 40 minutes, until the coffee cake is golden brown and a wooden toothpick inserted into the center of the cake comes out clean. Remove from the oven and set aside to cool in the pan on a wire rack for 10 minutes.

5. *To make the glaze:* In a small mixing bowl, whisk together the confectioners' sugar and lemon juice until well combined.

6. Using a serrated knife, separate the cake from the pan and invert onto a serving platter. Using a wooden toothpick, prick holes all over the surface of the cake and pour the glaze over the cake. Run a serrated knife around the edges of the pan to loosen the coffee cake and slice into squares. Return to the wire rack and allow to cool completely.

7. Transfer to a serving platter and serve at room temperature.

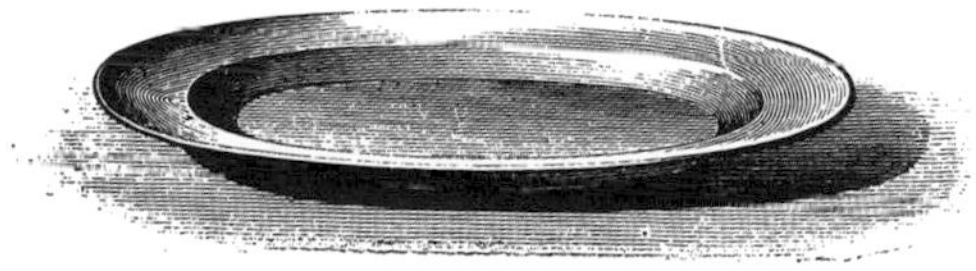

Peanut Butter and Jelly Coffee Cake

When I was a child, I always loved the sound Mama's oven door made when it opened and closed. It meant good things to me.

Mama told me once that one day, my morning baking would likely be focused on the preferences of others. For years now, I've made this coffee cake for the ones I love who adore peanut butter and jelly sandwiches.

Makes 1 9-inch square coffee cake

BATTER

Nonstick cooking spray, for greasing

All-purpose flour, for dusting

2 cups baking mix (I use Bisquick)

2 tablespoons granulated sugar

½ cup smooth peanut butter

⅔ cup buttermilk, room temperature

¼ teaspoon pure vanilla extract

1 large egg, room temperature, lightly beaten

½ cup jelly or jam (whatever flavor you have on hand)

GLAZE

⅔ cup sifted confectioners' sugar

1–2 tablespoons whole milk

GARNISH

Chopped peanuts, for sprinkling

1. Preheat the oven to 350°F. Grease a 9-inch square baking dish with the cooking spray and dust with some flour. Set aside.

2. *To make the batter:* In a large mixing bowl, using a hand mixer set at low speed, beat together the baking mix and granulated sugar for 30 seconds. Add the peanut butter and beat for 30 seconds, until well blended. Add the buttermilk and vanilla extract and beat for 30 seconds, until well blended. Add the egg and beat for 1 minute, until the batter is well blended and smooth.

3. Transfer the batter to the prepared baking dish and spread the jelly or jam over the batter, 1 tablespoon at a time. Bake for 30 minutes, until the coffee cake is golden brown and a wooden toothpick inserted into the center of the cake comes out clean. Remove from the oven and set aside to cool in the pan on a wire rack for 30 minutes.

4. *To make the glaze:* In a small mixing bowl, stir together the confectioners' sugar and 1 tablespoon of the milk. Add more milk, up to 1 tablespoon, as needed to reach a smooth consistency.

5. Drizzle the glaze over the coffee cake and sprinkle the peanuts over the top. Slice and serve warm.

RECIPES

Morning Savories

Morning Savories

I have always been a morning person. The tranquility of dawn gives me the solitude to think, write, read, and bake. To me, baking embodies the soul of morning—as an activity, it's quiet and creative, and it fills the new day with promise. I have such sweet memories of mornings from my childhood: my mother reading to me, enjoying bowls of hot cereal topped with her homemade fruit compotes on school mornings, and finding the occasional strips of bacon my father would leave for us on the warmer.

Mornings were holy to my entire family. Whenever one of us ran a new idea by my grandmother, she used to say, "It sounds credible now, but wait until the morning—morning brings clarity to everything."

When I was little, I distinguished our morning and midmorning meals by the times and days that they were served. Sometimes it all depended on the location or the occasion. There were the before-school breakfasts, the weekday breakfasts, the Saturday breakfasts, the Saturday breakfasts at My My's house, the country breakfasts, the Sunday morning breakfasts, Mama's brunches . . . so many different possibilities! Even today, with every breakfast or brunch I cook, I go back to a time when the women I knew and loved prepared delicious, filling, and comforting meals that gave our days the very best start.

We considered the first meal of the day to be the most important. My father was famous for saying that a waking body needed a good meal to push through the day—until the next good meal. I remember him saying, "A good meal helps you be your best self." Once, as my mother was preparing to serve a brunch for friends and family, she told me, "When women come to your house for coffee and talk, they also come for something good to eat." These were breakfast and brunch maxims that ran through the core of our family; I have never forgotten them.

Most of our breakfasts included some traditional items—perhaps a bacon dish, a sausage dish, an egg dish, and a plate full of golden toast. I can still hear the soft sizzle of bacon strips in the cast-iron pan and the cracking eggs. (Mama almost always scrambled her eggs, and Daddy always fried his.)

On the weekends, time wasn't at such a premium. I have fond and delicious recollections of the aromas and tastes that defined our weekend mornings and midmornings. Mama went out of her way to make them special—no matter the effort necessary to do so. She made us pancakes and waffles topped with homemade berry sauces, coffee cakes and pies laced with sugar and ground cinnamon, sweet bread loaves and rolls, and muffins chock full of nuts and home canned fruit. Mama's morning sweets highlighted our typical bacon and eggs and made them extra special.

Of course, this cookbook spotlights the breakfast and brunch sweets I remember from my childhood, but I would be remiss if I didn't include a small chapter containing some of my favorite morning savories. To me, the bacon, egg, and sausage dishes that gird a great morning meal are pillars of strength. Truth be told, some of my most vivid morning memories revolve around the classic savory portions of the meal.

A Good Cup of Coffee

Coffee has two virtues—it's hot and it's wet.

—Dutch proverb

If you're trying to impress a man with your cooking, you want everything you cook to taste better than he's ever tasted before. Even your coffee.

—Mama's proverb

I can't imagine a house without coffee. When I was growing up, coffee was the beverage of hospitality. Just after my parents asked a guest, "Can I take your coat?" they'd ask, "Would you like a cup of coffee?" Offering a cup of coffee is a simple gesture, but it sets a tone of warmth and welcome. And then there was the wonderful fresh aroma that perfumed our house as soon as Mama plugged in the electric percolator. Even though I was too young to drink it—our family considered coffee an adult beverage—I longed to have a cup of that rich, delicious coffee. I have distinct memories of my mother and aunt talking about it as though it was liquid gold. It's so versatile, they would say, that there isn't a dish that isn't that much better with it or a time of day when it's not appropriate to serve.

Both of my parents were passionate coffee drinkers. Daddy had his with lots of cream and sugar, and Mama took hers strong and black. Often, Mama would have Mary, the young girl who worked at the bakery inside our neighborhood grocery store, grind her coffee beans extra fine (Mary was known for keeping the grinder nice and clean). Sometimes Mama, who also had her own little grinder at home, would roast coffee beans in the oven and then grind them herself. Serving home-roasted coffee was one of her little pleasures. I guess for some people, a good cup of coffee is to their morning as a good bottle of wine is to their evening.

Thousands of recipes promise to deliver the perfect cup of coffee. I don't think you'll ever find that perfect cup, but I do think certain things can make one cup to taste better than another. Here are a few of my best tips:

* Serve the best-quality coffee you can.
* Make sure your coffeemaker and cups are sparkling clean. Residue from old coffee and soap detergent buildup will affect taste. Clean your coffeemaker and mugs with baking soda and water regularly.
* Because coffee is 95% water, start with clean, good-quality, distilled water. Mama used to buy gallon jugs of distilled water to use for her ironing and her coffee. Certain women in our neighborhood were known for serving watery, repulsive cups of coffee, but not my mother—it was important to her to provide people with a tasty meal.
* Don't stockpile coffee beans or grounds. Grinding fresh beans or buying freshly ground coffee always results in better coffee.
* Before you pour a cup of coffee, quickly stir the pot to redistribute its contents.
* So much depends on how you take your coffee. Most times, Mama offered her guests raw sugar and evaporated milk. To get the color and taste your guests are looking for, try offering a variety of creams, milks, and sugars.
* A good coffee experience is as much about aroma as it is about taste. Serve your coffee as soon as possible after brewing it.
* *Optional:* Add a chunk of rich, sweet chocolate to a cup of coffee for a bit of decadence in the morning.

A Good Cup of Instant Coffee

When you don't have the inclination (or the money) to buy the best beans to brew your coffee, instant coffee can be just as delightful. My Aunt Marjell, a wonderful cook and hostess, always served her guests instant coffee.

* Always use fresh, clean water.
* Use 1 rounded tablespoon of instant coffee per cup (of course, this will vary according to individual taste; Aunt Marjell used about 2 teaspoons per cup).
* Use very hot—almost boiling—water.
* Season with fresh whole milk, half-and-half, evaporated milk, or nondairy creamer and real sugar.
* Serve with a nice slice of homemade coffee cake to add a little intensity.

Sunday Morning Steaks and Cheesy Scrambled Eggs

IF YOU WANT TO BE CONSIDERED A REALLY GOOD COOK, YOU NEED TO have a morning steak recipe in your files. To me, the difference between an everyday breakfast and a good steak breakfast is like the difference between driving a Honda and a Cadillac—driving a Cadillac is *such* a rich experience. This is especially delicious served with buttered toast and Mama's Hash-Brown Potatoes (see recipe on p. 230).

Makes 4 servings

STEAKS

1 tablespoon vegetable oil

Salt and freshly ground black pepper, to taste

4 ½-inch-thick boneless ribeye steaks, room temperature

CHEESY SCRAMBLED EGGS

12 large eggs, room temperature

¼ cup evaporated milk (optional)

Salt and freshly ground white pepper, to taste

3 tablespoons unsalted butter

¾ cup shredded Cheddar cheese

1. *To make the steaks:* In a large cast-iron skillet over medium–high heat, warm the oil until it is hot but not smoking. Season the steaks with the salt and black pepper and add them to the skillet, taking great care not to overcrowd the skillet. Cook for 2 to 3 minutes, until they are browned. Turn over and cook for 2 minutes for medium–rare or 3 to 4 minutes for medium to medium–well. (To check the internal temperature of my steaks for doneness, I use a meat thermometer: 125°F for rare, 135°F for medium–rare, 145°F for medium, 155°F for medium–well, and 160°F for well done). Remove the skillet from the heat. Remove the steaks from the skillet and set them on a platter. Tent the platter with aluminum foil and let the steaks rest for 10 minutes.

2. *To make the eggs:* In a large mixing bowl, combine the eggs and, if using, the evaporated milk. (It's best to crack open each egg into a small bowl and then add the egg to the large bowl, as it's much easier to get out any little pieces of shell that way.) Season with the salt and white pepper. Using the tines of a fork, beat the mixture until it is smooth and well combined.

3. In a large heavy-bottomed nonstick skillet over low heat, melt the butter (make sure it does not brown). Swirl the butter to ensure the bottom and sides of the skillet are well coated. Add the egg mixture to the skillet. Sprinkle the cheese over the egg mixture. Let the mixture sit in the skillet for 30 seconds or so, until it thickens on the bottom.

4. Fold the egg mixture in the skillet and allow to cook for 10 seconds. Fold the mixture again and repeat until the eggs are fully cooked. Remove from the heat.

5. Divide the warm steaks and eggs evenly among 4 plates and serve hot.

Sunday-Best Sausage Bread Pudding

I AM ALWAYS SURPRISED WHEN PEOPLE SAY THEY HAVE MORNING DISHES that they reserve for holidays. Some tell me the tradition began in their families years ago, but I'm hard-pressed to recall such a memory or dish. When I was growing up, we did greet the winter cold and snow with hearty and fragrant soups and stews, had cooling treats to ward off the sun and heat of summer, and prepared fall dishes that took advantage of Michigan's harvest, but I don't remember saving anything that we liked to eat for a special time of year.

Perhaps the closest thing I can think of is this rich and decadent sausage bake, which we made throughout the year. Mama used to say, "Life is too short to shortchange yourself."

Makes 1 9-inch × 13-inch casserole

- Nonstick cooking spray, for greasing
- 5 cups day-old Italian bread, crusts removed, cut into 2-inch cubes
- 1 cup shredded Cheddar cheese
- 1 cup shredded Colby cheese
- 1 pound pork sausage
- 10 large eggs, room temperature, lightly beaten
- 1 cup half-and-half, room temperature
- 1 cup whole milk, room temperature
- ½ cup finely chopped green onions
- 2 teaspoons dry mustard
- ½ teaspoon salt
- Freshly ground black pepper, to taste

1. Grease a 9-inch × 13-inch casserole dish with the cooking spray and layer the bread cubes inside it. Sprinkle the shredded cheeses over the bread cubes. Set aside.

2. In a large nonstick skillet over medium–high heat, scramble the sausage into bite-size pieces and cook for 5 minutes, until the meat is browned and cooked through. Remove from the heat and transfer the sausage to a colander placed over a bowl to drain.

3. In a medium mixing bowl, whisk together the eggs, half-and-half, milk, green onions, and dry mustard. Season with the salt and black pepper and continue whisking until the ingredients are well combined.

4. Pour the mixture evenly over the bread cubes and shredded cheese in the casserole dish and sprinkle the sausage over the top. Cover with plastic wrap and refrigerate for at least 1 hour or overnight.

5. Remove the casserole dish from the refrigerator and allow it to come to room temperature for 30 minutes. Preheat the oven to 350°F.

6. Discard the plastic wrap and bake, uncovered, for 35 to 40 minutes, until a wooden toothpick inserted near the center of the pudding has only a few crumbs stuck to it when you pull it out. Remove from the oven and set aside to cool for 5 minutes.

7. Transfer to a serving dish or serve hot from the casserole dish.

"Life is too short to shortchange yourself." MAMA

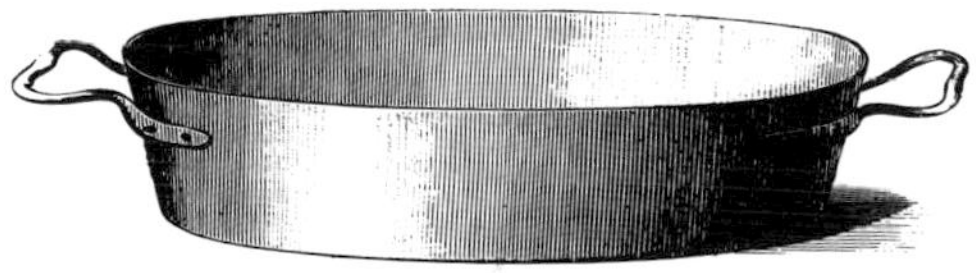

Mama's Hash-Brown Potatoes

THIS OLD-FASHIONED CLASSIC IMPARTS ITS GOODNESS TO EVERYTHING. Even after all these years, these potatoes are still pretty much everybody's favorite breakfast side dish.

Makes 4 servings

3 large russet potatoes, scrubbed and rinsed
Cold water, to cover
2 tablespoons unsalted butter
1 tablespoon vegetable oil
½ medium yellow onion, finely chopped
1 clove garlic, peeled and minced
Salt and freshly ground black pepper, to taste

1. Place the potatoes in a large saucepan and cover with the cold water. Place over medium–high heat and bring to a boil. Reduce the heat to medium and simmer for 15 minutes, until the potatoes are almost tender. Remove from the heat and drain. Set aside to rest until the potatoes are cool enough to handle.

2. Remove and discard the skins from the potatoes. Cut the potatoes into ½-inch cubes.

3. In a large, heavy skillet over high heat, warm the butter and oil, but take great care not to burn the butter. Reduce the heat to medium, add the onion, and cook, stirring constantly, for 2 minutes. Add the garlic and cook, stirring constantly, for 20 seconds.

4. Add the potatoes, salt, and black pepper and cook, shaking the pan occasionally to keep the ingredients from sticking and burning, for 4 minutes, until they begin to brown and form a tender golden crust on the bottom. Using a spatula, carefully turn over the potatoes, taking great care not to mash them. Continue cooking for 2 to 3 minutes, until the potatoes are fork tender and golden brown on both sides. Remove from the heat and serve immediately.

Mama's Ground-Turkey Sausage Patties

MAMA'S RECIPE FOR SAUSAGE PATTIES MAKES TURKEY ROUNDS THAT taste much better than the brands you buy at the store. As I recall, they were always moist and succulent, and a special addition to our table.

The patties are wonderful served with golden toast, scrambled eggs, and a slice of homemade coffee cake. Customize the seasonings to suit your taste or to accommodate the spices you have on hand. Make the patties smaller or larger or thinner or thicker according to your wishes. When I really want to impress somebody, I refrigerate the patties overnight to let the flavor of the spices soak into the meat. Some people use cooking oil to keep the patties moist, but others don't use anything at all. Personally, I always add a little butter to my sausage.

Makes about 4–6 servings

- 1 pound ground turkey (can substitute ground chicken or pork)
- ¼ cup finely minced yellow onion
- 1 tablespoon unsalted butter, room temperature, cut into small pieces
- 1½ teaspoons brown sugar
- 1½ teaspoons Worcestershire sauce
- 1 teaspoon dried sage, crushed
- ½ teaspoon ground fennel seeds
- ½ teaspoon crushed red pepper flakes
- ¼ teaspoon garlic powder
- ¼ teaspoon onion powder
- ¼ teaspoon ground thyme
- ¼ teaspoon dried marjoram
- ¼ teaspoon hickory-flavored liquid smoke
- ⅛ teaspoon freshly grated nutmeg
- ⅛ teaspoon ground allspice
- Nonstick cooking spray, for greasing

COOKS' NOTE: *The cooked patties freeze well if carefully wrapped. They'll store in the freezer for 1 month.*

1. In a large mixing bowl, combine all of the ingredients except the cooking spray. Using your hands, mix together the ingredients until they are thoroughly combined. Shape the mixture into small or medium-size patties.

2. Line a plate with several layers of paper towels and set aside.

3. Grease a large cast-iron skillet with a light coating of the cooking spray and warm the skillet over medium–high heat. Add the patties and fry, turning once, for 8 to 10 minutes, until they are golden on both sides and there is no pink in the middle (cooking times will vary depending on the patties' thickness). Take great care not to overcook the sausages, or they will dry out. Remove from the heat.

4. Transfer to the prepared plate to drain. Serve hot.

Hickory-Smoked Bacon and Grilled Cheese Sandwiches

I REMEMBER MY MOTHER'S GARDEN AS A VISION OF BEAUTY AND labor—planting, watering, weeding, pruning, and picking. Mama's garden was as much a part of my growing up as my rabbits, Snow White and Snow Ball, and my father's hunting beagles, Rodney and Bridgette.

Mama's garden had a wide block of flowers: backyard rows that hosted tulips; red, pink, and white roses; multicolored wind flowers; hyacinths; and daffodils. There were also rows of crowder peas; vines of green beans wrapped around sticks; okra pods; yellow and white squash; green and red peppers; sweet corn; sugar pumpkins; plots of collard, turnip, and mustard greens; and tomatoes.

When the garden was in full bloom, it teemed with color and fragrance. My mother always used to say that the flavor and color of fresh-picked food was infinitely superior to that of store-bought processed food. I have rich memories of her coming in the house with a bowl of ripe tomatoes to make a pot of delicious homemade tomato soup to serve alongside a platter of these Hickory-Smoked Bacon and Grilled Cheese Sandwiches.

Makes 4 servings

12 strips hickory-smoked bacon, room temperature

8 slices sourdough bread, lightly toasted

3 tablespoons butter, melted

1½ tablespoons Dijon mustard

4 slices Colby-Jack cheese

4 leaves romaine or other lettuce

1 large garden tomato, thinly sliced

1. Line a plate with several layers of paper towels and set aside.

2. Arrange the bacon strips in a single layer in a large, cold skillet. Place the cold skillet over medium–low heat and fry for 6 to 8 minutes, until the bacon strips are evenly browned and crisp. Remove from the heat.

3. Transfer the bacon strips to the prepared plate to drain and tent with aluminum foil to keep warm.

4. Using a pastry brush, brush the top of each slice of the bread with a liberal amount of the melted butter, taking care to spread the butter all the way to the edges. On 4 of the slices of bread, spread the Dijon mustard on top of the butter, place a slice of the cheese on top of the mustard, and place a leaf of the lettuce on top of the cheese. Arrange 3 strips of bacon on top of the lettuce and add 1 slice of the tomato. Top each sandwich with the remaining slices of bread, with the buttered side of the bread facing outward.

5. Place the sandwiches in a clean skillet over medium–low heat and press down on them. Cover and cook for 3 to 4 minutes. Turn over and brush the butter on the other side of the sandwich. Cook for 2 to 3 minutes, until the bread is toasted and the cheese has melted. Remove from the heat.

6. Transfer to a platter and slice each sandwich in ½. Serve warm.

COOKS' NOTE: *To add more deliciousness to my morning grilled cheese sandwiches with hickory-smoked bacon, I sometimes dress them up with fried or scrambled eggs on the side or nestled in the sandwich.*

Fried Green Tomatoes

WHEN I WAS A CHILD, FALL WAS ALWAYS MY FAVORITE SEASON. I LOVED hearing the leaves crunch under my feet on the sidewalk, staring up at the brilliant colors of a Michigan autumn, and inhaling the pungent aroma of sugar beets during the harvest. That aroma to this day invokes memories of my father's red dump truck and his seasonal job hauling sugar beets from a farm in Carrollton, Michigan, to the sugar plant just off M-13.

We picked the last of our garden bounty during the fall. I especially enjoyed it when my mother sent me to our garden to pick the last of the vegetables and fruits. To get me inspired, she'd describe the wonderful foods she'd can or freeze using the vegetables and seeds I gathered. Mama would paint a beautiful picture of the wind and snow of an approaching Michigan winter and the thought of walking into a house warm and fragrant with one of her garden meals.

I particularly remember being sent to the garden to pick the green tomatoes. My mother canned them into delicious chutneys or salsas or sliced them into perfect rounds to batter and fry. Those Fried Green Tomatoes gave our mornings a delicious lift. We loved them with our breakfasts and brunches, as side dishes that paired perfectly with our dinner meals, or as scrumptious late-night snacks. That's one of the reasons why I love them so much: Fried Green Tomatoes are delicious anytime.

Makes 4 servings

3 firm medium green tomatoes, cored and cut into ½-inch-thick slices

1 teaspoon coarse salt

½ teaspoon freshly ground black pepper

1 cup buttermilk, room temperature

¾ cup finely ground yellow cornmeal

¼ cup sifted all-purpose flour

½ teaspoon ground sweet paprika

Pinch granulated sugar

Vegetable oil, for frying

Mama would paint a beautiful picture of the wind and snow of an approaching Michigan winter and the thought of walking into a house warm and fragrant with one of her garden meals.

1. Gently season each tomato slice with the salt and black pepper on both sides and place the slices in a single layer in a large baking dish. Cover the slices with the buttermilk and refrigerate for about 20 minutes, gently turning over the slices at least once during the chill time.

2. Remove the baking dish from the refrigerator. Remove the tomato slices from the dish and place them on a wire rack to drain.

3. In a shallow, medium mixing bowl, combine the cornmeal, flour, paprika, and granulated sugar. Set aside.

4. Line a plate with several layers of paper towels and set aside.

5. In a large, heavy skillet over medium–high heat, place enough oil to cover the skillet's bottom to approximately a ¼-inch depth. Heat the oil until it begins to shimmer and reaches 360°F. Using heat-resistant tongs, dredge each tomato slice, 1 at a time, in the cornmeal mixture. Shake off any excess coating and slip the tomato slices into the skillet in a single layer. Fry for 3 minutes per side, until each tomato slice is golden brown and crisp. Remove from the heat.

6. Using a slotted spatula, transfer to the prepared plate to drain. Serve hot.

COOKS' NOTE: *Fried green tomatoes are delicious served by themselves or with a butter-based sauce.*

Corned Beef Hash

When I was a child, Paris, Tennessee—where Daddy grew up—was a frequent summer destination. We traveled there to visit his relatives and especially his mother, Mary Lee, and his Aunt Frances. The car trunk would be loaded with suitcases, gift boxes, and sandwiches we'd eat along the way, and we'd stop at service stations for cold soda pop, bags of hot peanuts, and chocolate candy bars chock full of nuts and crackly cereal. I remember devouring our store-bought finds with particular relish, because when you're on a car trip, the food at every stop always seems so divine.

Along the way, we would always stop at one particular diner for breakfast. Mama used to say that the food at this diner was as good as homemade food got and that the proprietors were like kin—warm and inviting.

The diner sold lots of pecan pie, fried chicken, catfish and shrimp baskets, and tall glasses of sweet tea. We always had the early-bird special: a giant plate of corned beef hash, two fried eggs served yolk-side up, and a big slice of wheat toast. It was a hearty, delicious meal designed for people on a long journey.

So many years later, I often think about my Tennessee kinsfolk and their warmth and company meals. I also think about that diner and its wonderful corned beef hash, and this is the recipe I use to recreate it.

Makes 4 servings

POTATOES

Nonstick cooking spray, for greasing

2 large russet potatoes, diced into ½-inch cubes

1 tablespoon vegetable oil

½ teaspoon dried basil

½ teaspoon dried oregano

½ teaspoon dried thyme

½ teaspoon salt, or to taste

¼ teaspoon freshly ground black pepper, or to taste

CORNED BEEF

2 tablespoons unsalted butter

¾ cup minced onion

2 garlic cloves, peeled and minced

2 cups cooked corned beef, cut into 1-inch cubes

Salt and freshly ground black pepper, to taste

2 teaspoons Worcestershire sauce

¼ cup heavy cream

4 large eggs, poached (see recipe on p. 244) or sunny-side up

2 tablespoons fresh parsley leaves, roughly chopped (optional)

1. Preheat the oven to 425°F. Grease a rimmed baking sheet with the cooking spray and set aside.

2. *To make the potatoes:* In a large mixing bowl, combine the potato cubes and the oil and, using your hands, mix them together until each cube is well coated. Sprinkle with the basil, oregano, thyme, salt, and black pepper and continue mixing until well combined. Set aside for 10 minutes.

3. Transfer the potatoes to the prepared baking sheet in a single layer. Bake, stirring once during the baking time to prevent sticking, for 20 to 25 minutes, until they are golden brown and crunchy. Remove from the oven and set aside.

4. *To make the corned beef:* In a large, heavy skillet over medium heat, melt the butter. Add the onion and cook, stirring constantly, for 3 minutes, until it becomes translucent. Add the garlic and cook, stirring constantly, for 1 minute, until the garlic is tender and fragrant. Add the corned beef, salt, and black pepper and cook, stirring constantly, for 3 minutes, until the corned beef browns. Add the potatoes and Worcestershire sauce and cook, stirring constantly, for 4 to 5 minutes.

5. Reduce the heat to low. Using the back of a spatula, press the mixture down, flattening it. Drizzle the heavy cream evenly over the top of the hash and cook for 10 to 15 minutes. Turn the mixture over, pat it down, and cook for 10 to 15 minutes, until the bottom of the hash is browned. Remove from the heat.

6. Divide the hash into 4 portions and transfer them to plates. Place 1 egg on top of each serving and sprinkle with the parsley, if using. Serve immediately.

Daddy's Griddle Cakes

THIS GRIDDLE CAKE RECIPE BELONGED TO MY FATHER'S MOTHER, Mary Lee, who was half Cherokee—she and all her sisters had long, dark, bone-straight hair. Daddy was very close to his mother. They looked alike, except that Daddy's complexion was chocolate brown, like his father's people.

Mama used to tell me that she had never seen a son write letters and send cards to his mother more than Daddy did. Other than my maternal grandfather, I can't think of a man who was more kind and forgiving than Daddy. Thinking back, I believe that's why he and Mama loved each other so much—they were cut from the same cloth.

On one of the few days when Daddy wasn't working—he worked full time for General Motors and had countless side jobs to supplement his income—he would sometimes make a plate of his mother's griddle cakes. I'd sit at the kitchen table and listen to him tell stories and watch him turn the cakes. His stories were usually about tools, old cars, hunting and fishing expeditions, and the Korean War. Daddy's stories were saltier than most of my mother's stories; Mama's stories were about living in the world as a woman, and his were about living in it as a man.

These griddle cakes are a wonderful side dish for any breakfast or brunch—great with a pat of butter, a drizzle of syrup or honey, and a strip or two of crispy bacon.

Makes about 10 griddle cakes

1 cup sifted all-purpose flour
½ cup white cornmeal
1 tablespoon firmly packed light brown sugar
½ tablespoon baking powder
½ tablespoon baking soda
½ teaspoon salt
1 cup whole milk, room temperature
½ cup half-and-half, room temperature
¼ cup vegetable oil, plus more for frying
1 large egg, room temperature, well beaten

On one of the few days when Daddy wasn't working, he would sometimes make a plate of his mother's griddle cakes.

1. In a large bowl, combine the dry ingredients: the flour, cornmeal, brown sugar, baking powder, baking soda, and salt. Mix well. Make a well in the center of the mixture and set aside.

2. In a medium mixing bowl, whisk together the wet ingredients: the milk, half-and-half, oil, and egg. Continue whisking until well combined.

3. Add the milk mixture to the flour mixture and stir until just moistened. (Do not overmix; the batter should be lumpy.)

4. In a large, heavy skillet over medium heat, place enough oil to cover the skillet's bottom to approximately a ¼-inch depth. Heat the oil until it begins to shimmer and reaches 360°F. Drop ladlefuls of the batter into the hot oil (the resulting griddle cakes should be about 4 inches in diameter), leaving space between each. Fry for 1 to 2 minutes, until the griddle cakes become puffy and bubbles appear on their surface. Using a spatula, turn each over and continue frying for another 1 to 2 minutes, until both sides are golden brown. Remove the griddle cakes from the oil and transfer them to serving plates.

5. Repeat step 4 until all the batter has been used. Remove from the heat.

6. Serve immediately.

Big Mama's Chicken and Waffles

COMBINING CHICKEN AND WAFFLES WAS AN ANOMALY IN OUR neighborhood. In fact, my great-aunt, Big Mama, was the only person I knew who did.

Big Mama told us that she had loving memories of growing up in the South, where her mother often made chicken and waffles for the family. I too have fond memories of Big Mama's luxurious Chicken and Waffles.

Makes 4 servings

CHICKEN

1½ cups buttermilk, room temperature

½ teaspoon garlic powder

½ teaspoon onion powder

¼ teaspoon salt

8 chicken tenders, boneless and skinless (about 1 pound)

1 cup all-purpose flour

½ teaspoon salt, or to taste

½ teaspoon freshly ground black pepper, or to taste

½ teaspoon ground sweet paprika

¼ teaspoon granulated sugar

Vegetable oil, for deep frying

WAFFLES

3 large egg whites, room temperature

Nonstick cooking spray, for greasing

2 cups sifted cake flour

1 tablespoon granulated sugar

2 teaspoons baking powder

¾ teaspoon baking soda

½ teaspoon salt

¼ teaspoon ground cinnamon

3 large egg yolks, room temperature

2 cups buttermilk, room temperature

4 tablespoons unsalted butter, melted and cooled

1 teaspoon vanilla extract

Waffle Syrup (recipe follows), for serving

1. *To make the chicken:* In a large mixing bowl, combine the buttermilk, garlic powder, onion powder, and salt and stir until well combined. Submerge the chicken tenders in the buttermilk mixture, turning them once to make sure they are evenly coated. Cover with plastic wrap and refrigerate for 3 hours or overnight.

2. In a shallow mixing bowl, combine the flour, salt, black pepper, paprika, and granulated sugar and stir until well combined. Remove the chicken tenders from the buttermilk mixture, allowing the excess liquid to drain from each chicken tender. Roll the chicken tenders evenly in the seasoned flour and allow them to rest in the shallow bowl for 10 to 15 minutes, until their coating has set.

3. Line a plate with several layers of paper towels and set aside.

4. In a large, heavy skillet over medium–high heat, place enough oil to cover the skillet's bottom to approximately a ¼-inch depth and heat the oil until it begins to shimmer and reaches 360°F. Slip the chicken tenders into the skillet in a single layer, working in batches as needed. Fry for 10 to 12 minutes per side, until each chicken tender is golden brown and crisp. After they are cooked, remove the chicken tenders to the prepared plate to drain and tent with aluminum foil to keep warm. Repeat until all chicken tenders have been fried. Remove from the heat.

5. *To make the waffles:* Using a hand mixer set at medium speed, beat the egg whites in a small mixing bowl until stiff peaks form. Set the bowl aside.

6. Preheat a lightly greased waffle iron according to the manufacturer's directions.

7. In a medium mixing bowl, sift together the dry ingredients: the cake flour, granulated sugar, baking powder, baking soda, salt, and cinnamon. Make a well in the center of the mixture and set aside.

8. In a separate medium mixing bowl, lightly beat the egg yolks. Add the buttermilk, butter, and vanilla extract and stir until combined.

9. Add the egg–buttermilk mixture to the flour mixture and stir until just moistened. (Do not overmix; the batter should be lumpy.)

10. Fold the stiff egg whites into the batter and set aside to rest for at least 5 minutes.

11. Pour a ladleful of the batter on the prepared waffle iron and cook according to the manufacturer's recommendations. Once the waffle is properly cooked, use the tines of a fork to lift it off the grid and place on a serving platter. Repeat until all the batter has been used.

12. Place 1 waffle on each of 4 serving plates and place 2 chicken tenders on each waffle. Drizzle each serving with a ribbon of Waffle Syrup and serve immediately.

Waffle Syrup

Makes 2 cups

1¼ cups water
1 cup granulated sugar
1 cup packed dark brown sugar
1 cup light corn syrup
¼ teaspoon ground cinnamon
⅛ teaspoon salt
1 teaspoon vanilla extract

1. In a large saucepan over medium heat, combine the water, granulated and brown sugars, corn syrup, cinnamon, and salt and bring to a boil. Reduce the heat to medium–low and simmer, stirring constantly, for 5 minutes, until the sugars have melted. Remove from the heat and stir in the vanilla extract.

2. Serve immediately or let cool and transfer to a tightly sealed container to store in the refrigerator for up to 1 week.

Eggs

When I was a kid, the sight of eggs and butter sitting out on the counter to warm to room temperature filled me with delight. I knew the air would soon be heavy with a tantalizing aroma—perhaps cake, a batch of brownies, sugar cookies, or one of my mother's delectable sweet loaves. With eggs, the possibilities were endless.

Eggs have always been essential to many of my favorite morning meals. As a side dish, eggs are not only delicious, but they are also sunny and versatile. I love them fried, scrambled, boiled, poached, baked, and as a key ingredient in wonderful morning dishes like omelets, frittatas, pancakes, and waffles. They give bacon, homemade sausage, and buttered toast its verve. On the pages that follow, I share with you a few of my favorite morning egg dishes.

Poached Eggs

WAY BEFORE IT WAS IN VOGUE, MY MOTHER WAS DEVOTED TO FITNESS. I remember standing in front of our black-and-white television set next to her doing jumping jacks per the instructions of Jack LaLanne. Sometimes, my mother was especially careful about what she ate—particularly when she was going somewhere special and wanted to wear a certain dress.

Poached eggs were wonderful for those occasions. Unlike scrambled or fried eggs, they don't need oil or butter—they're delicious all by themselves.

Makes 4 eggs

3 cups water (or enough water to cover the eggs by ½ inch)

½ teaspoon distilled white vinegar (optional)

¼ teaspoon salt (optional)

4 large eggs

Freshly cracked black pepper (optional)

1. Line a plate with several layers of paper towels and set aside.

2. In a medium saucepan over high heat, combine the water and vinegar and salt, if using, and bring to a boil. Reduce the heat to low and allow the water to simmer. Crack the eggs, 1 at a time, into a small bowl. Carefully transfer 1 egg at a time into the simmering water and cook, undisturbed, for 2½ minutes, until the egg whites are set but the yolks are still soft.

3. Using a slotted spoon, remove the eggs from the water and transfer them to the prepared plate to drain any excess water.

4. Transfer to serving plates. Serve immediately sprinkled with the pepper, if using.

COOKS' NOTE: *My Aunt Marjell doesn't care for vinegar in her poached eggs; she swears it gives them an odd aftertaste. My Aunt Helen wants me to tell you that sometimes you have to baste the tops of your poached eggs with the simmering water in order to get the flavor and doneness that you want.*

Eggs Benedict

THIS IS A PERFECT DISH TO BUILD A MORNING MEAL AROUND. A SERVING of Eggs Benedict adds class and dress to any early gathering.

Makes 4 servings

BASE

4 slices Canadian bacon

4 English muffin halves, well buttered on 1 side

HOLLANDAISE SAUCE

2 cups water

½ cup (1 stick) unsalted butter, melted and cooled

3 large egg yolks, room temperature

1 tablespoon warm water

1 tablespoon freshly squeezed lemon juice

¼ teaspoon salt

⅛ teaspoon freshly ground black pepper

ASSEMBLY

4 large Poached Eggs (see recipe on p. 244)

Dash ground sweet paprika

1. Line a plate with several layers of paper towels and set aside.

2. *To make the base:* In a large, heavy skillet over medium–low heat, cook the Canadian bacon slices for 2 to 3 minutes. Turn over the slices and cook for 2 to 3 minutes. Remove from the heat. Remove the Canadian bacon slices from the skillet and transfer them to the prepared plate to drain any excess grease. Tent with aluminum foil to keep the Canadian bacon slices warm.

3. Set the oven to broil. On a baking sheet, evenly space the English muffin halves. Place the baking sheet under the broiler for 2 to 3 minutes, until the English muffin halves are lightly crisped and golden. Remove from the oven and set aside.

4. *To make the hollandaise sauce:* Place the water in a saucepan over medium–high heat and bring to a boil.

5. In a medium heatproof glass bowl, vigorously whisk together the butter and egg yolks for 1 minute, until the mixture turns pale yellow. While whisking constantly, add the warm water, lemon juice, salt, and black pepper.

recipe continues

6. Once the water reaches a boil, reduce the heat to low and place the glass bowl over the saucepan, taking great care to ensure that the boiling water does not touch the bottom of the bowl or the ingredients in it. Cook, whisking constantly, for 2 to 3 minutes, until the mixture is thick and smooth. Remove from the heat.

7. *To serve:* Place a prepared English muffin half, buttered side up, on a serving plate. Place a slice of the Canadian bacon on top of each English muffin half, and place a poached egg on top of the Canadian bacon. Using a large spoon, drizzle a spoonful of the hollandaise sauce over the top of each egg and sprinkle the top of each with the paprika. Serve immediately.

COOKS' NOTE: *If I want my Eggs Benedict to really look fancy, I sprinkle a bit of chives or fresh parsley over them.*

Pan-Fried Egg and Bacon Sandwiches

When my cousins and I were growing up, our mothers always made sure our holidays were special. We always looked forward to the annual Fourth of July picnic on the river. Our at-home birthday parties always had plenty of balloons, candles, and homemade birthday cake served with freshly churned ice cream. My mother and I would dye Easter eggs at the kitchen table each year for our backyard Easter egg hunts. Every year, we'd have lavish family Christmas and Thanksgiving dinners at my grandparents' house. Sadly, it's different now. So many of us are scattered around the country or have passed away.

Even though things will never be the same, I maintain many of our old-fashioned customs, and I've even invented a few new ones. Now, we take the little kids to hunt for candy-filled eggs on the courthouse lawn. We always have a Christmas party on December 16, and for it, I decorate the house with many of the same decorations my mother and grandmother used in their homes. My late cousin Ryan, who spent his last Christmas with me, told me, "Patty, this is the best Christmas I've had since childhood. Everything is so blue and green and red and orange and twinkly. It looks so festive in here." It was just what I wanted to hear.

Now that I'm older, and usually operating on my last nerve—my three- and four-year-old grandchildren live with me—I prefer get-togethers that are small, intimate, and easy. Among them are my Sandwich Nights, which I hold once a month or so. We get together to laugh, eat sandwiches and popcorn, play games, and watch kid-friendly movies. My hope is that the kids will always remember these nights.

Sometimes, I make these Pan-Fried Egg and Bacon Sandwiches for our Sandwich Nights. Everybody loves them!

Makes 4 sandwiches

8 thick slices bread

1 clove garlic, peeled and cut in half

2 teaspoons unsalted butter, melted and cooled

8 strips thickly cut smoked bacon

4 large eggs

Salt and freshly ground black pepper, to taste

4 slices of Monterey Jack or Cheddar cheese, room temperature

4 tablespoons mayonnaise (optional)

Pan-Fried Egg and Bacon Sandwiches *CONTINUED*

1. Set the oven to broil and place the rack about 5 inches from the heat source.

2. On a baking sheet, evenly space the slices of bread. Rub each slice of bread with the cut sides of the garlic clove. Using a pastry brush, brush each slice of bread with the butter. Place the baking sheet under the broiler for 1 to 2 minutes, until the slices of bread are lightly crisped and golden. Remove from the oven and place 2 slices each on 4 serving plates.

3. Line a plate with several layers of paper towels and set aside.

4. Arrange the bacon in a single layer in a large, cold skillet. Place the cold skillet over medium–low heat and fry for 6 to 8 minutes, until the bacon strips are evenly browned and crisp. Remove from the heat.

5. Transfer the bacon strips to the prepared plate to drain and tent with aluminum foil to keep warm.

6. Drain all but 1 tablespoon of the bacon fat from the skillet and return it to medium–low heat. Add 2 of the eggs to the skillet and fry, undisturbed, for 2 to 3 minutes, until the whites are set. Lightly season the eggs with the salt and black pepper. Using a spatula, turn over the eggs and lay 1 slice of the cheese on top of each egg. Cook, undisturbed, for 1 to 2 minutes, until the cheese has melted but the egg yolk has not completely set. Remove the eggs from the skillet and place them on a plate.

7. Repeat step 6 with the other 2 eggs. Remove from the heat.

8. Using a spatula, transfer 2 strips of bacon to 1 of the slices of bread on each plate. Place 1 egg on top of each bacon-topped slice of bread. If using, spread the mayonnaise on the other slice of bread on the plate and gently press the bread on top of the eggs and bacon. Serve immediately.

COOKS' NOTE: *I always give my cooked bacon strips an extra pat with a paper towel, to ensure that all of the unwanted grease is gone.*

Miss Lola's Scrambled Eggs

JUST BECAUSE A WOMAN STAYS HOME KEEPING HOUSE, IT DOESN'T MEAN she can't be sophisticated, knowledgeable, and interesting. Miss Lola Choyce kept house, yet she lived one of the most avant-garde lives that I had ever seen.

Miss Lola had a pretty baby face and a plump hourglass figure. Mama used to say that Miss Lola was a contrast in womanhood—on one hand, she was a grande dame of the feminine arts, with excellent skills in stitchery, rose gardening, hospitality, and home cooking. On the other, she had an unconventional lifestyle and values as contemporary as that of any modern woman's. Miss Lola's younger boyfriend, Lucky, was what my mother called a *street man.* Mr. Lucky paid Miss Lola's bills and gave her spending money. On some mornings while Mama and I were visiting Miss Lola, Mr. Lucky would stroll in, drop a wad of paper money in Miss Lola's lap, and either go back out or head upstairs to his bedroom in the back of the house (Miss Lola had explained that the vibrant afternoon sun that streamed in her bedroom window would keep him awake).

My mother would always bring a doll or book to keep me busy, but I loved to listen to the conversations Mama and Miss Lola had. Miss Lola told captivating stories about men and women and relationships—fornicating preachers, cheating housewives, and men who were so stingy with their money that no woman with an ounce of dignity would have anything to do with them. But I especially liked hearing her stories about the relationship she had with Mr. Lucky.

According to Miss Lola, Mr. Lucky had other women stashed around town. Some were young, some were attractive, some were streetwise, and some were just barhopping party girls. Miss Lola referred to Mr. Lucky's other women by their first names—Bernice, Julia, Vanette, and Key-Key. When Miss Lola spoke their names, there was no animosity in her voice. In fact, Miss Lola and her "wife-in-laws" seemed to get along like sisters.

Once, when Mama was engrossed in learning a new tatting stitch Miss Lola was patiently teaching her, I quietly followed Mr. Lucky into Miss Lola's kitchen. I'll never forget what I saw. Miss Lola's morning kitchen looked like a picture in a book, so lacy and lemon-yellow perfect. The Formica top on her kitchen table glistened in the sun, and her lacy handiwork adorned everything from the curtains to the countertop. Mr. Lucky, who had broad shoulders and walnut-colored skin, was helping himself to Miss Lola's chafing dishes. He fixed

recipe continues

himself a heaping plate of bacon, golden-fried potatoes, and eggs so yellow and perfect-looking that they could have slid off the pages of a cookbook. I didn't know what he'd been doing in the streets all night, but standing over Miss Lola's warming dishes, Mr. Lucky looked like a man who was pleased to be home.

Mr. Lucky looked at me. As I recall, he was on the short and solid side, and handsome like a rock star; his face carried the well-groomed look of Little Richard. He said, "Have some?" and pointed to Miss Lola's beautiful eggs.

Of course, my good manners gave me the perfect response: "No, thank you."

Mr. Lucky said, "You sure? Eggs're Lola's specialty; you haven't tasted an egg until you taste one of Lola's."

Who knows why certain events turn solid in your mind, and others melt away like warm butter? From that morning forward, whenever I played house, I patterned my imaginary kitchen after Miss Lola's, and I pictured my imaginary husband looking like Mr. Lucky, with strong, broad shoulders and pretty white teeth. And when I cooked imaginary eggs for my imaginary husband, they were as perfect as the ones warming in the beautiful chafing dishes in Miss Lola's sunny kitchen.

Makes 4 servings

12 large eggs (2–3 per serving), room temperature

½ cup half-and-half, room temperature

Salt and freshly ground black pepper, to taste

2 tablespoons unsalted butter, for frying

1. In a medium mixing bowl, slightly beat the eggs and then whisk in the half-and-half. Add the salt and black pepper and whisk until combined.

2. In a heavy skillet over medium heat, melt the butter. As soon the butter starts to foam, reduce the heat to medium–low and pour the egg mixture into the hot pan. As soon as the eggs begin to solidify on the bottom, scrape the bottom of the skillet and fold the eggs onto themselves. Continue scraping and folding until the eggs are cooked to suit your taste. Immediately remove the skillet from the heat and remove the eggs from the skillet.

3. Serve immediately on warmed plates.

Cheesy Scrambled Eggs

Miss Lola taught Mama all kinds of beautiful tatting knots—the Venus Love Knot, the Spanish Rose, the Sunburst, and the Pineapple Stitch, to name a few. Mama's handiwork started showing up all over the our house: stitched around the borders of her aprons, our kitchen curtains, face cloths, and the doilies that she threw on the backs of our chairs and love seats.

Mama didn't keep up with Miss Lola the way she kept up with her other girlfriends. I believe Miss Lola, as skilled in the old-fashioned domestic arts as she was, was too modern for Mama, who really was just an old-fashioned, red-lipstick-and-white-pearls kind of girl who thought it was ludicrous to openly share a man with a host of other women.

I can't tell you Miss Lola's whereabouts; we lost contact with her years ago. But long after I grew up, I heard that she was still living an unconventional life and keeping her relationship with Mr. Lucky open. Even though he'd settled down and married a quiet woman named Lucille, he still paid Miss Lola's bills and still dropped wads of paper money in her lap.

To add a luscious, rich twist to Miss Lola's Scrambled Eggs, add about 1⁄4 cup of freshly grated Cheddar cheese to the recipe when the eggs are about halfway done.

Old-Timey Brunch Chicken Salad

My Aunt Marjell is a bona fide brunch queen. Mama used to tell me, "The best cooks are women who enjoy feeding people as much as they enjoy entertaining them. You can taste it in the things they serve."

When I think of chicken salad, I think of old-fashioned sit-downs with girlfriends who come for talk and food. I think about women sitting together over card games and discussing books, wayward lovers, financial distresses, and divorces. This simple, old-fashioned chicken salad recipe graced many of the family brunches that the women in my family hosted. It has a touch of curry powder, a seasoning that my mother swore by. Of course, if you don't like its flavor, you can omit it.

Makes 4–6 servings

CHICKEN

Nonstick cooking spray, for greasing

1 whole chicken (3–3½ pounds)

Salt and freshly ground black pepper, to taste

Unsalted butter, room temperature

1 small onion, peeled and quartered

1 cup celery leaves

1 small clove garlic, peeled and finely sliced

1 dried bay leaf, broken in half

SALAD

Salt and freshly ground black pepper, to taste

2 teaspoons freshly squeezed lemon juice

½ teaspoon curry powder

⅓ cup mayonnaise, or more or less as desired

¼ cup half-and-half, cold

2–3 stalks celery, chopped

1 cup seedless green grapes, halved

1 cup toasted walnuts, roughly chopped

1 bunch chives, chopped

GARNISH

2 tablespoons freshly chopped parsley leaves

1. Preheat the oven to 350°F. Grease a rimmed baking sheet with the cooking spray and set aside.

2. *To make the chicken:* Empty its cavity and rinse the chicken inside and out. Dry it thoroughly with paper towels and trim off any excess fat around the cavity. Place the chicken, breast side up, on the prepared baking sheet and season it with the salt and black pepper. Rub the butter all over the chicken and stuff the cavity with the onion, celery leaves, and garlic. Place the broken bay leaf inside the cavity.

3. Bake for 45 minutes to 1 hour, until the chicken juices run clear and its skin is golden brown; a meat thermometer inserted into the inner thigh and not touching the bone should register around 160°F. Remove from the oven and set aside the baking sheet on a wire rack to cool completely.

4. *To make the chicken salad:* Strip the meat from the chicken carcass and discard the skin and bones. Dice the meat into bite-size pieces and place them in a large serving bowl.

5. Season the chicken with the salt and black pepper and evenly sprinkle it with the lemon juice and curry powder. Add the mayonnaise and half-and-half and gently stir until well combined. Gently fold in the celery, grapes, walnuts, and chives until just combined. Cover with plastic wrap and chill in the refrigerator for at least 1 hour.

6. Garnish with the parsley and serve cold.

Sausage, Egg, and Cheese Ring

When I set this pretty and delicious ring on the table, somebody always has the impression that I've been in the kitchen all day—cooking and sculpting it. Of course I haven't, but I don't tell them that. You know how some people are—they're gonna think what they want to think.

Makes 4–6 servings

1 egg yolk

1 teaspoon water

Nonstick cooking spray, for greasing

1 pound breakfast sausage

4 ounces cream cheese, room temperature, cut into ½-inch cubes

½ teaspoon garlic powder

½ teaspoon dried sage

½ teaspoon crushed fennel seeds

¼ teaspoon dried marjoram

Pinch freshly grated nutmeg

5 large eggs, room temperature

2 tablespoons whole milk, room temperature

Salt and freshly ground black pepper, to taste

4 tablespoons unsalted butter

1 (8-count) tube refrigerated crescent roll dough, separated

1 cup freshly grated Cheddar cheese

1. In a small mixing bowl, whisk together the egg yolk and water until they are well combined. Set aside.

2. Preheat the oven to 350°F. Grease a rimmed baking sheet with the cooking spray and line it with parchment paper. Set aside.

3. In a large mixing bowl, combine the sausage, cream cheese, garlic powder, sage, fennel, marjoram, and nutmeg and mix well.

4. Place a large, heavy skillet over medium-high heat. When the skillet is warm, add the sausage mixture. Cook, stirring constantly, until the sausage is cooked through. Remove from the heat. Using a large slotted spoon, transfer the mixture to a colander resting over a pan, allowing any grease to drain.

5. In a medium mixing bowl, whisk together the eggs and milk. Season with the salt and black pepper.

6. In a large, nonstick skillet over medium-low heat, warm the butter. Pour the egg mixture into the skillet. As soon as the eggs begin to solidify on the bottom, scrape the base of the skillet and fold the eggs onto themselves. Continue scraping and folding until the eggs are cooked to suit your taste. Immediately remove the skillet from the heat and remove the eggs from the skillet.

7. Place the pieces of crescent roll dough in a circular formation on the prepared baking sheet; their straight ends should be touching and their pointed ends should be aiming outward, like a star. Spoon an even portion of the sausage mixture on each crescent roll in the circle. Evenly sprinkle the cheese over the sausage mixture and evenly sprinkle the egg mixture over the cheese. Wrap the pointy ends of the crescents over the sausage, cheese, and eggs toward the center of the ring and fold in. Brush the tops of the crescent dough with the egg wash from step 1.

8. Bake for 20 to 25 minutes, until the crescent rolls are golden brown. Remove from the oven and set aside to cool in the pan on a wire rack for 5 minutes.

9. Using a wide spatula, loosen the ring from the baking sheet and slide it onto a cake pedestal. Serve hot.

Miss Ruby's Table-Talk White Bread

YEARS BEFORE I WAS BORN, A LADY NAMED RUBY BROWN RAN A boardinghouse for men around the corner from my grandmother's house. But even if you didn't know for a fact that Miss Ruby's was a place for men only, you'd know for sure as soon as you stepped inside her kitchen and caught a whiff of the heady aromas that had set into the fixtures—fried onions, minced garlic, and roasted bell peppers. As the story goes, Miss Ruby's cooking became so popular that as her male boarders got married off, the boardinghouse became a haven for single young women, who paid their rent with the money they earned by cooking meals for single men. They made so much food, in fact, that there was plenty left over.

My friend Sandra Moore once told me that she'd attended a B.B. King concert and the great bluesman had told a story about the best slice of apple pie that he'd ever eaten. He said that it had been baked by a Saginaw woman named Ruby, but he couldn't remember her last name. I told the story to my Aunt Marjell, who immediately said, "I bet he wasn't talkin' about nobody but Ruby Brown. Miss Ruby brought one of the best apple pies I've ever eaten to one of our Civitan meetings."

This recipe for Table-Talk White Bread came from Ruby Brown's recipe files. I absolutely love the smell of homemade bread—on a cold or rainy day, the intoxicating aroma pulls people into the house like a magnet. This bread is tender inside, has a lovely golden-brown crust outside, slices easily, and gives the kitchen a cozy scent.

Makes 1 9-inch × 5-inch × 3-inch loaf

2¼ teaspoons (1 ¼-ounce package) active dry yeast

¾ cup warm water (110°F–115°F)

1 tablespoon plus ⅛ teaspoon granulated sugar (divided)

½ cup warm whole milk (110°F–115°F)

2 tablespoons unsalted butter, melted and cooled

1 teaspoon salt

3–4 cups all-purpose flour, plus more for dusting

Vegetable oil, for greasing

1 large egg yolk, room temperature, mixed with 2 teaspoons water (optional)

1. In a large mixing bowl, slowly sprinkle the yeast over the warm water. Sprinkle ⅛ teaspoon of the granulated sugar over the yeast and stir until the mixture is well combined, the sugar dissolves, and the yeast becomes foamy. Add the milk, butter, remaining granulated sugar, and salt and stir until well combined.

2. Add 2 cups of the all-purpose flour to the large mixing bowl and stir until well combined. Continue adding the flour, ¼ cup at a time, until the mixture leaves the sides of the bowl and comes together to form a soft dough.

3. Turn out the dough onto a lightly floured work surface. Fold and press the dough for 5 minutes, until it becomes smooth and supple. (If needed, lightly dust flour over your work surface to keep the dough from sticking.) Form it into a smooth ball. Place the ball of dough in a well-greased bowl and turn it so all sides of the dough are greased. Cover with plastic wrap and set aside to rest and rise in a warm, draft-free place for 1½ hours, until the dough has doubled in size.

4. Grease a 9-inch × 5-inch × 3-inch loaf pan with the vegetable oil.

5. Remove the dough from the bowl, return it to the floured work surface, and gently punch it down. Fold and press the air out of the dough for 5 minutes. Shape the dough into a rectangle and place it into the prepared pan. Set aside to rest and rise again for 40 minutes.

6. Preheat the oven to 350°F.

7. Brush the top of the bread with the egg wash, if using. Bake for 35 to 45 minutes, until the bread is golden brown and sounds hollow when gently tapped. Remove from the oven and set aside to cool in the pan on a wire rack for 10 minutes.

8. Remove from the pan, slice, and serve.

COOKS' NOTE: *This bread is perfect for dipping into gravy, making sandwiches, and serving as plain old toast. It makes a lovely base for French toast as well.*

Miss Rose's Bacon Quiche

My father's mechanic friend, Gerry Horn, lived in the country and had a yard full of old cars and car parts. Daddy loved to tinker with old engines and carburetors and braking mechanisms, so to him, Mr. Gerry's yard was paradise. When we turned down Mr. Gerry's gravel road, Daddy would light up like a kid in a candy store.

Mr. Gerry's wife, Rose, was a retired elementary school teacher. I remember her talking to me in the tone of someone who had spent many years in the company of small children. She often asked me about my school life and wanted to know who my best friends and favorite teachers were. She talked to me about problem solving and life goals and assured me that in the scheme of things, school would last only a short time. She told me, "The early bird always gets the best twigs."

Like my mother, Miss Rose loved to knit, crochet, needlepoint, can fruits and vegetables, cook, and bake. Unlike Mr. Gerry and Daddy, Miss Rose wasn't gone on old cars and car parts, but she tolerated the car parts that littered her backyard. "The way I see it," she once told Mama, "there are worse things that a man can do." Miss Rose had been married much longer than my mother and had many sage observations.

Miss Rose's hospitality started the moment we pulled into the driveway. The Horns' house in the woods was a welcoming place, with wooden floors, a big fireplace, an old-fashioned butler's pantry stocked with mason jars full of Miss Rose's colorful canning, and a friendly cat named Pete. Everybody seemed happy there. While my father and Mr. Horn were engaged in car talk, Mama and Miss Rose entertained themselves at the kitchen table, drinking cups of hot coffee and exchanging needlepoint patterns and recipes. I have fond memories of sitting beside Mama on the long mahogany bench that ran the length of their table, enjoying Miss Rose's oven-baked delights and listening to Miss Rose's cautionary tales.

I am so glad that my mother got Rose Horn's quiche recipe. It's delicious and very easy to make, and it's a wonderful breakfast or brunch entrée to serve to company. This quiche goes well with most of the recipes in this book. Its crust recipe calls for a combination of butter and vegetable shortening. The butter gives the crust flavor, and the shortening gives it flakiness.

Makes 1 9-inch quiche (8 servings)

CRUST

1 cup all-purpose flour, plus more for rolling

¼ teaspoon salt

⅓ cup unsalted butter, cold, cut into ½-inch cubes

2 tablespoons vegetable shortening, cold

3–4 tablespoons ice water

1 (32-ounce) bag dried beans, for blind baking

FILLING

9 strips crisp cooked bacon, drained and crumbled

1 medium yellow onion, minced

1 (8-ounce) jar button or portobello mushrooms, drained, thinly sliced

1 cup freshly grated Cheddar cheese

¼ cup freshly grated sharp Colby cheese

1 teaspoon fresh thyme, chopped

Salt and freshly ground black pepper, to taste

1 cup whole milk, room temperature

4 large eggs, room temperature, lightly beaten

⅓ cup half-and-half, room temperature

⅛ teaspoon freshly grated nutmeg

1. *To make the crust:* In a medium mixing bowl, sift together the dry ingredients: the flour and salt. Using your fingers, a pastry blender, or the tines of a fork, cut the butter and shortening into the flour mixture until it resembles peas. Gently and very gradually sprinkle 3 tablespoons of the ice water into the dough and massage it in. The dough should hold together; if not, add more ice water, 1 teaspoon at a time. Gather the dough into a ball and pat it into a disk. Tightly wrap the disk in plastic wrap and refrigerate for at least 1 hour. (The disk will keep for 3 days in the refrigerator and up to 3 months in the freezer.)

2. Turn out the dough onto a floured work surface. Using a floured rolling pin, roll out the dough into a 12-inch-wide circle about ¼ inch thick. Fit the dough into a 9-inch pie plate and trim the excess edges from the plate, leaving enough to fold 1 inch of dough under itself. Flute the crust edges according to your preference and prick the bottom of the dough with the tines of a fork. Refrigerate for 15 minutes.

3. Preheat the oven to 375°F.

recipe continues

4. Remove the dough from the refrigerator. Fit a large piece of parchment paper on top of the dough and fill the pie plate with the dry beans. Bake for 10 minutes. Remove from the oven and remove the beans and parchment paper from the pie plate.

5. Return to the oven and bake for 10 minutes, until the crust is lightly golden. Remove from the oven. Set the crust aside on a wire rack to cool completely.

6. *To make the filling:* In a medium mixing bowl, combine the bacon, onion, mushrooms, Cheddar and Colby cheeses, and thyme. Season with the salt and black pepper and stir until well combined.

7. In a mixing bowl with a spout or a large measuring cup, combine the milk, eggs, half-and-half, and nutmeg and stir until well combined. Set aside.

8. Spread the bacon mixture evenly on the bottom of the cooled crust and evenly pour the milk mixture over it. Bake for 30 to 40 minutes, until the quiche is golden brown and a wooden toothpick inserted into the middle comes out almost clean (the quiche should have some jiggle to it). Remove from the oven and set aside on a wire rack to cool for 15 minutes.

9. Slice the quiche into 8 wedges and serve warm.

Pop's Angel Biscuits

Biscuits were a mainstay in my family. You'd think that by now I'd be used to the warm, comforting touch that they bring to a meal. I can't resist a good biscuit, especially when it's served hot from the oven. I like to slather mine with melted butter and homemade jam. When homemade biscuits are dressed that way, they give a table down-home charm.

My maternal grandfather, Pop, was known for his angelic biscuits—he had an incredibly gentle touch with the dough. I have fond memories of rushing to my grandparents' house to get a helping of my grandfather's light and feathery biscuits. He once told us, "In the old days, a plateful of biscuits graced all of my family's morning meals." Back then, they filled all of their biscuits with fresh butter and homemade jelly or sorghum molasses.

Makes 10–12 biscuits

- Nonstick cooking spray, for greasing
- 1 cup all-purpose flour, plus more for rolling
- 1 cup cake flour
- 2 teaspoons granulated sugar
- 2 teaspoons baking powder
- ½ teaspoon baking soda
- ½ teaspoon salt
- 3 tablespoons lard, vegetable shortening, or unsalted butter, cold
- ½–1 cup whole milk, very cold

1. Preheat the oven to 400°F. Lightly grease a baking sheet with the cooking spray and set aside.

2. In a large mixing bowl, sift together the dry ingredients: the all-purpose and cake flours, granulated sugar, baking powder, baking soda, and salt. Using your fingers, a pastry blender, or the tines of a fork, cut the lard into the flour mixture until it becomes coarse, like cornmeal.

recipe continues

3. While stirring constantly, add the milk, taking care to add just enough to moisten the flour. When a soft dough that pulls away from the sides of the bowl forms, it has reached the proper consistency. Gently knead the dough in the bowl 2 or 3 times.

4. Turn out the dough onto a lightly floured work surface. With floured hands, knead lightly for about 2 minutes, until the dough's surface is no longer damp. Form the dough into a ¼- or ½-inch-thick square.

5. Using a 2-inch round biscuit cutter, cut the dough into 10 to 12 circles. Place the dough circles on the prepared baking sheet about 1 inch apart.

6. Bake for 10 to 12 minutes, until the biscuits are golden brown. Remove from the oven and set aside to cool on the baking sheet for 5 minutes.

7. Transfer to a serving platter and serve warm.

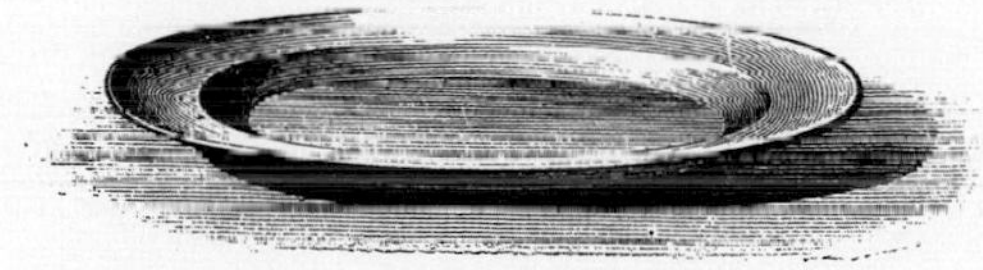

Acknowledgments

I AM SO THANKFUL for the environment that my parents, Ruth and M.C. Pinner, provided to me. It was filled with books, gardens, old tractors, dump trucks, girl talks with Mama, recipes, food preparation, and lessons in how to be properly perceived as a lady.

I am grateful to my aunts, Marjell, Helen, and Betty Jean, who have shared their recipes and cooking methods with me. Not long ago, I was planning a meal for someone I really wanted to impress. Aunt Marjell told me to bring the menu to her house while I ran some errands. When I returned, she had made everything on the list—she'd put together a delicious, old-fashioned supper that I didn't have the experience to prepare. She instructed me to warm the food when I saw his car pull up. Sure enough, my intended loved the food and devoured "my" cooking with relish. I think about that day often. What Aunt Marjell did for me that day was exactly what my mother would have done for me. I am still tickled by it and thankful for the kind of love she has for me.

I am also thankful for my cousins. They all love to cook. They all have their specialties, and I would be hard pressed to say who cooks the best. I especially thank my cousin Michelle, who never tires of food talk on the phone or in person.

I thank my cooking friends—Susan Howell, Cheri Dodge, Pamela Wyrick, Jocelyn Gordon, Edgina Foreman, and Sherry Hannah—for their recipes and cooking wisdom.

Perrin Davis, thank you for your patience and your editing, and for spearheading the effort to bring this beautiful cookbook to its finish. Thank you, so much, for all that you have done.

Thank you, Doug Seibold, for pairing me with such a wonderful editor.

Thank you, Cassandra Greenwald, my copyeditor, for your incredible cooking knowledge and wonderful help. Your cooking observations and queries are ones that I will use in my own cooking.

Thank you, Morgan Krehbiel, for designing a warm and beautiful cookbook around the recipes. Your design gives this lovely book so much homespun appeal.

Sally Ekus, thank you for everything.

Lisa Ekus, my agent, I thank you for being with me from the beginning. You have certainly changed my life.

Index

About the Author

PATTY PINNER is a home cook who lives in Saginaw, Michigan, with her son and grandchildren. Patty has written two prior cookbooks: *Sweets: Soul Food Desserts and Memories*, which the *New York Times* selected as one of its recommended cookbooks of the year, and *Sweety Pies: An Uncommon Collection of Womanish Observations, with Pie*. Selected recipes from *Sweety Pies* were featured in Oprah Winfrey's *O, The Oprah Magazine*. Patty's books have been nominated for International Association of Culinary Professionals and James Beard Foundation cookbook awards.

In Patty's own words, "Cooking relaxes me. Cooking gives me glory."

SKYSCRAPER STYLE

26. CHRYSLER BUILDING (overleaf)

A. The stainless steel on the cresting of this skyscraper of 1928-30 designed by William Van Alen is actually mounted on wooden forms (not visible) which were prepared in a shipyard.

SKYSCRAPER STYLE

Art Deco New York

CERVIN ROBINSON
ROSEMARIE HAAG BLETTER

New York OXFORD UNIVERSITY PRESS 1975

Library of Congress Catalogue Card Number: 74-22885
Printed in the United States of America

PREFACE

In the last quarter century architectural historians have turned their attention to a number of past periods ranging from Italian Renaissance to High Victorian, from Shingle Style to Art Nouveau. Subsequently Modern architects who read them have commendably aimed to adopt into their own discipline what seemed the strengths of some of these styles of the past, whether these were Renaissance modular principles or Victorian naturalism. At the same time there has always been some suspicion that architects, instead of adopting the principles, were still merely copying the surface appearances of styles. We might say therefore that this book is not intended as a pattern-book.

Its subject is precisely what, in the thirties, the proponents of the International Style were revolting against in America. It was this Beaux-Arts architecture of the skyscraper which then seemed, of all architectures, the one which least understood the direction in which the twentieth century should go. Ultimately the International Style did in some ways succeed in being the antithesis it meant to be; in others it now looks surprisingly to have been the same job done to a different and more successful sales pitch.

The authors might have chosen to show what seemed the best of Art Deco architecture throughout the U.S. If they had, the book would have been little more than an amused once-over-lightly. It aims instead to point to the intentions of the architects who practiced Art Deco as well as to the sources of the style and to illustrate the wealth of buildings that New York City, the epitome of the Art Deco metropolis, its Gotham, still possesses. The book does not say everything about architecture in New York between the wars; it will not have the last word on the style. It aims instead to be an introduction to the study of Art Deco architecture.

The authors' interest in the subject was first aroused in the sixties: one of us took a photograph in 1966 of three of the buildings this book deals with, a view from the roof of the Seagram Building which has long since been closed off by new construction. This picture appeared in *Architectural Forum* at the end of that year and appears here as the frontispiece to the first essay. The other author turned her attention to these New York buildings in 1968 while in the process of doing a research paper on Expressionism in American architecture as part of a doctoral program in the Columbia Art History Department. Thereafter, because of other commitments, we did not immediately pursue the subject. In the years that followed, some books and articles on Art Deco appeared. Most treated architecture tangentially—the exception being David Gebhard's work on the West Coast Moderne. We resumed our work on Art Deco architecture in 1971 when the John Simon Guggenheim Memorial Foundation gave a grant under which the pictures for the book could be taken.

The authors are indebted to others besides the Foundation for help of many kinds in the preparation of the book . . . above all to Alfred Frazer for suggesting it to us in the first place and especially to James F. O'Gorman and Edgar Kaufmann, Jr., who were kind enough to read the text at, respectively, an early and a late stage in its writing; also to Reyner Banham, Peter Blake, James Marston Fitch, Adolf K. Placzek, and G. E. Kidder Smith; to William H. Jordy, E. J. Kahn, Jr., Henry-Russell Hitchcock, George R. Collins, Philip C. Johnson, Rockwell K. DuMoulin, Kenneth Frampton, Wallace K. Harrison, Mrs. Liselotte Kahn, Herbert Lippmann, Robert Djerejian, George E. Thomas, and Ludwig Glaeser; to the following institutions and their staffs: first and foremost the Avery Architectural Library at Columbia —especially to Neville Thompson, the New York Public Library, the library of the New York Historical Society, the New York Chapter of the A.I.A., and the National Institute for Architectural Education; and finally to Sebastian Mazzola and his staff at the Plan Desk of the City Department of Buildings, whose records and help are always so valuable to research in Manhattan.

New York
October 1974

C. R.
R. H. B.

CONTENTS

SKYSCRAPER STYLE

BUILDINGS AND ARCHITECTS

Major sections of New York City—the financial district, the midtown area, Central Park West, and Washington Heights, not to speak of Ocean Parkway in Brooklyn and Grand Concourse in the Bronx—are studded with buildings done in a style which few have bothered to notice until recently. With the exception of a few examples like the News and McGraw-Hill buildings, which were considered just short of International Style, the Empire State because it was the world's tallest building, or Rockefeller Center because of its ambitious program, these structures, which had gone up in the late twenties and the thirties, had become pariahs of modern architecture. Seen in the light of the purist ethic of the Modern Movement, their gaudy efflorescence of color and ornament looked gauche. But in America of the late twenties and thirties Art Deco was the overwhelmingly prevailing modernism. The European International Style that had developed by the late thirties was not widely applied in America. Today, when we have had twenty years of the austere architecture ushered in by Skidmore, Owings & Merrill's Lever House, it may be refreshing to re-examine an architecture that aims to be popular, entertaining, and urbane.

The prevalent New York City architecture of the twenties and thirties also, in fact, reflects an international style, one that for a time was much more widely accepted than *the* International

Gotham: the spire of the Chrysler Building (William Van Alen, 1928-30), seen between the RCA Victor tower, left (Cross & Cross, 1930-31) and one of the towers of the Waldorf-Astoria, right (Schultze & Weaver, 1930-31).

Style. Images of some of these buildings, like the Waldorf-Astoria, the Chrysler and the RCA Victor buildings, or the Empire State, helped crystallize our image of Gotham, the city of skyscrapers and urban chic, without which such a film as *King Kong* would be difficult to imagine. The distinctive forms of the Chrysler and Empire State have assumed the familiar characteristics of landmarks, an associational value in which they will not easily be replaced by the twin shafts of the World Trade Center. Many of these buildings are well worth taking a second look at before they disappear from our rapidly changing cityscape. Smaller stores and restaurants have long since gone. But such larger projects too as the Ziegfeld Theater, the House of Detention for Women, and a series of pier buildings have gone in the last few years, and the McGraw-Hill Building awaits a somewhat uncertain future.

Art Deco appeared on the Main Streets of towns large and small in America, but it was first of all a style of the large cities. Used for a wide variety of urban building types, it was primarily a commercial style. It was thought by American architects, and with some justification, to be an international style and one in which, by the second half of the twenties, they had achieved pre-eminence because of their skyscrapers[1]—a building type much admired in Europe but not much built there until after World War II. In America there was some ambivalence about the skyscraper. If it was America's great achievement, it was also only justifiable in areas with the highest land values,[2] and the prime example of such an area was New York City.

There are several standards by which one can judge the impact of an architecture. One can look at its direct stylistic influence on subsequent architecture, as we have done with the International Style. If that is the standard, Art Deco has had (so far) just about no influence at all. Or one can look at its impact on the cities in which it occurs. Paris, for instance, has scarcely been affected by the buildings Le Corbusier built there in the twenties and thirties. Berlin was decisively affected by its early Modern buildings; Amsterdam more so. And the impact of Art Deco on New York City was greater still.

Architectural criticism can ask what intentions lie behind a building, and then (provided the intentions are not irresponsible) can ask to what extent they have been fulfilled. Stated most briefly, the occasion for Art Deco in New York City was a building boom that started in 1925 and lasted until 1931; and the intention of New York architects was to unite several separate ideas in the design of the skyscrapers called for in the boom years. The buildings they designed were marked by European decorative influences but were also affected by certain ideas from Chicago, by the theater, and by an image of a future New York that had long had popular currency. The career of this architecture was probably also determined by the fact that its journalism was weak. Finally, it was marked, and perhaps most significantly, by the training that New York architects had received.

Education

The Beaux-Arts educational system was criticized in the 1930s and after as an ingrown, Francophile system which put the handling of India ink on stretched paper above training in building and had its students designing the most useless of monumental buildings, and in styles of the past. But, however monumental these student projects were, the buildings involved were meant as public amenities; their grandeur was intended to be both accessible to the general public and comprehensible to it. These were qualities the Art Deco skyscrapers would have. Student projects were supposed to surmount simply utilitarian needs: "It is sometimes necessary," wrote John Harbeson in the twenties, "to add interest to a plan composed almost entirely of useful rooms; at such times one's ingenuity is given a real test."[3] As for style, architects trained under this system can sound downright hapless with regard to that. This is Raymond M. Hood (1881-1934, MIT, Ecole des Beaux-Arts[4]):

> My experience, which in reality consists of designing only two skyscrapers [the Tribune tower and the American Radiator Company building], does not justify my expressing an opinion as to whether a building should be treated vertically, horizontally or in cubist fashion. On the contrary, it has convinced me that on these matters I should not have a definite opinion. To use these two buildings as examples, they are both in the "vertical" style or what is called "Gothic," simply because I happened to make them so. If at the time of designing them I had been under the spell of Italian campaniles or Chinese pagodas, I suppose the resulting compositions would have been "horizontal." . . . Nothing but harm could result if at this stage in our development the free exercise of study and imagination should stop, and the standardizing and formulating of our meager knowledge and experience should now take its place.
>
> It might be proper to say something precise about the different styles, but I am as much in the air about style as I am about everything else.[5]

Perhaps the aspect of Beaux-Arts training that was of most significance to design in the late twenties and the thirties was the special order and manner in which student projects were done.

The student started with an *esquisse,* a sketch made at the beginning of a project in which he committed himself to a general form for his solution. "It is done in a short and fixed time, usually nine hours, and is made 'en loge.' This means literally 'in the box' or booth . . . the spirit of this requirement is that the student shall make his sketch without the aid of books or advice."[6] Then, "in the development of a problem, the elements indicated in the esquisse (rooms or open spaces in plan, motives in elevation), may be changed considerably in proportion, but no such elements may be left out, and none may be added."[7] Thus the most important decisions were made at the beginning of design and without any give and take among fellow students. The rest was filling in. The major student projects were organized as competitions at which students were not present to defend their drawings. In the atelier criticisms were eventually given, but were clearly one-sided affairs: "A man who is a good architectural critic is apt to be temperamental—most talented people are. A temperamental man is not always at his best—his moods fluctuate, and so does his efficiency, as his spirit is buoyant or depressed. . . . It is for this reason that it is well at the very beginning to form habits of preparing things for the critic with an eye to his comfort."[8] So the architect was taught to show his cards at the beginning of the game; and his training included neither collaboration nor verbal defense of his designs.

The original esquisse, if properly done, committed the student to a great deal, but the details were left purposely vague. This was not an architecture in which carefully thought out detail could be multiplied to make a whole. The esquisse approach presumably accounts furthermore for a lack of connection between the mass of some Art Deco buildings and their detail. It also explains how, once a French exposition, the 1925 Paris Exposition Internationale des Arts Décoratifs et Industriels Modernes, had signaled to French-trained and Francophile American architects that modernism was now acceptable in France, a variety of modern decorative influences could fall into place like the last piece that would complete the puzzle of the New York skyscraper style, Art Deco.

Design in the Early Twenties

The shape which New York buildings took once the boom started was influenced both by a design which the Finn Eliel Saarinen had submitted to a competition held in 1922 for a new

Eliel Saarinen, Chicago Tribune Building competition entry, 1922.

Chicago Tribune Building[9] and by a New York zoning ordinance passed in 1916 which required building setbacks. Saarinen's highly regarded entry was taken to be style-less and was thought in the twenties finally to have freed architects from what had seemed the inevitable alternatives in skyscraper design, Gothic solutions on the one hand and vertically stretched Classical ones on the other.[10] New York Art Deco skyscraper design started off on the Saarinen model, which was then repeatedly modified in response to the zoning law. This law required setbacks, which were to start at a height dependent on the width of the street, and allowed a tower of unlimited height on part of the building site; it was understood to encourage a certain shape of building: a ziggurat-crowned prism surmounted by a tower or two towers side by side. Architects had high hopes in the early twenties that it would transform their city desirably; but because of the law's complexity and because building activity did not pick up for some years after the war, the precise shape of things to come was uncertain even as late as 1924. As a result of interest in the law's ultimate effect there appeared in the architectural journals of the day a number of articles on the subject; at least seven were printed in the first half of the twenties.[11]

Of these the most interesting to the present-day reader is one published in 1923, which illustrated the results of a study by the firm of Helmle & Corbett of the building shape which the zoning law would encourage on a full New York City block.[12] The results were drawn in perspective by the professional renderer Hugh Ferriss (1889-1962, Washington University). In one rendering the maximum shape allowed by the law was shown, its tower rising into the clouds (Fig. 1). Then a series of modifications of this "envelope" were given, made with the exigencies of daylight (Fig. 2) and the realities of steel-frame construction (Fig. 3) and of rental (Fig. 4) in mind. A further rendering (not illustrated here) showed the final, logically arrived at shape given an "architectural" treatment by the application of columns to its base and crown (a treatment apparently not recommended by the architects but offered out of fair-mindedness). A final drawing showed how the Manhattan of the future would look when such buildings had been widely built.

This high hope of things to come from a zoning law is alien to us. Since World War II we have looked to the architect to be mostly in control of his work, though we know he may have to compromise here and there. In the twenties, however, circumstances seem to have been expected to play a larger role. An ar-

Figure 1

Figure 2

Figure 3

Figure 4

Helmle & Corbett, zoning envelope studies, renderings by Hugh Ferriss.

chitect would apologize for the top of his building because he had rushed in the design of it: "When the 17th story masonry work was being built, we were still studying the top of the building at ½″ scale. I merely insert this to ask for a little indulgence on the part of people who might otherwise be inclined to be very critical of the result."[13] Or a critic would say that the top of a building had been improvised at the last moment when considerable evidence was available that this was simply not so.[14] Design both then and now may well in reality be made up of a similar mixture of intention and compromise; but it was certainly considered to be more at the mercy of circumstance then.[15]

One reason for this feeling that events were out of control was a radical change in architectural practice. Architects trained to build monumental buildings such as theaters, embassies, and city halls, found themselves in the second half of the twenties in the midst of a commercial building boom which required maximum rental space and immediate return on investment. In 1927 Edwin Avery Park wrote:

> If the question be asked "What is architecture in this country today?" one can only answer it is not what it once was. It certainly is not what it was, say ten years ago. Times have changed and many architects heave sighs. There is no more fun in the game. . . . The architect might as well never have wasted his time learning to design. His job is now that of financial engineer, his time spent in cutting, scraping and shoe-horning, trying to produce something, without time to worry too much over how the thing will look. . . . Art and architecture no longer function upon a basis of patronage. Architecture is competing in the great modern struggle to survive through fitness.[16]

The steel structure of the buildings put up in the late twenties and early thirties was accepted as something given. But finding the proper form of cladding for a skeleton frame was felt to be a major task. For this architects turned to a source of design outside architecture and to a theory. The first was stage design, which in the twenties had an importance that now, when both television and set-less motion pictures compete with theater, it no longer has. The theory, a German one that the forms for the parts of a building should be derived from the parts of original, that is, primitive buildings (in particular, that the proper form for a wall was that of a woven mat), presumably came to New York architects by way of Chicago, along with the skeleton frame.[17] In New York Art Deco, forms taken directly from the theater appear in lobbies and at building entrances, or the lower floors of high buildings are given forms like painted sets facing onto the street. On other buildings the cladding of steel frames is given a fabric pattern or a woven form, or in some cases looks explicitly like hanging curtains. The designer and writer Paul T. Frankl (1887-1958) referred to such walls as "brick tapestries hung from the sky."[18] In a number of ways the Art Deco had the characteristic of being an architecture of "both-and." Decorative forms, for instance, might be both primitive and modern or both traditional and exotic. The top of a building could be both pagoda-form and a frozen fountain,[19] and the architecture would thereby seem either the richer in meaning, or the more imprecise in intention.

When twenties architects considered dealing with sections of the city larger than single buildings, the ideal of a city with multilevel traffic arteries appealed to them. A multilevel solution to the city's traffic problems was proposed in 1923 to the Regional Plan Association by a committee chaired by Harvey Wiley Corbett (1873-1954, University of California, Ecole des Beaux-Arts). Pedestrians were to pass through shopping arcades at the second-story level of the city's buildings. These arcades were to be connected by bridges crossing the roadways between. Automobile traffic would be at ground level; parking might cover the whole of the area under the city's buildings if that proved necessary. Underpasses were to occur at major intersections, and rail traffic would be underground. Though such visions as this had a popular ancestry in the frontispieces to Moses King's *Views of New York* published before the First World War, the committee's image, it claimed in its report, was that of Venice:

> From an architectural viewpoint and regard to form, decoration, and proportion, the idea presents all the loveliness, and more, of Venice. . . . Venice is the adaptation of a city to the necessities of the terrain on which it is built. The New York of the future will be an adaptation of the metropolis to the needs of traffic, freeing the city from the unsightly congestion and turmoil of the present. Pedestrians will move about through the arcaded streets, out of danger from traffic, protected from the snows of winter and the glare of the summer sun. Walking would become a pastime. . . . Shopping would be a joy.[20]

Fragments of this multilevel image appeared in several Art Deco buildings. The most ambitious attempts to realize it were made in studies for Rockefeller Center, but it did not appear in the complex as built.

A final ingredient of Art Deco is suggested by a restoration of King Solomon's Temple and Citadel which Helmle & Corbett drew up about 1925. A full-scale replica was to be built at the 1926 Sesquicentennial Exhibition in Philadelphia, where the public was to be able to rub elbows with employees dressed as ancient Israelites and later, having left the buildings, was to see them go up in simulated flames. This construction was apparently never built. Who was to have paid for it if it had been or what it was to have advertised, if anything, we are not told. The image is clear, though—an eye-boggling and exotic (yet educational) environment open to the public. The project strikes us as tawdry, but its character was to be an element in the Art Deco buildings to come. By a slight shift of locale it could evoke the images of Babel and Babylon that were associated with the New York skyscraper. Enough was thought of it for it to be published in *Pencil Points;*[21] it was sent to an exhibition of American work held in Berlin at the beginning of 1926; and Corbett lectured on it a year or two later.

In 1925 there was, quite apart from the Paris Exposition, increasing contact with the foreign architectural world, and the building boom began. The number of new office buildings built in 1925—fifteen—was not matched in any year after World War II till 1957. The number built in 1926, thirty, has not been matched since.[22] At the end of 1925 American architects put together an exhibition of their work and of America's architectural past for the Berlin Akademie der Künste.[23] In some respects this exhibition was made up of the sort of material that might be buried in a time capsule. It did, however, sum up what seemed significant in the work of the early twenties. Among New York efforts (which were selected by Harvey Wiley Corbett and Alfred Bossom [1881-1965], an English architect working in New York at the time) the show included the studies of the zoning envelope and of the multilevel traffic solution as well as of Solomon's Temple. In a selection of current New York buildings two were Art Deco, one virtually complete and the other a project. The first was McKenzie, Voorhees & Gmelin's Barclay-Vesey Building. The second was described as a "new building for an insurance company" by Buchman & Kahn. This was clearly their Insurance Center Building for 80 John Street.

Art Deco Beginnings

Construction of the Barclay-Vesey Building (1) had begun in 1923. Brickwork was started in 1924. In the summer of 1925 the editor of *The American Architect* wrote one of the architects, Stephen Voorhees (1878-1965, Princeton), that it was the finest modern building in America. It opened early in 1926 as an equipment and administrative center for the New York Tele-

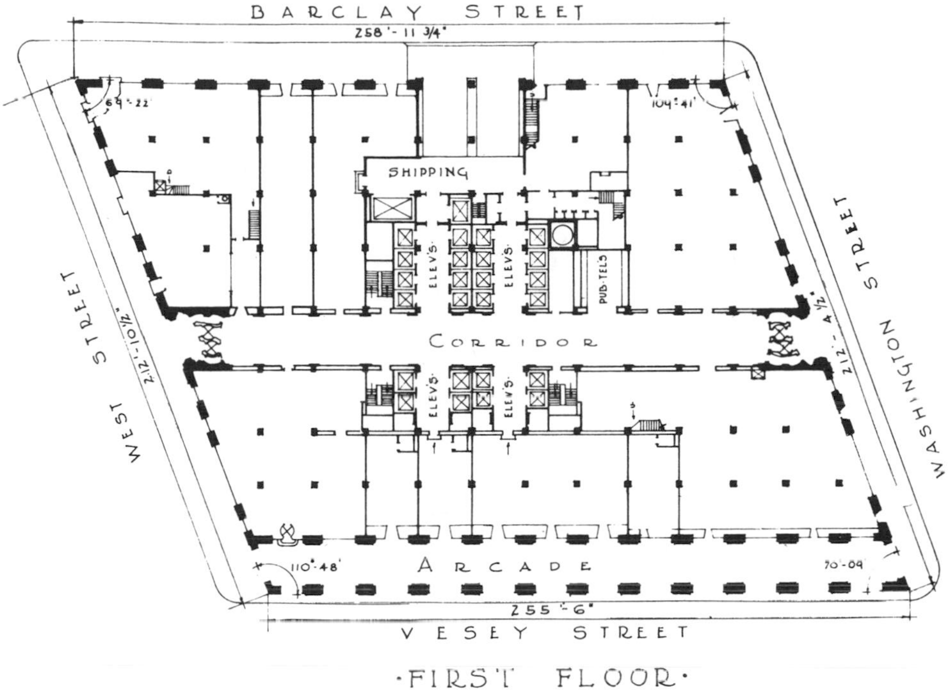

McKenzie, Voorhees & Gmelin, Barclay-Vesey Building, 1923-26, plan.

phone Company. The general form of the building had been determined by the zoning ordinance; its height was that at which the cost of space in the building met the market value of such space elsewhere in the city, a suitably hard-nosed criterion.[24] The tower of the building was on the model of Saarinen's Tribune entry and was treated with buttresses (1A). On the exterior of the building decoration in the form of fruit, animals, and human figures appears in low relief (1B). This ornament was said by some to be descriptive of the products formerly sold on the site, where there had been a produce market, and was also said to be "derived from marine sources, suggesting the proximity of the sea and maritime commerce."[25] The presence of aborigines and elephants among the fruit was not explained. Fruit continues on the lobby walls (1D). The elevator doors are demonstrably handcrafted (1E). Lewis Mumford wrote that "the main hall . . . is as gaily lighted and decorated as a village street in a strawberry festival."[26]

At street level on the south side is an arcade within which the sidewalk passes (1C and plan) and onto which shops were intended to open. Because the Barclay-Vesey was some distance from other office buildings at the southern tip of Manhattan, this covered way seems never to have had much success as a shopping arcade. But it was built as a compromise solution to the city's plan

Buchman & Kahn, Insurance Center Building, 1926-27 (photograph of model).

to widen Vesey Street here,[27] and it seems to have been the first appearance of an element of the multilevel traffic plan.

The designer of the Barclay-Vesey Building, Ralph Walker (1889-1973, MIT), had clearly committed himself to most of this before the 1925 Exposition took place. But the executive floor may have been affected by that event. The anteroom there has a cornice which, though as foliate as the lobby below, in being faceted seems to derive from German Expressionist sources (1G). What this cornice may be is a first sign that, because of the 1925 show, modern styles were becoming acceptable. "Trivial reminiscences of the Gothic have fallen away," wrote Fiske Kimball, "puerile suggestions of historic style no longer mar the interior. As in the best German work, all is smelted anew in the creative spirit."[28] McKenzie, Voorhees & Gmelin should have been the more accessible to German ideas in that one partner, Paul Gmelin (1859-1937), was German born and trained. The boardroom is paneled. Between the panels decorative tree trunks seem to rise to a foliate cornice and to a similar grill above the door (1F). Today we are prepared to think of a boardroom as something of a jungle; evidently in the twenties its occupants, and Ralph Walker too, considered it something closer to Adam's hut in Paradise.

Construction on the second Art Deco building exhibited in Berlin, the Insurance Center Building, was not to start until March 1926. It was represented by a rendering, it seems, and by a photograph of a model. These show a clean-lined setback office building. Raised vertical lines at the setbacks help it to avoid successfully the appearance of a stack of boxes. What is not quite apparent, at least in the photograph of the model, is the character of the decoration towards the bottom of the building. A form of zigzag band occurs there which was repeated frequently in the Art Deco architecture to come (3). Like the cornice in the Barclay-Vesey anteroom, it may not have come directly from a particular building at the Paris Exposition; such forms can have been available from a number of sources. Ely Jacques Kahn, the architect of the building, wrote much later of the Furniture Exchange Building, built in 1926, that in designin its cornice he had "had in mind the texture of fabric."[29] But another possible source for such zigzags could have been the work of Adolfo Best-Maugard, a Mexican artist who had exhibited and lectured in New York and who brought out a book on design in 1923[30] (an English translation was published by Knopf in 1927[31]). Such designs as Best-Maugard's, if they were of in-

Buchman & Kahn, Furniture Exchange Building, 1926, detail.

fluence, would have had the appeal of being both primitive and modern.

In 1926 too forms that clearly had come from Paris appeared on the Lowell, an apartment house on East 63rd Street by Henry C. Churchill (1893-1962, Cornell) and Herbert Lippmann (b. 1889, Columbia). It exhibited a number of the characteristics of the Art Deco architecture that would develop. One was the quality of being almost a stage set carefully related to the street onto which the building faced. Others were the use of handicrafts and of color. The building, otherwise brick-clad, was faced on its ground-floor street front with glazed terra-cotta. The façade was in a modernized Classical form, in color, and for the most part in two dimensions. In only a few places, as in a form of pediment over the main doorway and in some pilasters, did it swell from the wall (4*). A contemporary reviewer wrote: "It is not by accident that the façade gives the momentary impression of being a back-drop, but rather an intentional declaration that the architects believe a façade can be more successfully painted, so to speak, on a building than modelled on one. . . ."[32] The façade is perhaps also characteristic in incorporating the entrance to a restaurant which the building contained, emphasizing the building's multiple purpose. The metalwork for the lamps at either side of the main doorway was done by Walter von Nessen; the mosaic above was designed by Bertram Hartman and executed by the Ravenna Mosaic Company. Gates had been made for the restaurant by Edgar Brandt and metal doors for the building by his New York company, Ferrobrandt. This was clearly a craft-oriented modernism. The year before, Ferrobrandt, under Jules Bouy, had made wrought-iron gates that could have come directly from Paris for the Cheney Brothers Silk Store designed by Howard Greenley (2A and B). Here a screen at the entrance to the building itself (the Madison-Belmont of Warren & Wetmore) was also done by Ferrobrandt (2C).

The Insurance Center, the Barclay-Vesey, and the Lowell suggest three courses which New York Art Deco architecture was to take. The first building had walls composed of woven patterns in terra-cotta; the firm of Buchman & Kahn, which designed the Insurance Center, put up a series of buildings with more explicitly woven forms in color in the following years. The second was a massive building with crag-like forms and brick walls which (to viewers of the time) were especially appropriate to the steel-framed building—they were "veneers of thin wall hung over skeleton frames";[33] the firm that designed the telephone company building made a house style of this type of volume hung with walls that became ever more explicitly hung in folds. The third was a building the facing of whose lower floors had the character of a stage set carefully related to the street.

Kahn and Others

Ely Jacques Kahn (1884-1972, Columbia, Ecole des Beaux-Arts) was the son of an Austrian-born importer of glass and mirrors; his elder sister Rena Rosenthal was, in the twenties, an importer of European arts and crafts. In 1915 Kahn joined a firm, previously Buchman & Fox, that had long specialized in commercial

* Buildings illustrated in the separate color section are marked with an asterisk in the list of buildings which starts on page 83.

buildings. By the middle twenties Kahn was doing a series of large, soundly designed[34] commercial buildings in the city, for which he had developed a vigorous, personal style of decoration. For a time in 1927 and 1928 they appear with woven forms in brightly colored terra-cotta on their walls. The masterpiece was his office building at the bottom of Park Avenue (6A). The color there, which appeared on the setbacks, was meant to be seen from the surrounding streets as the building's only exterior decoration. This colored terra-cotta was designed with the help of Leon Victor Solon (1872-?), an English-born artist and architectural writer. Solon had written on the colors used in classical antiquity;[35] and those on the Park Avenue Building were intended to reproduce the Greek primaries.[36] Its owners showed some qualms about this use of color on an exterior and, according to Kahn, Raymond Hood was brought in to reassure them that what was being proposed was good. Colored terra-cotta was also used on two other buildings, one on West 39th Street of 1927 (7) and the other at 261 Fifth Avenue of 1928-29 (21A). Eventually exterior color was used less by Kahn. However, he continued to use painted plaster, brass, and brightly colored mosaics in building lobbies whose lines suggest the headlong flow of the citizens of Gotham to and from their work (21B, 24). Kahn put up over thirty buildings in the seven years from 1925 to 1931.[37] Many were in the garment district south of Times Square (16, 80, 81). Some were in the printing district east of Grand Central Station, and some were insurance buildings northeast of Wall Street. One was for the film industry (24A and B). Only the Squibb Building (40) was what could be called a skyscraper. A reason for the consistent quality of Kahn's work, despite the variety of purposes for which these buildings were built, was that many of them were designed for two real estate promoters, Abe Abelson and Louis Adler,[38] who apparently recognized the soundness of the buildings Kahn was doing, while imposing few preconceptions on him as to what the appearance of buildings should be.

The firm of McKenzie, Voorhees & Gmelin, which after the completion of the Barclay-Vesey Building became Voorhees, Gmelin & Walker, also did a great many buildings for one client, the telephone company. They put up a series of buildings throughout the city in the late twenties, many with curtain-like brick walls and faceted lintels and copings (44, 45, 46). But their work was not confined to the telephone company. In 1928-30 they did a headquarters for Western Union with shaded orange

Joseph Urban, Ziegfeld Theater, 1926-27.

brick walls (27A and B). The entrances to the Western Union Building are in proscenium form and contain curtain-like screens in glass and bronze. In 1929-30 Voorhees, Gmelin & Walker did a headquarters for the Salvation Army (36A) incorporating an office tower, a women's dormitory, and a temple, again in massive volumes hung with brick and stone in the manner of curtains. Within the theater-like temple (36B) the faceted ceiling is cut out in willow patterns to overcome any illusion of weight. The walls of a building at the corner of Wall Street and Broadway built for Irving Trust in 1929-32 were even more explicitly curtain-like (54B and C). The interiors of a main banking room on the ground floor (54D) and of a lounge at the top of the building (54H) are faceted spaces. Such spaces seemed (to other architects as well as to Voorhees, Gmelin & Walker) the appropriate form for the destination of the hurrying citizens of the city.

The stage-set character of Art Deco buildings was demonstrated at its most explicit in the Ziegfeld Theater by the Austrian born and trained designer Joseph Urban (1872-1933). Urban, who was older than most of the New York Art Deco architects, had first come to this country in connection with the Austrian exhibit at the 1904 Louisiana Purchase Exposition in St. Louis and had returned to America to stay in 1911. By the twenties he had a reputation as a versatile designer of interiors and of stage sets for Boston and New York opera companies as well as for Ziegfeld productions. He showed an assurance in his designs that his younger colleagues lacked, and his buildings seem less enamored of a skyscraper formula than do others. His Ziegfeld Theater was striking in terms of our concern in having a façade in the form of a proscenium reflecting the real proscenium within (though not its particular form). This façade was described at the time as "a brilliant attempt to bring the stage in stone onto the street."[39]

Skyscrapers

In the twenties the archetypical modern American building was the skyscraper. The first real skyscraper to be started in the twenties was the Chanin Building of Sloan & Robertson begun in 1927.[40] (One of the last skyscrapers of the boom was to be the Empire State; the briefness of the period in which most of the Art Deco buildings were built is underlined by the fact that construction began on the Empire State six days after completion of the Chanin). As had been the case with the Barclay-Vesey and with the first skyscraper apartment building, the Panhellenic tower (see below), the Chanin's point of departure was Saarinen's Tribune entry (its top is to the left in color plate 57). It shared with other New York Art Deco buildings a carefully developed relationship to the street (9A and B), and its architects were clearly concerned that interiors have a popular and educative character rather than being simply useful. It also enjoyed a

William Van Alen, building on the northeast corner of Seventh Avenue and 33rd Street.

limited realization of the multilevel ideal. The lobby contained shops and restaurants; in the basement was a Baltimore and Ohio Railroad Motor Coach depot (accessible to buses by an entrance on the south side of the building).[41] From the basement too there was access to the Grand Central subway station. On the fiftieth floor, high above, there was a theater,[42] and above that an executive office level for the Chanin brothers, whose construction firm had put the building up, and an observation deck. The street level lobby in marble and brass was designed to offer the casual visitor as rich and eventful a welcome as would a movie palace of the period (9C, D, and E). The decorations in the lobby by René Chambellan (1893-1955) reportedly tell "symbolically . . . the story of a city in which it is possible for a man to rise from humble station to wealth and influence by the sheer power of his mind and hands"[43] (9C). A visitor to the Chanin organization was met by wrought-iron gates whose themes were energy, apparently, and machinery, art and money (9F). All of this was optimistic, instructive, and crafted—an impressive amenity accessible to the public.

From a hostile viewpoint the nadir of Art Deco design was probably the Chrysler Building. In 1928 announcement was made of the impending construction of a Reynolds Building designed by William Van Alen (1882-1954, Pratt, Paris Prize[44]). This was to be "surmounted by a glass dome, which, when lighted from within, will give the effect of a great jewelled sphere."[45] Before construction started, the lease on the site (from Cooper Union) and the plans were sold to Walter Chrysler. The plans were then somewhat modified—the building was lowered and its crowning motif changed. It was constructed in 1928-30. In the early years of the decade Van Alen had done a number of steel-framed buildings, many of them for Child's Restaurants, whose use of clearly nonstructural, though masonry, curtain walls and window frames set virtually at the surface of the wall was designed to express the nature of their construction.[46] In several store designs he had earned a reputation for doing the startling and dramatic thing.[47] If that was what was expected of him, his Chrysler did not disappoint. Proscenium-like entrances hold glass and metal screens lit from behind and decorated with fabric patterns (26H and I). Inside, within the triangular concourse (see plan), coved lighting over exits and elevator lobbies appears in the form of raised curtains (26J). "And as it is a commercial proposition, embodying the emblazonment of automotive progress," wrote the architect and critic Kenneth Murchison (1872-1938, Columbia, Ecole des Beaux-Arts) of the completed building, "why should the architect have hesitated a moment in being the Ziegfeld of his profession. . . ?"[48] In the basement there are shops, and connection was made with the IRT subway system, one which the subway company itself vigorously but unavailingly opposed. The exterior walls above the lowest floors have what was described at the time as the form of a basket-weave (26G).[49] Higher up, at the base of the tower, the building is pinched out at its corners (at a level which includes a decorative frieze of automobile hub caps and mudguards) in an attempt to overcome an optical illusion in which buildings that had horizontally banded towers seemed broader at their tops than at their bases[50] (26F). Within the crowning motif of the building was a luncheon club, whose main dining room had a German Expressionist character (26N). Still higher, above the club's gymnasia, there was originally an observation level, also Expressionist in character, where Walter Chrysler's original handmade tools (now in Detroit) were on display—again the educative touch.

The first apartment skyscraper was John Mead Howells' Panhellenic tower designed on the model of Saarinen's Tribune Tower project[51] and built off 49th Street near the East River in

William Van Alen, Chrysler Building, 1928-30, plan.

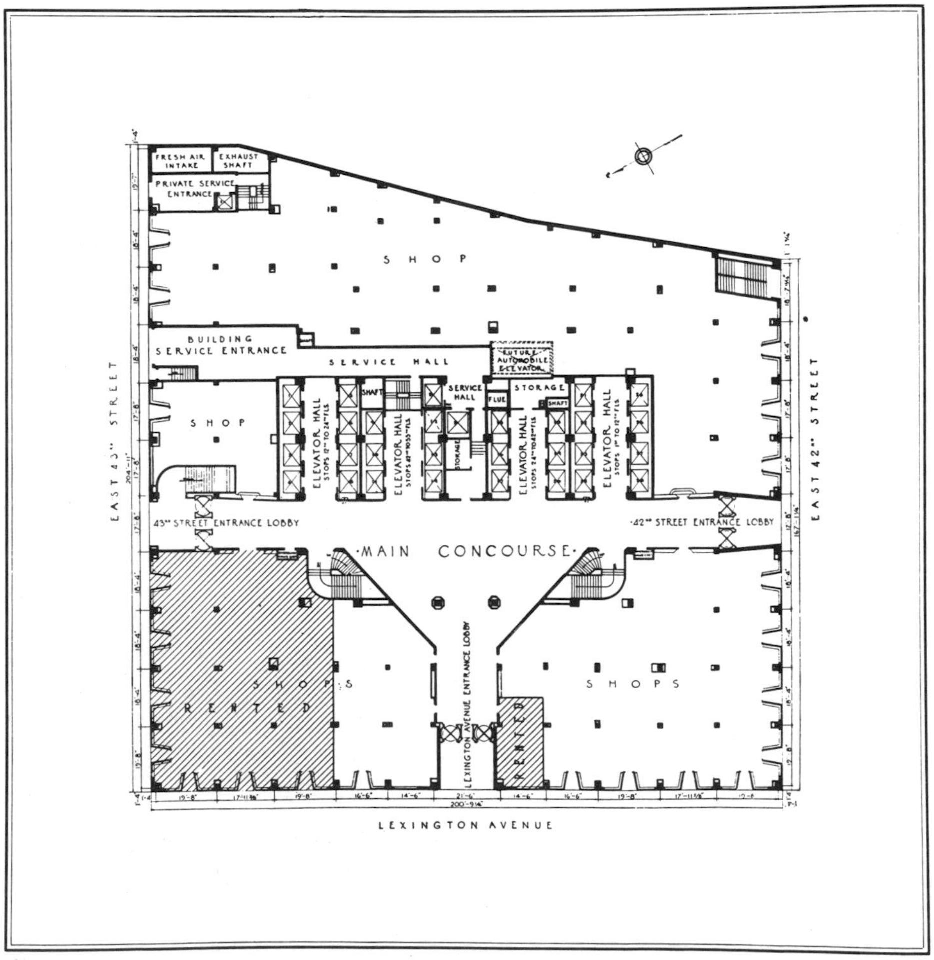

FIRST FLOOR PLAN

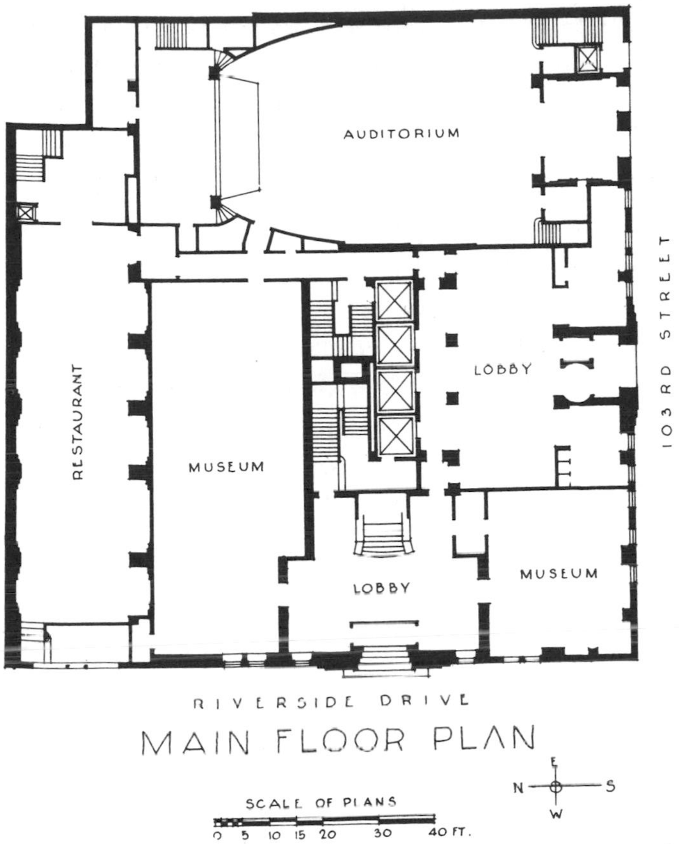

Helmle, Corbett & Harrison and Sugarman & Berger, Master Building, 1928-29, plan.

1927 (8). In 1928-29 a skyscraper apartment hotel was built on Riverside Drive to designs of Helmle, Corbett & Harrison and Sugarman & Berger (19A and B). It incorporated a museum for the Russian painter and theatrical designer Nicholas Roerich, studio space and an auditorium for the Master Institute of United Arts, and a restaurant (see plan). The building struck its architects as remarkable because it used shaded brick, starting with deep purple at the base of the building and rising to light grey at the top.[52] This shading was an optical device, used on a number of Art Deco buildings, which was said to make a building look taller and to give a viewer the illusion of sunlight even on an overcast day.[53] The Riverside Museum was designed to be artificially lit—such lighting was an innovation at the time. It also seems remarkable now that the Master Institute included among its faculty and lecturers Alfred Bossom, Claude Bragdon, Norman Bel Geddes, Robert Edmund Jones, Lee Simonson, and Adolfo Best-Maugard,[54] all of whom seem to have had significant though

Howells & Hood, 3 East 84th Street, 1928, rendered by Donald Douglas.

oblique impact on New York architectural design in the twenties.

From 1928 on there arose on Central Park West a series of large apartment houses, seven in all, which still make of that avenue a showplace for Art Deco. Of these the most interesting, in some ways, are the three designed by Schwartz & Gross (20, 64, 66), each with its distinctive ground-floor and crowning motifs. Throughout the late twenties and early thirties Art Deco was being applied too to an ever greater range of building types. In the Stewart & Company building of 1928-30 (25) designed by Warren & Wetmore (altered by Ely Kahn for Bonwit Teller) and in Starrett & Van Vleck's Bloomingdale's addition of 1930 (56) it was applied to the department store. A skyscraper garage was built in 1929-30, the Kent Columbus Circle Garage (43) by Jardine, Hill & Murdock; and there was a stock exchange façade in 1930, the Curb Exchange of Starrett & Van Vleck (59). Louis Allen Abramson and F. P. Platt & Brother designed a number of buildings for the Horn & Hardart chain of automated restaurants (29, 69, 70). There was also an Art Deco prison, the House of Detention for Women (55), 1929-32, by Sloan & Robertson, and an Art Deco church, the Fourth Church of Christ Scientist, 1931-32 (93), by Cherry & Matz.

Hood

An architect who built few buildings—some four Art Deco ones[55]—but who was as highly regarded as any New York architect of the twenties was Raymond Hood. In 1928 a small apartment house was put up to his designs on East 84th Street just off Fifth Avenue (14). On it appeared for the first time the recessed metal spandrels between vertical masonry strips (the spandrels derived ultimately from Sullivan's) that were to become a standard feature of many Art Deco skyscrapers. As this building was rendered for publication, it was represented as modern (an automobile is seen being unloaded in the foreground), but its stone facing is depicted as time-worn.[56] A desirable permanence seems thereby to have been suggested. Hood himself thought in longer time spans than we would consider practical. "The skyscraper problem is new," he wrote, "we have practically no traditions and, after all, serious architectural study is a new thing in this country; so it is fortunate that up to the present no one has formulated too strict a set of rules for our guidance. Another hundred years may, of course, change this. . . ."[57]

By designing the News Building of 1929-30 in a form ap-

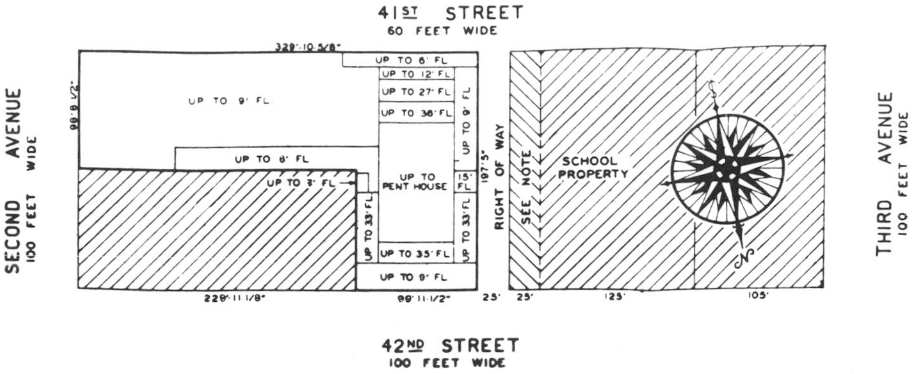

DIAGRAM OF AIR AND LIGHT CONDITIONS AT VARIOUS FLOORS

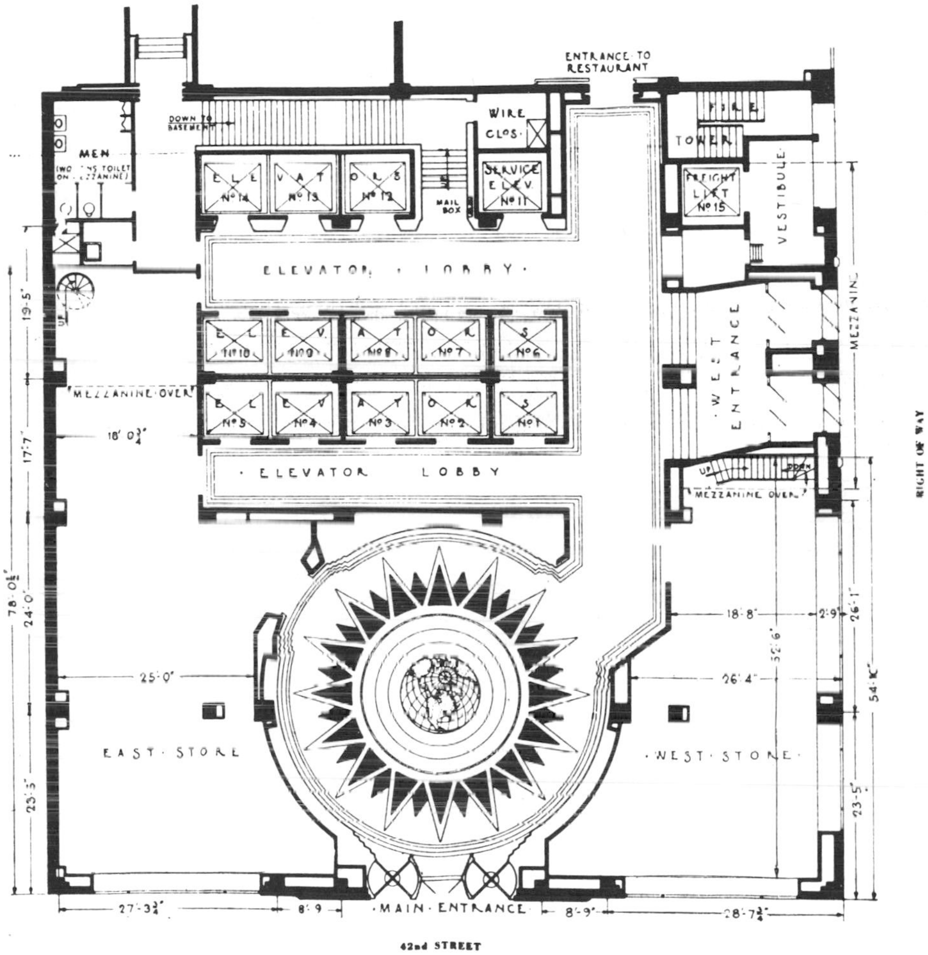

PLAN OF FIRST FLOOR

Howells & Hood, News Building, 1929-30, plans.

proaching that of a slab, Hood escaped the skyscraper formula of a prism with setbacks and a tower above. No sharp distinction was made between tower and base (35). Critics have considered this and Hood's McGraw-Hill Building (82) as International Style. But the News at its base is enriched with decorative bronze (35A and D). In its lobby (see plan) a globe revolves below a faceted ceiling of black glass (35F). The intention was in no way International Style. Hood's purpose in striping the exterior of the building (35B and C) was the same as his purpose in making his earlier American Radiator Building black—to hide the windows. "A wall that pretends to be a wall hates to be shot full of holes," as Edwin Avery Park paraphrased his thought.[58] In the McGraw-Hill Building of 1929-30 Hood turned to a machine aesthetic in the streamlined lobby and ground-floor exterior (82A). Yet his surfacing material for the building above was the colored craft material, terra-cotta, of the first Art Deco buildings.[59] Hood's final achievement was at Rockefeller Center, where it can be assumed that the slab of the RCA Building (90A) owes its form to Hood and to his News Building. It should be noted that at the Center the design is rationalized. Just as the crowning gesture of the Chrysler Building (26D) became transformed on the Empire State Building, 1930-31, of Shreve, Lamb & Harmon,[60] (76) to the symbolically functionalist form of a dirigible mooring mast, so the form of Hood's slab at Rockefeller Center follows function, as it were. All office space in the slab is to be no more than approximately twenty-seven feet from a window, and so the building is sculpted back as banks of elevators fall off.

The Center succeeds especially well at reaching some of the goals it shared with previous Art Deco buildings. The relation of the Fifth Avenue buildings of the Center, with the RCA Building behind them, to the avenue itself is especially successful (97, 102, 103). The Center, with its shops, arcades,[61] restaurants, theaters, skating rink, and tours, is accessible and popular as none of our postwar office buildings on their aloof plazas have, it is true, even aimed to be. Understandably, because of the length of time over which it was designed and built, the Center has one foot in the earlier craft-oriented Art Deco and another in the machine-oriented later phase. Though the Center retained the crafted metal spandrels of the earlier buildings (90C), it otherwise made an uncertain shift from the craft to the machine aesthetic. In the process, the work of artists who were employed to embellish the Center, work no longer satisfactorily a part of the architecture, became less than adequate as art standing on its own.

Much has been written about the process by which Rockefeller Center was designed by the group of architects involved: Benjamin Wistar Morris, Reinhard & Hofmeister, Corbett, Harrison & MacMurray, and Hood, Godley & Fouilhoux.[62] Arcades, elevated walkways, and pedestrian bridges played a part in a variety of early schemes, but they were lost in the Center as built. The individual architects, starting from scratch, as with a Beaux-Arts design problem, could devise radically varied designs for the Center.[63] But there is an inescapable similarity between the Center as eventually built and a major early solution by Benjamin Wistar Morris and Reinhard & Hofmeister at a time when the centerpiece of the whole was still to be a Metropolitan Opera House.[64] In both, a promenade splitting the central block leads to a plaza in front of the principal building. In collaboration, the architects—perhaps because collaboration in the first, crucial stage of design had not been part of their training—could at best only develop a solution already decided on, that is, develop another man's esquisse. A description of the Associated Architects' office procedure points only to efficiency at getting plans out as needed rather than to getting the best from each designer.[65] It is as though the Center were both the greatest achievement of Art Deco and the Waterloo of the Beaux-Arts architect.

Elsewhere Art Deco became in these years of the Depression the style of neighborhood movie house remodelings, of block after block of small apartment houses in the Bronx, and of government buildings like Cross & Cross's Federal Building (101). It was the style of the Kress's (106), Grant's and Woolworth's on New York's main street just as it was their style on the Main Streets of hundreds of other towns in a slump. In 1939, Harvey Wiley Corbett was at last able to realize his dream of Solomon's Temple when he designed New York's Criminal Courts Building, the Tombs (112). But by this time those who took their architecture seriously had long since turned their attention to the International Style.

Journalism

At its start New York Art Deco had a good press. Lewis Mumford said that the Barclay-Vesey Building (apart from its "strawberry festival" ornament) was "clear and logical, inflexibly committed to its programme."[66] Of Ely Kahn's Park Avenue Building he wrote, ". . . one building like this, which faces the entire problem of design, and has a clear unflinching answer for each question, may well serve to crystallize all the fumbling and uncertain elements in present-day architecture."[67] The building was written up in the *Architectural Record* by the very same Leon Solon who had had a hand in its design.[68] One cannot have a better press than that.

Yet the architectural journalism of the day was in some ways less than adequate for the architecture it served. American architectural magazines in the twenties were only beginning to unite pictures with words. They started the decade with entirely separate sections of text and plates, and during the twenties text and pictures never quite succeeded in coming together. Texts rarely referred precisely to photographs as illustrations of their arguments; there was certainly not the present-day custom of using descriptive captions and of writing in a text only what can be attested to by a picture. Worse, illustrations were sometimes assigned to an article mistakenly, as though, say, any modern buildings could illustrate any article on modern architecture.[69]

The journalism of Art Deco, as an architecture of "both-and," tended to be imprecise. There was no one good reason for doing something; a design might have several explanations, all acceptable. This did not hurt design, but it encouraged a journalism which was not incisive and adopted no particular critical stance. Art Deco and its journalism were a pushover for the International Style critics with their verbal attack and defense, their sloganeering, and their emphasis on simplification rather than ambiguity. They implied that the Art Deco architect had had International Style intentions but that his resolve had failed him. Henry-Russell Hitchcock, in the thirties one of the definitive spokesmen of the International Style, wrote in 1929 that the Stewart Store (25) was really quite good, but for the small amount of decoration on it. He doubted one could find a better building of comparable purpose in any European capital. He strongly recommended a view of the back of the building—"one of the finest bits of engineering architecture in New York"[70]—and, surprisingly, seemed to think the setbacks an indulgence of the architects. Douglas Haskell liked the Empire State Building, but he thought it had been at its best as a mere steel frame and had regressed when its curtain wall was added.[71]

For all the inadequacy of its journalism, the Art Deco was meant to be a consistent style. It was clearly not intended to be one of a number of styles which the architect might choose from, depending on the job and the client.[72] Even those who were hostile to it in the thirties understood this. Philip Johnson wrote that it had failed in its intention to be a style for two reasons:[73] that it had not had a consistent attitude to ornament, and that it had not lasted for ten years.[74] From our vantage point we can see that perhaps it did have a consistent attitude to ornament (though clearly to Johnson the only acceptable, consistent attitude would have been repudiation of it). As for those obligatory ten years, why, by the time the last buildings illustrated in this book were built, it had lasted ten years, and a little over.

Cervin Robinson

NOTES

1. An approving view of the skyscraper was expressed by Thomas E. Tallmadge in *The Story of Architecture in America* (New York: W. W. Norton, 1927), pp. 295-96.
2. American views hostile to the skyscraper appear in George C. Nimmons, "Skyscrapers in America," and in William Stanley Parker, "Skyscrapers Anywhere," both in *Journal of the American Institute of Architects*, 11 (Sept. 1923), 370-72. G. H. Edgell takes them to be inevitable in *The American Architecture of To-Day* (New York and London: Charles Scribner's Sons, 1928), pp. 358 and 362.
3. John F. Harbeson, *The Study of Architectural Design* (New York: Pencil Points Press, 1926), p. 127. This was the publication in book form of a series of articles which had appeared in *Pencil Points* over a period of years. The series had started in 2 (Jan. 1921), 19.
4. Throughout this text the school at which an architect studied is given after his dates. Where several names form the name of a firm, dates and schools are given in a footnote.
5. Raymond M. Hood, "Exterior Architecture of Office Buildings," *Architectural Forum*, 41 (Sept. 1924), 97.
6. Harbeson, p. 7.
7. Harbeson, p. 78.
8. Harbeson, p. 17.
9. It was also no doubt influenced by other even more progressive foreign entries to the same competition, which was published as *The International Competition for a New Administration Building for the Chicago Tribune, MCMXXII* (Chicago: The Tribune Company, 1923).
10. For the response to Saarinen's entry see Tallmadge, p. 290.
11. John Taylor Boyd, Jr., "The New York Zoning Resolution and its Influence upon Design," *Architectural Record*, 48 (Sept. 1920), 193-217; Harvey Wiley Corbett, "High Buildings on Narrow Streets," *American Architect*, 119 (8 June 1921), 603-8, 617-19; Aymar Embury II, "New York's New Architecture, the Effect of the Zoning Law on High Buildings," *Architectural Forum*, 35 (Oct. 1921), 119-24; Irving K. Pond, "Zoning and the Architecture of High Buildings," *Architectural Forum*, 35 (Oct. 1921), 131-34; Harvey Wiley Corbett, "The Influence of Zoning on New York's Skyline," *American Architect*, 123 (3 Jan. 1923), 1-4; Harvey Wiley Corbett, "Zoning and the Envelope of the Building," *Pencil Points*, 4 (April 1923), 15-18; and "Effect of New York Zoning Resolution on Commercial Buildings," *American Architect*, 125 (18 June 1924), 547-51.
12. Corbett, "Zoning and the Envelope of the Building."

13. Raymond Hood, "The American Radiator Company Building, New York," *American Architect*, 126 (19 Nov. 1924), 470.
14. See Kenneth M. Murchison, "The Chrysler Building as I See It," *American Architect*, 138 (Sept. 1930), 28 and 30.
15. Such an accepting attitude had a place in training too: Harbeson, pp. 71 and 72: ". . . having made a bad esquisse, . . . there is nevertheless a great value in carrying the problem through to a finish . . . the constant need for ingenuity to counteract the bad qualities of such an esquisse . . . is a real training for the problems of office work, where site, questions of construction, or the idiosyncrasies of a client frequently prevent an easy 'parti' and call for a display of ingenuity."
16. Edwin Avery Park, *New Backgrounds for a New Age* (New York: Harcourt Brace & Co., 1927), pp. 141-42.
17. See p. 61 of the Bletter essay, on Semper.
18. Paul T. Frankl, *New Dimensions: The Decorative Arts of Today in Words and Pictures* (New York: Payson & Clarke, 1928), p. 55.
19. Claude Bragdon, *The Frozen Fountain* (New York: Alfred A. Knopf, 1932), p. 11: "A building a fountain: how clarifying a point of view! . . . The needle-pointed *flèche* of the Chrysler tower catches the sunlight like a fountain's highest expiring jet."
20. Thomas Adams, *The Building of the City*, Regional Plan, Vol. II (New York: Regional Plan of New York and its Environs, 1931), p. 309.
21. "Dr. John Wesley Kelchner's Restoration of King Solomon's Temple and Citadel, Helmle & Corbett, Architects," *Pencil Points*, 6 (Nov. 1925), 69-86.
22. See Gordon D. MacDonald, *Office Building Construction, Manhattan 1901-1953* (New York: Real Estate Board of New York, 1952), and Samuel B. Ruckley, *Rebuilding Manhattan: A Study of New Office Construction* (New York. Real Estate Board of New York, 1972).
23. A catalog was published: *Ausstellung neuer amerikanischer Baukunst, Januar 1926*, Berlin, Im Verlage der Akademie der Künste zu Berlin.
24. The design of the building (apart from "elements contributing to the service of beauty") was explained in a manuscript of 1925, "A Big Building in New York," written by Stephen Voorhees for the "Princeton Engineering Journal" and in the possession of the New York Telephone Company. However, no "Princeton Engineering Journal" seems to have existed at the time.
25. Park, p. 150.
26. Lewis Mumford, "American Architecture Today," *Architecture*, 57 (April 1928), 185.
27. See "The Arcade," *Telephone Review* (Sept. 26, 1926), in possession of New York Telephone Company.
28. Fiske Kimball, *American Architecture* (Indianapolis and New York: Bobbs-Merrill, 1928), p. 216.
29. Ely Jacques Kahn, unpublished manuscript in the Avery Architectural Library, Chapter II, pp. 27-28.
30. Adolfo Best-Maugard, *Metodo de Dibujo, Tradición, Resurgimiento y Evolución del Arte Mexicano* (Mexico, Departmento Editorial de la Secretaría de Educación: 1923). As a student Best-Maugard had drawn up primitive designs for Franz Boaz. He had decided that all such primitive patterns could be reduced to a few elements and that by practicing such elements the person who was untrained in art could teach himself.
31. Adolfo Best-Maugard, *A Method for Creative Design* (New York and London: A. A. Knopf, 1927).
32. H. R. Shurtleff, "Apartment Hotel at 28 East 63rd Street," *Arts*, 11 (1927), 41.
33. Park, p. 151.

34. It is difficult some fifty years after the event to judge how well designed for its purpose a building may have been. We do know that Kahn was used repeatedly by a few clients to design a variety of specialized buildings. Despite the obvious care he gave to decoration, articles by Kahn rarely speak of it except in the most general terms. Instead, he tends to emphasize the need to satisfy the specialized needs of different clients. See Ely J. Kahn, "Economics of the Skyscraper," *Architectural Record,* 63 (April 1928), 298-301, and "Civilized Architecture," *Architectural Forum,* 52 (June 1930), 785.
35. Leon V. Solon, *Polychromy: Architectural and Structural, Theory and Practice* (New York, Architectural Record), 1924.
36. Kahn, unpublished manuscript, II. 4.
37. See *Ely Jacques Kahn,* Contemporary American Architects Series (New York: Whittlesey House, 1931), for illustrations of many Kahn buildings.
38. Kahn, unpublished manuscript, II. 7-11.
39. Tallmadge, p. 286.
40. John Sloan, 1888-1954, New York University; T. Markoe Robertson, 1868-1952, Yale, Ecole des Beaux-Arts. Though the Chanin was not intended to reach a record height, it had a greater number of stories than the Woolworth, the last building that had done so.
41. "B. O. Motor Coach Station, New York," *Architectural Forum,* 53 (Dec. 1930), 743, 744.
42. See R. W. Sexton, "A Theater on the Fiftieth Floor," *Architectural Forum,* 52 (May 1930), 727-30.
43. C. Adolph Glassgold, "The Decorative Arts," *Arts,* 15 (April 1929), 286.
44. The Paris Prize was awarded each year after a competition by the Society of Beaux-Arts Architects. The winner was sent, expenses paid, to the Ecole in Paris.
45. *American Architect,* 134 (Aug. 20, 1928), 269.
46. See Leon V. Solon, "The Passing of the Skyscraper Formula of Design," *Architectural Record,* 55 (Feb. 1924), 135-44, and Francis S. Swales, "Draftsmanship and Architecture, V, as Exemplified by the Work of William Van Alen," *Pencil Points,* 10 (Aug. 1929), 526.
47. Swales, 526.
48. Kenneth Murchison, "The Chrysler Building as I See It," p. 24.
49. Eugene Clute, "The Chrysler Building, New York," *Architectural Forum,* 53 (Oct. 1930), 403.
50. Clute, 404. Other buildings were given entasis, presumably to overcome this illusion: Urban's New School building, for instance, and, for that matter, the News, which shouldn't have had the problem.
51. It also clearly drew from Hood's American Radiator Building just as the latter had in part drawn from Corbett's Bush Terminal Building. But the primary liberating influence came from the Saarinen design.
52. Harvey Wiley Corbett, "Architecture of the Master Building," *Archer,* numbers 3 and 4 (1929), 26.
53. Henry S. Churchill, writing on "The State Tower Building in Syracuse," *Architectural Forum,* 50 (Jan. 1929), 1.
54. See announcements in issues of *Archer,* 1927-29.
55. This does not include his Rex Cole showrooms (of which one at least still stands in Bay Ridge as a Porsche-Audi salesroom).
56. "Aquatint Rendering by Donald Douglas," *Pencil Points,* 8 (Nov. 1927), 660. Douglas was a designer in Hood's office.
57. Raymond M. Hood, "Exterior Architecture of Office Buildings," *Architectural Forum,* 41 (Sept. 1924), 97.
58. Park, p. 149.

59. Not that terra-cotta was ever completely abandoned by Art Deco architects. A description of terra-cotta manufacture of the time can be found in W. A. Starrett, *Skyscrapers and the Men Who Build Them* (New York: C. Scribner's Sons, 1928), pp. 224, 235.
60. Richard H. Shreve, 1877-1946, Cornell; William Frederick Lamb, 1884 1952, Williams, Columbia, Ecole des Beaux-Arts; Arthur Loomis Harmon, 1878-1958, Chicago Art Institute, Columbia.
61. These are arcades, if passageways without arches but with shops can be described as shopping arcades.
62. Benjamin Wistar Morris, 1870-1944, Columbia, Ecole des Beaux-Arts; L. Andrew Reinhard, 1892-1964, Beaux-Arts Institute of Design; Henry Hofmeister 1890-1962, Beaux-Arts Institute of Design; Wallace K. Harrison, b. 1895, Ecole des Beaux-Arts; William H. MacMurray, 1868-1941; Frederick Augustus Godley, 1886-1961, Yale, MIT, Ecole des Beaux-Arts; Jacques André Fouilhoux, 1879-1945, Ecole Centrale des Arts et Manufactures. William H. Jordy, *American Buildings and Their Architects: The Impact of European Modernism in the Mid-Twentieth Century* (Garden City, N.Y.: Doubleday, 1972), p. 428, gives a useful summary of the literature on Rockefeller Center.
63. For Hood's, see Walter H. Kilham, Jr., *Raymond Hood, Architect—Form Through Function in the American Skyscraper* (New York: Architectural Book Publishing Co., 1973), p. 159. Plans of this Hood scheme and some others were published in Raymond Hood, "The Design of Rockefeller City," *Architectural Forum,* 56 (Jan. 1932), 1-7.
64. This was illustrated (Fig. 5) in Winston Weisman, "Who Designed Rockefeller Center?" *Journal of the Society of Architectural Historians,* 10 (March 1951), 14.
65. Wallace K. Harrison, "Drafting Room Practice," *Architectural Forum,* 56 (Jan. 1932), 77-80 and 81-84.
66. Lewis Mumford, "American Architecture Today," *Architecture,* 57 (April 1928) 185.
67. Mumford, 188.
68. Leon V. Solon, "The Park Avenue Building, New York City," *Architectural Record,* 63 (April 1928), 289-97.
69. Two examples of this casual attitude to illustration are: Samuel Chamberlain, "In Search of Modernism," *American Architect,* 131 (5 Jan. 1927), 71-74, and Talbot Faulkner Hamlin, "The International Style Lacks the Essence of Great Architecture," *American Architect,* 143 (Jan. 1933), 12-16. For that matter, in the Mumford article cited above a general view, identified as of the Park Avenue Building, one of the two buildings being discussed in the article, is in fact not a view of that building but of Kahn's Insurance Center Building.
70. Henry-Russell Hitchcock, "The Stewart Building," *Arts,* 16 (Oct. 1929), 124-27.
71. Douglas Haskell, "The Empire State Building," *Creative Art,* 8 (April 1931), 242-44.
72. This seems to have been true for whole buildings but not necessarily for every interior in them. The executive floor of Hood's McGraw-Hill Building was not Art Deco; and in the Cloud Club in the Chrysler Building only the main dining room was in the style.
73. Philip Johnson, "The Skyscraper School of Modern Architecture," *Arts,* 17 (May 1931), 575.
74. What he said precisely was that "a style must be worthy of continuing at least a decade."

J. M. van der Meij, Scheepvaarthuis, Amsterdam, 1912-16.

THE ART DECO STYLE

"Some of this modern mess you have created and never stop to analyze is really beautiful."

Artist addressing the public in Edwin Avery Park's *New Backgrounds for a New Age,* 1927

Definition

In 1927, in *New Backgrounds for a New Age,* Edwin Avery Park insisted that a new age had dawned and should be expressed in art and architecture. He found that art was proclaiming our civilization, but to his dismay architecture and interior design seemed to be lagging behind. Describing the cultural milieu of the designer, for example, he wrote: "He will dance and dine to jazz, read 'Ulysses,' have himself psychoanalyzed, listen to Debussy, appreciate Cézanne, and ride in an aeroplane. But he will be installing an Empire suite in some wealthy lady's apartment. We have nothing to say for ourselves."[1]

This was written just as American architects were beginning to come to grips with the jazz age. Barely three years after Park's statement, a series of distinctive Art Deco skyscrapers altered the New York skyline, and hundreds of Art Deco shops, restaurants, and building lobbies exuded the spirit of modernity. The cityscape and its public interiors had changed, and the change could be seen by both the tourist and the office worker.

What made Art Deco buildings unique? What are the characteristics that differentiate them from architecture done in a Neogothic or Neoclassical manner? Did Art Deco in fact develop an idiom that would justify our calling it a style? The strength of the Beaux-Arts tradition in New York, still alive in the early twenties, would lead one to suspect that most architects, from the outset, were not interested in an overtly revolutionary style or a total break with the past, but more in a rephrasing of given modes.

Art Deco architecture depends first of all on a traditional form of an American commercial style: the skyscraper as it had evolved from its beginnings in Chicago in the late nineteenth century. No structural innovations or drastic changes in interior subdivision of spaces were introduced (except perhaps that internal walls were now often used as mere partitions to provide flexibility for office floors).[2] Louis Sullivan's precepts, stated in "The Tall Office Building Artistically Considered" of 1896, apply to most Art Deco skyscrapers as well. There is a ground floor with shops, banks, and other services amply spaced and with a "main entrance that attracts the eye to its location"; the exterior of the ground floor is treated in a "liberal, expansive, sumptuous way." The office floors are expressed uniformly; Sullivan had said to "make them look alike because they are all alike." The attic is dealt with emphatically to show that "the series of office tiers has come definitely to an end."[3] This basic three-part division was maintained in most Art Deco skyscrapers, with some minor additions. First, the multi-functional treatment of the ground floor, taken for granted by Sullivan, in many Art Deco buildings is expanded to include a more complex traffic circulation: access to subways, bus stops, and parking garages is now often incorporated into the planning of the lower section of a structure. Second, the zoning law affected the massing of tall buildings. In place of Sullivan's overhanging cornice, there appear a variety of stepped-back shapes, which are, when seen from afar, actually more distinctive as terminating points than Sullivan's flat roofs. There were, to be sure, later variations in the way architects dealt with the setback requirements, such as the less conventional arrangement of the building mass in the Daily News Building, or the gradual system of setbacks in the building group of Rockefeller Center, beginning with the low elevation of the structures along Fifth Avenue; the full height of the RCA Building is not achieved abruptly. By the time Rockefeller Center was designed, the idea of the tall building as a single slab had been changed by an approach to massing which kept the building more within human scale at its street façade or at least more within scale of the older urban fabric.[4] Naturally, these later projects were also larger than any that had been executed before, and the effect of their scale must have been an important concern of their architects.

Sullivan had also believed that the chief characteristic of the tall office building was its loftiness. This he described as its "dominant chord. . . . It must be tall, every inch of it tall. The force and power of altitude must be in it, the glory and pride of exaltation must be in it. It must be every inch a proud and soaring thing. . . ."[5] Indeed, in Sullivan's own tall buildings this is usually expressed by piers which rise uninterruptedly from the second floor to the attic level with recessed spandrels and windows. Precisely this effect is sought after in most Art Deco skyscrapers; whether the piers are classicizing and heavily articulated, or Gothicizing, more slender, and triangular, they almost always form the dominant vertical feature.

The most obvious element of Art Deco architecture is its use of sumptuous ornament, and the lush textures and color achieved by combining several materials, such as stone, brick, terra-cotta, and metal. Again, there is an aspect of this which can be tied to nineteenth-century architecture. Concentration of dynamic ornament around entrances and at the attic zone, with more structured ornamental patterns in spandrels, is also a feature of Sullivan's tall buildings and can be found with variations in Art Deco skyscrapers.

Color and ornament had, of course, been used extensively in Victorian architecture. John Ruskin in *The Stones of Venice* (1851-53) treats ornament in a way that is comparable to its use in Art Deco architecture—its primary justification is to delight. He wanted an ornament that was visually and sometimes even physically accessible. A similar obviousness and palpability resides in Art Deco decoration, as it does in any populist expression. As to the relation between ornament and structure, Ruskin was for an expression of structure, but not for an engineering aesthetic. He believed that ornament should not conceal construction, but neither should construction be revealed blatantly:

> . . . it may sometimes, on the one hand, be necessary to conceal [the masonry] as far as may be, by delicate and close fitting, when the joints would interfere with lines of sculpture or of mouldings, and it may often, on the other hand, be delightful to show it, as it is delightful in places to show the anatomy even of the most delicate human frame: but *studiously* to conceal it is the error of vulgar painters, who are afraid to show that their figures have bones; and studiously to display it is the error of the base pupils of Michael Angelo, who turned heroes' limbs into surgeons' diagrams. . . .[6]

Ruskin saw the nonstructural wall areas between piers as a "wall veil," much as the twentieth-century architect would use the term "curtain wall." Instead of using the International Style's general mode of revealing structure by means of a glazed curtain wall, Art Deco architects "express" structure in Ruskin's sense in their opaque curtain walls.

At the same time it must be pointed out that color used in Art

Deco buildings does not always rely on the natural color of materials, as Ruskin had also recommended. Glazed tiles and polychrome terra-cottas are often used, in bright, vibrant, and startling colors. Sometimes whole buildings are shaded, beginning with a dark-toned brick at ground level and shading into lighter and lighter tonalities toward the top. Harvey Wiley Corbett's Master Institute and Riverside Museum (19), for example, changes from a dark purple below to a greyish color at the top; a similar effect is achieved in Schwartz & Gross' apartment house at Central Park West and 66th Street (64A). In other instances, large, bold ornament is used near the building's top, as in Kahn's office building at 2 Park Avenue (6A). The scale of this daring, vivid design was consciously geared to perception from a distance (Ruskin had also insisted that ornament remain readable from various vantage points).[7] A small-scale design in muted colors would have virtually disappeared from several blocks away. Thus, the Art Deco architect was not only concerned with giving the passerby and office worker an elevating experience by enhancing entrance area and lobby space with a profusion of ornament. He was equally concerned with having the building remain readable from a distance and with its general effect in the skyline, and therefore used unusual terminations at the top and ornament scaled to distance, effects that are today perhaps no longer as readily apparent, with the occlusion of so many Art Deco skyscrapers by later, taller buildings.

A similarity between nineteenth-century theory and contemporary developments was noted by Talbot Hamlin in an essay of 1932, "Is Originality Leading Us Into a New Victorianism?" He believed that behind the search for originality which he saw in all twentieth-century styles lay a theory of expressionism formulated by Ruskin and the French architectural theorist, Viollet-le-Duc. Despite the continued validity of nineteenth-century ideas, Hamlin found in contemporary architecture the same ferment of taste that had troubled the Victorians. He saw as the chief causes of a degradation of taste the following:

1. The commercialization of the search for originality in order to make new markets for new manufactured goods. This led inevitably to the fact that manufacturers and builders made things and houses to satisfy the masses, who are always the least educated, the least cultured parts of the population.
2. An innate love of richness and decoration on the part of the buying public that results so easily in excess and complexity.
3. A cultural condition, showing in politics, literature, and religion, of unprecedented hypocrisy, arrogance, distortion of values, and dishonesty.
4. The endless facility of the human mind in rationalization, that enables it to apply almost any given theory to almost any given facts.[8]

Ely Jacques Kahn as early as 1929 had similarly criticized the facile rush to novel forms: "The essential is honesty; the danger is the belief that freedom suggests acceptance of anything which is merely different. As any period has discovered there is always a great volume of freak, shoddy work being produced that cannot be avoided. Just now the tendency to jumbled, explosive geometric forms has led some designers to eccentricities that will quite as promptly be cast aside."[9]

These are in fact the problems any post-aristocratic architecture must face, problems that not only developed because of the rise of a nouveau riche class, but that are a deeper and an intrinsic part of the question of taste in a mass society, where style is no longer decreed from above by an aristocratic class. The attempts of the nineteenth-century design reformers notwithstanding, no one in modern society, not even the architect or artist, seems to have proper standing to legislate taste.

The design of architectural ornament is commonly the first indication of whether a building is Art Deco. It is in the specific arrangement of patterns that Art Deco is most directly indebted to the Paris 1925 Exposition Internationale des Arts Décoratifs et Industriels Modernes. However, some caution is called for, since the 1925 exhibition was itself already highly eclectic, and it is often quite difficult to tell whether a pattern should be classified as Cubist or Expressionist. In any case, many of the ornamental terra-cotta panels, spandrels, or metal screens of Art Deco architecture have the stylized floral patterns (9B, 9B, 70) and strident geometrics combining harsh angular forms with sections of circles and other softly curving shapes that are familiar from Art Deco crafts (9D, 9E, 26L).

Another of the more novel aspects of the style is the use of faceted, crystalline forms leading to an entrance, like a modern version of a Gothic splayed doorway (44, 46, 89). Sometimes faceting occurs at the ceiling, as in lobbies and lounges (35, 36), or, most visibly, in the crowning features of a building (54, 80). The source of this type of detailing appears to be German Expressionist architecture. Such sculptural effects were more typical of the earlier, arts-and-crafts oriented and Gothicizing aspect of the style. By the thirties one can also find more Constructivist effects, as in the top of the McGraw-Hill Building (82) or the Century and Majestic apartments (87, 96). But, as with many of the features of Art Deco architecture, one is not entirely certain that these forms are in fact Constructivist, for such interpenetrating forms could just as readily be traced to Frank Lloyd Wright.

Art Deco is, then, basically an eclectic style that makes simple definitions difficult. Most important, the style should not be defined solely in terms of its newer aspects—such as its ornament, streamlined forms, etc.—but must be seen together with its conservative elements—the older, commercial skyscraper architecture of which it is a continuation and the Beaux-Arts background of many of the Art Deco architects. All these characteristics coalesce in Art Deco architecture in a new way.

Art Deco architecture in New York was created mostly for big business. Yet the result was not an austere corporate imagery, but an architecture that was good advertising, meant to entertain and draw in the public. Together with Neoclassical features and the dry repetitiveness of commercial floors, there is also the Romantic interest in sensory experience through texture, color, and decoration. The Art Deco architect was not interested in the dematerialized ascetic expression of the International Style. Even when he conceived of his walls as "curtain-walls," they have the look of masonry walls, of traditional construction, with down-to-earth tactile effects. The passerby is supposed to empathize with the building as if it were some obvious, theatrical gesture taken from a Baroque painting. Such buildings are enticing on a common level like the ruddy cheeks of a Rubens Madonna. Mysteries of volume, ambiguities of transparent space, and forms hovering heavenward—subtleties found in International Style architecture—are absent from Art Deco design, which often attempts to provide the kind of style and elegance the contemporary public was more likely to have encountered in the theater or in films than in real life. Sometimes such attempts misfired and looked shrill. But the more successful ventures are examples of a decent pluralistic architecture.

Such conclusions, while based on Art Deco architecture in New York, represent general principles of the style. For example, Forrest F. Lisle, discussing Chicago's Century of Progress Exposition of 1933, writes in a similar vein:

> Contrary to most historical and critical assessments of American architecture of the 1930's, Moderne architecture [his term for Art Deco] can be shown to have been the logical and thus, perhaps, "proper" stylistic choice, for America to have made in view of the nation's institutions, traditions, and ideals . . . it is demonstrable that basic to the development and acceptance of the Moderne was the existence of, and regard for, democratic, egalitarian, middle-class, commercial, free-enterprise, popular culture values and comprehensions.[10]

The sources of the Art Deco style of the Century of Progress fair he describes as follows:

4. THE LOWELL

Henry S. Churchill and Herbert Lippmann faced the ground floor of this steel-framed apartment house with glazed terra cotta. Build in 1926 between Park and Madison on 63rd Street, the building incorporated a French restaurant, the Passy, which is still in business there. The mosaic above the entrance was designed by Bertram Hartman. Octagonal decorative panels were popularized by the Paris Exposition des Arts Décoratifs et Industriels of 1925 but had been used earlier by Secession designers.

6. THE PARK AVENUE BUILDING

A. The glazed terra-cotta at the top of this 1927 building by Ely Jacques Kahn was intended to reproduce the primary colors of Greek antiquity. The building is seen here with the Empire State Building (76) behind.

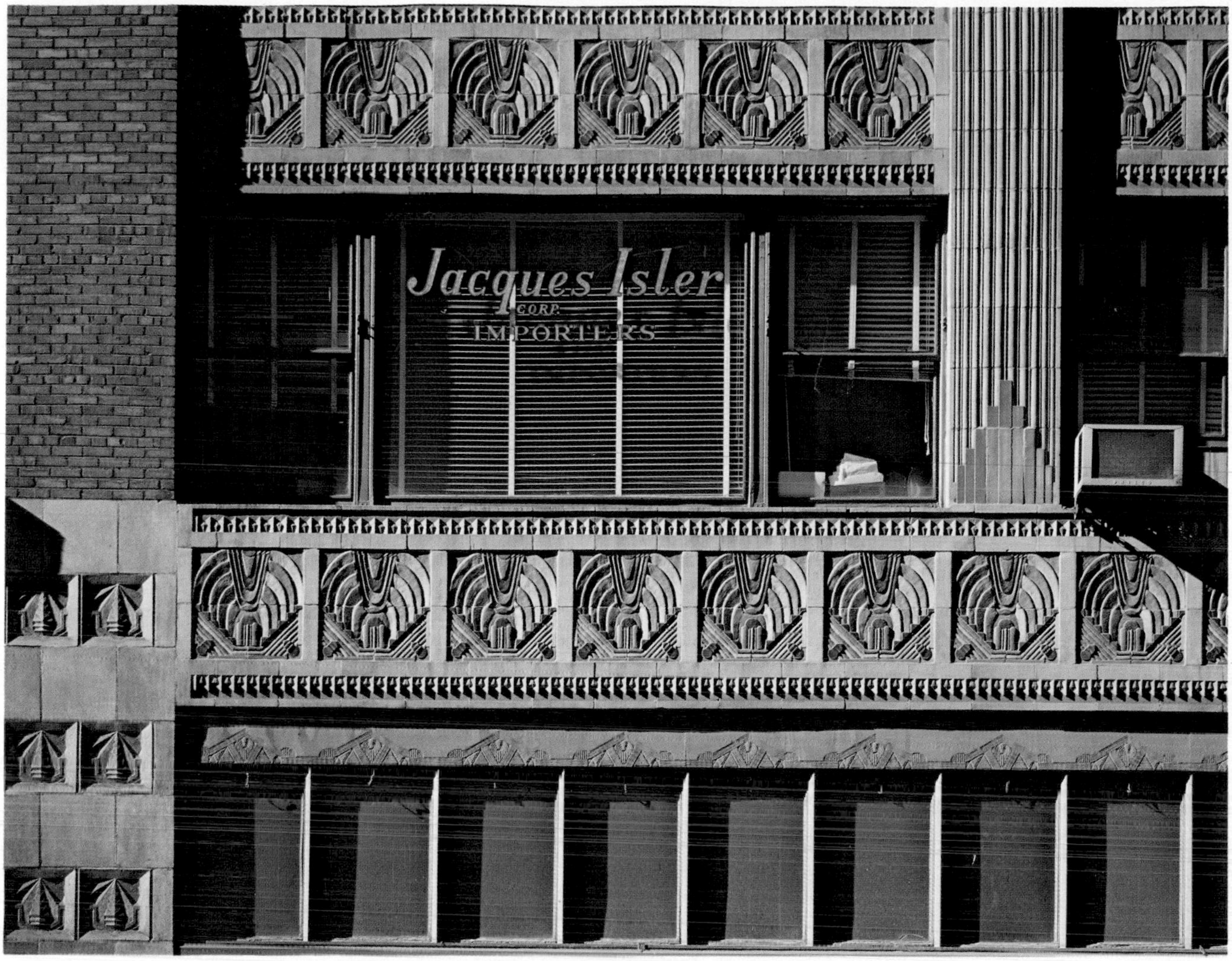

7. 42 WEST 39TH STREET

Buchman & Kahn built a second building in 1927, this one in the garment district and with glazed terra-cotta towards its base. The use of sumptuous and colorful ornament and the juxtaposition of a variety of materials is apparent here as in Kahn's Park Avenue building.

24. FILM CENTER BUILDING

A. The forms in the elevator lobby of this building of 1928-29 by Ely Kahn derive from fabric design. But their effect is to suggest the flow of the citizens of Gotham on their way to and from work. Horizontal striping, such as appears here, had been popularized by the 1925 Paris Exposition, but, like so much else of the Art Deco, had been used earlier by Viennese designers.

26. CHRYSLER BUILDING

B and C. The elevator doors and interiors of the cabs feature veneers of a variety of woods. The cabs came in four patterns, one of which is illustrated here.

35. THE NEWS BUILDING

A. Raymond Hood's building of 1929-30 is clad in alternating strips of white and red: white brick verticals—and windows with red shades below recessed spandrels of red and black brick.

This apartment building a few blocks south of Grand Central Station was designed by Bowden & Russell and built in 1930. Bright scales of color in terra-cotta appear on the tower of the building. The Chanin (9) and the Chrysler Building (26) are to the left beyond it.

57. THE TOWN HOUSE

64. CENTRAL PARK WEST AT 66TH STREET

A. Schwartz & Gross's apartment house of 1930 was one of a number of Art Deco buildings that had curtain walls of brick which shaded from a dark color at the base of the building to a light one at the top. The building was thereby to seem taller and to give the impression of being sunlit even on an overcast day.

60. TWENTIETH-CENTURY FOX BUILDING

A. A stained-glass window was set between the vestibule and lobby of the New York headquarters of a Hollywood movie company.

This building by Louis Allen Abramson is on 181st Street not far above the George Washington Bridge. Decorative bands appear on its stone-surfaced façade. The top band is in glazed terra-cotta. The lower, broader one is finished in metallic surfaces.

70. HORN & HARDART

82. McGRAW-HILL BUILDING

A. The streamlined entrance to this building of 1930-31 by Raymond Hood marks it as a late Art Deco building, but in its use of color it suggests the earlier craft phase of the style. An address sign originally set below the company's name is missing.

> . . . the Paris 1925 Fair, Frank Lloyd Wright, cubism, machine ethics, Mayan forms, Pueblo patterns, Dudok, the Viennese Secession, modern interiors, the zoning-law setback. This large number of weakly related sources, readily identified as underlying the Moderne in America, begins to suggest the loose, broad, inclusive, less intense, rather indiscriminate, thus democratic, perimeters of the modern movement *here* as opposed to the impersonal, reductive, exclusive, more idealistic, more moralistic thrust of avant-garde Europe at this time.[11]

Despite the recent flurry of publications on Art Deco art, there has been to date no general book on the architecture of that period.[12] Those books on Art Deco art that do mention buildings do so peripherally and are often quite misleading: while earlier historians had neglected Art Deco in favor of the International Style, several authors of contemporary Art Deco books go now to another extreme and suggest that everything produced in the twenties and thirties is Art Deco, including International Style architecture.[13] The reader is never told exactly how someone like Corbusier, Gropius, or Mies is supposed to fit into the Art Deco style. We will have a more workable model of the styles of the twenties and thirties if we assume that there was an esoteric style, that is, the International Style, alongside of which developed a more popular style which has been named variously Art Deco, Modernistic, Jazz Modern, Zigzag Modern, Style 1925, the Twenties Style, the Thirties Style, Streamlined Modern, etc.[14] The most commonly used term at the moment is Art Deco (and so we have chosen to use it, despite its obvious inadequacies with respect to architecture because originally it implied only the decorative arts), a name that is based on the 1925 Paris Exposition Internationale des Arts Décoratifs et Industriels Modernes. In its own day this style was referred to in America, after some initial vacillations between "modernist" and "modernistic," as Modernistic from about 1928 onward.[15]

One of the major reasons why Art Deco has not previously become a standard chapter in architectural histories is that it was never as revolutionary as the International Style—some traditions were broken by the Art Deco architect but others were left intact. Its promoters did not want to upset the viewer—they wanted to find an *acceptable* modern style; one could call the Art Deco architect an avant-garde traditionalist. And while the architectural results were on occasion vulgar, the intention was to create a mass modern. In place of the undecorated, glazed, stuccoed, and severe façades of the International Style, the Art Deco architect provided rich textures, architectural ornament, and polychrome effects, a clear bridge to the architecture of the past.

Art Deco never looks intellectual and cool like the International Style, but is instead lavish and opulent, qualities that have a direct appeal to the senses. The style became acceptable to middle-of-the-road patrons of commercial architecture, many of whom seemed to have few convictions about architectural expression. Most of these real estate developers gave their architects free rein, as long as the style was new without being shocking. Art Deco became the style of such smart stores as Bonwit's, Bloomingdale's, and Tiffany's, it became the corporate style for the New York Telephone Company, of the elegant Waldorf-Astoria Hotel, of the garment district, of the Horn & Hardart automated restaurant chain, and of the movie palaces where officer workers and café society mingled.

Because Art Deco occupies a position somewhere between a "high" and a vernacular style—although a mass style, it was urbane and never possessed the naïveté of a folk style—its forms did not often spring from native creativity. It borrows from here and there and deserves a prize for eclecticism, a feature which has made it most elusive to analyze. Given its popular, eclectic nature, we should expect a long list of variables and sources, to which we will turn shortly.

Whether or not Art Deco became an American style—a phase that differs from European Art Deco—there are regional differences apparent to even a casual visitor to, say, Los Angeles or Philadelphia. In Los Angeles Art Deco was more strongly affected by the Mission style, by a precocious car culture, and by Hollywood.[16] In California, also, the building types in the style are more varied, and Art Deco does not remain as much restricted to high-rise buildings as elsewhere. Philadelphia's Art Deco is closer to that of New York City but often has a more forcefully expressed ornament. In fact, speculating on a modern style to come, an editor of *The American Architect* thought that any new styles of the future would not be national at all but regional.[17] It is conceivable, however, that there is a national style with regional variations. We present the New York Art Deco buildings as specific examples within this wider context.

If we rely for dating Art Deco on its varied terminology, we must assume that the Twenties Style, for instance, began in 1920 and ended in 1929. Of course, historical development is not that obliging. Another name, the "Style 1925," is much more specific, perhaps too precise. This appellation derives from the central event of the period, the Paris 1925 exposition. However, it is obvious that the style did not spring full-fledged into existence when the gates to the exposition opened, nor did it end suddenly when the exposition closed. Most authors on Art Deco crafts are agreed on 1925 as a pivotal and crucial date: they see the exhibition as both the climax and the popularization of the style and hence the beginning of its eclipse.[18]

For New York Art Deco architecture the conventional dating must be revised. Art Deco was not used here extensively until after the impact of the 1925 Paris exposition was felt. To be sure, a few early examples were erected between 1923 and 1927, but the style attained its greatest popularity between 1928 and 1931. There are in addition some structures that were begun in the late thirties. In any case, if we want to identify a high point of this popular style, it must be placed in the late twenties and early thirties. This is considerably later than the peak in arts and crafts; in part because architecture, being tied to a multitude of economic requirements, usually responds to a new style more slowly than the other arts, and in part because architectural training in New York had remained close to the Beaux-Arts tradition and its conservative method of education.

Alfred H. Barr, in the catalogue of the Museum of Modern Art's *Modern Architecture—International Exhibition* of 1932, sees Art Deco architecture clearly as a style, but as a style not worthy of the Museum of Modern Art. He finds that the Paris 1925 exposition had had more disturbing effects than the Chicago Tribune Tower competition of 1922:

> Only recently has the deluge of modernistic decoration from Vienna, Paris, Stockholm, and Amsterdam begun to diminish, but not before our more advanced architects, already stimulated by Saarinen's success, had accepted the modernistic mode with enthusiasm and ornamented their buildings with zigzags and chevrons instead of Gothic crockets and Classical moldings. The modernistic style has become merely another way of decorating surfaces.[19]

Barr goes on to say that he hopes for a "genuine" new style, a style which will eliminate the confusion of the past, a style that will use light surfaces, open plans, a style that will emphasize volume over mass, and that will be without ornament—all clearly International Style principles. There are two significant points in Barr's statement. First, he calls the Art Deco architects "advanced" even though he does not approve of their style, indicating that the Art Deco architect was neither conservative enough to be dismissed outright by the Museum of Modern Art, nor, on the other hand, avant-garde enough to be in the museum's good graces. Further, it is interesting that Barr, while correctly identifying the eclecticism of Art Deco architecture, mentions only the newer European sources and fails to point out the older American precedents for the style. Of course, it must be remembered that he was writing at a time when the avant-garde insisted on a revolutionary credo and regarded the past as a confusing or irrelevant factor. In any case, let us now examine more specifically the European influences Barr mentions.

The French Influence

If we want to explore the multifarious sources for Art Deco architecture, it is best to begin with the 1925 Paris exposition, which in itself epitomized the style's characteristic quality of pastiche. To understand why the style of the 1925 exposition was not entirely novel, but was rather made up of novelties, we must first clarify the reason for the exhibition. In 1910 at the Paris Salon d'Automne an exhibition of German crafts had been held which met with great popular success (crowds had to be controlled by the police) and also made French artists and artisans realize that French production had not kept pace with the German arts and crafts development.[20] As early as 1907 the German Werkbund had been founded for the furtherance of the relation between architects, artists, craftsmen, and industry.[21] In France, on the other hand, design at the time was fairly conservative. This "design gap" was seen as an economic and competitive disadvantage, and to overcome it, plans were made, beginning in 1912, for an exhibition to be held in 1915 in Paris that would be an answer to Germany's dominance in the design field.[22] World War I interrupted the original plan. In 1922 it was resurrected, but the exhibition did not take place until 1925. By this time Germany was no longer just a competitor in the production of modern design; it was a conquered enemy nation, and what had originally been intended as an economic contest took on political overtones. The exhibition was ostensibly international, but Germany was invited too late for adequate organization and preparation and it declined. Thus Germany, the original cause of this design contest, was excluded, and the comparative merit of French and German design could not be evaluated at all. The political implications of the exposition are even clearer when the general layout of the site is examined: the main intersection at the exhibition grounds was reserved for the major nations allied with France during World War I—Britain, Belgium, Italy, and the United States.[23] The scheme was not carried out completely as planned only because the United States declined participation. Herbert Hoover, then Secretary of Commerce, wrote that America could not take part because no modern design was being produced there.[24] If Hoover's response seems odd, it can be partly understood in the light of the equally odd participation requirements set up by the exposition committee. Any works submitted were supposed to possess new inspiration and real originality, and any imitations of ancient styles were "strictly prohibited."[25] The understandable result of such a bureaucratic approach to new creation and disregard for normal stylistic development was that most of the works submitted frenetically displayed their novelty. It was modernity by official decree: let there be a new style.

On the other hand, this eagerness to be modern contrasts curiously with an equal reluctance to include examples of the revolutionary architecture of that period, especially the International Style. The products of the Bauhaus were not shown because they were German, but what is the explanation for the absence of

L. H. Boileau, Pavilion of the Bon Marché department store at the 1925 Paris show.

J. Hiriard, Tribout & Beau, Pavilion of the Galeries Lafayette, 1925 Paris show.

de Stijl design? And why did Corbusier have to occupy by night a peripheral site for his *L'Esprit Nouveau* pavilion after having been tipped off that it would be given to another entrant?[26] Why did the commissioners have a six-foot palisade fence erected around his pavilion obscuring it from view?[27] Together with Melnikov's pavilion for the Soviet Union, Corbusier's pavilion was the most avant-garde work of architecture of the whole exhibition. The reason for this reluctance was, it seems, that really revolutionary forms were not sought—only a popularized image of a modern style.[28]

This becomes especially clear when we consider that the demand for newness does not seem to have extended to the architecture of the exhibition itself. While most of the buildings have the rich ornamental reliefs and decorative screens typical of Art Deco, the architectural grouping and massing is, almost without exception, Neoclassical in spirit. The buildings are most commonly based on centralized plans, or they exhibit bilateral symmetry, with flanking wings and stepped roofs that ascend to a crowning pinnacle. In fact, one of the major entrances, from the Place de la Concorde, is, with its forest of pylons, strangely reminiscent of a National Socialist or Fascist scheme. Thus, the architecture itself was quite conservative, and any newness was carried by the surface ornament. It is in the decorative surfaces of this architecture that the "style" and the motifs characteristic of Parisian Art Deco have all been brought together: stylized fountains, zigzag borders, and dense floral fields packed into octagons, into spandrels, and into other geometric forms. There were some exceptions: both the Danish pavilion by Kay Fisker and the Dutch pavilion by J. F. Staal had a rich texture produced not through decorative panels but through an intricately organized pattern of exposed bricks, the latter in the manner of the Expressionist Amsterdam School. Further, Josef Hoffmann's Austrian pavilion, with its horizontally articulated bandings that were integrated with the structure, was austere in the context of the other pavilions.[29] In the courtyard of the Austrian pavilion was the only German design of the exposition, a "greenhouse" by Peter Behrens done in German Expressionist fashion with faceted, crystalline glass sections. Behrens' pavilion was there only because he had been invited by Hoffmann to participate in the Austrian entry (Behrens was teaching in Vienna at the time). Ely Jacques Kahn writing of the electrifying effect the 1925 Paris exposition had on him, singles out the Austrian and "German" pavilion as especially striking.[30]

Thousands of visitors from the United States came to the 1925 Paris exposition.[31] And just as France had been stimulated by the German exhibition of 1910, so the United States was inspired by this one. Although Hoover had not sent American representatives to the show, it was apparently not because he thought the exhibition unimportant but because he seems to have been truly convinced that the United States could not have come up with original designs. Even before the opening of the Paris exposition, he appointed a commission to visit Paris and write up a report for the benefit of American manufacturers. The commission in turn invited trade associations to appoint delegates, so that in the summer of 1925 eighty-seven delegates from such organizations as the American Institute of Architects, the Architectural League of New York, the Furniture Designers' Association, the American Construction Council, the Association of National Advertisers, the Society of Arts and Crafts, the Society of Interior Decorators, the New York State Department of Education, the Illuminating Engineering Society, the Silk Association of America, and United Women's Wear, as well as delegates from the Metropolitan Museum and from the New York Times, visited the exposition.[32] On their return the delegates made reports to their respective trade associations and published articles in trade papers on the exposition. The commission seems to have been completely taken in by the image France had wanted to convey ever since the successful German show of 1910. In a general report, one of the commissioners writes that German manufacture had been important because of the Werkbund until 1914, but that since the war—and here he quotes from a French writer—"France has taken a leaf from Germany's book."[33] The French intention to regain dominance in design met with complete success—commercial success, that is. Most visitors, like the American commissioners, did not inquire into the origins of the new styles presented at the exposition and naturally assumed that they were French. The show was so successful that to this day, several historians of the Art Deco style treat it as a primarily French phenomenon, rather than the eclectic one it was.

From the visual and written evidence one must conclude that it was the general impact of the Paris exposition—not individual French architects such as Robert Mallet-Stevens, André Lurçat, or Pierre Chareau—that affected American architects the most. The style of the exposition was further popularized in New York City by an exhibition of modern French furniture at Lord and Taylor's in 1928. Organized by Ely Jacques Kahn, the show included ensembles by such designers as Chareau, Ruhlmann, Jourdain, and Sue et Mare.[34] Henry-Russell Hitchcock commented in 1928 that within a year of the Paris exposition Art Deco products had been introduced to New York, although through commercial channels "rather than through architects and decorators."[35] Then in 1929, when zigzags were already flooding the market, the Metropolitan Museum held an exposition organized by Richard Bach, a curator of industrial arts and one of Herbert Hoover's commissioners for the Paris 1925 exposition. The Metropolitan show was an exhibition of contemporary American design called "The Architect and the Industrial Arts." Apparently because no American interior furnishings were available in the new style, most were designed by the architects themselves, including, among others, Raymond Hood, Ely Jacques Kahn, Ralph T. Walker, Joseph Urban, Eugene Schoen—all New York architects—John Root of Chicago, and Eliel Saarinen of Detroit.[36] The exhibition was scheduled to run for six weeks, but on the first Sunday after it opened 10,000 people came to see it, and it was held over for half a year. Thus, in 1929, when Art Deco architecture had already begun to make a strong showing in New York City and had already been accepted by the public, the Metropolitan Museum put its stamp of approval on it.

The Viennese Influence

Since the 1925 exposition took place in Paris, there has often been an automatic assumption that Art Deco represents a populariza-

Josef Hoffmann, Palais Stoclet, Brussels, 1905-11.

tion of Cubism. One can point to the Cubists' transformation of a coherent picture space into an oscillating surface, a feature apparent in some examples of Art Deco ornament. On the other hand, flat, two-dimensional articulation of ornament is also common in Art Deco. And specific details of the Art Deco style—its jagged points, chevrons, triangles, and tightly packed fields of flowers—have no precedent in Cubism at all.

Several characteristics of Art Deco have their origin in Art Nouveau—not the sinuous type of Art Nouveau, but the Glasgow type and especially the Viennese version, the Secession style. The Secession style was perhaps more architectonic in a traditional sense than any other form of the Art Nouveau. Its architecture retained a clear, classically-inspired form; richness was achieved by using precious materials like marble, lush colors, and architectural ornament that usually appeared in restricted areas or was subjected to a regular geometric structure without the whiplash that marked the Art Nouveau style in most of its other phases. The major architects of the Secession style were Otto Wagner, Joseph Olbrich, and Josef Hoffmann.[37] More important than specific works of these architects in the promulgation of the Secession style was the Wiener Werkstätte (Vienna Workshop) founded in 1903 under Hoffmann's leadership. It produced arts and crafts objects designed by artists and architects and executed in its own workshops—by 1905 the Werkstätte employed more than one hundred workers.[38] Right from the beginning, its products—whether jewelry, fabrics, or china—could easily be con-

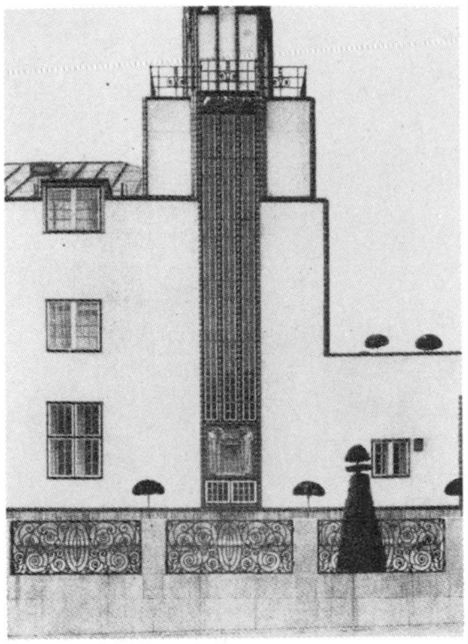

Palais Stoclet, exterior detail.

fused with Art Deco objects. There are the same bold fabric designs, pendants set in geometric frames, and rectangular and polygonal porcelain objects with vertical sides. Exemplifying the unified Wiener Werkstätte style is the Palais Stoclet in Brussels (1905-11), a villa designed by Hoffmann and with interior decoration by Wiener Werkstätte artists like Gustav Klimt. The building's exterior is fairly restrained; the smooth, marble-veneered walls with corners and windows emphasized by a dark metallic molding anticipate the "cool" materials favored in the thirties. The stepped tower with its Neoclassical statues and urns heaped with metallic flowers prefigures other aspects of the Art Deco style. The dining room of the Palais Stoclet was of yellow marble with a black and white marble floor and held a severe-looking set of dining chairs with octagonal metal sconces on the wall. The austerity was broken only by a magnificent frieze, designed by Klimt, that consisted of a mosaic of majolica, hammered metal, enameled pieces, opals, coral, and other stones.[39] Sheldon Cheney, in *The New World Architecture* of 1930, calls Viennese design "the smartest examples of Modernism thus far achieved. The Viennese seem to have made elegance the first test of success." Of Hoffmann's Palais Stoclet he writes that with its smooth, metal-trimmed walls it must have made carriages look out of date, and that motor cars would look completely appropriate next to it.[40]

Josef Hoffmann, Palais Stoclet dining room.

Joseph Urban, New York branch of Wiener Werkstätte, entrance rotunda, 1919.

In 1915 the Wiener Werkstätte was joined by Dagobert Peche, a young architect who brought to the geometric style of the Secession a playful manner in a Rococo spirit and prefigured in many of his designs the more frivolous side of Art Deco.[41] Wiener Werkstätte products were well known in Europe through their frequent illustration in periodicals and through such exhibitions as the 1914 Werkbund exhibition in Cologne at which Hoffmann and Peche had each designed a room for the Austrian pavilion. The Wiener Werkstätte also opened up branches in several cities, including Berlin, Zurich (this shop was designed and run by Peche from 1917 until 1919), and New York. The New York branch, on Fifth Avenue, was opened in 1919 under the management of the Austrian-born Joseph Urban.[42] The shop itself was a showpiece of the Secession style, and although it was not a financial success, its influence on New York architecture and design was important.[43] Leon Solon, a friend of Kahn's, wrote in 1923, in an article on the New York Wiener Werkstätte in the *Architectural Record*, that its style is usually called Art Nouveau but that it anticipates a new decorative feeling in architecture.[44] And Paul Frankl, like Urban an Austrian and active as a designer in New York, says: ". . . Joseph Urban's initiative in bringing the work of the Wiener Werkstätte to America may be considered one of the initial stepping stones in the development of our modern art movement. It succeeded in bringing many ideas, if only for a time, before the American public."[45]

The German and Central European Influence

Despite Germany's absence from the 1925 Paris exposition, its influence was not totally diminished. Not all roads led to Paris, and architects had their own ways of keeping informed. Ely Jacques Kahn, for example, during trips to Europe visited exhibitions not only in Paris, but also in Austria and Germany.[46] There seems to have been a general interest in German architecture, for an editor of *The American Architect* reports in 1925 that readers had requested illustrations of more German work.[47]

César Klein, bedroom for Wolfgang Gurlitt, Berlin, 1919.

Walter Gropius, Sommerfeld House, Berlin, 1921-22, stairwell.

What was of interest to American architects in German architecture of this period was probably not the works in the International Style, nor the more utopian designs of Expressionist architects.[48] It was more likely the popularized versions of Expressionism that seem to prefigure the Art Deco style of the later twenties. For example, in 1919 the Expressionist artist César Klein designed a bedroom for a Berlin house that seems like full-fledged Art Deco but in its German context is classified as Expressionist. And Walter Gropius' Sommerfeld House in Berlin of 1921-22, in its exterior and especially interior decorations carved by Bauhaus students, has as its *leitmotiv* triangles and chevrons, including triangular lighting fixtures—the very forms that became typical in the Art Deco style.

The faceted, crystalline ceilings of Voorhees, Gmelin & Walker's Irving Trust and Salvation Army buildings (54, 36) were prefigured in Bruno Taut's recreation room for a single men's residence in Berlin of 1919-20, in a dance casino at the Scala Palace in Berlin by Walter Würzbach and the sculptor Rudolf Belling of circa 1920, and in a restaurant used in Fritz Lang's 1922 film *Dr. Mabuse, the Gambler*.

Fiske Kimball in *American Architecture* (1928) wrote of the German influence: ". . . a reflux from abroad is favoring the

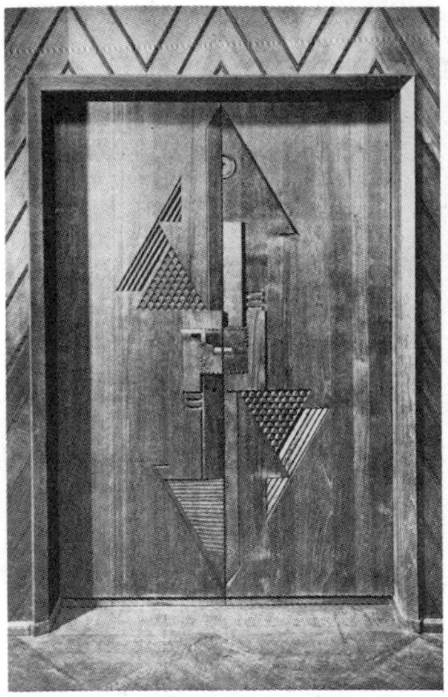

Sommerfeld House, detail of carved door by Joost Schmidt, a Bauhaus student.

drift from the classic. Certain American artists have recognized the creative liberty secured by the Germans, and are trying to free themselves from the bondage of academic detail while preserving the American heritage of simplicity and unity of form."[49]

Perhaps most congenial to the Beaux-Arts trained New York architects was a conservative interpretation of the Expressionist style which appeared in the so-called North German brick style, which resurrected the Hanseatic Gothic tradition of brick architecture and added some Expressionist overtones. Ornament is usually ingrained; that is, the structural unit, the brick itself, is used to introduce decoration by varying color tonalities and by changing the normal alignment of the bricks so that they project in angular patterns from the wall. The overall impression this type of architecture produces is of an earthy, hand-crafted texture. The March 1925 issue of *The American Architect* published illustrations of North German Expressionism—Fritz Höger's Chilehaus (1922-23) and Hans and Oskar Gerson's Ballinhaus (1923), both in Hamburg.[50] The Expressionism of these brick structures was often mixed with such Gothicizing features as triangular piers, as in Höger's Chilehaus; this device came to be used in many Art Deco buildings in New York as well.[51]

Peter Behrens, to whom Gropius, Mies, and Corbusier had been apprenticed during his earlier, better-known classicizing period,

Restaurant scene with faceted ceiling from Fritz Lang's *Dr. Mabuse, the Gambler*, 1922.

Fritz Höger, Chilehaus, Hamburg, 1922-23, detail showing some of the brick textures.

after World War I also turned to a medievalizing Expressionism. His "Dombauhütte" (cathedral lodge) designed for the Munich crafts show of 1922 is symptomatic. Although the medieval masons' lodge was only the workshop associated with the construction of a cathedral, Behrens designed his in the form of a chapel with interwoven, angular forms of varicolored brick suggesting a return to the integration of crafts with architecture and a superiority of handicrafts over machine work.[52] In Behrens' design for the I. G. Farben Dyeworks at Höchst, executed between 1920 and 1924, the Medieval and Expressionist styles appear split: the exterior of this large industrial complex is conservatively articulated in a Neomedieval style, whereas the multilevel entrance hall is an Expressionist transformation of a soaring Gothic interior. The material is brick throughout. On the exterior, brick is used in horizontal bands. In the hall the brick colors intensify toward the top, from a blue-green below to an orange-yellow above, a crescendo effect that terminates in star-shaped skylights. This building was illustrated in *The American Architect* in 1925, almost as soon as it had been completed,[53] and it may well be the source for the shaded brick structures in New York.

Höger, Chilehaus, general view.

Germany was not the only source for vaguely Expressionist, medievalizing, folkloristic, or handicraft tendencies in early Art Deco architecture. A national romanticism seems to have af-

Peter Behrens, I. G. Farben, Höchst, 1920-24, main hall.

fected the old Hanseatic League from Scandinavia to Holland during the first quarter of the century. Ragnar Östberg's Stockholm Town Hall with its vernacular overtones (1909-23), P. V. Jensen Klint's Expressionist Grundvig Church in Copenhagen (1913, 1921-26), and Eliel Saarinen's classicizing Helsinki railroad station (1905-14) are all part of this romantic and colorful style,[54] as are J. M. van der Meij's proto-Art Deco Scheepvaarthuis in Amsterdam (1912-16) and the more idiosyncratic expressionist works of such Amsterdam School architects as Michel de Klerk and Willem Dudok.[55] De Klerk's hous-

Van der Meij,
Scheepvaarthuis.

ing was illustrated here in 1922 in the *Journal of the American Institute of Architects* and in 1925 in the *Architectural Record*.[56] And in 1923 the *Architectural Forum* had shown some buildings by Dudok.[57] Cheney in *The New World Architecture* had this to say about Dutch architecture: ". . . for nearly a decade—until Germany actively resumed building and overtook her two or three years ago—Holland showed the most Modernistic face to the world of any of the nations. And for a new architecture with a most pronounced national or racial flavor you must even today go to the Dutch cities."[58] After 1927, when the Art Deco style in New York intensified, the volume of European material shown in American periodicals also increased. Evidence of the influence of the Expressionist brick style is especially strong in Voorhees, Gmelin & Walker's Western Union Building (27; 1928-30), with its unusual animated-looking brick panels.

A further aspect, the use of vivid color, found especially in the earlier examples of Art Deco, can be related to German Expressionist architecture in general, not just to the North German brick style.[59] Influenced by such Expressionist artists as Kandinsky, Bruno Taut had used vibrant colors in his housing projects from 1914 on.[60] Behrens' already mentioned use of glazed bricks in the interior of the Hoechst Dyeworks is another instance of an Expressionist color scheme. Many publications in America testify to a similar interest. Leon Solon published in the *Architectural Record* of 1922 a series of articles on polychromy in architecture.[61] And although they dealt largely with the use of color in Greek architecture (in this sense they still reflected the Beaux-Arts taste of the early twenties), they also introduced the general idea of a brightly ornamented architecture. Solon's essays were subsequently published as a book in 1924.[62] In an article in a 1921 issue of the *Architectural Record*, Alfred Bossom, in discussing the work of the artist Nicholas Roerich, claimed that more color had been appearing in recent architecture.[63] And one wonders whether it was Roerich's idea to have the exterior of the Master Institute and Riverside Museum (formerly Roerich Museum) shade from a purple brick at the base to a light grey brick at the top. Another article, "Architectural Polychromy" by C. Howard Walker, appeared in the March 1923 issue of the *Architectural Record*,[64] and in October 1925 W. Francklyn Paris, in reviewing the 1925 Paris exposition, wrote that "expressionists" held center stage and goes on to characterize the new style. He believed that mass in modern architecture must remain undisguised, that it must consist of straight lines and sharp angles; and since applied

Hans Poelzig, Grosses Schauspielhaus, Berlin, 1919, foyer.

decoration had become taboo (his analysis in this respect does not seem to describe the style of the 1925 Paris show), he called for color and rich materials to take its place.[65] In a similar vein Ely Jacques Kahn wrote in "On the Use of Color" of 1928 that color contrasts in architecture could eliminate carving and crockets. In another essay the following year, "On Decoration and Ornament," Kahn wrote that color must be used in proportion to the distance of the observer.[66] This indicates that perceptual effects of color were considered, that is, the intensity of the color used depended on the distance it was to be from street level and the observer. A concern for color is also apparent in most of Raymond Hoods' work up until about 1930. The Daily News Building has piers of white vitreous brick with spandrels of dark red and dull red brick patterns, and the window shades were red to harmonize with the spandrels. And Hood's blue-green glazed terra-cotta spandrels in the McGraw-Hill Building were described in 1931 as producing a good "atmospheric" quality under all types of weather conditions.[67] And as late as 1934 Sheldon Cheney, in his *Expressionism in Art,* wrote that although Victorian luxuriousness was missed in modern architecture, the bareness of the new architecture could be enriched in the idiom appropriate to the time by using a greater range of color.[68]

In German Expressionist architecture the interest in using color sprang originally from the desire to use colored glass that would transform light into a mystical experience, a light mysticism comparable to Gothic mysticism. However, in utopian Expressionist projects this signaled not so much religious feeling as a spiritual transformation of society. In Expressionism concern for light and for color usually went together. When building was again possible after World War I and the inflation that had followed, glass was usually found to be too costly, so that the dream of a colored glass architecture was changed into polychrome brick or colored stucco surfaces. Indirect lighting, with the source of light not revealed, often became a substitute in executed buildings for light seen through colored glass. A master of early examples of indirect lighting was Hans Poelzig. His Grosses Schauspielhaus of 1919 in Berlin uses indirect lighting for the columns of the foyer and in the theater itself. This was shown in a 1923 issue of *The American Architect.*[69] The use of indirect lighting of lobbies and the dramatic nighttime lighting of pinnacles, such as in the Barclay-Vesey Building, the RCA Victor Building, and the Chanin Building, is an effect that may have been borrowed from the Expressionist projects for glass architecture illuminated at night.[70] Or it may be a device borrowed from the theater. As early as 1921 Kenneth Macgowan, in *The Theatre of Tomorrow* (a book found in Voorhees, Gmelin & Walker's library), discusses Poelzig's Grosses Schauspielhaus and his set designs for *The Golem*, and makes a special point of German stage lighting as practiced by Max Reinhardt, Adolphe Appia, and Gordon Craig. The use of chiaroscuro lighting producing deep spatial effects is contrasted with Leon Bakst's flat, almost two-dimensional stage sets. The latter are depicted as somewhat outmoded.[71] In the January 1925 issue of the *Architectural Record*, in an article on "New Dimensions in Architectural Effects," Herbert Kroly wrote that the new zoning law was not nearly as important as the new effect that could be achieved through using color and light. Referring to the gilding used on Raymond Hood's American Radiator Building of 1924, he writes: "The gilding of these stories suggests . . . bewildering possibilities as to the future use of surfaces with colors, glows, and lights in order to convert the high places of New York, as seen from distant streets, into a wonderland of elaborate, fanciful and vivid masses and patterns."[72] Again, as for Kahn, the stated reason was to make the tops of skyscrapers visible at ground level and from far away. Harvey Wiley Corbett, in a 1930 article, "Design in Office Buildings" in *The Architectural Forum*, further reinforces a call for nocturnal lighting: he demands a wider use of color and proposes that buildings be flooded with harmonizing hues at night.[73] Such dramatic effects, when applied to an office building, are no longer comparable in intention to German Expressionism. They appear here simply as devices borrowed from the theater, dramatic devices that seem to coalesce with the equally theatrical sculptural and ornamental program of several Art Deco buildings; the drama of life in the modern metropolis is depicted as taking place not in its churches, schools, or city hall but in the office skyscraper. Kahn, in his essay "On the Use of Color," writes that the ". . . Dream of a colored city, buildings in harmonious tones making great masses of beautiful patterns, may be less of a vision if the enterprising city developer suspects the result."[74] This is Kahn, the public relations man, speaking about a dream world with commercial value.

Some American artists, architects, and historians were familiar enough with central European architecture and design to allow them to see the Paris 1925 show not as the first creative outburst of a new style, but as the eclectic amalgam of styles that it was. This is clear from an essay by Leon Solon; he writes that the exhibition has fallen short of expectations because unusual forms were procured at any cost. He acknowledges the desire to create advertising value, but sees in much of what was shown a French interpretation of central and northern European styles.[75] Leo Friedlander, an architectural sculptor like Solon, wrote in a 1927 *Architectural Forum* that the seed of the new movement "was sown in Austria 28 years ago. Its influence first spread to Germany, then to Scandinavia, Holland, Finland, Servia, Belgium and France."[76] And Ely Jacques Kahn in a 1929 issue of *Creative Art* wrote:

> It is commonplace to the ignorant to assume that so-called modernism is a mushroom growth of the day, possibly a recollection of 1925 in Paris—still more dimly a shaking of the old bones of the L'Art Nouveau. So much has already been said in this connection that it is trite to refer to the thirty years of development in Austria, Germany, Belgium, and the more recent Renaissance in France.[77]

The historian Fiske Kimball in his *American Architecture* of 1928 stated the same idea more briefly. He believed that an "impulse from abroad was given by the Paris exposition of decorative arts in 1925, where surviving elements of the *art nouveau*, which had remained in solution, were precipitated by reagents from Vienna."[78] And Sheldon Cheney in *The New World Architecture* of 1930, discussing the new European style, is the harshest critic of the 1925 exhibition:

> And why is there no weighty evidence from France? As early as 1925, Paris spread out the buildings of the Exposition of Decorative Arts, avowedly to bring to focus contemporary French effort outside the traditional styles—and to bring world Modernism into agreement with the graceful French talent. But that affair, and sporadic outcroppings here and there, . . . have only gone to show that outside a few inspired engineers and one or two imported radical architects, the impotent Beaux-Arts men still control France. Even the Exposition proved the French to be adapters of the Viennese thing, softening down the squared masses into sweeter and more graceful forms—with the sensuous delicacy of the Viennese touch a little spread toward the luxurious and grandiose. . . .
>
> . . . The French Modernists, as a matter of fact, have fattened themselves a bit over-assiduously on the Blue-Danube seductive grace, until Paris passes on to the Americas and to England and points more remote a hall-marked French decorative mode that is really sweetened and popularized Viennese.[79]

Extending this food analogy, one might say that to Cheney the 1925 exhibition is Viennese pastry served up as gingerbread.

American Influence

As has been noted before, the Art Deco architect did not look only to Europe for inspiration. Within the American tradition the work of Louis Sullivan and Frank Lloyd Wright is central. Sullivan's use of a luxurious but tightly organized ornament within a generally classicizing massing of form can be seen as a prototype for comparable Art Deco features. His emphatic use of vertical piers with recessed spandrels is another element common in Art Deco skyscrapers. Further, Sullivan's accent on building entrance and building top by means of a dynamic ornament (usually spandrels are ornamented also, but with a pattern more rigid and geometric than that used for entrance and top) becomes general practice in most Art Deco skyscrapers.

The references among writers of the twenties to the wall as a veneer or a curtain[80] can be traced to ideas circulated by the Chicago School, ideas which, together with Sullivan's placement of architectural ornament, derive from the theories of the nineteenth-century German architect Gottfried Semper. John Wellborn Root translated and published one of Semper's essays—"Development of Architectural Style"—in the *Inland Architect* of 1890. Earlier, during a discussion of the Illinois State Association of Architects, published in the *Inland Architect* in 1887, Semper had been quoted by one of the speakers.[81] Louis Sullivan had been present at this meeting. Also, Dankmar Adler, Sullivan's partner, was fond of reciting Semperian *bons mots*. Semper in one of his essays on the evolution of architectural form, "The Four Elements of Architecture," had proposed four basic components: the hearth as the first social gathering place, the basement to raise the hearth off the damp ground, a roof with supporting poles to protect the fire against rain, and lastly an enclosure of textiles, animal skins, wattle or any other filler either hung from the frame or placed between the supporting poles.[82] These concepts, proposed to explain past architectural development, were often interpreted as a recipe for new architecture, hence the interest in creating curtain walls that look like woven tapestries (6A, 21A, 26G). Semper had also developed notions of dynamic distribution of ornament in architecture: areas of greatest dynamic stress (actual and apparent), such as entries and roof lines, were seen as being in tension and therefore received emphatic fields of decoration. Sullivan seems to have followed Semper in his organization of ornament.[83]

The use of extensive ornament at the ground floor and near the top in Art Deco buildings is thus tied to a nineteenth-century tradition that lends them scale at close range as well as from a distance and makes them appear less dehumanizing than the unarticulated top and the bland elevator lobby which characterize most current office buildings.

Frank Lloyd Wright, Midway Gardens, Chicago, 1914. Detail of interpenetrating sculptural ornament and textured concrete blocks.

Frank Lloyd Wright, A. D. German Warehouse, Richland Center, Wisconsin, 1915. Detail of patterned blocks facing top storey.

Although Frank Lloyd Wright had not yet executed any of his skyscraper projects by the twenties, his influence on the Art Deco style was considerable and may be perceived in his very early development of an abstract, usually geometric ornament. This appeared first in the stained glass panels of his prairie houses, then in the tiles used in the Coonley House (1908) that imitate textile patterns, and it becomes part of an ingrained architectural ornament in the patterned concrete blocks of the Midway Gardens (1914), in the lava blocks of the Imperial Hotel (1916-22), and in the various concrete blocks for his California houses of the early twenties.[84] Both of Paul Frankl's books, *New Dimensions* of 1928 and *Form and Re-Form* of 1930, begin with illustrations from Wright's California houses.

Another American stylistic ingredient of Art Deco architecture, the Pre-Columbian influence, had been interpreted by Wright in his A. D. German Warehouse (1915) and in his Hollyhock House (1920). Wright's use of ornament within clearly defined zones and canted walls seems to have been inspired by Mayan architecture. However, there is little direct reference to any Pre-Columbian design in New York Art Deco,[85] except perhaps in the ornament of Edward Sibbert's Kress Building (106) and, possibly, the decorative detailing of Starrett & Van Vleck's Bloomingdale store (56). In Art Deco crafts the frequent stepped design of appliances and furniture is assumed to derive from Mayan or Aztec pyramids. Similar stepped formations in architecture, on the other hand, depend more likely on the New York City zoning law that required such setbacks.[86]

There was, though, in the Art Deco period a certain interest in primitivism, a tendency common among early twentieth-century styles. The 1923 *Architectural Record* carried an article titled "A

Frank Lloyd Wright, Hollyhock House, Hollywood, 1920.

Primitive Basis for Modern Architecture," which claimed that the American Indians were the first Cubists. However this claim was illustrated with works in a New Mexico Mission style.[87] An exceptional exoticism is the Egyptian cornice of Schwartz & Gross' apartment house on Central Park West (20B). More often references to primitive or exotic styles are difficult to classify and, at least in New York, they flourished more readily in interior decoration. Winold Reiss, an Austrian-born designer, executed two New York interiors, both no longer in existence, the Crillon Restaurant in peasant motifs[88] and the Congo Room at the Hotel Alamac with chairs whose backs consisted of flat panels in the shape of black and white aborigines and with walls covered with jungle murals and masks.[89]

Popular Cultural Influences

Because from its very beginning Art Deco was not an abstruse style, it not only drew inspiration from earlier architecture, but was especially open to influences from stage and screen in which high art had already been digested and popularized. *The American Architect* published in 1920 the following editorial:

> The important motion picture producers are fast realizing the commercial value of good architecture. This fact is becoming evident in the recent presentation of "feature films." Among those legends which announce the various people who shared responsibility in the production of a scenario, it is becoming customary to include the name of the architect who designed the exteriors and planned the arrangement and decoration of rooms which serve as a background for the story. Architects will appreciate this recognition of their cooperation in these matters.[90]

This is an indication that architectural design was being made part of the film, and that architecture could affect public taste through film. In fact, in 1921 the *Journal of the American Institute of Architects* published an essay about *Caligari* and its use of exaggerated space and lighting.[91] Sets from the theater and film began, in fact, to influence taste, and designs by Norman Bel Geddes or Lee Simonson were as much discussed as the plays themselves.[92] And in 1922 the *Architectual Record* illustrated Claude Bragdon's and Norman Bel Geddes' theater design.[93]

The German Expressionist film was especially precocious in using artists and architects as set designers, and such films as *The Cabinet of Dr. Caligari* (1919) and *The Golem* (1920) contain many formal elements that came to be called Art Deco at a later time. *Caligari* was shown in the States in 1921, and although it was

Scene from *The Cabinet of Dr. Caligari* (Robert Wiene, director), 1919. This view shows the use of distorted space and exaggerated light and shadows.

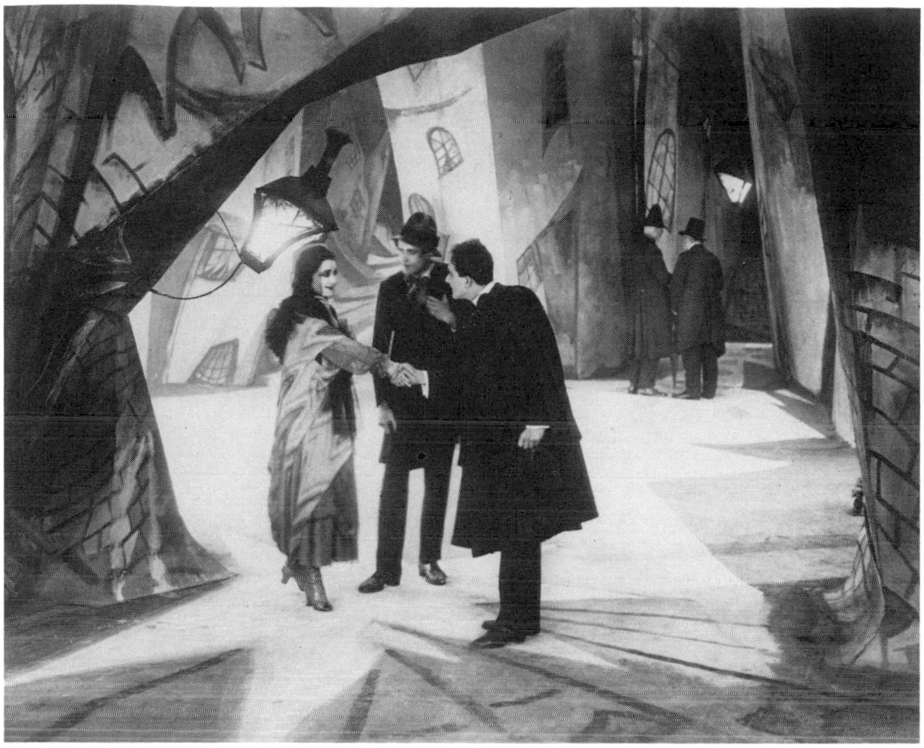

Interior scene from *Caligari*. In contrast to the angular exterior setting, this shows softly rounded forms. Both formal treatments are ingredients of Art Deco.

seen by comparatively few people, it was nevertheless the most widely discussed film of the time. . . . "It is a matter of record that no picture, not even *The Birth of a Nation,* ever created quite as much comment, argument, and speculation in one month's time as did *The Cabinet of Dr. Caligari.*"[94]

The Golem, with Expressionist sets designed by the architect Hans Poelzig, was also released here in 1921. Writing in *Theatre Magazine*, a reviewer said that "this is another of the spectacular German films that have recently been imported into this country, thereby breaking the nightly rest of Hollywood."[95] The impact of such films on Hollywod fostered an influx of European film-makers. Erté, the French designer, also came to Hollywood to do the sets for the film *Paris 25*.[96] A later film like Fritz Lang's *Metropolis* (1926) contained Art Deco details, especially in its interior architectural design (Lang had originally studied architecture before becoming a film director), but the views of his Metropolis with its ominous buildings, viaducts and overpasses, and airplanes whirring between skyscrapers prefigure the futuristic images of the modern metropolis later created by Hugh Ferris. In *Metropolis* the imagery of the modern city also has come full circle, for Lang was influenced in the creation of his sets by a view of the Manhattan skyline seen on a boat trip to the States in 1924:

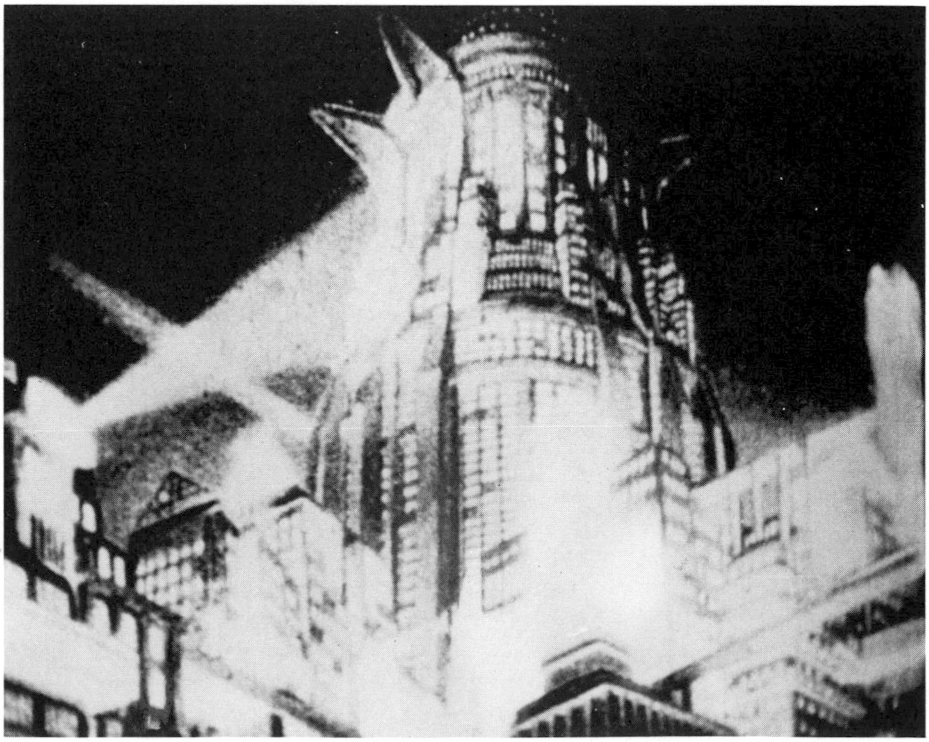

Night view of city from *Metropolis* (Fritz Lang, director), 1926.

Night club entrance from *Metropolis*.

I first came to America briefly in 1924 and it made a great impression on me. The first evening, when we arrived, we were still enemy aliens so we couldn't leave the ship. It was docked somewhere on the West Side of New York. I looked into the streets—the glaring lights and the tall buildings—and there I conceived *Metropolis*.[97]

A large exhibit of contemporary design held at Macy's in 1928 and called "Art in Trade Exposition" (organized by the Art in Trade Club) brought many of the divergent sources of the Art Deco style together under one roof. There were rooms by the Austrian Josef Hoffmann, by the German Bruno Paul, by the Italian Gio Ponti, by French designers and design groups—Leleu, Dufrêne, and D.I.M.—by the New York architect Eugene Schoen, and by Kem Weber, a German who had settled in Los Angeles where he worked both as an architect and a Hollywood set designer.[98] The popularization of the Art Deco style through the Paris exposition of 1925, through films, and through the shows at Lord and Taylor's and Macy's in 1928 makes clear that from the beginning Art Deco was seen as a marketable modern style.

A Period of Science, Industry, and Business

What figure the poet might employ to describe the skyscraper, dwarfing the church, outpointing the cathedral spire, I do not know. There is an epic implication in man's defiance of the laws of gravity, and beauty in the naked lift of uprising steel and concrete. But the purpose of the skyscraper is not poetic. Perhaps Commercialism is a new God, only too powerful and too appealing, to Whom men are building today their largest, costliest, and most laudatory structures. In this service they are building higher and ever higher, concentrating more and more activity into less of ground space, stealing light and air from their neighbors, piously recording in their structures the Exploitation that is [a] right-hand attribute of Commercialism.

At any rate, the skyscraper is the typical building of the twentieth century. New York City . . . sees the rise of scores of business buildings larger, more honest in methods of construction and in purpose (for the cathedral in coming times, as now, can be little more than a show place, a piece of insincerity), and more expressive of contemporary living. Business rules the world today, and as long as business can best be served where many offices are concentrated in one small area, in buildings designed as machines for the efficient discharge of buying, selling, trading, banking, law disputes, gambling, and exploitation, business architecture will be supreme.[99]

Contemporary writers agreed in characterizing their period. For Edwin Avery Park, writing in *New Backgrounds for a New Age* of 1927, America was a new world of science, industry, and business;[100] he believed that American art of the future would be a reflection of industrial democracy. Paul T. Frankl wrote similarly in *New Dimensions* of 1928: "Our age is one of invention, machinery, industry, science, and commerce."[101] For both writers the times were distinguished by a triumvirate of science, industry, and business, not art. In 1928 Frankl was still overwhelmed by the rapid pace of industrialized society, and he saw art as an antidote to the world at large: "The great complexity of things about us is quite worrying. Human nature cannot keep pace with modern invention. And, while complexity is a characteristic of our mechanical lives, it is the opposite of this that we seek for in aesthetic enjoyment. The opposite of complexity is simplicity."[102] But by 1930, in *Form and Re-Form*, he seems to have come to terms with complexity and speed. Instead of counteracting it in aesthetic expression, he now proposes to articulate it. For him the spirit of American democracy manifests itself in freedom, frankness, freshness, directness, compression, and speed.[103] The subversion of traditional values by the frenetic rhythms of science and industry had not even been questioned by Park, who had written: "Houses are less important than motor cars, and furniture less again than hot water, thermostats and scientific kitchens. Utility and mobility we seek."[104]

New industrial materials were beginning to make an impact on architecture, particularly interiors and furniture design, in a manner reminiscent of the Victorian period's unabashed and inventive use of materials like cast iron and papier-mâché for furniture. Paul Frankl wrote admiringly of this trend that "industrial chemistry today rivals alchemy! Base materials are transmuted into marvels of new beauty."[105] Formica was used for interior walls: vitrolite, a heavy black glass, was employed especially in hotels, restaurants, and theaters (as in Frederick Kiesler's Film Guild Cinema, for instance). Monel metal, a copper and nickel alloy, was used for soda fountains and furniture trim. Bakelite was probably among the best-known of the early plastics and was used for a wide variety of manufactured goods. Synthetic cork plates could be employed as wall or floor coverings, and aluminum leaf replaced silver leaf and was used for the ceilings of the staircases in the Chrysler Building.[106]

By around 1930 the designs of Art Deco architects began to be affected by an overwhelming realization that the machine and industry are overriding factors in modern life.[107] Sheldon Cheney's estimate in *The New World Architecture* is brightly optimistic:

> There will ultimately be machine-developed energy to solve all men's work problems, with no more labor than is involved in passing control. The ele-

ments themselves will be tamed, weather tempered, transportation become effortless, cleanliness universal, the works of the intellect and of the artistic faculties will be transported instantaneously to all. Living will be speeded, concentrated, regulated, as never before.

There is no turning back. There is no hindering the swiftness of humanity's advance toward that time. No one can foresee the organization that will turn all this to the good of the human soul, when the old pivots on which individual life has turned—labor, making a living, money, protective nationalistic governments—are scrapped. We only know that increasingly now the problem of nobly utilizing leisure time becomes all-important. We are past the possibility of challenging the machine, of curbing it, of attempting escape from it. We must live in a way that crowds into a week what used to be the experiences of a year, that makes a half-hour's work of what used to occupy our grandparents for a day. We must move by machinery, communicate by it—live by it.[108]

Architects now turned to a machine aesthetic, as the Futurists, Constructivists, and International Style architects had done before them. As in the latter groups, the machine was mythologized and romanticized. No direct influence from these movements is suggested. Antonio Sant'Elia's Futurist architectural designs of 1913-14 were not publicized in America. If we can speak of Futurist or Constructivist tendencies in the later Art Deco style, they came indirectly through International Style architecture, which by the thirties was beginning to affect the Art Deco style. The hand-crafted, Expressionist-influenced, and exotic quality of the earlier Art Deco style disappeared and was replaced by severer, Neoclassic forms with much less ornament and almost no color. Upward-rushing, Gothic-inspired piers are no longer the norm. Horizontal features appear more frequently—in part adapted from the International Style and in part suggesting the streaking image of vehicles flashing by. Terra-cotta decoration gives way to smoothly articulated surfaces with an occasional rounded, streamlined corner, sheathed in shining metal. Such streamlining effects are often seen as having been influenced by similar methods in car design. By 1931 streamlining had affected architecture, as in the entrance to the McGraw-Hill Building (82A) and in the foyer of Joseph Urban's auditorium for the New School (51E). But strangely, as late as 1932 Norman Bel Geddes was still complaining that streamlining had not yet made any inroads into commercial car design.[109] Streamlined forms had actually been used by Eric Mendelsohn in sketches and executed buildings in the teens and throughout the twenties, most of which had been published here by 1930. Mendelsohn had wanted to suggest in a generalized sense the dynamics of modern industry; the one executed example

Eric Mendelsohn, sketches for industrial buildings, most of which contain streamlined forms, from Sheldon Cheney, *The New World Architecture*, 1930.

that prefigures a specific motif of the later streamlined style is his interior of the Universum Cinema (1927-28) in Berlin. Its parallel horizontal triple-line bands leading toward the screen appear to be a direct precedent for the similar motif in the entrance to the McGraw-Hill Building.

When Mendelsohn visited the United States in 1924 he spent two days as the guest of Frank Lloyd Wright at Taliesin. While on a walk near Taliesin they drew designs in the sand on the banks of a river, Wright a garage with an imaginary superstructure, Mendelsohn a sketch with rounded contours. That evening and the next morning Mendelsohn made architectural sketches from which Wright selected several for himself.[110] The younger architect's impact on Wright can perhaps be seen in some of the latter's streamlined designs for the Broadacre City project and the Johnson Wax Administration Building, both of the thirties.

Also, in 1934 the Museum of Modern Art held a "Machine Art" exhibition. In the catalogue for the show, Alfred H. Barr elevated the product of the machine to a Platonic archetype:

> The beauty of machine art is in part the abstract beauty of straight lines and circles made into actual tangible surfaces and solids by means of tools, lathes and rules and squares. In Plato's day the tools were simple handworker's implements but today, as a result of the perfection of modern materials and the precision of modern instruments, the modern machine-made object approaches far more closely and more frequently those pure shapes the contemplation of which Plato calls the first of the "pure pleasures."[111]

The austerity and machine imagery of the later Art Deco style with its greyer, more impersonal look (see Cross & Cross' Tiffany Building or Corbett's Criminal Courts Building, both of 1939), also fits in better with the Depression. The lushness of the earlier style might have looked too frivolous during the thirties, and the dramatic pyrotechnics of the earlier Art Deco gave way to a stylization of the workaday world.

The End of a Period

What was responsible for the demise of Art Deco architecture? The Depression played a large role. By the late thirties most of the Art Deco structures going up were no longer corporate but mostly federal or municipal buildings. Then the beginning of World War II resulted in a steep decline of new building.

However, even before the onset of World War II, taste was beginning to shift in favor of the International Style. Starting in 1932, with the publication of Henry Russell Hitchcock's and Philip Johnson's *The International Style* and the already-mentioned Museum of Modern Art International Architecture exhibition, it became clear that a European style had evolved that was regarded as more advanced by the most prestigious architectural historians. In the exhibition catalogue for the Museum of Modern Art show, the Art Deco architects were, as mentioned earlier, singled out as the adversaries of the new style. In another Museum of Modern Art publication, *What Is Modern Architecture?* of 1942, the characteristics assigned to the International Style by Hitchcock and Johnson are still stated unequivocally as design principles for modern architecture in general. However, by 1944, in the catalogue of yet another Museum of Modern Art exhibit, *Built in USA—1932-1944*, the assurance of the earlier statements is beginning to be qualified and some doubt about the universal validity of the International Style appears. Elizabeth Mock, looking back to the Museum of Modern Art catalogue of 1932 in her foreword, finds that the analysis of aesthetic principles is still correct; however, she goes on to say:

> But the book had its weakness. Although modern materials and construction and modern living preferences were recognized as the basis of the new es-

thetics, there is little hint of their endless possibilities for development, nor of the effect such development would inevitably have upon design. The Museum placed great importance on "volume," achieved through non-committal, dematerialized wall planes, absence of projecting cornice, flush doors and flush ribbon windows, whereas modern architecture has always had, at least potentially, a freedom and flexibility far beyond those limits.[112]

In any case, the Museum of Modern Art had played an important role in paving the way for the acceptance of the International Style in this country. In 1933, shortly after the International Style had been pinpointed and codified by Hitchcock and Johnson, Talbot Hamlin published a succinct attack on it in an essay in *The American Architect* called "The International Style Lacks the Essence of Great Architecture." He begins bitterly:

The climax of the propaganda that has surrounded the birth of an architecture of today has been the development of a movement called the International Style. This, its sponsors claim, is architecture indeed, the only valid method of building under the present social system. To this International Style as to the god of a new religion they offer a service of adulation artfully compounded of the methods of modern publicity, and the ethical and religious passion of a Ruskin.[113]

And comparing the salient features of great architecture of the past with those of the International Style, Hamlin writes:

. . . the sense stimulus is the primary element; and the more intellectual the content that is required for its appreciation, the more esoteric the art. The layman—for all great architecture is sooner or later loved by the layman—is not an engineer, a philosopher, or a sociologist, except in the most elementary manner. . . . He likes to have a feeling that things "work." But it's a qualitative, not a quantitative, interest. And it is true of both Greek and Gothic architectures that they appeal to this "qualitative" and not "quantitative" kind of thought. The layman can make them his own. And this is distinctly not true of the International Style, which aims most definitely at the other ideal.

It is not quantitative functionalism that is at the root of great architecture. It is not abstruse intellectual content of any kind. . . . It is not conformity to any theory. It is never the result of labored and self-conscious puritanism. It is never a denial of joy in life.

Examination of Greek and Gothic work, it seems, reveals an exuberance of color and form that is instinct with the delight of creation. It is not enough merely to build, these architectures seem to say, nor even to build well and with at least approximate honesty. Human desires demand more; over this framework, within it, imagination must play richly, not only to arrange, but to decorate, yet so beautifully that decoration itself shall seem to flow out of necessary form. To be beautiful, gracious, enticing—to take the bare limbs of building and make them flower like cherry trees in spring—is not this the engendering power of great architecture?

Thus great architecture has disciplines that are more stimuli than inhibitions. It can be helped, but never created, by structural expression; yet structural expression carried to the limit would often spoil it. . . . The root of great architecture is like the root of any created beauty, deep in the matrix of human consciousness. It is spontaneity, delight in form. It is a superfluity—almost always a sense of "more than enough." It is the play of creative minds that makes living and building a delight as well as a task. It is the dance of Siva.

Can it be that the International Style has never learned how to play?[114]

Using Hamlin's definition, we could say that if the International Style is one of "less is more," then Art Deco is a style of "more than enough."

A Skyscraper Fantasy

Let us end with a fantasy to end all Art Deco fantasies. When Frank Lloyd Wright was excluded from participation in the Chicago Century of Progress Fair to be held in 1933, he was invited by the American Union of Decorative Artists and Craftsmen to address them at Town Hall. Before the meeting Raymond Hood (one of the commissioners of the Chicago Fair) took him to dinner at the Crillon restaurant (designed by Winold Reiss). Afterwards, at Town Hall, Wright delineated three hypothetical proposals for fair architecture.[115] One of these, for a skyscraper, seems like the archetypal Art Deco multi-functional, theatrical, science-fiction building:

Build a great skyscraper in which the Empire State Building might stand free in a central interior court-space which would be devoted to all the resources of the modern elevator. . . .

Instead of glass for enclosure—some of our many light, transparent glass substitutes might be used. The multitudinous areas thus created could be let to the various exhibitors. The entire feature of the top stories could be garden observatories, pleasure places. . . . This tower construction of steel might rise from the triple-decked parking terraces, one corner of the terraces projecting and extending into the lake two ways at right angles to make piers and harbors for all water craft. Beneath the lake nearby where the reflections of the tower would fall, powerful jets of the lake itself rising by way of inserted power pumps to great height. All to be illuminated by modern light-projecting apparatus, projecting toward the tower and projecting from it. The lake thus at contingent points becoming a series of great fountains irradiated by light.

The Lake Front Park itself would thus become merely landscape adjunct to the great modern structure . . . about a half mile high.

The clouds might naturally or artificially drift across its summit. Or effects be created by aeroplanes laying down colored ribbons of smoke to drift across it.[116]

Rosemarie Haag Bletter

NOTES

1. Edwin Avery Park, *New Backgrounds for a New Age* (New York: Harcourt, Brace & Co., 1927), p. 50.
2. Paul T. Frankl, *Form and Re-Form* (New York: Harper & Brothers, 1930), p. 77.
3. Louis H. Sullivan, "The Tall Office Building Artistically Considered," reprinted in *Kindergarten Chats and Other Writings* (New York: Wittenborn, 1968), p. 205.
4. Sullivan had anticipated such later massing in his unexecuted design for a Fraternity Temple of 1891.
5. Sullivan, p. 206.
6. John Ruskin, *The Stones of Venice* (London: Smith, Elder & Co., 1851), vol. I, pp. 59-60. For further discussion of Ruskin's theory of ornament see Kristine Ottesen Garrigan, *Ruskin on Architecture—His Thought and Influence* (Madison: University of Wisconsin Press, 1973).
7. Ruskin, p. 238.
8. Talbot Faulkner Hamlin, "Is Originality Leading Us Into a New Victorianism?" *American Architect,* 141 (Feb. 1932), 70.
9. Ely Jacques Kahn, "The Province of Decoration in Modern Design," *Creative Art,* 5 (Dec. 1929), 886.
10. Forrest F. Lisle, Jr., "Chicago's 'Century of Progress' Exposition: The Moderne as Democratic, Popular Culture," abstract of paper presented at Twenty-Fifth Annual Meeting of the Society of Architectural Historians, San Francisco, January 26-30, 1972 (part of a program on Moderne Architecture, chaired by David S. Gebhard), *Society of Architectural Historians Journal,* 31:3 (Oct. 1972), 230.
11. Ibid.
12. To date there are two publications dealing with architecture. One is David Gebhard and Harriette von Breton, *Kem Weber—The Moderne in Southern California 1920 through 1941* (Santa Barbara: The Art Galleries, University of California, 1969). The same text was reprinted in David Gebhard, "The Moderne in the U.S. 1920-1941," *Architectural Association Quarterly,* 2 (July 1970), 4-20. The illustrations, however, are not the same as in the *Kem Weber* catalogue—the former illustrate the text on the Moderne in Southern California. Gebhard has also written a brief text for *The Richfield Building: 1928-68* (Los Angeles: Atlantic Richfield Company, 1970).
13. For example, Theodore Menten in his *The Art Deco Style* (New York: Dover, 1972) includes Corbusier's Voisin Plan, Gropius' Teachers' Housing at the Dessau Bauhaus, and Bruno Taut's exhibition hall at Magdeburg in Art Deco. And Yvonne Brunhammer in *The Nineteen Twenties Style* (London: Paul Hamlyn, 1966) calls her section on architecture simply "The In-

ternational Style" and proceeds to discuss the Werkbund, Gropius, and Taut as part of Art Deco.

14. Terminology is best discussed in Bevis Hillier, *Art Deco* (London: Studio Vista, 1968), p. 10 ff. The most comprehensive bibliography on Art Deco crafts appears in Bevis Hillier, *The World of Art Deco* exhibition catalogue, Minneapolis Institute of Arts, 1971.
15. Park still refers in 1927 to the new movement as "modernist" (p. 7). However, the following year Paul Frankl in *New Dimensions* (New York: Payson & Clarke, 1928) refers to "modernistic" effects (p. 18), and Leon Solon in "The Park Avenue Building, New York City," (*Architectural Record*, 63 (April 1928), 289-301) uses the terms "modernist" and "Modernistic." By 1932 the Museum of Modern Art in a catalogue for the *Modern Architecture International Exhibition* of 1932 refers several times to the "modernistic style," now in a perjorative sense.
16. See Gebhard text of *Kem Weber*.
17. Editorial, "A Regional Style of Architecture," *American Architect*, 117 (Feb. 4, 1920), 151-52.
18. While most authors agree that 1925 represents a central date, there is no clear indication why specific dates for the beginning of the style were chosen: Giulia Veronesi in *Style and Design, 1909-1929* (New York: Braziller, 1968) begins her discussion with the Art Nouveau style; Brunhammer, like Veronesi, sees the beginning of the style in 1909, but her stated reason is that 1909 is the date of Peter Behrens' AEG factory and the first Futurist manifesto (what these have to do with Art Deco is never explained); and Martin Battersby in *The Decorative Twenties* (New York: Walker & Co., 1969) fixes the beginning at 1910, although nearly all his illustrations are from the twenties.
19. *Modern Architecture—International Exhibition*, p. 13.
20. Veronesi, p. 219, and Rudolph Rosenthal and Helena Ratzka, *The Story of Modern Applied Art* (New York: Harper & Brothers, 1948), p. 77.
21. The Werkbund exerted its influence through its periodical, *Die Form*, through the Werkbund yearbook, and through exhibitions. See Julius Posener, *Anfänge des Funktionalismus—Von Arts and Crafts zum Deutschen Werkbund* (Berlin: Ullstein Bauwelt Fundamente, 1964). And Ulrich Conrads, editor, *Programmes and Manifestoes on 20th-century Architecture*, transl. by Michael Bullock (London: Lund Humphries, 1970).
22. Elie Richard, "Genèse d'une Exposition," Exposition Internationale des Arts Décoratifs et Industriels Modernes, Paris, Avril-Octobre 1925, *Catalogue Général Officiel* (Paris: Imprimerie de Vaugirard [1925]), unpaged. This also contains a map of the exhibition. See also Battersby, p. 17 and Judith Applegate, *Art Deco* (New York: Finch College Museum of Art, 1970), unpaged.
23. *Report of Commission appointed by the Secretary of Commerce to visit and report upon the Intl. Exposition of Modern Decorative and Industrial Art in Paris 1925*, p. 16.
24. Frankl, *Form and Re-Form*, p. 1.
25. *Report of Commission* . . . , p. 17.
26. Veronesi, p. 219.
27. *Le Corbusier und Pierre Jeanneret*, ed. and transl. by O. Stonorov and W. Boesiger (Zurich: Dr. H. Girsberger & Co., 1930), vol. I, pp. 100 and 102. It is really not very surprising that the commission erected this fence since it was part of Corbusier's program in the pavilion to reject the decorative arts.
28. It is also curious that, although the exposition was to be of decorative *and* industrial arts, there was in fact very little industrial art shown.

29. Further exceptions to the decorative frenzy of most of the pavilions were the designs by Tony Garnier and Auguste Perret.
30. Ely Jacques Kahn, unpublished manuscript, Avery Library, Columbia University, section II, p. 32.
31. Rosenthal and Ratzka, p. 17.
32. *Report of Commission . . .* , p. 5.
33. Ibid., p. 14.
34. Rosenthal and Ratzka, p. 176 and Kahn, unpublished manuscript, II, p. 36.
35. Henry-Russell Hitchcock, "Some American Interiors in the Modern Style," *Architectural Record*, 64 (Sept. 1928), 235.
36. Metropolitan Museum of Art, *The Architect and the Industrial Arts—An Exhibition of Contemporary American Design*, Feb. 12 to March 24 and continued to Sept. 2, 1929 (1929). See also Rosenthal and Ratzka, pp. 178-79; Kahn, manuscript, II, p. 32; and Arthur Tappan North, *Raymond Hood*, Contemporary American Architects series (New York: McGraw-Hill, 1931), p. 70.
37. Charles Rennie Mackintosh's work in Glasgow may also be seen as prefiguring the Art Deco style. However, his work does not seem to have the same continuity with the twenties that we can find in Hoffmann's architecture and the designs of the Wiener Werkstätte. Some of the more classicizing work of Joseph Olbrich at the Darmstadt Artists' Colony, such as the Ernst-Ludwig Haus and the entrance to the wedding tower, might also be included in a list of sources for Art Deco.
38. *Die Wiener Werkstätte—Modernes Kunsthandwerk*, exhibition catalogue (Vienna, 1967), p. 13.
39. Rosenthal and Ratzka, p. 59.
40. Sheldon Cheney, *The New World Architecture* (London, New York, and Toronto: Longmans, Green & Co., 1930), pp. 25 and 186.
41. See Max Eisler, *Dagobert Peche* (Vienna and Leipzig: Gerlach & Widling, 1925). Peche designed black-and-white-striped furniture as early as 1915. Striped furniture in starkly contrasting colors became a fad in the twenties (Veronesi claims that such designs in Art Deco derive from designs by Leon Bakst made between 1919 and 1923; p. 42).
42. Rosenthal and Ratzka, p. 173. According to these authors Wiener Werkstätte products, together with silks by Paul Poiret (p. 42), had been imported by John Wanamaker's as early as 1913.
43. Leon V. Solon, "The Viennese Method for Artistic Display—New York Galleries of the Wiener Werkstätte," *Architectural Record* 53 (March 1923), 266-71.
44. Solon, p. 266.
45. Frankl, *New Dimensions*, p. 76.
46. Kahn, manuscript, II, p. 31.
47. Egerton Swartwout, "Review of Recent Architectural Magazines," *American Architect*, 127 (March 15, 1925), 279.
48. However, some of the more fantastic designs of this period, Mies' and Poelzig's skyscraper projects, had been illustrated in Walter Curt Behrendt's article "Skyscrapers in Germany," *Journal of the American Institute of Architects*, 11 (Sept. 1923), 365-70.
49. Fiske Kimball, *American Architecture* (Indianapolis & New York: Bobbs-Merrill, 1928), p. 209.
50. *American Architect*, 127 (March 15, 1925), 281. The illustrations of the Chilehaus and the Ballinhaus were taken from *Moderne Bauformen*. The Chilehaus was illustrated again in the same year in "Gleaned from the

Foreign Architectural Press," *American Architect*, 128 (1925), 551-52. The Chilehaus was also illustrated in Frankl's *New Dimensions*. For further illustrations of German Expressionist architecture see also Wolfgang Pehnt, *Expressionist Architecture* (New York and Washington: Praeger, 1973), Eng. trans. by J. A. Underwood and Edith Küstner.

51. Triangular piers had also been used by Bruno Taut in a series of buildings designed for Magdeburg. Earlier American Neogothic skyscrapers, such as Cass Gilbert's Woolworth Building of 1913, had also used such piers. In this instance it is, therefore, difficult to say whether their use in Art Deco derives from American Neogothic architecture or from German Gothicizing Expressionist architecture, or both.

In the case of Voorhees, Gmelin & Walker, the German influence can be clearly established because of Gmelin's German background. The firm's library contained many books on contemporary German architecture, as well as a collection on German and American stage and cinema design. Among them: Eric Mendelsohn, *Amerika* (Berlin, 1926); Hermann Muthesius, *Die Schöne Wohnung* (Munich, 1922); Oliver Saylor, ed., *Max Reinhardt and his Theater* (New York, 1924); Paul Zucker, *Theater und Lichtspielhäuser* (Berlin, 1926); Fr. Kranich, *Bühnentechnik der Gegenwart* (Munich and Berlin, 1929); Günther Herkt, *Das Tonfilm Theater* (Berlin, 1931); Joseph Urban, *Theaters* (New York, 1929); Kenneth MacGowan and Robert Edmond Jones, *Continental Stagecraft* (New York, 1922); Sheldon Cheney, *The Art Theater* (New York, 1917); R. W. Sexton and B. F. Betts, *American Theatres of Today* (New York, 1927, 2 vols.), and many others.

A somewhat vaguer relationship between an American architect and a central European influence can be seen in Harvey Wiley Corbett's interest in Frederick Kiesler's designs. Kiesler, a Viennese-born architect who had been a member of the Berlin G group and the Dutch de Stijl movement before coming to America, in 1926 exhibited plans for his Endless House at the New York Theater Guild, where Corbett saw them and began taking an interest in Kiesler. According to Kiesler himself, he worked for two years in Corbett's architectural firm (Thomas H. Creighton interview with Kiesler, "Kiesler's Pursuit of an Idea," *Progressive Architecture*, 42 (July 1961), 105-16). However, Wallace K. Harrison claimed in a private interview that Kiesler never joined Corbett's office officially but that Corbett fostered Kiesler's career and took a special interest in Kiesler's design for the Eighth Street Playhouse (1929; today much altered), which seems to owe a debt to Mendelsohn's Universum Theater in Berlin.

52. This goal is explicitly stated by Behrens himself in his opening speech of the exhibition, "Die Dombauhütte," *Deutsche Kunst und Dekoration*, 26 (Jan. 1923), 221-30.

53. Peter Behrens "Administration Buildings for Industrial Plants," *American Architect*, 128 (August 1925), 167-74. This essay contains an illustration of the I. G. Farben main hall. See also Peter Behrens, "Seeking Aesthetic worth in Industrial Buildings" (transl. by Arthur Woltersdorf) *American Architect*, 128 (Dec. 5, 1925), 475-79. This essay deals primarily with Hans Poelzig's and Behrens' own work and contains, among others, an illustration of a brick office building by Hans Poelzig in Hanover with a dominant zigzag motif. Behrens' work was again extensively illustrated in Shepard Vogelgesang, "Peter Behrens, Architect and Teacher," *The Architectural Forum*, 52 (May 1930), 715-21. The much more idiosyncratic brick Expressionism of Bernhard Hoetger—as, for example, in his Paula Modersohn-Becker House of 1926—did not seem to receive the same publicity here as the work of

Behrens, Poelzig, or Höger. However, the brick detailing over the entrance to the RCA Victor Building is perhaps comparable to some of the sculptural brick surfaces of the Modersohn-Becker House.

54. Saarinen's station was published in the States after his *succès d'estime* with his Tribune Tower competition design of 1922 and arrival in America the following year (see Albert Christ-Janer, *Eliel Saarinen*, foreword by Alvar Aalto [Chicago: University of Chicago Press, 1948], p. 132).
55. F. R. Yerbury, ed., *Modern Dutch Buildings* (London: Ernest Benn, 1931). This gives a good overview of Dutch work considered important in the early thirties. Suzanne Frank's unpublished dissertation, "Michel de Klerk (1884-1923)—An Architect of the Amsterdam School" (Columbia University, 1969), contains useful information on Van der Meij's Scheepvaarthuis.
56. Clarence Stein, "Amsterdam, Old and New," *Journal of the American Institute of Architects,* 10 (October 1922), 310-28, and F. C. Brown, "De Dageraad," *Architectural Record,* 57 (Jan. 1925), 72-73. See also Edith Elmer Wood, "Recent Housing in the Netherlands," *Architectural Record,* 53 (Feb. 1923), 173.
57. Editorial, "Some Buildings in a Dutch Housing Community—W. M. Dudok, Architect," *Architectual Forum,* 38 (May 1923), 235-38.
58. Cheney, p. 29.
59. In books on Art Deco crafts the vibrant colors that became fashionable in the twenties are usually ascribed to the influence of Leon Bakst's stage and costume design for Diaghilev's Russian Ballet. However, we should remember that the French Fauves and the German Expressionists had utilized bright colors before Bakst. Bakst should be seen in this context as a popularizer, not an originator.
60. Bruno Taut in his postwar utopian books frequently proposed the use of color shading in architecture, where the color becomes lighter toward the top of the building, a device applied by Behrens in the I. G. Farben main hall (mentioned earlier) and used in the later twenties in several brick buildings in New York. Taut's work was probably known to American readers. For example, Taut's Glass House for the Cologne *Werkbund* Exposition of 1914 was illustrated in the context of a discussion on glass products (Editorial, "Glass as a Decorative and Structural Product," *American Architect,* 132 (Oct. 5, 1927), 456); Ely Jacques Kahn also seems to have been familiar with Taut's work (Ely Jacques Kahn, "Sources of Inspiration," *Architecture,* 60 (Nov. 1929), 251); and Talbot Hamlin refers to Taut as an architect distinct from the International Style movement and praises Taut's book *Modern Architecture* of 1929 (see Talbot Faulkner Hamlin, "The International Style Lacks the Essence of Great Architecture," *American Architect,* 143 (Jan. 1933), 12).
62. Leon Solon, "Principles of Architectural Polychromy," *Architectural Record,* 51, (1922), 1-7, 93-100, 189-96, 285-91, 377-86, 465-75.
62. Leon Solon, *Polychromy* (New York: Architectural Record, 1924).
63. Alfred C. Bossom, "Nicholas Roerich," *Architectural Record,* 50 (Aug. 1921), 83.
64. C. Howard Walker, "Architectural Polychromy," *Architectural Record,* 53 (March 1923), 272-78.
65. W. Francklyn Paris, "The International Exposition of Modern Industrial and Decorative Art in Paris," *Architectural Record,* 58 (Oct. 1925), 365-85.
66. Ely Jacques Kahn, "On Decoration and Ornament," in Arthur Tappan North, *Ely Jacques Kahn* Contemporary American Architects Series (New York: McGraw-Hill, 1931), pp. 21 and 24.
67. North, *Raymond Hood,* p. 14. Henry-Russell Hitchcock wrote in 1932 that

Hood's polychrome façade for the Patterson House at Ossining was suggestive of the "fantasies of the German expressionists" (Museum of Modern Art, *Modern Architecture*, p. 130).

68. Sheldon Cheney, *Expressionism in Art* (New York: Liveright, 1934), p. 378.
69. Roi L. Morin, "Design and Construction of Theaters—Part V—The Auditorium," *American Architect*, 123 Jan. 1923), 57-58, 66-67.
70. Indirect lighting and nighttime illumination of buildings had become widespread by the time of the 1925 Paris exhibition (see particularly the Polish Pavilion by Joseph Czajkowski, which had a glass superstructure that was illuminated at night).
71. Kenneth Macgowan, *The Theatre of Tomorrow* (New York: Boni & Liveright, 1921).
72. Herbert Kroly, "New Dimensions in Architectural Effects," *Architectural Record*, 57 (Jan. 1925), 94.
73. Harvey Wiley Corbett, "Design in Office Buildings," *The Architectural Forum*, 52 (June 1930), 779.
74. Kahn, "On the Use of Color," Arthur Tappan North, *Ely Jacques Kahn*, p. 24.
75. Leon Solon, "Will the Exposition Regain Artistic Leadership for France?" *Architectural Record*, 58 (Oct. 1925), 391-93. Alfred Bossom in "The Rebirth of Art and Architecture in Europe," expressed a counterview "European art and architecture are being reborn on the banks of the Seine. The Exposition . . . has been compared to the Italian Renaissance." (*American Architect*, 128 [Aug. 26, 1925], 161).
76. Leo Friedlander, "The New Architecture and the Master Sculptor," *The Architectural Forum*, 46 (Jan. 1927), 1.
77. Ely Jacques Kahn, "The Province of Decoration in Modern Design," *Creative Art*, 5 (Dec. 1929), 885.
78. Fiske Kimball, *American Architecture* (Indianapolis and New York: Bobbs-Merrill, p. 210.
79. Cheney, *The New World Architecture*, pp. 29 and 175.
80. Park refers to veneers of thin walls hung over skeleton frames (p. 151) and to walls that are merely curtains hung on a great frame (p. 126). W. A. Starrett, *Skyscrapers and the Men Who Build Them* (New York and London: Charles Scribner's Sons, 1928), mentions "curtain walls" specificially (caption for illustration opposite page 222).
81. Godfried [sic] Semper, "Development of Architectural Style," transl. and arranged by John W. Root, *The Inland Architect and News Record*, 14 (Dec. 1889), 76-78; 14 (Jan. 1890), 92-94; 15 (Feb. 1890), 5-6; 15 (March 1890), 32-33. Illinois State Association of Architects "Discussion," *The Inland Architect and News Record*, 9 (March 1887), 26. In an obituary for Semper (J. T. C., "Gottfried Semper," *The American Architect and Building News*, 7, part I, [Jan. 31, 1880], 36-37 and part II, [Feb. 7, 1880], 43-44) the importance of his *Der Stil* is pointed out and all of his essays published in foreign periodicals known to the author are listed.
82. Semper discusses this in his essay *Die vier Elemente der Baukunst* (Braunschweig, 1851).
83. Semper's importance for Sullivan was pointed out in the twenties by Fiske Kimball in "Louis Sullivan—An Old Master," *Architectural Record*, 57 (April 1925), 289-304.
84. Wright's works of this period were discussed in the following essays, among others: Louis H. Sullivan, "Concerning the Imperial Hotel, Tokyo, Japan," *Architectural Record*, 53 (April 1923), 332-52; A. N. Rebori, "Frank Lloyd Wright's Textile-Block Slab Construction," *Architectural Record*, 62 (Dec. 1927), 449-56; and Douglas Haskell, "Organic Architecture: Frank Lloyd

Wright," *Creative Art*, 3 (Nov. 1928), li-lvii. Wright himself published a series of essays, "In the Cause of Architecture," in the *Architectural Record* of 1928 (vol. 63, pp. 49-57, 145-51, 350-56, 481-88, and 555-61).

85. The *Architectural Record* did publish a well-illustrated article on Mayan architecture by S. K. Lothrop, "The Architecture of the Ancient Mayas," (57 [April 1925], 491-509). However, the essay seems purely archaeological; there is never any intention of this style's application for contemporary architecture.
86. Hillier in *The World of Art Deco*, pp. 26-32, develops an elaborate theory that American architects may have identified with the political situation in Mexico and, therefore, imitated Mexico's architecture. We have found no evidence for this, at least in New York. The stepped design of many Art Deco crafts is often referred to as "Aztec." Paul Frankl, however, calls his stepped pieces of furniture "skyscraper furniture"; crafts design in this instance, in other words, was imitating skyscraper design under the set-back law, not Aztec forms. If architects in New York ever had in mind Pre-Columbian architecture, it came as an afterthought.
87. Rose Henderson, "A Primitive Basis for Modern Architecture," *Architectural Record*, 54 (August 1923), 189.
88. See Frankl, *New Dimensions*, p. 45.
89. See Park, p. 141 and ill. 62.
90. Editorial, "Current News—Motion Picture Producers Recognize Efforts of Architects in the Productions," *American Architect*, 117 (Feb. 4, 1920), p. 157.
91. Ben J. Lubschez, "The Cabinet of Dr. Caligari," *Journal of the American Institute of Architects*, 9 (Jan. 1921), 213-16. The importance of *Caligari* as well as *The Golem* is also discussed in Macgowan, *The Theatre of Tomorrow*, p. 119.
92. Rosenthal and Ratzka, pp. 170-71. They also mention the great impact *Caligari* had.
93. *Architectural Record*, 52 (1922), 170.
94. Lewis Jacobs, *The Rise of the American Film* (New York: Teachers College Press, 1968), p. 303.
95. Frank Vreeland, "Worth While Pictures of the Month," *Theatre Magazine*, 36 (Sept. 1921), 175.
96. Hillier, *Art Deco*, p. 37.
97. P[eter] Bogdanovich, *Fritz Lang in America* (New York: Praeger, 1967), p. 15. At the American opening of *Metropolis* in 1927 10,000 people queued up in front of the Rialto Theater (Paul M. Jensen, *The Cinema of Fritz Lang* [New York: A. S. Barnes, 1969], p. 58).
98. Rosenthal and Ratzka, p. 175.
99. Cheney, *The New World Architecture*, p. 120.
100. Park, p. 41.
101. Frankl, *New Dimensions*, p. 16.
102. Ibid.
103. Frankl, *Form and Re-Form*, pp. 3, 5.
104. Park, p. 77.
105. Frankl, *Form and Re-Form*, p. 163.
106. Ibid., p. 165.
107. See Klaus-Jürgen Sembach, *Style 1930* (New York: Universe Books, 1971), and Sheldon and Martha Cheney, *Art and the Machine* (New York: Whittlesey House, 1936).
108. Cheney, *The New World Architecture*, 75.
109. Norman Bel Geddes, *Horizons* (Boston: Little, Brown & Co., 1932). But see Clement Edson Armi, "The Formation of the Torpedo Tourer," *Society of*

Architectural Historians Journal, 29 (Dec. 1970), 339-46. He shows that racing cars and "future cars" had applied streamlining from about 1910 onward, affecting even the design of commercial vehicles to some extent. Only the very obvious airflow shapes characteristic of the thirties seem to be new.

110. Oskar Beyer, ed., *Eric Mendelsohn: Letters of an Architect*, introduction by Nikolaus Pevsner, transl. by Geoffrey Strachan (London, New York, Toronto: Abelard-Schuman, 1967), pp. 71-74.

111. A[lfred] H. B[arr], Jr., Foreword, *Machine Art*, Museum of Modern Art, N.Y., March 6–April 30, 1934, unpaged.

112. Elizabeth Mock, Foreword, *Built in USA—1932-1944*, Museum of Modern Art, N.Y., 1944, p. 12.

113. Talbot Hamlin, "The International Style Lacks the Essence of Great Architecture." *The American Architect*, 143 (Jan. 1933), 12.

114. Ibid., p. 16.

115. Howard McKee, "*Frank Lloyd Wright and the Chicago World's Fair of 1933*," unpublished paper, Avery Library, Columbia University, 1964, p. 12. Wright's Town Hall lecture took place in 1931.

116. Frank Lloyd Wright, *An Autobiography* (New York: Duell, Sloan and Pearce, 1943), p. 353.

A SELECTED LIST

of 115 Art Deco buildings in New York City including the major buildings and representative examples of minor building types

Buildings 13, 17, 23, 29, 30, 33, 37, 38, 41, 47, 52, 48, 62, 78, 79, 84, 91, and 111 are not illustrated. Buildings marked with an asterisk are illustrated wholly or partly in the color section following p. 40.

1923

1. Barclay-Vesey Building. McKenzie, Voorhees & Gmelin, 1923-26. Barclay, Vesey, Washington, and West Streets.

1925

2. Cheney Brothers Store. Ferrobrandt and Howard Greenley, 1925. Madison Avenue at 34th Street.

1926

3. Insurance Center Building. Buchman & Kahn, 1926-27. John, Platt, and Gold Streets.
4. *The Lowell. Henry S. Churchill and Herbert Lippmann, 1926. 63rd Street between Park and Madison.
5. 420 Madison Avenue. Dennison & Hirons, 1926-27. Between 48th and 49th Streets.

1927

6. *Park Avenue Building. Buchman & Kahn, 1927. At 32nd and 33rd Streets.
7. *42 West 39th Street. Buchman & Kahn 1927. Between Fifth and Sixth Avenues.
8. Panhellenic Tower. John Mead Howells, 1927-30. First Avenue just east of 49th Street.

9. *Chanin Building. Sloan & Robertson, 1927-30. Lexington Avenue at 41st and 42nd Streets.
10. Manufacturers Trust Branch, Eighth Avenue and 43rd Street. Dennison & Hirons, 1927-28?
11. International Magazine Company Building. Joseph Urban, 1927-28. Eighth Avenue at 56th and 57th Streets.

1928

12. Beaux-Arts Institute of Design. Dennison & Hirons, 1928. 44th Street between First and Second Avenues.
13. Fort Wadsworth Towers. H. I. Feldman, 1928. West 188th Street and Wadsworth Terrace.
14. Apartments, 3 East 84th Street. Howells & Hood, 1928. Off Fifth Avenue.
15. Apartments, 68th Street and Third Avenue. George & Edward Blum, 1928.
16. 275 Seventh Avenue, Buchman & Kahn 1928. At 25th and 26th Streets.
17. Apartments, 22nd Street and Second Avenue. George & Edward Blum, 1928.
18. Fuller Building. Walker & Gillette, 1928-29. 57th Street and Madison Avenue.
19. Master Building. Helmle, Corbett & Harrison and Sugarman & Berger, 1928-29. Riverside Drive and 103rd Street.
20. Apartments, Central Park West and 94th Street. Schwartz & Gross, 1928-29.
21. 261 Fifth Avenue. Buchman & Kahn, 1928-29. At 29th Street.
22. Broadway Block Building. Schultze & Weaver, 1928-29. At Broadway and 51st and 52nd Streets.
23. Allied Arts Building. Buchman & Kahn, 1928-29. 45th Street between First and Second Avenues.
24. *Film Center Building. Buchman & Kahn, 1928-29. Ninth Avenue at 44th and 45th Streets.
25. Stewart & Company (later Bonwit Teller) Store. Warren & Wetmore (altered by Ely Jacques Kahn), 1928-30. Fifth Avenue at 56th Street.
26. *Chrysler Building. William Van Alen, 1928-30. Lexington Avenue at 42nd and 43rd Streets.
27. Western Union Building. Voorhees, Gmelin & Walker, 1928-30. Hudson, Thomas, and Worth Streets and West Broadway.
28. The Navarre. Sugarman & Berger, 1928-30. Seventh Avenue and 38th Street.

1929

29. Horn & Hardart, Sixth Avenue and 45th Street. F. P. Platt & Brother, 1929.
30. Apartments, 68th Street and Second Avenue. George & Edward Blum, 1929?
31. Wadsworth Manor. H. I. Feldman, 1929. Wadsworth Terrace at 190th Street.

32. Apartments, 240 East 79th Street. Godwin, Thompson & Patterson, 1929. Between Second and Third Avenues.
33. Corn Exchange Branch. Fellheimer & Wagner, 1929. St. Nicholas Avenue between 167th and 168th Streets.
34. Office building, 501 Madison Avenue. Robert D. Kohn and Frank Vitolo, 1929-30. At 52nd Street.
35. *News Building. Howells & Hood, 1929-30. 42nd and 41st Streets and Second Avenue.
36. Salvation Army Building. Voorhees, Gmelin & Walker, 1929-30. 13th and 14th Streets between Sixth and Seventh Avenues.
37. Downtown Athletic Club. Starrett & Van Vleck, 1929-30. West and Washington Streets between Morris Street and Battery Place.
38. Apartments, Park Avenue and 79th Street. Sloan & Robertson, 1929-30.
39. The Eldorado. Margon & Holder, 1929-30. Central Park West at 90th and 91st Streets.
40. Squibb Building. Buchman & Kahn, 1929-30. Fifth Avenue at 58th Street.
41. Bricken-Continental Building, Buchman & Kahn 1929-30. Broadway, Seventh Avenue, and 41st Street.
42. Essex House. Frank Grad, 1929-30. Central Park South between Sixth and Seventh Avenues.
43. Kent Columbus Circle Garage. Jardine, Hill & Murdock, 1929-30. Columbus Avenue and 61st Street.
44. Telephone Building, East 13th Street. Voorhees, Gmelin & Walker, 1929-30. On Second Avenue.
45. Telephone Building, West 17th and 18th Streets. Voorhees, Gmelin & Walker, 1929-30. Between Seventh and Eighth Avenues.
46. Telephone Building, West 50th Street. Voorhees, Gmelin & Walker, 1929-30. Between Ninth and Tenth Avenues.
47. Hollywood Theater. T. W. Lamb, 1929-30. 51st Street between Broadway and Eighth Avenue.
48. Beaux-Arts Apartment Hotel. Murchison & Hood, Godley & Fouilhoux, 1929-30. 44th Street between First and Second Avenues.
49. Barbizon Plaza. Murgatroyd & Ogden, 1929-30. Central Park South, 58th Street, and Sixth Avenue.
50. National Title Guaranty Company. Corbett, Harrison & MacMurray, 1929-30. Montague Street between Clinton Street and Cadman Plaza, Brooklyn.
51. New School for Social Research. Joseph Urban, 1929-30. 12th Street between Fifth and Sixth Avenues.
52. City Bank Farmers Trust Building. Cross & Cross 1929-31. William, Hanover, and Beaver Streets and Exchange Place.
53. Southgate Apartments. Emery Roth, 1929-31. 52nd Street east of First Avenue.
54. Irving Trust Building. Voorhees, Gmelin & Walker, 1929-32. Wall and New Streets and Broadway.
55. House of Detention for Women. Sloan & Robertson, 1929-32. Sixth and Greenwich Avenues and 10th Street (demolished).

1930

56. Bloomingdale's on Lexington Avenue. Starrett & Van Vleck, 1930. At 59th and 60th Streets.
57. *The Town House. Bowden & Russell, 1930. 38th Street between Lexington and Park Avenues.
58. 21 West Street. Starrett & Van Vleck, 1930. Morris and Washington Streets.
59. Curb Exchange façade. Starrett & Van Vleck, 1930. Trinity Place between Thames and Rector Streets.
60. *Twentieth-Century Fox Building. Joseph J. Furman, 1930. 56th Street between Ninth and Tenth Avenues.
61. West Side Elevated Highway. Architectural design by John Sloan, 1930. Between Canal Street and Riverside Park.
62. Hotel Carlyle. Bien & Prince, 1930. Madison Avenue at 76th and 77th Streets.
63. Office tower, southeast corner 40th Street and Madison Avenue. Kenneth Franzheim, 1930.
64. *Apartments, Central Park West at 66th Street. Schwartz & Gross, 1930.
65. New Amsterdam apartments. Margon & Holder, 1930. 86th Street and Amsterdam Avenue.
66. Apartments, Central Park West and 84th Street. Schwartz & Gross, 1930.
67. Apartments, 40 West 86th Street. J. M. Felson, 1930-31. Between Central Park West and Columbus Avenue.
68. The Ardsley. Emery Roth, 1930-31. Central Park West and 92nd Street.
69. Horn & Hardart, 33rd Street. Louis Allen Abramson, 1930-31. Between Seventh Avenue and Greeley Square.
70. *Horn & Hardart, 181st Street. Louis Allen Abramson, 1930-31. Between Wadsworth and St. Nicholas Avenues.
71. RCA Victor Building. Cross & Cross, 1930-31. Lexington Avenue and 51st Street.
72. Sears Roebuck Building. Frank S. Parker, 1930-31. Ninth Avenue and 31st Street.
73. American Savings Bank, 42nd Street. Hirons & Mellor, 1930-31. Between Sixth Avenue and Times Square.
74. Waldorf-Astoria. Schultze & Weaver, 1930-31. Park and Lexington Avenues and 49th and 50th Streets.
75. 500 Fifth Avenue. Shreve, Lamb & Harmon 1930-31. At 42nd Street.
76. Empire State Building. Shreve, Lamb & Harmon, 1930-31. Fifth Avenue and 33rd and 34th Streets.
77. 29 Broadway. Sloan & Robertson, 1930-31. Morris Street and Trinity Place.
78. Newsweek Building. Robert D. Kohn, 1930-31. 49th and 50th Streets and Madison Avenue.
79. Hotel Edison. H. J. Knapp, 1930-31. 47th Street between Duffy Square and Eighth Avenue.
80. Bricken-Casino Building. Firm of Ely Jacques Kahn, 1930-31. Broadway and 39th Street.

81. 1400 Broadway. Buchman & Kahn, 1930-31. 38th and 39th Streets.
82. *McGraw-Hill Building. Hood, Godley & Fouilhoux, 1930-31. 42nd and 41st Streets between Eighth and Ninth Avenues.
83. Broadway Fashion Building. Sugarman & Berger, 1930-31. Broadway at 84th Street.
84. Daily Commerce Building. Buchman & Kahn, 1930-31. 44th Street and Third Avenue.
85. 60 Wall Tower. Clinton & Russell, Holton & George, 1930-32. Pine, Pearl, and Cedar Streets.
86. Northeast corner 45th Street and Lexington Avenue. F. R. Stuckert, 1930-32.

1931

87. Majestic Apartments. Office of Irwin S. Chanin, 1931. Central Park West and 71st and 72nd Streets.
88. Earl Carroll Theater. George Keister, 1931. Seventh Avenue at 50th Street.
89. Long Island Area Headquarters, New York Telephone Company. Voorhees, Gmelin & Walker, 1931. Bridge and Willoughby Streets, Brooklyn.
90. RCA Building. Associated Architects, 1931-33. Rockefeller Plaza and 49th and 50th Streets.
91. Americas Building. Associated Architects, 1931-32. Sixth Avenue and 51st Street.
92. Radio City Music Hall. Associated Architects, 1931-32. Sixth Avenue and 50th Street.
93. Fourth Church of Christ Scientist. Cherry & Matz, 1931-32. Ft. Washington Avenue and 185th Street.
94. Metropolitan Life, North Building. H. W. Corbett and D. E. Waide, 1931-33. Park Avenue, Madison Square, and 24th and 25th Streets.

1932

95. Provident Loan Society Branch, 72nd Street. Renwick, Aspinwall & Guard, 1932. Between Amsterdam and Columbus Avenues (demolished).
96. Century Apartments. Office of Irwin S. Chanin, 1932. Central Park West and 62nd and 63rd Streets.
97. British Empire Building and Maison Française. Associated Architects, 1932-33. Fifth Avenue and 49th and 50th Streets.
98. City of New York Central Substation. 1932. 53rd Street between Sixth and Seventh Avenues.
99. City of New York Greenwich Substation. 1932. West 13th Street and Greenwich Avenue.

1933

100. Midtown Theater. Boak & Paris, 1933. Broadway between 99th and 100th Streets.

101. Federal Office Building. Cross & Cross, 1933-35. Vesey, Church, and Barclay Streets and West Broadway.
102. Palazzo d'Italia. Associated Architects, 1933-35. Fifth Avenue and 50th Street.
103. International Buildings. Associated Architects, 1933-35. Fifth Avenue and 50th and 51st Streets.
104. City of New York Smith Street Substation. 1933. Second Place and Smith Street, South Brooklyn.

1934

105. East River Savings Bank. Walker & Gillette, 1934-35. Trinity Place and Cortlandt and Dey Streets.

1935

106. Kress Building. Edward F. Sibbert, 1935. Fifth Avenue and 39th Street.
107. Piers 88, 90, and 92. 1935 (demolished).
108. Apartments, 80th Street and West End Avenue. George F. Pelham 2nd, 1935-36.

1936

109. Time & Life Building. Associated Architects, 1936-37. Rockefeller Plaza and 48th and 49th Streets.

1938

110. Horn & Hardart, 57th Street. Ralph B. Bencker, 1938. Between Sixth and Seventh Avenues.
111. Provident Loan Society Branch, 43rd Street. Renwick, Aspinwall & Guard, 1938. Between Lexington and Third Avenues.

1939

112. Criminal Courts Building. H. W. Corbett, 1939. Center, White, Baxter, and Leonard Streets.
113. Joan of Arc Junior High School. Eric Kebbon, 1939-40. 92nd and 93rd Streets between Columbus and Amsterdam Avenues.
114. Airlines Building. John B. Peterkin, 1939-40. 42nd and 41st Streets and Park Avenue.
115. Tiffany Building. Cross & Cross, 1939-40. Fifth Avenue and 57th Street.

PLATES

1. BARCLAY-VESEY BUILDING

A. This building just north of the Trade Center towers was one of a great number built by telephone companies throughout the country in the 1920s. Bell System policy seems to have called consistently for progressive design; this building by McKenzie, Voorhees & Gmelin was the first in the Art Deco style. Housing both equipment and corporate offices, it stood out as the largest telephone building in the world, and to contemporary architects was remarkable also in having—as it seemed to them—neither in its massing nor in its decorative detail any trace of an historical style. A photograph of it served as frontispiece to English-language editions of Le Corbusier's *Towards a New Architecture*. The lot is in the shape of a parallelogram; the tower is square. Hence the twist between the base of the building and the tower.

B. Aborigines and the company's bell appear among plant forms above the entrances

C. Exotic animals and plants are carved on the arches of the building's arcade (originally a shopping arcade) and over the windows above.

D. The main lobby was described by Lewis Mumford as being "as gaily . . . decorated as a village street in a strawberry festival."

E. Elevator doors off the ground floor lobby are demonstrably hand-wrought.

F. Decorative relief is continued on a grill above the door of the board room on the executive level.

G. Decorative relief also appeared on the lintel of a door leading from an anteroom to the board room and on the plaster coving above it. The coving is remarkable in evidently being German Expressionist in origin.

H and I. Within the boardroom, the furniture, such as the table shown here, is in a vertical arts and crafts style—vertical as in some of the "skyscraper" furniture of the period.

2. CHENEY BROTHERS STORE

A and B. The French ironworker Edgar Brandt established a New York branch called Ferrobrandt under the direction of Jules Bouy. These gates were made by Ferrobrandt for a silk store of 1925 on Madison Avenue cater-cornered from Altman's.

C. The building in which Cheney Brothers had their ground-floor shop, the Madison-Belmont by Warren & Wetmore, also had an entrance screen by Ferrobrandt.

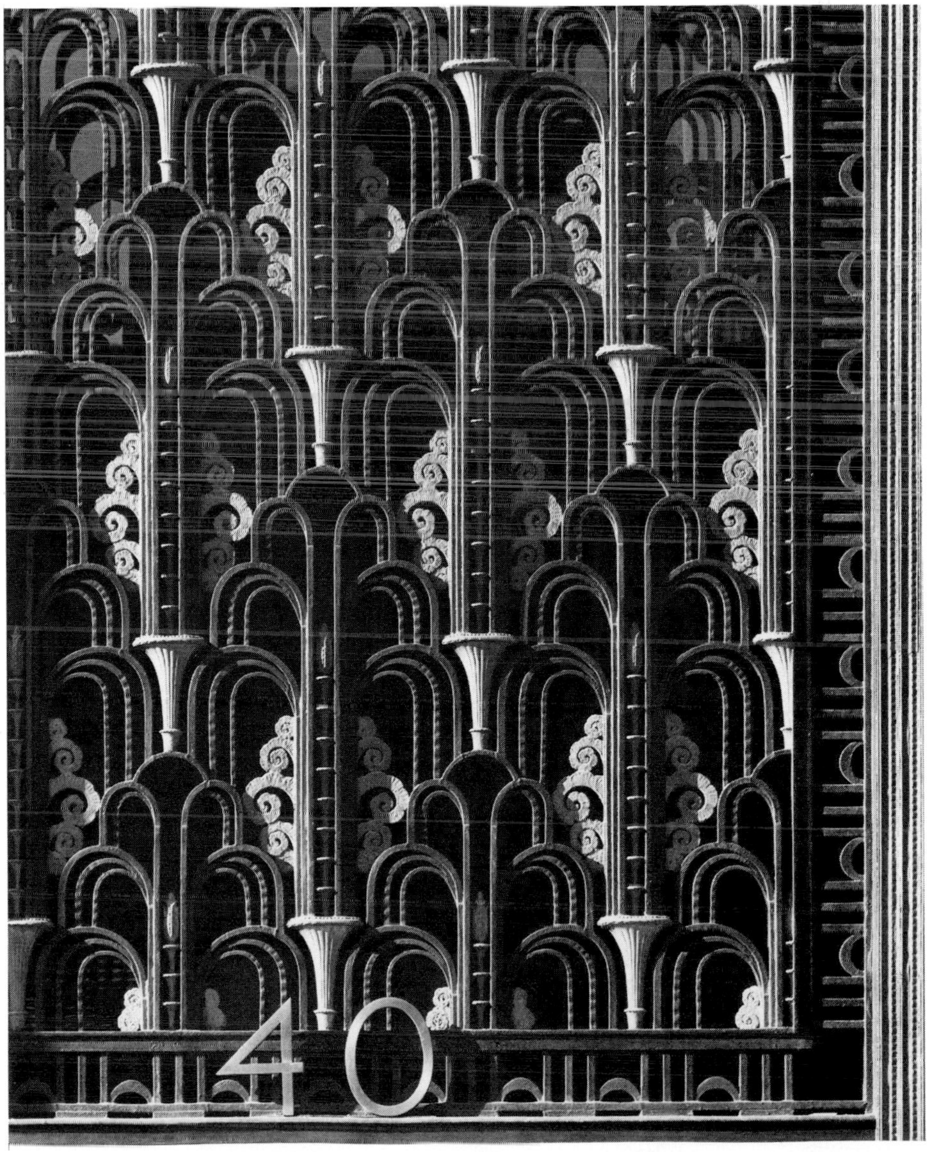

3. INSURANCE CENTER BUILDING

A form of zigzag which became a common feature of New York Art Deco buildings first appears on this one of 1926, designed by Buchman & Kahn for the district just to the north of Wall Street. This zigzag probably comes ultimately from textile sources as did (according to the designer, Ely Jacques Kahn) the design of the cornice of the slightly earlier Furniture Exchange Building (on Lexington Avenue between 32nd and 33rd Streets; see p. 15). The Insurance Center Building was the first of a cluster of Kahn buildings in Downtown Manhattan which would eventually surround and largely hide this first one.

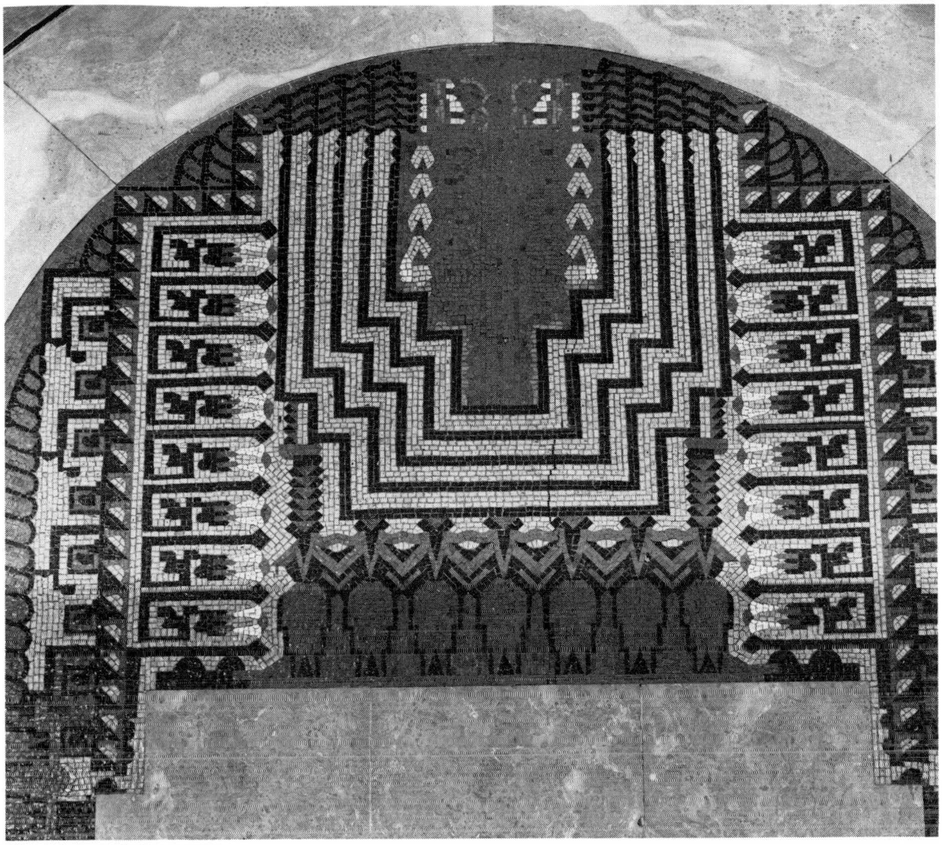

6. THE PARK AVENUE BUILDING

B. The masterpiece of the New York Art Deco, Ely Kahn's office building of 1927 for the lower end of Park Avenue, has towards its top glazed terra-cotta cladding whose colors were carefully designed to be effective from a distance (see exterior view in color section). In the lobby original mosaics are still in place, but the original lamps and the main ceiling decoration are no more. Lewis Mumford wrote of the building: "One swallow may not make a summer; but one building like this, which faces the entire problem of design, and has a clean, unflinching answer for each question, may well serve to crystallize all the fumbling and uncertain elements in present-day architecture."

5. 420 MADISON

Flat fields of curvilinear ornament, a characteristic of architectural design at the 1925 Paris show, made their appearance in New York on this small office building on Madison Avenue by Dennison & Hirons, built in 1926-27.

B. Decorative terra-cotta panels were by René Chambellan. The building, erected in 1927-28, is a short distance north of the UN Building.

8. PANHELLENIC HOTEL

A. John Mead Howells' orange brick and terra-cotta tower was one of a number of buildings, including the Barclay-Vesey Building and Raymond Hood's earlier American Radiator Building, which looked to Eliel Sarrinen's Chicago Tribune entry as a pattern for the style-less skyscraper.

9. CHANIN BUILDING

A. This office tower of 1927-30 at 42nd Street and Lexington Avenue near Grand Central was built by and for the Chanin Brothers' construction firm and still contains its headquarters. Sloan & Robertson were the architects. Their style-less inspiration was again Saarinen's Tribune tower—the top of the Chanin appears in plate 57 in the color section, to the left of the Chrysler Building (26) and the Town House. Though it had more floors than the Woolworth, the world's tallest building at the time the Chanin was designed, the latter was not as tall.

B. A flat band of plant forms in terra-cotta appears three floors above street level. The building immediately to the right is Shreve, Lamb & Harmon's 500 Fifth Avenue (75).

C. Allegorical figures in the vestibules are by the sculptor René Chambellan.

D. Brass radiator grills, each with a different design, are set in the walls of the lobby (as they are below the allegorical figures in the vestibules). Here, as on 420 Madison (5), spiralling forms predominate.

E. This window onto the Chanin lobby was originally that of a Longchamps Restaurant. The fan-shaped details in flat decorative panels are perhaps an expressive version of Minoan or Egyptian decoration.

F. At the executive level, metal gates include machine forms, the outline of a violin, and, at the base, stacks of money. The dynamic forms of this gate are reminiscent of the expressive ornament of the nineteenth-century designer Christopher Dresser, as is much Art Deco design.

G. A private bathroom has coved lighting. Glass doors close off a bathtub with shower.

10. MANUFACTURER'S TRUST BANK

This branch bank a block west of Times Square was built in 1927-28 to designs of Dennison & Hirons. Floral panels are incorporated into a Classical framework. The characteristic Art Deco spiral forms predominate. In the panels which top the pilasters, one can also detect a lingering relationship to Ionic or Corinthian volutes.

11. INTERNATIONAL MAGAZINE BUILDING

A block south of Columbus Circle, this building of 1927-28 was designed by the Austrian-born designer Joseph Urban, who handled the Art Deco style, ultimately German and Austrian in its sources, with more assurance than his younger American colleagues and seemed to have none of their urge to build high. As in the Manufacturer's Trust Bank (10), Art Deco motifs are superimposed on a Neoclassical style: zigzags appear on urns.

A. The design of this building, the headquarters of the Beaux-Arts educational system in America, was determined by a competition. The first, second, and third prize winners were Frederic C. Hirons, Harry Sternfeld of Philadelphia, and William Van Alen, each of whom as a student had also won the Paris Prize to the Ecole in Paris. The winning Hirons design was erected in 1928. The Art Deco pilaster capitals are of Near Eastern and Greek inspiration.

12. BEAUX-ARTS INSTITUTE OF DESIGN

B. Statues were to have been mounted above the blocks at the second-floor level.

A. This small apartment house just off Fifth Avenue was designed by Raymond Hood and built in 1928 for Colonel Patterson of the Daily News.

14. 3 EAST 84TH STREET

B. On it appear for the first time the recessed metal spandrels that were to be a feature of many Art Deco skyscrapers to come.

15. 210 EAST 68TH STREET

This was one of a number of large apartment houses designed by George & Edward Blum, buildings across whose façades bands of terra-cotta ornament were sparsely stretched to give some individuality to what were essentially anonymous buildings.

16. 275 SEVENTH AVENUE

This building of 1928 was one of many designed by Buchman & Kahn for New York's garment district. It was in the public lobbies of these buildings that exuberant inventiveness in design was given free rein—especially in their molded plaster ceilings.

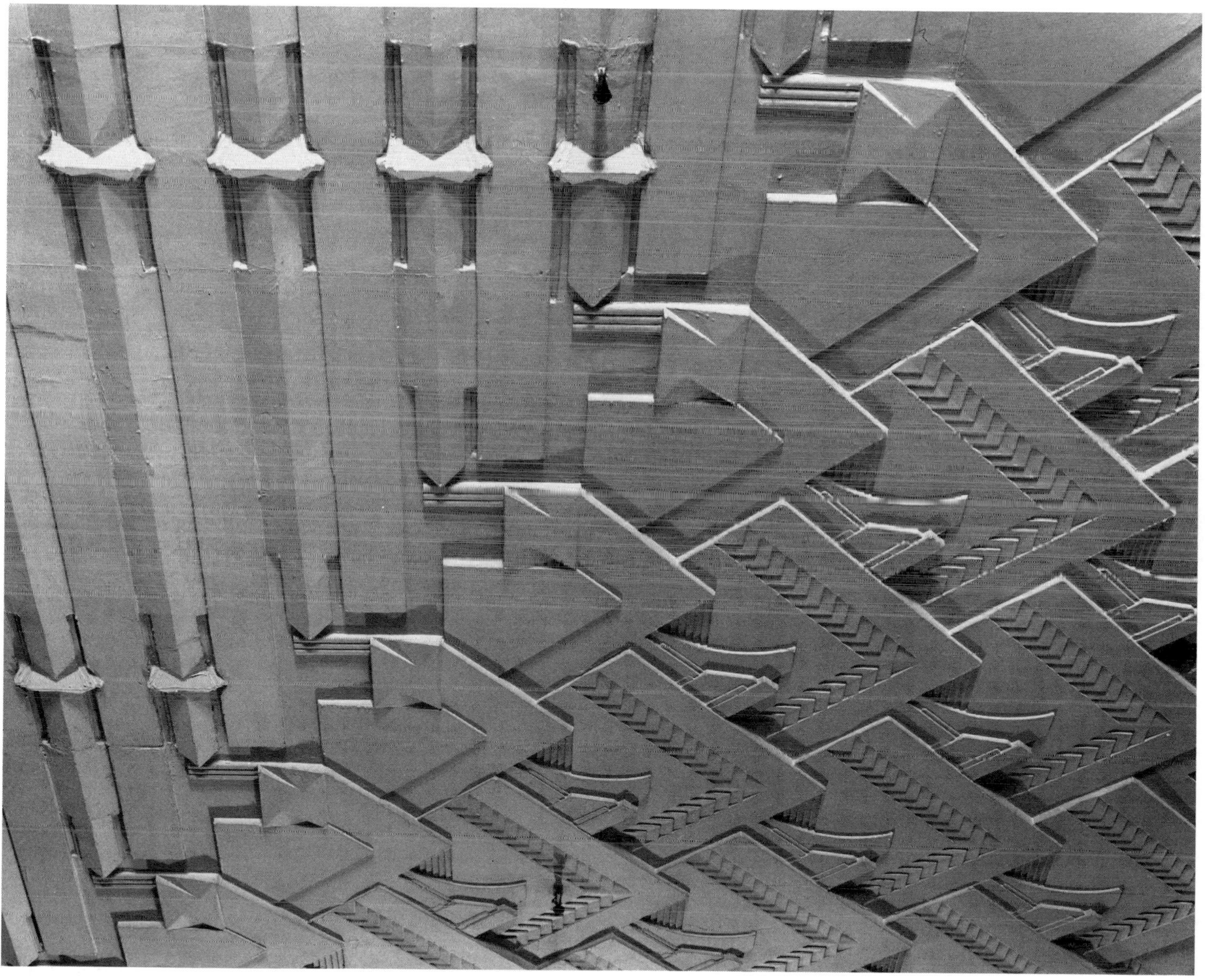

18. FULLER BUILDING

A. Like the Chanin (9), this building of 1928-29 on 57th Street was built for the headquarters of a construction firm (the Fuller Company's previous headquarters had been the Flatiron Building). The top is in black and white stone, which, with its forceful color contrast, has a primitive quality. The architects were Walker & Gillette. The building to the left is Ely Kahn's Squibb Building (40).

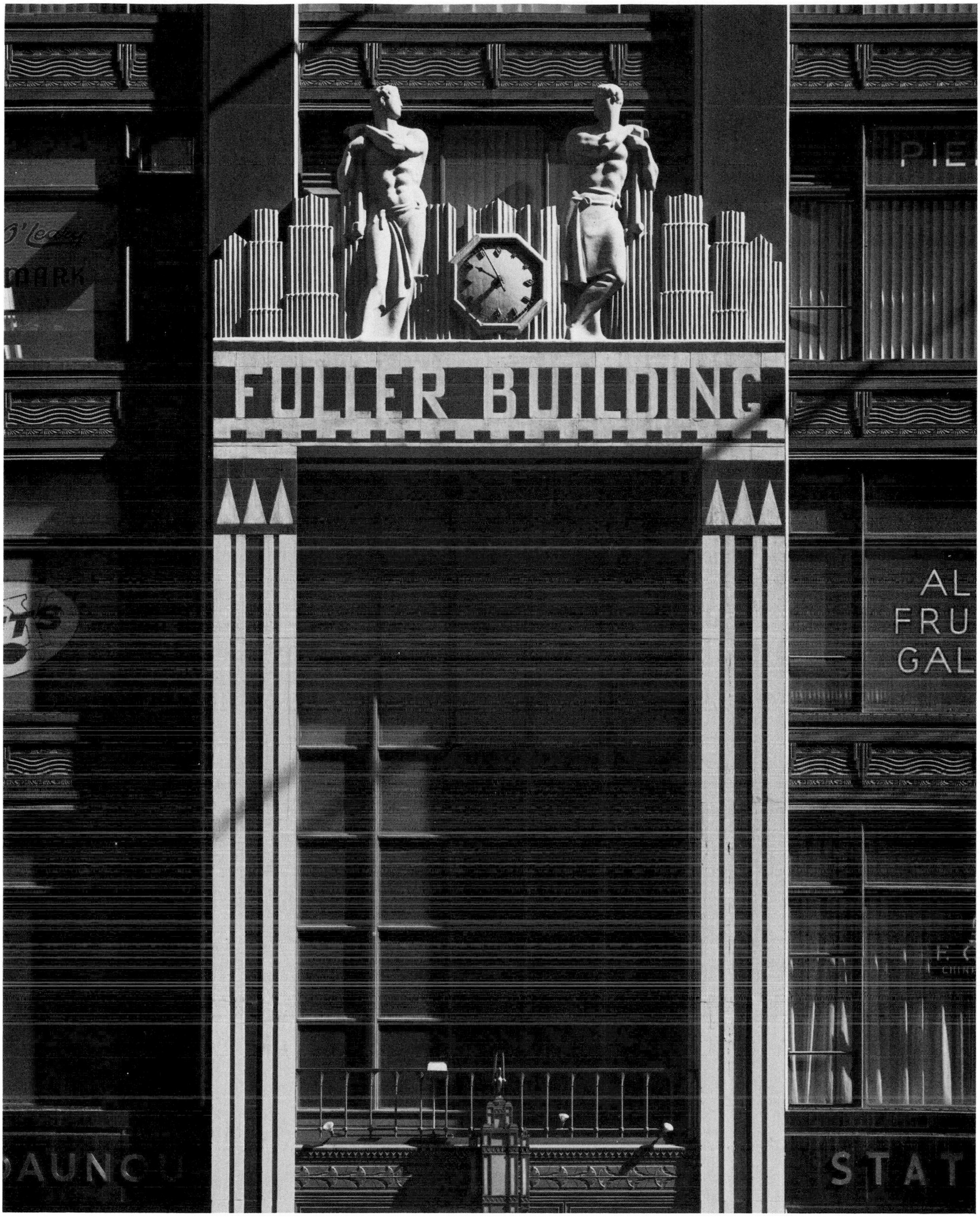

B. The entrance is surmounted by figures by Elie Nadelman which were added after 1931. Here too the ubiquitous Art Deco octagon is imposed on a clock.

19. MASTER BUILDING

A. This tower, the highest on Riverside Drive after the Riverside Church, was built in 1928-29 as a museum, art school, and apartment hotel combined. Designed by Helmle, Corbett & Harrison and Sugarman & Berger, it was one of a number of buildings of the twenties which had a curtain wall of brick shaded from a deep tone at the base to a lighter one at the building top. In this instance the base is in a dark purple brick which shades to a light grey at the crown. Inside, the museum space was innovative in being artificially lit. The Riverside Museum has now moved and the Master Institute of United Arts no longer exists. The Equity Theater is housed in what were the Institute's auditorium and the apartment hotel's restaurant.

B. The crowning motif is an early example of a faceted shape at a building's top, a device also used by Ely Kahn (see his Bricken-Casino building, 80). The faceted forms here, together with the shaded brick, suggest a German Expressionist influence.

A. This red brick and terra-cotta apartment tower of 1928-29 at 94th Street was the first of a series of apartment buildings that Schwartz & Gross designed for Central Park West addresses.

20. 336 CENTRAL PARK WEST

B. The terra-cotta cornices at the top of the building and its water tower housing seem to have been inspired by Egyptian precedents.

21. 261 FIFTH AVENUE

A. Forms appear at their most explicitly woven on the façade of this garment district loft building at 29th Street by Buchman & Kahn. It was built in 1928-29.

B. Inside, the lobby still retains its molded plaster ceiling and, more surprisingly, its original lights.

22. BROADWAY BLOCK BUILDING

A. This small commercial building of 1928-29 on Broadway above Times Square was designed by Schultze & Weaver, the architects who were to design the Waldorf-Astoria (74). On its façade irregular Art Deco octagons serve as capitals for the pilasters. In the distance can be seen the Paramount Building.

B. Construction began on the Paramount building in 1926 to designs of C. W. & George L. Rapp of Chicago in a style which was not Art Deco. Before completion the architects (or their clients) had been converted, and they added a clock tower surmounted by an illuminated glass ball; it is only these parts of this building that are in the style.

24. FILM CENTER BUILDING

B. This building of 1928-29 by Ely Jacques Kahn is on Ninth Avenue west of Times Square. It was designed to house a variety of activities which involve the handling of motion picture film. The forms of molded plaster and stone on the wall and ceiling of this vestibule and of the brass radiator grill below derive from fabric design. (For a view of the lobby beyond see the color section.)

A. This building of 1928-30 was no sooner finished to designs of Warren & Wetmore than it passed into the hands of Bonwit Teller and was remodeled for them by Ely Kahn. His contribution included the replacement of exuberant metal screens at the entrances with the more restrained ones that are still in place there.

25. STEWART & COMPANY STORE

B. At the top of the Fifth Avenue façade he left the chic figures and the urns above them intact.

26. CHRYSLER BUILDING

D. At its completion this building of 1928-30 by William Van Alen was the tallest in the world. The cresting at its top now contains radio transmitting equipment. E. In the tower below the spire, the topmost enclosed story originally formed an observation floor. Below that was a private luncheon club, the Cloud Club (still there; see below), and its gymnasia; a duplex apartment for Walter Chrysler, who had built the building; and early offices of Time, Inc.

F. At the base of the tower proper the building is pinched out at its corners and widens to a service floor at the 30th story, where there is a frieze of automobile hub caps and mudguards and, at the corners, winged radiator caps. The widening was meant to overcome an optical illusion from which the towers of horizontally striped towers were found to suffer: their tops appeared larger than their bases. Raymond Hood also took measures to overcome the illusion in his News Building (35) to the right, even though it did not have horizontal stripes—its terminal screen is curved in perceptibly.

G. Lower on the building, curtain walls have what was described at the time as the form of a basket-weave.

I. The entrance screen on the west side of the building still retains its crenellated band but lacks the black glass it once held as well as the original variety of textured glass above.

H. Entrances at ground level are in the form of proscenia and contain glass and metal screens.

J. The lobby is triangular in shape (see plan, p. 22) and, at exits and above the elevator lobbies, has coved cold-cathode lighting in the form of raised curtains.

K. The ceiling mural is by Edward Trumbull. The lines shown here were said to represent natural forces.

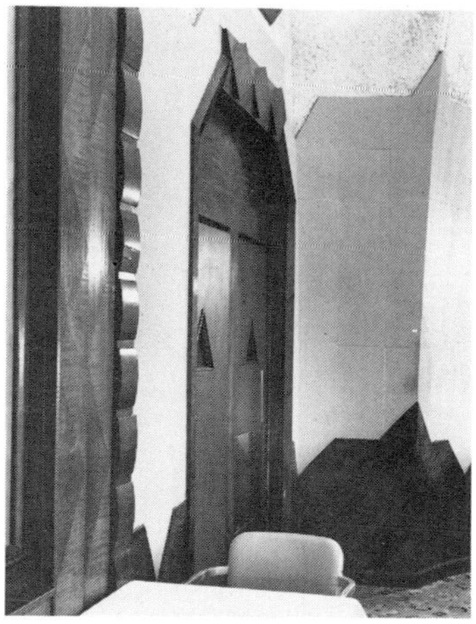

N. The main dining room of the Cloud Club towards the top of the building has lost its original furniture but is otherwise intact.

M. Staircases, which give access to the second floor and to the basement, are topped with ceilings finished in aluminum leaf.

L. The interiors of the elevator cabs feature wood veneers (see color section for another example).

27. WESTERN UNION BUILDING

B. The mass of the building, in shaded orange brick and with a variety of chevrons in its decorative brickwork, forms an effective terminal to the view up West Broadway from above the new Trade Center towers.

A. The entrance to this building of 1928-30 by Voorhees, Gmelin & Walker is of brick, bronze, and glass and in proscenium form. The use of brick above the doorway in a textured and idiosyncratic fashion probably derives from German Expressionist and Dutch sources.

28. THE NAVARRE

This building of 1928-30 by Sugarman & Berger in the garment district south of Times Square has one entrance to its elevator lobby and a second entrance which originally led to a second-floor banking room (now an Off-Track Betting office).

31. WADSWORTH MANOR

A and B. This is a virtuoso brick and terra-cotta building of 1929 on Washington Heights by H. I. Feldman. Many modest apartment buildings followed the same course in the years to come. The triangular piers here, often used at this time, can be found earlier in Neogothic buildings and in German Expressionist brick buildings.

32. 240 EAST 79TH STREET

Godwin, Thompson & Patterson followed the example of the Lowell (4) in making a stage set in glazed terra-cotta of the ground floor of this East Side apartment house of 1929.

34. 501 MADISON AVENUE

A detail of the building by Robert D. Kohn and Frank E. Vitolo is shown. Kohn was the architect of the Newsweek Building and of the extensions which carried the older Macy's Store of De Lemos & Cordes to Seventh Avenue. 501 Madison was built in 1929 30.

B and C. Raymond M. Hood's building of 1929-30 escaped the standard formula for twenties skyscrapers of a tower set on a ziggurat by taking the area of tower the zoning law allowed in a form approaching that of a slab.

35. THE NEWS BUILDING

D and E. At ground level there is a wealth of decoration, particularly in bronze. (See color section also.)

35E.

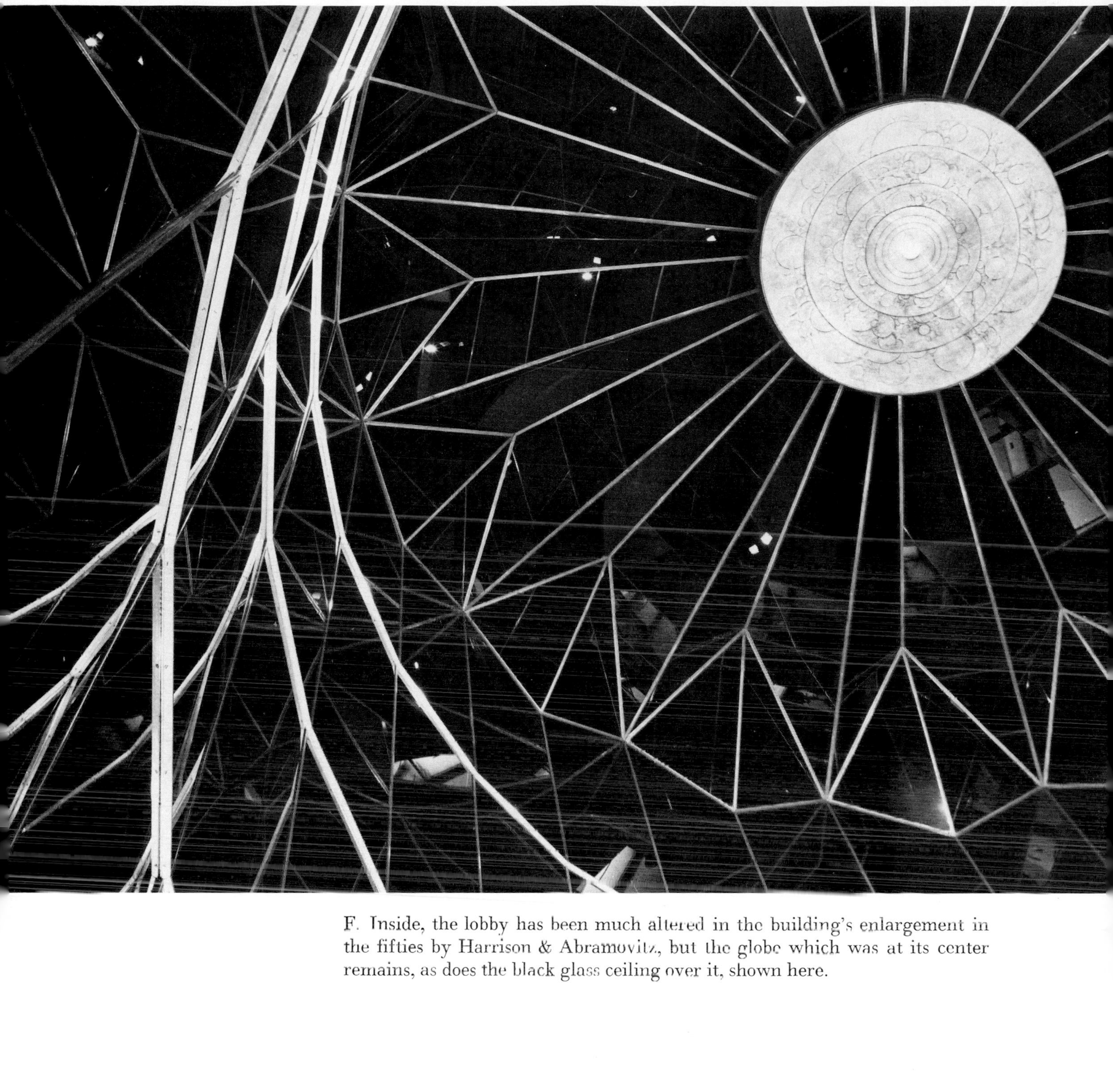

F. Inside, the lobby has been much altered in the building's enlargement in the fifties by Harrison & Abramovitz, but the globe which was at its center remains, as does the black glass ceiling over it, shown here.

A. This complex, designed by Voorhees, Gmelin & Walker and built in 1929-30, comprised a Territorial Headquarters Building (right), a Girl's Dormitory (rear), and a Temple (center).

36. SALVATION ARMY BUILDINGS

B. The interior of the Temple has a ceiling pierced in a willow pattern, through which lights shine.

40. SQUIBB BUILDING (with Walker & Gillette's FULLER BUILDING [18] behind)

This Fifth Avenue office building of 1929-30 by Ely Jacques Kahn is one of the few buildings he designed that had much of a tower above its setbacks. It is catercornered from Grand Army Plaza and is probably best known to New Yorkers for the F.A.O. Schwartz store on its ground floor.

42. ESSEX HOUSE

Frank Grad's hotel of 1929-30 faces across Central Park South with this composition, which contains a profusion of the volute motif.

43. KENT COLUMBUS CIRCLE GARAGE

Jardine, Hill & Murdock designed some automated parking garages—automatic in the sense that cars were not driven by an attendant after being placed on the buildings' elevators. One was near Grand Central Station. This garage is northwest of Columbus Circle. The shop window is an alteration. The Century Apartments (96) can be seen to the left of the garage.

TELEPHONE BUILDINGS

Throughout the twenties the telephone company was expanding rapidly and put up many new buildings. These three by Voorhees, Gmelin & Walker were all built in 1929-30.

44.
This one, with crystalline forms and zigzags, is on East 13th Street. It is an expansion of an earlier two-story building.

45.

One is on West 17th and 18th Streets west of Seventh Avenue.

46.

A third with faceted forms and willows is on West 50th Street.

48. BEAUX-ARTS APARTMENT HOTEL

These two apartment blocks face each other across 44th Street west of the UN. They have long been highly regarded by the progressive probably in part because they were horizontally banded at a time when this was favored by International Style critics and also presumably because, being on both sides of the street, they were responsible for a closer-to-total environment than other, single blocks. They were named after the Beaux-Arts Institute of Design (12) next door. The doormen no longer dress as gendarmes, and the lobbies have been altered.

49. BARBIZON PLAZA

A and B. This building of 1929-30 by Murgatroyd & Ogden was topped by a glass roof when first built. It still dominates the view north on Sixth Avenue in the Fifties.

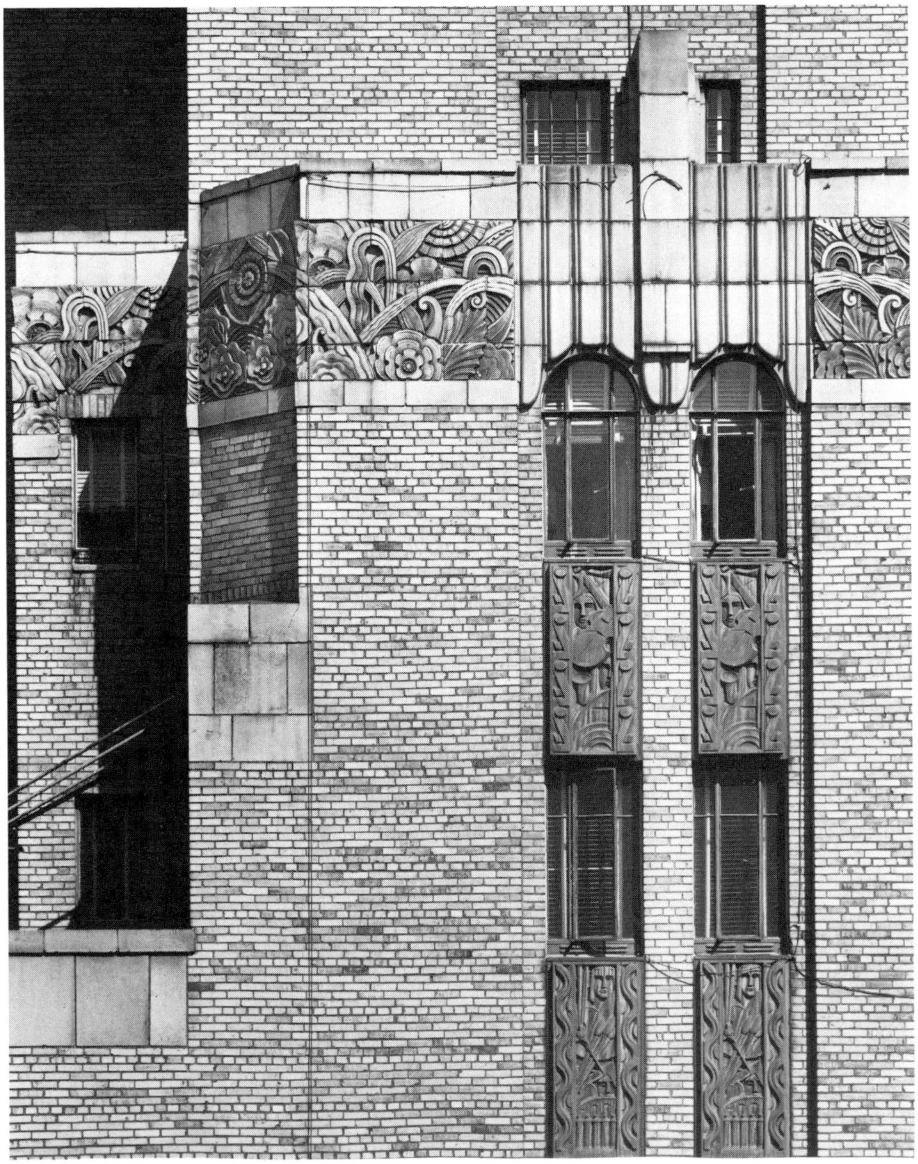

50. NATIONAL TITLE GUARANTY COMPANY

Like the Chanin Building (9), this Brooklyn bank building of 1929-30 by Corbett, Harrison & MacMurray has buttresses above its lowest floors. Lamps which were originally in front of the building are no longer there, and the bank interior has been completely altered.

51. NEW SCHOOL FOR SOCIAL RESEARCH

A. Joseph Urban designed this building, the horizontally striped façade of which slopes back to overcome the optical illusion which would make its top appear broader than its bottom. It was built in 1929-30. B and C. Inside, the ceiling of the auditorium, though without stalactites, suggests its parentage in the Berlin Grosses Schauspielhaus of Hans Poelzig. It was described as being formed of perforated plaster.

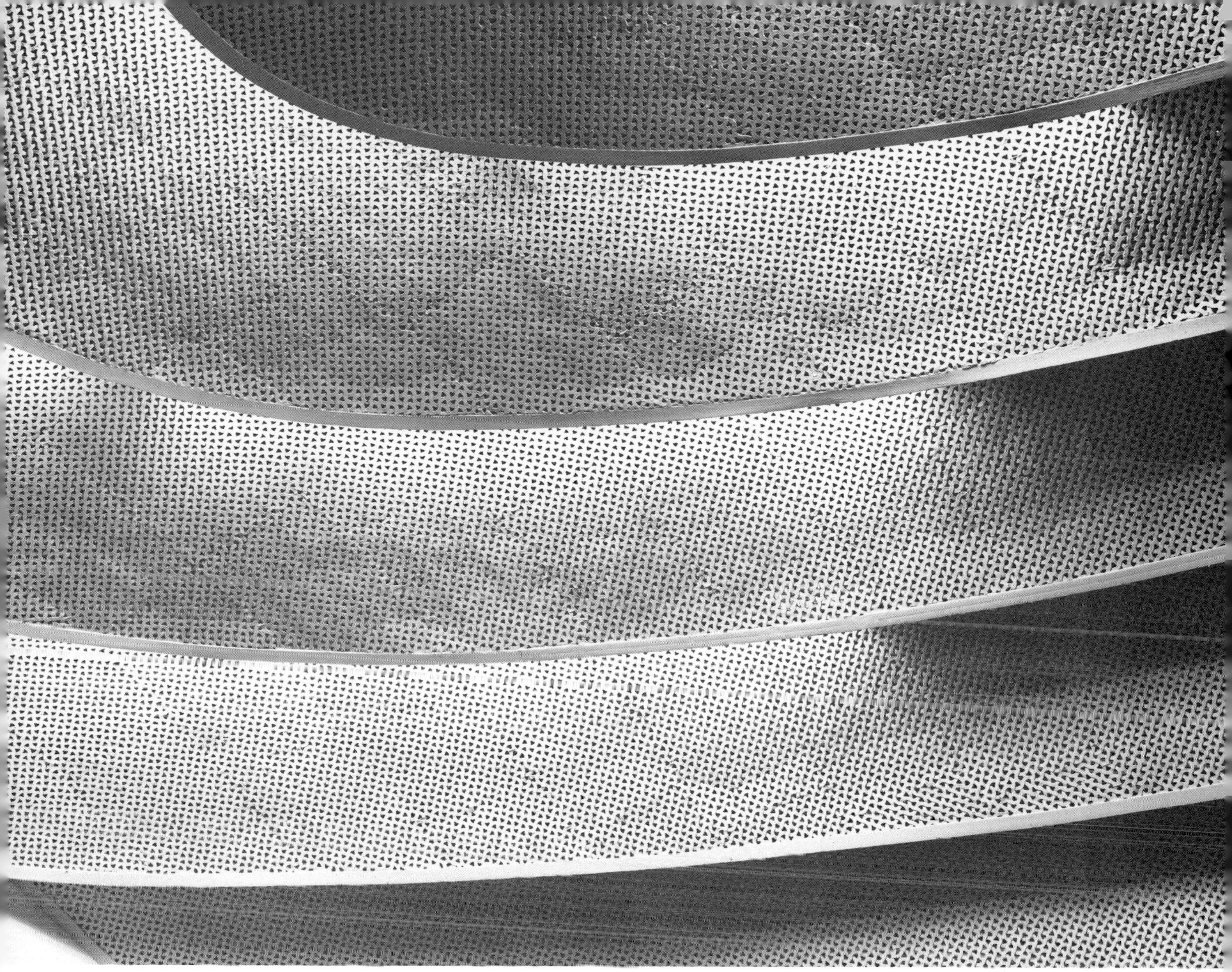

D and E. In the auditorium lobby the building's German origins are also suggested by the lettering of the commemorative plaque.

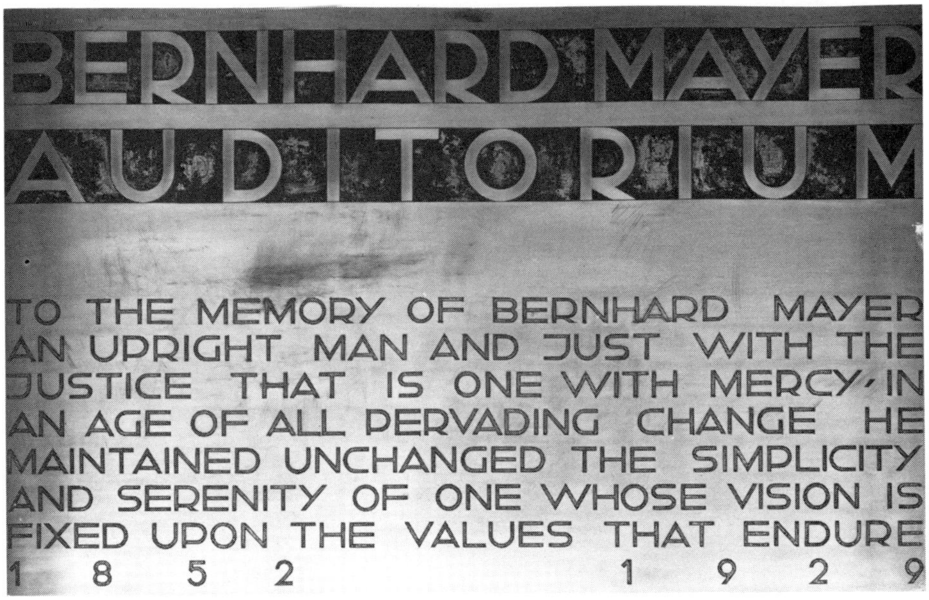
BERNHARD MAYER
AUDITORIUM
TO THE MEMORY OF BERNHARD MAYER
AN UPRIGHT MAN AND JUST WITH THE
JUSTICE THAT IS ONE WITH MERCY · IN
AN AGE OF ALL PERVADING CHANGE HE
MAINTAINED UNCHANGED THE SIMPLICITY
AND SERENITY OF ONE WHOSE VISION IS
FIXED UPON THE VALUES THAT ENDURE
1 8 5 2 1 9 2 9

53. SOUTHGATE APARTMENTS

A and B. Two of a variety of entrances to this apartment complex on East 52nd Street next to the river are shown. The buildings were designed by Emery Roth and built in stages from 1929 to 1931.

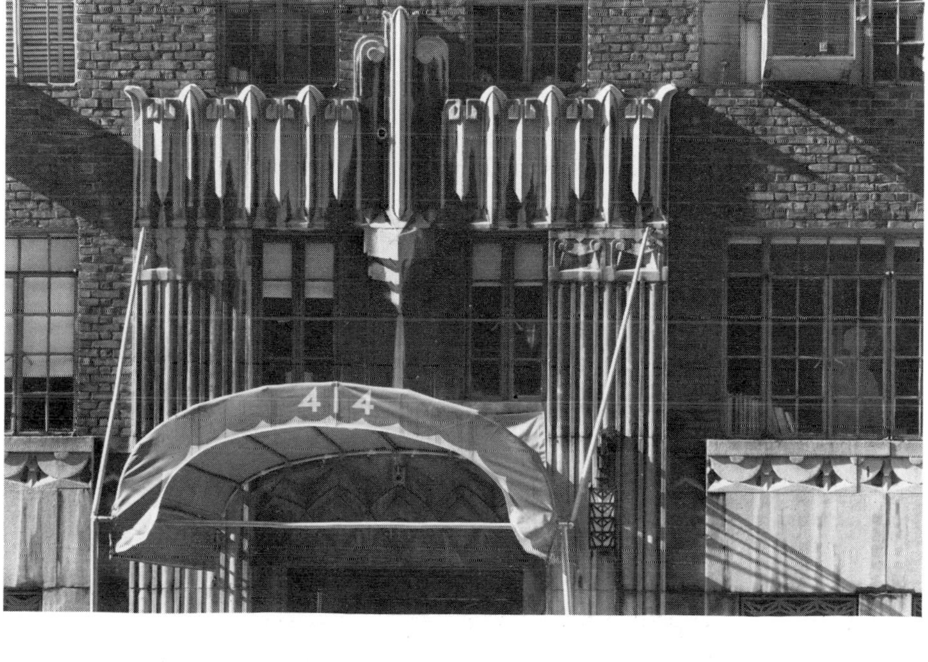

54. IRVING TRUST BUILDING

A. This bank headquarters building of 1929-32 by Voorhees, Gmelin & Walker is at the head of Wall Street opposite Trinity Graveyard.

B and C. Its curtain wall is in fabric folds and incised with a fabric pattern.

D. The main banking room has walls and ceilings sheathed in red and gold mosaics designed by Hildreth Meière. E and F. The vault gates and register grills have a sort of pattern that the writer Claude Bragdon suggested the designer generate from magic squares, moves in chess games, and the like.

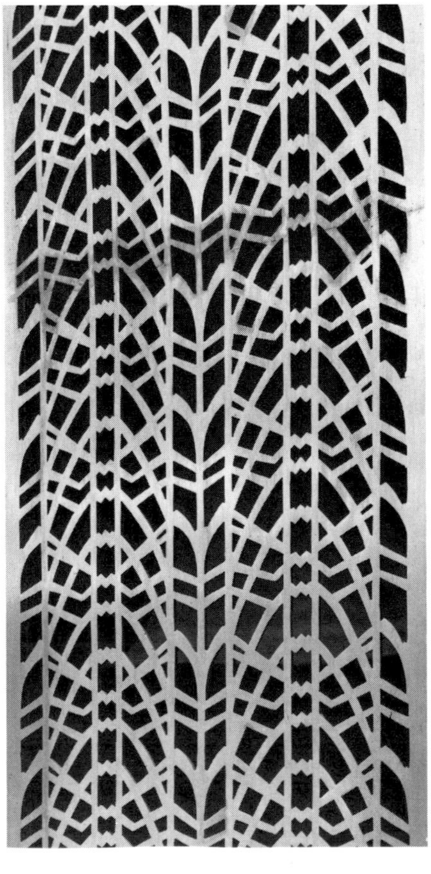

G. At the top of the building's faceted tower appear large windows.

H. The high, faceted-ceilinged lounge within the top of the tower is virtually intact except that the original boldly patterned wall covering has been replaced.

A and B. Sloan & Robertson's brick-sheathed prison in the Village, built in 1929-30, was recently razed.

55. HOUSE OF DETENTION FOR WOMEN

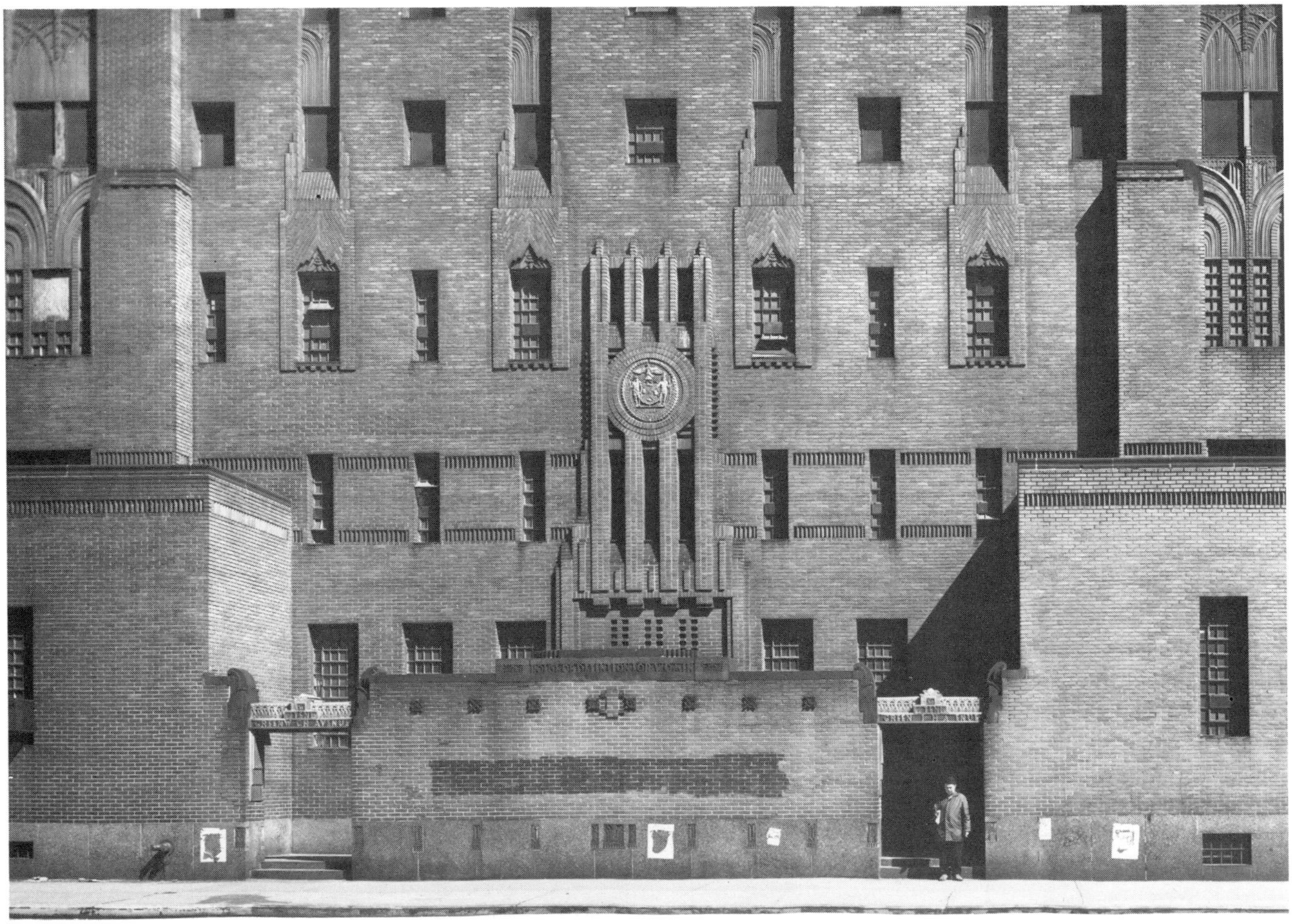

56. BLOOMINGDALE'S

A. In 1930 Bloomingdale's built this extension of their store west to Lexington Avenue. Starrett & Van Vleck were the architects.

B. The first two floors are in black terra-cotta and marble, those above in terra-cotta and brick (now painted). The forms of the terra-cotta may have been inspired by Precolumbian design.

59. CURB EXCHANGE FACADE

This façade was added in 1930 by Starrett & Van Vleck to a pre-existing exchange building just west of Trinity Graveyard. The Curb has since become the American Stock Exchange.

60. TWENTIETH-CENTURY FOX BUILDING

B. Joseph J. Furman was the architect in 1930 of this building on West 56th Street for a Hollywood movie company. Whether or not he was also responsible for the building's interiors is not known. The lobby (see color section) was preserved into the present because for many years its walls were hidden by frames for posters. The movie company has left the building since these pictures were taken.

C. The walls of an upstairs screening room were unfortunately painted over.

61. WEST SIDE ELEVATED HIGHWAY

This roadway, recently much in the news for its present decrepitude, was finished in 1930. John Sloan of Sloan & Robertson had some role in its design. Plaques such as this one were mounted at cross streets to announce the pier beyond and were presumably part of his contribution.

63. 22 EAST 40TH STREET

This office building of 1930 by Kenneth Franzheim was characteristic in that its lower floors, in this case in polished and unpolished black marble, were treated as a sort of stage setting especially related to the street.

64.

APARTMENTS

B and C. A series of apartment houses was built on Central Park West and on the West Side in the years around 1930. This one at 66th Street by Schwartz & Gross had curtain walls of brick which shaded from purple just above the base of the building to yellow at the top (see color section).

65.

A and B. On 86th Street, Margon & Holder also put up a mammoth apartment house at the corner of Amsterdam Avenue, the New Amsterdam.

66.
A and B. A second Schwartz & Gross apartment house at 84th Street and Central Park West had large sprout-like forms at its base and at its top.

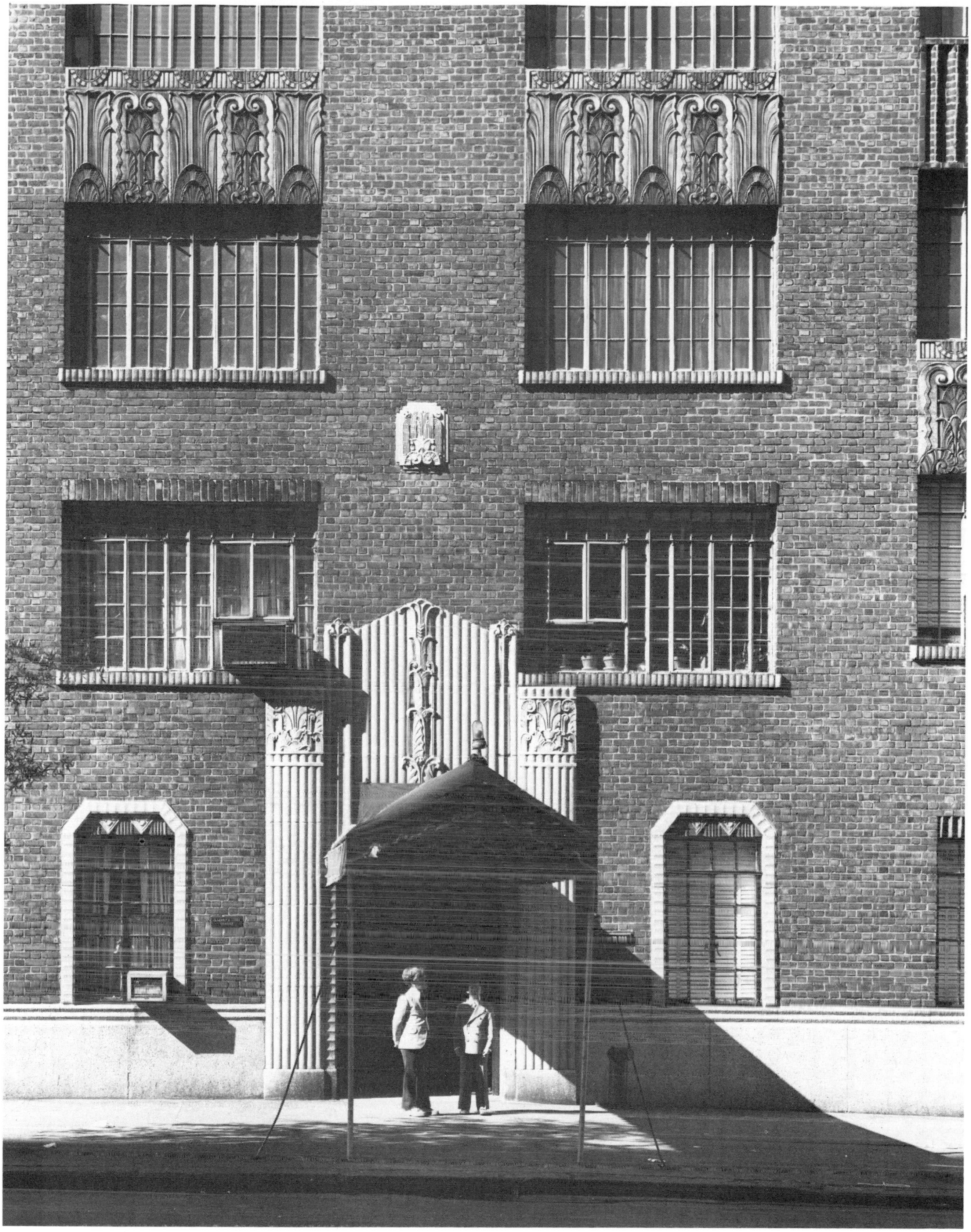

67.
On 86th Street between Central Park West and Columbus Avenue J. M. Felson erected a smaller apartment house with a brick curtain wall and a set of terra-cotta spandrels.

39A and 68A.

On two adjacent blocks farther north, at Central Park West and between 90th and 92nd Streets, Margon & Holder and Emery Roth put up two apartment buildings. One had pointed, fountain-like finials and bronze at its base (39B).

39B.

68B.
The other had a simpler tower and bands of decorative sandstone and colored concrete skirting its base.

96, 87A and B.

Two Central Park West buildings by the Office of Irwin Chanin, each a block wide, had twin towers and the sort of interlocking fins at their crowns and curved forms behind which would in the thirties be a familiar feature of the design of such products as radios. These were the Century, a few blocks north of Columbus Circle, and the Majestic, across 72nd Street from the Dakota.

87A.

87B.

69. HORN & HARDART

This building for the chain of automated restaurants was built in 1930-31 to designs of Louis Allen Abramson. Standing on 33rd Street near what was Penn Station, it suggests that by this date there was feedback to New York from elsewhere in America. The details here, especially the figures knocking heads on either side of the building, come from the Richfield Building in Los Angeles, whose architects, Morgan, Walls & Clements, apparently got them in turn from Josef Hoffmann's Palais Stoclet in Brussels.

71. RCA VICTOR BUILDING

A. Cross & Cross designed this office tower—now the GE Building—in materials similar in color to those of Saint Bartholomew's Church, which it adjoins. The building to the left is Schultze & Weaver's Waldorf-Astoria (74).

B and C. Above the windows and doors at street level appear zigzag forms presumably representing the vibrating Victrola needles of the RCA Victor Company. The light illuminating the clock and supported by two scrawny arms is, like the GE clock face, a replacement but an Art Deco one.

71C.

Art Deco was the house st, of this company, which thereby helped disseminate it throughout the country. This particular building, just south of the General Post Office, was designed by Frank S. Parker and built in 1930-31.

72. SEARS ROEBUCK BUILDING

73. AMERICAN SAVINGS BANK

Hirons & Mellor put up this small bank building on 42nd Street between Sixth Avenue and Times Square in 1930-31. It has since ceased to be a bank.

75 and 76. 500 FIFTH AVENUE and EMPIRE STATE BUILDING

Shreve, Lamb & Harmon were putting up their tower at 500 Fifth Avenue just north of the Public Library in the same years (1930-31) in which their Empire State Building was being erected.

A and B. The Empire State Building passed beyond the early, craft-oriented Art Deco skyscrapers in that many of its forms were made to seem machined and in that its crowning device was functional, if only symbolically so. The building retained the cast metal spandrels of earlier buildings on its exterior.

MANUFACTUR
RIVERBOAT
LONGCHAMPS
Riverboat

C. Inside, bridges crossed the lobby. Originally these were not enclosed in glass as they are now, and their ceilings stepped up to a surface from which hung a chandelier.

77. 29 BROADWAY

Sloan & Robertson designed this building for a narrow site towards the very bottom end of Broadway. It was built in 1930-31. A metal screen that hung in the entrance way is no longer in place.

In 1930-31 Ely Jacques Kahn put up two buildings on one block just south of Times Square. One is L-shaped in plan; the other sits within the angle of the L. The first, whose crown appears here at the upper right, faces south.

80 and 81. BRICKEN-CASINO BUILDING and 1400 BROADWAY

The Bricken-Casino building, tucked within the L, asserts itself more stridently with a finned crowning motive and a virtuoso performance in setbacks.

82. McGRAW-HILL BUILDING

C. Below the Mendelsohnian crown, where the lettering has been painted over, columns are sheathed in metal and spandrels are of blue-green terracotta. (See color section.)

B. Raymond Hood's building for the publishing company was built farther west on 42nd Street than other office buildings have been for the reason that zoning would not permit its printing plant closer to the midtown commercial center. Whereas the News Building tower (35) had been designed in the form of a slab perpendicular to the street, the McGraw-Hill has what is virtually a slab parallel to it. The building was built in 1930-31.

83. BROADWAY FASHION BUILDING

This office building with stores on its ground floor is on Broadway just south of 86th Street. It is of the modest sort which characteristically found a place on the Main Streets of most American towns in the thirties, though this one keeps an extra share of elegance by the large amount of glass on its façade in relation to the light framework in which it is set. Sugarman & Berger designed the building, erected in 1930-31.

85. 60 WALL TOWER

A. This office tower of 1930-32 is a block away from its address—it is connected to a Wall Street building by a bridge. Presumably because it became more important in the Depression to rent space than to advertise a company, the building was named after the address rather than the company that built it, Cities Service. Nevertheless, the familiar company logotype is much in evidence. At the entrances there also appears a model of the building. Sculptural models were much used in design in the twenties and thirties; one suspects that both owners and architects hated to do away with them after design was completed, hence such a use as this. The architects here were Holton & George. B. The building is topped with a crystalline lighting fixture.

C. Metal flowers appear above the lobby cigar stand.

D. There are aggressively non-structural corbels at the top of a pilaster in the lobby.

E. The elevator system was innovative in having double-decker cabs, one half of each going to odd floors, the other to even ones, from two lobbies one above the other. The system is common now, but was not profitable in the thirties, and its use was discontinued. Until recently the upper half of some original cabs, such as this one, could be seen.

This building by an architect named Stuckert was built in 1930-32 and represents the Art Deco at its most modest, both in stature and in quality. Originally, rather than holding a Zum Zum's, it housed a Bickford's.

86. LEXINGTON AVENUE AT 45TH STREET

88. EARL CARROLL THEATER

This building, part of honky-tonk west of Rockefeller Center and north of Times Square, was built in 1931 as a theater for demure girlie shows of the day. George Keister was the architect.

89. LONG ISLAND AREA HEADQUARTERS BUILDING

This brick curtain wall with metal window frames set in front of it covers a large telephone company building of 1931 in downtown Brooklyn. Voorhees, Gmelin & Walker designed it. The virtuoso brickwork, as explicitly tapestry-like as any by the firm, also suggests the brickwork of North German Expressionist buildings.

90A. These buildings, all part of the Rockefeller Center complex and built between 1931 and 1935, accounted for most of the construction work undertaken after the Depression had made itself felt. They were designed by several architectural firms working in collaboration and calling themselves the Associated Architects. The setbacks at the sides of the slab of the RCA building are not there in response to the zoning law but to the decreasing number of elevator shafts on the upper floors.

90, 92, 97, 102, 103. RCA BUILDING, RADIO CITY MUSIC HALL, BRITISH EMPIRE BUILDING, MAISON FRANCAISE, PALAZZO D'ITALIA, INTERNATIONAL BUILDINGS

97A, 102, 103. The row of low blocks on Fifth Avenue (the British, French, Italian, and International buildings) were the Associated Architects' way of relating the Center to the smaller scale of Fifth Avenue. The (former) Time & Life Building (109) is behind them.

90.B. The rear of the Center on Sixth Avenue, where in the thirties there was an elevated railway, shows no such consideration as was shown on Fifth Avenue.

90C. The RCA Building still had the cast metal spandrels of the earlier, craft-oriented Art Deco.

90D, 97B, 90E. Otherwise, the buildings' aesthetic was not a craft one and art was expected to stand on its own. It did not always do so successfully at the Center.

92A and B. The Radio City Music Hall offered its own complete vision of high life.

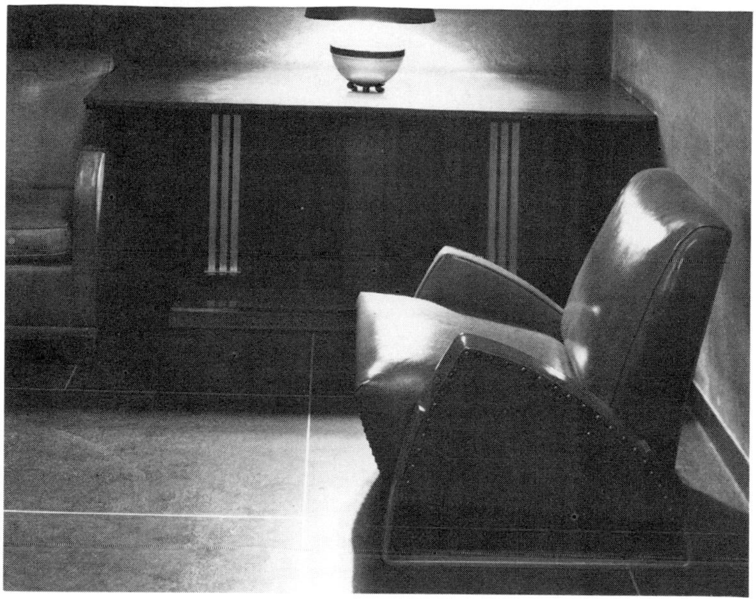

92C and D. It also included the comforts of home.

93. FOURTH CHURCH OF CHRIST SCIENTIST

A and B. Cherry and Matz, specialists in church architecture, did this building in upper Manhattan a few blocks above the George Washington Bridge. It was built in 1931-32 and is at the side of Ft. Washington Park in an area which contains many modest Art Deco apartment houses. The church has recently become a synagogue.

94. METROPOLITAN LIFE, NORTH BUILDING

This large office tower of 1931-32 was, according to early renderings, to have been much higher, a real temple of Babel. It stands between Madison Square and Park Avenue. H. W. Corbett and D. E. Waide were the architects.

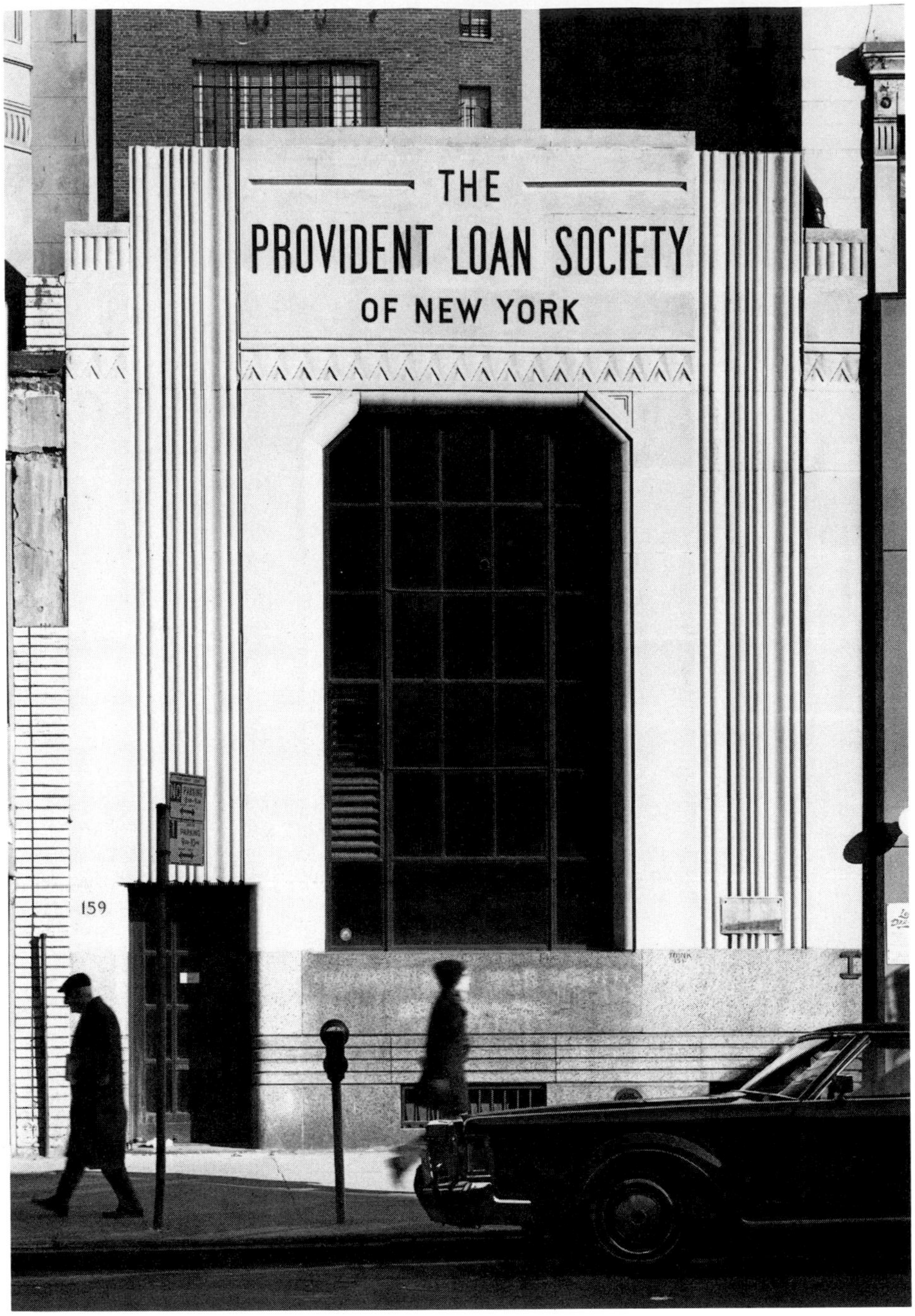

95. PROVIDENT LOAN SOCIETY BRANCH, 72ND STREET

This is one of a great many small loan offices built for this firm. All aim to suggest, by their large-scaled forms, the security of their vaults. Several were done in the Art Deco style by Renwick, Aspinwall & Guard. This one, built in 1932, made way a short while ago for a paint store.

98, 99, 104. CITY OF NEW YORK SUBSTATIONS

These small buildings are part of the Independent Subway system. Each houses unmanned machinery which converts alternating current into direct current for the subway. The buildings illustrated here were built in 1932 and 1933. The first is near Rockefeller Center, the second in the Village, and the third in Brooklyn.

NO
PARKING

100. MIDTOWN THEATRE

This small movie theater on Broadway above 96th Street was designed by Boak & Paris and built in 1933.

101. FEDERAL OFFICE BUILDING

A. This stone-faced block dating from 1933-35 was designed by Cross & Cross. It stands just north of the new Trade Center buildings and east of the Barclay-Vesey Building (1).

B. At its corners it has an eagle, a flag, and that international nationalist symbol of the time, a fasces.

105. EAST RIVER SAVINGS BANK

This narrow building on Trinity Place just north of the chain of plazas that extends from the Chase Building to the Trade Center was designed by Walker & Gillette and built in 1934-35. The bronze lettering at about eye level on the building has been replaced since this picture was taken by a modish 1970s logotype.

106. KRESS BUILDING

A. This office building and store has a high-ceilinged sales room on its ground floor and several sub-grade floors with a luncheonette and cafeteria. It was designed by Edward Sibbert and built in 1935. B. The decoration on the front is perhaps Mayan in character—each decorative knob depicts a category of merchandise sold in the store.

107. PIER BUILDING

This structure, built in 1935, was recently torn down, a casualty of the shift away from ocean liner travel.

108. APARTMENTS, 80TH STREET AND WEST END

Drape shapes in stainless steel appear at the top of this building of 1935-36 designed by George F. Pelham 2nd.

110. HORN & HARDART, 57TH STREET

This restaurant was designed by Ralph Bencker, a Philadelphia architect who also designed many H & H's in Philadelphia (and the N. W. Ayer Building in that city as well). This New York building, faced in terra-cotta, was built in 1938.

112. CRIMINAL COURTS BUILDING

This structure of 1939 is known as "the Tombs" after its predecessor, a prison in the Egyptian style. It houses both courts and prison and was designed by Harvey Wiley Corbett. It stands just north of Foley Square and backs onto Columbus Park.

113. JOAN OF ARC JUNIOR HIGH SCHOOL

This building in the West Nineties is largely featureless except for this luxuriant growth at its entrance. The school was designed by Eric Kebbon and built in 1939-40.

114. AIRLINES BUILDING

This building, also of 1939-40, only recently ceased to serve its original purpose as an airlines ticket office. It was designed (by John B. Peterkin) to serve a number of other uses as well. It still houses a garage in its basement and was meant to have, as well as restaurants, a theater in space that has long been occupied by a Horn & Hardart.

115. TIFFANY BUILDING

A and B. By the time Cross & Cross designed this building (erected in 1939-40) at the corner of Fifth Avenue and 57th Street, the Art Deco had largely returned to the classical forms it had originated in. The Fuller Building (18) appears to the left of it in A, the Stewart store (25) (now Bonwit Teller) to the right in B.

PHOTO CREDITS

Permission to reprint material from copyright sources among the following is gratefully acknowledged:

Eliel Saarinen, Chicago Tribune Building competition entry, from *The International Competition for a New Administration Building for the Chicago Tribune, MCMXXII* (Chicago: The Tribune Company, 1923), Plate Number 13.

Helmle & Corbett, zoning envelope studies, renderings by Hugh Ferriss, from Harvey Wiley Corbett, "Zoning and the Envelope of the Building," *Pencil Points*, 4 (April 1923), 16.

McKenzie, Voorhees & Gmelin, Barclay-Vesey Building, plan, and Helmle, Corbett & Harrison and Sugarman & Berger, Master Building, plan, from Plate 8, Part II of Volume I, and Plate 4, Part VII of Volume III of *American Architecture of the 20th Century*, Oliver Reagan, ed. (New York: The Architectural Book Publishing Company).

Buchman & Kahn, Insurance Center Building, photograph of model, from *American Architect*, 129 (April 20, 1926), 454.

Joseph Urban, Ziegfeld Theater, photograph by Sigurd Fischer from *Architectural Record*, 61 (May 1927), 388.

William Van Alen, Chrysler Building, plan, from *Architectural Forum*, 53 (October 1930), 412.

Howells & Hood, 3 East 84th Street, rendering by Donald Douglas, *Pencil Points*, 8 (November 1927), 660.

Howells & Hood, News Building, plans, *Architectural Forum*, 53 (November 1930), 542

L. H. Boileau, Bon Marché Pavilion, and J. Hiriard, Tribout & Beau, Pavilion of the Galéries Lafayette from M. Roux-Spitz, *Exposition des Arts Décoratifs Paris 1925* (Paris: Albert Lévy, 1928), plates 52 and 54.

Josef Hoffmann, Palais Stoclet, general exterior and dining room, from Josef Hoffmann, *Wendingen* (Amsterdam: "de Hooge Brug," 1920), pp. 4, 11.

Josef Hoffmann, Palais Stoclet, exterior detail, and Eric Mendelsohn's sketches for industrial buildings, from Sheldon Cheney, *The New World Architecture* (New York, 1930), pp. 182, 96.

Interior of Wiener Werkstätte, by Joseph Urban, New York, from *Architectural Record*, 53 (March 1923), p. 269.

César Klein, Bedroom for Wolfgang Gurlitt, Berlin, from *Junge Kunst*, 5 (1923), n.p.

Walter Gropius, Sommerfeld House, Berlin, stairwell and door, from *Staatliches Bauhaus Weimar 1919-1923* (Weimar and Munich: Bauhausverlag, 1923), ill. 117 and 45.

Scene from *Dr. Mabuse*, from Siegfried Kracauer, *From Caligari to Hitler* (Princeton, N.J.: Princeton University Press, hardback reprint ed., 1966), ill. 6.

Fritz Höger, Chilehaus, Hamburg, general view, from Gustav Adolf Platz, *Die Baukunst der Neuesten Zeit* (Berlin: Propyläen-Verlag, 1930), plate XI.

Fritz Höger, Chilehaus, detail, from *Moderne Bauformen*, 24 (1925), plate 15.

Peter Behrens, I. G. Farben, Höchst, main hall, from Paul Joseph Cremers, *Peter Behrens—Sein Werk von 1909 bis zur Gegenwart* (Essen: G. D. Baedeker Verlag, 1928), plate 7.

Hans Poelzig, Grosses Schauspielhaus, Berlin, foyer, from *Wasmuths Monatshefte für Baukunst* (1920-21), plate 14.

Frank Lloyd Wright, Midway Gardens, Chicago, detail from *Architectural Record*, 62 (Dec. 1927), 454.

Frank Lloyd Wright, A. D. German Warehouse, Richland Center, Wisconsin, and Hollyhock House, Hollywood, from Henry-Russell Hitchcock, *In the Nature of Materials 1887-1941—The Buildings of Frank Lloyd Wright* (New York: Duell, Sloan, and Pearce, 1942), ill. 204, 235. Better illustrations of the Wright buildings would have been used if difficulties raised by the Taliesin Foundation, which retains copyright on much Wright material, had not prevented it.

Scenes from Robert Wiene's *The Cabinet of Dr. Caligari* and scenes from Fritz Lang's *Metropolis*, courtesy of The Museum of Modern Art, New York, Film Stills Archive).

The color photographs of the Chrysler Building were first published in *Architecture PLUS* (May-June 1974).

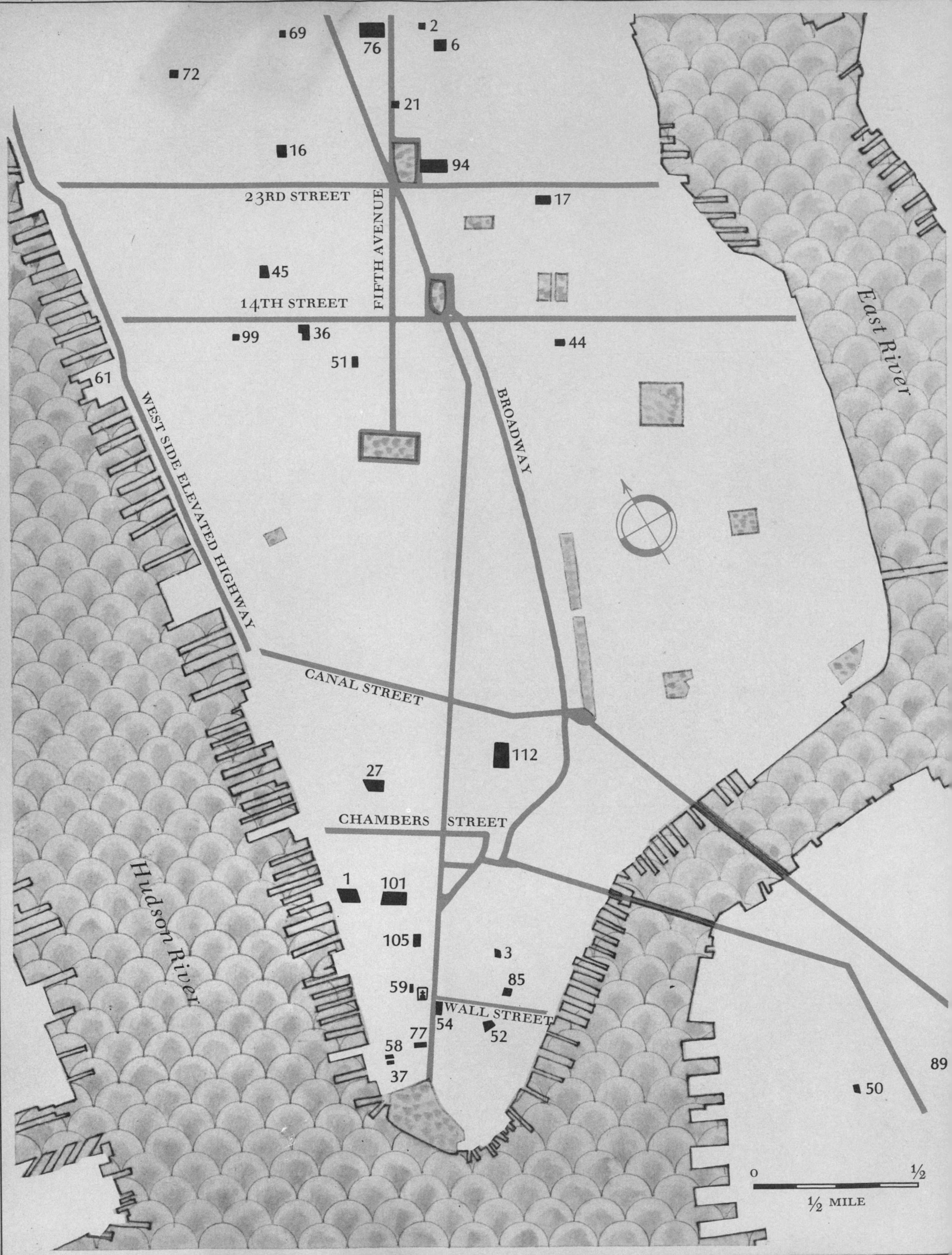

69
76
2
6
72
21
16
94
23RD STREET
17
FIFTH AVENUE
45
14TH STREET
99
36
44
51
61
BROADWAY
East River
WEST SIDE ELEVATED HIGHWAY
CANAL STREET
112
27
CHAMBERS
STREET
1
101
Hudson River
105
3
59
85
WALL STREET
54
52
77
58
37
89
50
0
½
½ MILE